THE DOS OPERATING SYSTEM

LEONARD LINDENMEYER
ANNE ARUNDEL COMMUNITY COLLEGE

boyd & fraser publishing company

CREDITS:

Acquisitions Editor: James H. Edwards
Marketing Manager: Eileen Pfeffer
Manufacturing Coordinator: Tracy Megison
Production Assistant: Jean Castro

A Division of South-Western Publishing Company
Danvers, MA 01923

International Thomson Publishing
boyd & fraser publishing company is an ITP Company.
The ITP trademark is used under license.

Manufactured in the United States of America

Library of Congress Cataloging-in-Publication Data

Lindenmeyer, Leonard.
The DOS operating system / Leonard Lindenmeyer.
p. cm.
Includes index.
ISBN 0-87835-752-1
1. Operating systems (Computers) 2. PC-DOS (Computer file)

I. Title.
QA76.76.063L538 1994 91-30455
005.4'46--dc20 CIP

2 3 4 5 6 7 8 9 10 D 6 5 4

CONTENTS

PREFACE

DOS as an operating system for personal computers is now more than 10 years old. Its capabilities have been steadily expanded over the years as hardware has become more sophisticated. Table P.1 below highlights the addition of features with the release of each version of DOS.

When originally developed, DOS actually referred to PC-DOS, developed for the IBM personal computer (PC) by Microsoft Corporation. Later, Microsoft developed DOS for various IBM-compatible computers such as those manufac-

TABLE P.1 The History of DOS

Version	Year	Characteristics
1.0	1981	Original operating system for the IBM PC
1.1	1982	Double-sided floppy drive support
1.25	1982	MS-DOS for non-IBM computers
2.00	1983	Hard drive support introduced
2.10	1983	IBM PC Jr. computer support included
2.11	1983	Standard Version 2 for non-IBM customers
3.00	1984	Support for IBM AT 1.2 MB disk drives
3.10	1984	Software support for computer networks
3.20	1986	Floppy disk support for 3.5-inch disks
3.30	1987	IBM PS/2 computer family supported
4.00	1988	IBM DOS Shell introduced
4.01	1989	Updates and corrections to Version 4.00
5.00	1991	New DOS Shell, smaller nucleus, memory management introduced
6.00	1993	Includes disk compression feature nearly doubling storage capacity, anti-viral utility, multiple boot options, and improved backup and restore programs.

tured by Texas Instruments, Zenith, and many others. This DOS was referred to as MS-DOS because it was a generic version of DOS created for these compatibles. Each of these copies was slightly different; they were tailored to the particular compatible for which Microsoft had done the development.

ABOUT THIS BOOK

This book is about DOS as an operating system. It can be used to learn PC-DOS for an IBM microcomputer; it can also be used to learn MS-DOS for any one of a wide variety of compatible computers.

This book is intended for a full-semester intermediate or advanced DOS course normally taught at the freshman or sophomore level in college today. It is also intended for personal computer users who want to learn more about the DOS operating system for their personal computer.

This book is designed to help you learn DOS. The vast majority of personal computer users buy their computers to use with one or more software application packages such as a word processor, a spreadsheet, or database management. As a result, many users learn to use only a small subset of the DOS commands. How do we learn to use any software? You can read several books; you can study the commands; you can memorize all the parameters associated with the commands; but, no matter how much of this you do, the way most of us learn software is by *using* it. You must sit in front of the machine and use the software to solve problems. There is no substitute for hands-on learning. This book takes you step by step through examples so that you learn by doing. In addition to hands-on material, each chapter contains questions and problems on the material covered. Where appropriate, each chapter also contains a section called Common Mistakes, which helps new users avoid typical errors and understand why these cause problems.

A NOTE TO THE READER

This book is a result of teaching and working with hundreds of students who have learned to use DOS. Based on that experience, several unique features have been incorporated into this book. First, it is organized around the major functions performed by DOS. Command groups are organized around these major DOS functions. Second, the concept of system defaults is discussed. The primary purpose of the book is to teach DOS, but a second purpose is to help you understand an operating system and how it works. To do that, you must understand the concept of system defaults. Third, each chapter that discusses a group of commands also discusses some of the most common mistakes made by a user. You can't use DOS without making mistakes. When you make a mistake, you must understand the mistake and know how to correct it. Finally, there is a section devoted to installing a system and setting up your computer. The purpose of this section is to help you install, organize, and manage your own computer system.

ORGANIZATION OF THE BOOK

This book is organized into four main parts. Part I, An Introduction to DOS, discusses hardware control features built into the microcomputer and some standard function key features built into DOS. Learning to use the function keys at the command level, along with learning something about hardware controls, will make you more efficient at the keyboard. In addition, Part I discusses some standard defaults built into DOS. A default is an assumption the system makes when you execute any command. These assumptions are vital to your understanding of how your computer works. Part I also introduces the idea of command groups to help the reader organize and understand the DOS commands by function and to aid in understanding the purpose behind each command.

Part II introduces internal DOS commands. It presents examples of the use of each internal command and shows practical applications of each command. Part II also shows some common mistakes users make when typing these commands.

Part III discusses external DOS commands, by far the largest group of commands. Fortunately, all these commands need not be learned at one time. The commands in each command group are organized and discussed from the most used to the least used. In that way the reader can learn commands in small groups by skipping from chapter to chapter. The commands are summarized in Appendix F by function to help you scan for features if you are looking for specific capabilities when using your computer.

Part IV discusses system management. This part includes specific recommendations, hints, and other suggestions for setting up your personal computer. Suggestions include installation guidelines, protection features, and the setup of an AUTOEXEC.BAT file and a CONFIG.SYS file to control the boot process. These suggestions also include some built-in protective features that help get you back on line when problems with your computer arise. Part IV need not be used at all in the course, or it could be used to tie the concepts together.

ACKNOWLEDGMENTS

Perhaps the most difficult portion to write of any book is the acknowledgments. You may leave someone out. You may not give someone or a group of people the emphasis they deserve. Where do you begin? Perhaps the best way to start is by reflecting on the experiences that led to the creation of this book, which involved so many helpful people.

My first experience with microcomputers was in 1977. I can still recall the hours I spent learning to use my first software package. I can recall days spent learning to use the CP/M operating system on my Apple computer. Since 1977, I have worked with and taught many people in both operating systems courses and other courses. I also operate a consulting practice in which I help clients learn to use their microcomputers. Many of these teaching experiences have had an influence on this book. To list them all would require that I have a perfect memory; it would also require many pages in this book!

For these reasons my thanks must first go to my students, for without them, I would never have learned enough to write this book. Anyone who has ever taught knows that to teach a subject, you must know it well. You must be able to answer questions that you often don't think of yourself. By teaching the subject, you are forced to learn more because you must answer the students' questions. Many times their questions arise because they use a different computer from the one you use, or because they raise issues that you never considered. Their questions also arise because they think of things in a different way. Therefore, my first thanks go to all my students who, through their learning, have stretched my learning.

Two students deserve special mention. They have not only been good students, they have also worked with me for several years and have contributed much to this book; and so, to Catherine Bosse and Ann Walkinshaw I want to offer a special thanks. Their work, their inspiration, their standards of excellence, and their critiques have done much to improve this book. Without them it might never have been completed.

Next I must thank my clients. As a group, they have presented me with a wide range of problems to solve over the years. These problems have involved many different types of computers, software packages, and operating systems. Through this experience I have gained a greater understanding of the similarities and differences between operating systems. And through this experience, I have learned ways to make it easier to use a computer.

Without the experience gained in working with both students and clients, this book could not have been written. All of my course development efforts in my teaching have stemmed from experience with these two groups of people. To all of them I give many thanks.

Finally, I would like to thank Jim Edwards, the acquisitions editor for boyd & fraser, and his staff. The writing and development of a textbook is a lengthy task. Without a good working relationship with the publisher, it can become a chore. The people of boyd & fraser have been particularly helpful throughout this entire process.

Len Lindenmeyer
Annapolis, Maryland
January 1993

LIST OF TABLES

List of Figures

PART I

AN INTRODUCTION TO DOS

CHAPTER 1

DOS AS AN OPERATING SYSTEM

INTRODUCTION

What is DOS? What is PC-DOS? MS-DOS? How do they differ? **DOS** stands for *Disk Operating System.* An **operating system** is a program, or, more correctly, a group of programs that makes your computer hardware work. When you buy a computer, you purchase both hardware—the system unit, the monitor, and the keyboard—and an operating system compatible with your hardware. If you buy an IBM PC or an IBM compatible, you get a DOS operating system, either PC-DOS or MS-DOS. The operating system software that you buy and the version of that software must be compatible with your hardware; in other words, it must be able to work with your computer hardware.

PC-DOS is the operating system that works with IBM personal computers. MS-DOS is the operating system that works with IBM-compatible personal computers. A wide variety of compatible computers are available in the marketplace today. In fact, compatibles represent the single largest class of personal computers sold. Brands such as Compaq, Hewlett-Packard, Dell, Gateway, Zeos, AST Research, Packard Bell, Compuadd, and many others are available from retail stores and mail order channels. Regardless of manufacturer brand, they typically come supplied with DOS as an operating system. Today, they will probably come supplied with MS-DOS Version 5.0. They may also be supplied with Windows as a Graphical User Interface (GUI). The operating systems, however, are not interchangeable. PC-DOS for an IBM will not work with a Texas Instruments or other compatible. Likewise, MS-DOS for a Texas Instruments compatible will not work with an IBM personal computer.

COMPATIBILITY

What is meant by the term *compatible computer?* It is a very general term with a somewhat hazy meaning. **Compatibility** is the extent to which you can exchange software and data between two computers. If two computers are 100 percent compatible, software that runs on the first computer will also work on the second computer. Likewise, a diskette with files written by the first computer can be read by the second computer. In general, there is never 100-percent compatibility between computers made by two different manufacturers.

The term *compatible* is generally used to describe microcomputers that have a degree of compatibility with the IBM series of personal computers. The term has been used as a selling feature by smaller computer manufacturers who claim that their computers are compatible with the IBM PC. When the sales brochures or salespeople say this, they use the term very generally and are never specific as to what it really means. Keep in mind that no non-IBM computer is 100 percent compatible with an IBM personal computer. There is always some software package or application program written for an IBM personal computer that will not function correctly on a compatible. The IBM PS/2 line of computers are not compatible in many ways with many other computers today because of their microchannel I/O architecture. In general, compatibility usually means that files can be interchanged between an IBM personal computer and a compatible computer. During the period when all IBM and compatible computers were using 5 1/4-inch, 360 kilobyte diskettes, the term compatible had a very important and specific meaning. It meant that the computers were **file compatible.** Today even file compatibility has lost some of its meaning, because there are now several different disk-formatting standards. High-density 3 1/2-inch diskettes cannot be read by computers with 3 1/2-inch double-density diskette drives. As a result, we must be very specific when talking about file compatibility between two microcomputers.

Two personal computers can also be **boot compatible.** A computer that is boot compatible can be booted up from a boot disk prepared on an IBM computer, and vice versa. Not too many compatibles meet this test of compatibility.

Finally, our two hypothetical computers are **software compatible** when an application program written for the IBM personal computer will function 100 percent effectively on the compatible computer. Many compatible computers meet this test for software compatibility. However, the fact that *one* application is interchangeable on two computers does not mean that *all* application programs will be interchangeable.

So, when we use the term *compatible computers* today, it is important to be specific. What do we mean by this compatibility? Are the computers file compatible, boot compatible, or software compatible? If the computers run DOS, whether PC-DOS or MS-DOS, they will generally be file compatible. In most cases, particularly with widely used application software, microcomputers are also software compatible. Whether the compatibility goes beyond this test will probably require some testing and investigation on your part. If you always use the same computer and never need to transport data from one computer to another, compatibility is of no importance to you. However, most people need to interchange data between computers (for example, if they have one model at home and another at work). If you have this need, you must understand the basics of compatibility.

There are ways to overcome the compatibility problem. If you own an IBM compatible, the version of DOS supplied with the computer may include an emulator. **Emulators** are products that help bridge the compatibility gap. They can consist of software only, or a combination of hardware and software. Whatever its form, the emulator is a product that makes two computers more compatible. Generally, emulators are focused on allowing software products written for one computer to function 100 percent effectively on the compatible computer.

At the other end of the spectrum, two computers can be 100 percent *incom-*

patible. An Apple Macintosh computer running System 7 of its operating system is 100 percent incompatible with an IBM computer running PC-DOS. Software written for the Macintosh cannot be interchanged with the IBM, or vice versa. Likewise, data written on a diskette by the Macintosh cannot generally be read by the IBM, and vice versa.

But even this situation is changing. The new line of Powerbook computers from Apple can be provided with software to read and recognize diskettes formatted under DOS. As more systems are networked, and as users develop needs for interchanging data files across operating system platforms, products—both software and hardware—will be developed to meet those needs. Many networks today include a mix of equipment running different operating systems.

Compatibility is a topic treated far too lightly in most books and magazine articles. If you don't understand it all now, don't worry. This book will deal with the issue in much greater depth.

The focus will be on the specific compatibility issues: file compatibility, boot compatibility, and software compatibility. As a DOS user you can do a number of things to bridge the compatibility gap. The range of diskette formats available, as well as the number of software applications, make compatibility an important topic to understand.

VERSIONS OF DOS

PC-DOS was first released in 1981 for the original IBM Personal Computer (PC). PC-DOS was a joint development effort between IBM and Microsoft Corporation. The IBM PC proved to be so popular that by 1982 a small number of manufacturers introduced to the market several other computers that were compatible with the PC. As a result, Microsoft released MS-DOS for these IBM compatibles (the *MS* stands for Microsoft). The popularity of the IBM PC, coupled with the rapidly expanding market for PCs and the demand for software applications, was a major factor in forcing suppliers to maintain a degree of compatibility among personal computers. Without the compatibility that existed in the early years of the IBM PC, it is doubtful that the personal computer market would have expanded as rapidly as it did. Table 1.1 provides a brief history of the development of DOS and the major features included with the release of later versions.

There are many more versions of DOS than are shown in this table. Users of Texas Instruments computers, for example, may be running Version 2.11 or 2.13 of MS-DOS. Users of Panasonic PCs may be running Version 3.18. These versions are very similar to Version 2.10 or Version 3.10 for the IBM in Table 1.1. These DOS versions for Texas Instruments and Panasonic, however, have some unique features associated with them. As we said earlier, there is no 100 percent IBM PC-compatible computer.

TABLE 1.1 The History of DOS

Version	Year	Characteristics
1.0	1981	Original operating system for the IBM PC
1.1	1982	Double-sided floppy drive support
1.25	1982	MS-DOS for non-IBM computers
2.00	1983	Hard drive support introduced
2.10	1983	IBM PC Jr. computer support included
2.11	1983	Standard Version 2 for non-IBM customers
3.00	1984	Support for IBM AT 1.2 MB disk drives
3.10	1984	Software support for computer networks
3.20	1986	Floppy disk support for 3 1/2-inch disks
3.30	1987	IBM PS/2 computer family supported
4.00	1988	IBM DOS Shell introduced
4.01	1989	Updates and corrections to Version 4.00
5.00	1991	New DOS Shell, smaller nucleus, memory management, file recovery features introduced
6.00	1993	Includes disk compression feature nearly doubling disk storage capacity, anti-viral utility, multiple boot options, and improved backup and restore programs.

LEARNING DOS

How do we learn about something as complicated as an operating system? Obviously, it is not a lesson to be learned in a day, a week, or even a month. Neither is it something to be learned only by reading. To learn DOS and to be proficient in applying it to your computing problems requires some work. The main thing it requires is sitting in front of a computer, typing, and applying DOS to your computer needs. Reading is fine, but you can't leave out a healthy dose of hands-on experience as you learn to apply the many features incorporated into DOS. So, when you want to learn to use a new DOS command, whether it be TREE, XCOPY, REPLACE, or FORMAT, turn on your computer, open your book, and start typing. You'll be surprised at how quickly you'll learn, and how much you'll retain, if you combine your reading with hands-on work at the keyboard.

The power that resides in the computer sitting on your desk is incredible. DOS, along with this book and the skills you will acquire, will unlock the power and potential inside your computer, regardless of the type of computer you own. Your computer can assist you in a thousand ways to function more effectively and productively, both at work and at home.

A FEW SIMPLE CONVENTIONS

The next section discusses a few simple conventions that are introduced in this text to make it easy to follow the exercises. These simple conventions clearly spell out what the user types, and the machine responses that result. As you read, these conventions will make it clear what you should type when creating or modifying a file, and what the system's responses will be. The conventions are as follows:

1. The **system prompt** is always shown in normal text, just as it appears below.

   ```
   C:\>
   ```

   This is the normal DOS prompt, which shows that the default drive is C:, the default directory is the root directory (indicated by a blackslash [\]) , and the standard DOS prompt > (the greater-than sign) is displayed indicating the computer is ready to receive your input. If your system does not display this prompt, you can make it do so by including the command

   PROMPT pg

   as part of your AUTOEXEC.BAT file. If your system has a different default drive such as D or E, your system will display that letter instead of the drive letter C.

2. The characters you should type when issuing a command or creating or modifying a file are always shown in bold print, as displayed below.

   C:\> **DIR [Enter]**

   In this command, which tells the computer to display the directory listing of files, the characters DIR appear in bold print, indicating that you type DIR. [Enter] indicates that you should press the Enter key, which may be labeled with a bent arrow on your keyboard. From here on, this book will not include [Enter], but you must press the Enter key after typing every command in order for DOS to execute the command. Generally, when you are required to press keys such as the Enter key, the key or key combination will be presented in brackets [ ]. In these instances, press the key indicated, but do *not* type the brackets. See Step 4 below.

3. The system response to typing a command is always displayed in color. The example below shows a typical sequence, including display of the DOS prompt, display of the command you type, and system's response to the command.

```
C:\> CHKDSK C:

  21135360 bytes total disk space
     53248 bytes in 3 hidden files
     38912 bytes in 16 directories
  14256128 bytes in 474 user files
   6787072 bytes available on disk

      2048 bytes in each allocation unit
     10337 total allocation units on disk
      1704 available allocation units on disk

    655360 bytes total memory
    491904 bytes free
```

4. Finally, at times you must type a control sequence of characters, such as Ctrl-C. Such a sequence of keystrokes is required, for example, to switch from input mode in EDLIN to command mode. When the user is required to type this kind of sequence, it will be shown in brackets like this [Ctrl-C]. This sequence indicates you must hold down the Control [Ctrl] key while you press the letter C. Then release both of these keys.

QUESTIONS AND PROBLEMS

1. What is DOS and why do computer users need it?
2. What is the difference between PC-DOS and MS-DOS?
3. What does the term *compatibility* refer to?
4. Why is file compatibility important to someone using one brand of microcomputer at work and a different brand at home?
5. Does exchanging files between two different types of microcomputers require that they be running the same version of DOS?
6. Why is the version of DOS running on your computer important?
7. What version of DOS introduced support for 3 1/2-inch diskette drives?
8. What version of DOS introduced the DOS Shell?
9. Why might the same version of DOS on two different manufacturer's computers contain slightly different sets of files?
10. Can utilities be added to supplement DOS's capabilities on any personal computer?

CHAPTER 2

HARDWARE AND SOFTWARE

INTRODUCTION

In addition to providing the user with many software programs, DOS also provides some direct hardware control features. These features are extremely useful in situations in which you need to control your computer's screen or printer. You can implement these features through keyboard control sequences, or through function key sequences.

Figure 2.1 shows a picture of the standard IBM keyboard. The position of various keys used in keyboard control sequences is identified. Note that the Esc, Alt, and Ctrl keys are on the left side of the keyboard, with the balance of the hardware control keys on the right. Some keys on the numeric keypad serve a dual role. The numeric keys 2, 4, 6, and 8 are numeric keys when the Num Lock key is toggled into numeric mode. If the Num Lock key is pressed again, it places the numeric keypad in cursor control mode. In this mode, the numeric keys 2, 4, 6, and 8 represent cursor control left and right, as well as up and down. On the far left of the keyboard are the 10 function keys. (F1 through F10).

Figure 2.2 shows the IBM enhanced keyboard, sometimes referred to as the PC/AT keyboard. The position of various keys used in keyboard control sequences is identified. Note that here, too, the Esc, Alt, and Ctrl keys are on the left side of the keyboard, with the balance of the control keys on the right. Again, some keys on the numeric keypad serve a dual role. Just as they do on the standard keyboard, the numeric keys can be toggled from numeric mode to cursor control

FIGURE 2.1 Standard IBM keyboard showing hardware control keys

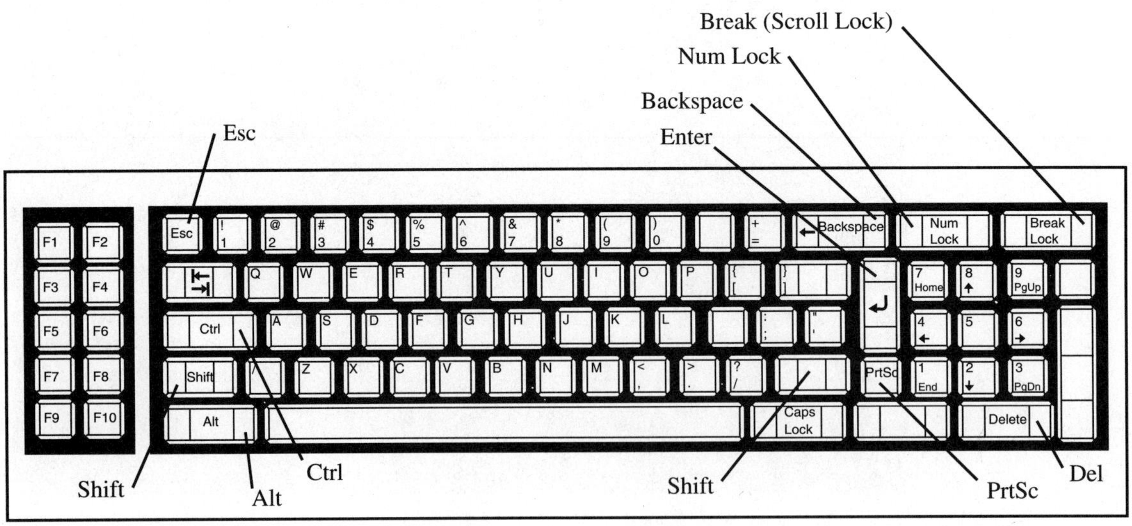

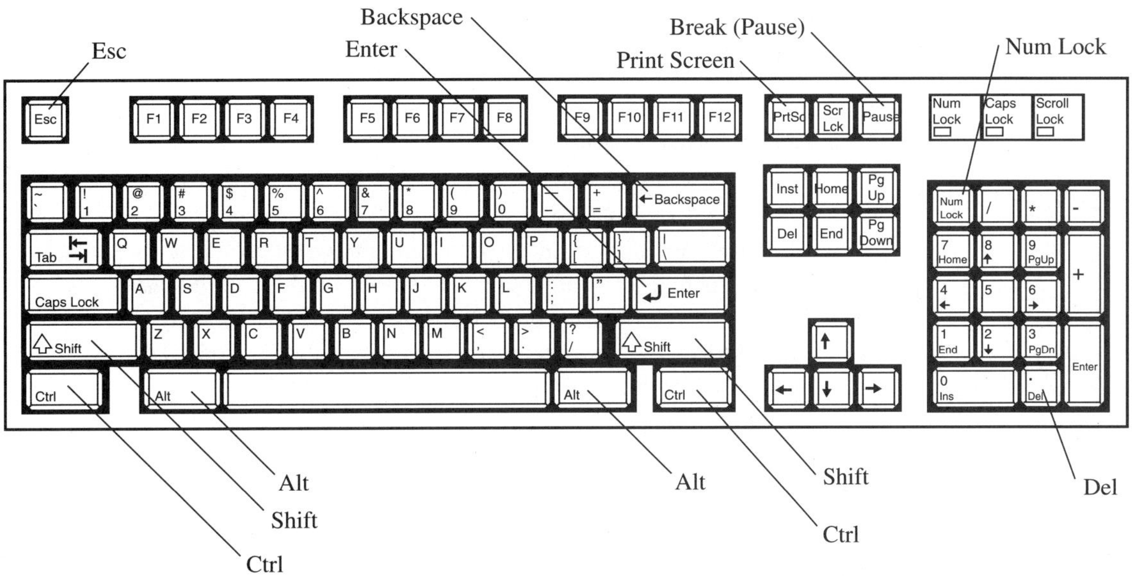

FIGURE 2.2 Enhanced IBM keyboard showing hardware control keys

mode and back again. Note that on the enhanced keyboard, a separate set of cursor control (arrow) keys has been added just to the left of the keypad section of the keyboard. You will usually control the cursor with these separate cursor keys rather than with the numeric keypad cursor keys if your computer is equipped with an enhanced keyboard. Note too that the function keys have been moved from the far left side of the keyboard to a position above the main typewriter section of the keyboard.

KEYBOARD CONTROL SEQUENCES

Table 2.1 shows hardware controls that are available via a variety of keyboard sequences. These keyboard sequences and some sample applications are discussed below. Your keyboard may not have some of the keys listed. If so, there is usually a substitute key for the one mentioned, or a second sequence that implements the same function. Try these functions on your keyboard and note the ones that work for you. You will find many of them very useful as your knowledge and skill with DOS increases.

All input and output devices are buffered with a special memory that is used when reading or writing data to or from a device. The keyboard is no exception. Part of your hardware includes what is referred to as the **keyboard buffer.** On most microcomputers this is a 132-character memory that stores the commands or characters that you type prior to pressing the Enter key. It is easy to determine what is in the keyboard buffer when using DOS. Just press the F3 function key and DOS shows you what is stored in this 132-character memory. Some of the keyboard and function key sequences discussed below use the keyboard buffer.

MULTIKEY SEQUENCES

These sequences are implemented by pressing the key shown, if it is a single key. In the cases where a key combination is shown [Ctrl-C] for example, the user would hold down the Ctrl key while pressing a C. When executing a key combination like [Ctrl-C], it is not necessary to type a capital C. [Ctrl-C] can be implemented as [Ctrl-C] or as [Ctrl-c].

Note that several of the functions listed in Table 2.1 can be implemented in two or more ways; for instance, Ctrl-C and Ctrl-Break do the same thing. Learn whichever one is the easiest to remember. In the case of these two, Ctrl-C is usually easy to remember because "C" stands for "cancel," and Ctrl-C cancels the command currently executing. This command, which you may use any time, will

TABLE 2.1 **Keyboard Control Sequences**

Key Sequence	Function
Ctrl-C	Cancel the command or program that is currently in execution.
Ctrl-Break	Same as Ctrl-C.
Ctrl-P	Puts the printer in echo mode.
Ctrl-Prtsc	Same as Ctrl-P.
Ctrl-S	Temporarily suspends processing and freezes the display screen.
Ctrl-Num Lock	Same as Ctrl-S.
Shift-Prtsc	Dumps the information on the display screen to your printer.
Ctrl-Alt-Del	Warm boot of the operating system.
Esc	Cancels the current line or command stored in the keyboard buffer.
Ins	Puts the keyboard in insert mode for inserting characters into a command.
Del	Deletes a single character from the keyboard buffer.
Backspace	Backspaces one character and deletes that character from the buffer.
Pause	Same as Ctrl-S.
Caps Lock	Toggles the keyboard between uppercase and lowercase.
Num Lock	Toggles the numeric keypad between numeric mode and cursor control mode.

cancel the program currently in execution and return the screen to the DOS prompt. It can terminate the execution of COM files, EXE files, and batch (BAT) files. In some cases there is a delay in canceling, because DOS waits for the completion of input/output (I/O) operations. If the cancellation does not occur immediately, it will normally be because either disk or printer operations are in progress.

To test the Ctrl-C operation, copy a group of files using wildcard addressing. Once the copy is in progress, issue a Ctrl-C to cancel the operation before all the files are copied.

The Ctrl-P sequence puts the printer into echo mode. When you issue this sequence, you must follow it by pressing the Enter key. You should hear the printer respond, indicating that the printer has connected. When the printer is in echo mode, everything that appears on the display screen is "echoed" to the printer. The Ctrl-P sequence is a toggle. This means that issuing the sequence the first time puts the printer into echo mode. If you issue a second Ctrl-P, the printer is toggled out of echo mode.

The Ctrl-P sequence is very useful if you need a log of a computer session. Such a log is useful if you are learning to perform an operation and you would like a record of everything that you typed, as well as all the responses from the computer, including error messages, names of files copied, and so on. Use echo mode if you want to display batch file listings, for example, and want the name of the batch file listed with each. You can also use the Ctrl-P sequence to obtain a file listing that will scroll across your screen because it is several pages in length.

The Shift-Prtsc sequence is used to dump the contents of the display screen to the printer when the information of interest will fit on the display screen without scrolling. Short directory listings, directory listings in wide mode, and short batch files are some of the items for which you might use Shift-Prtsc.

The Ctrl-S sequence freezes the screen contents so that you can read information as it scrolls across the screen. This command has some limited usefulness. With the speed of modern computers, the screen display frequently scrolls so quickly that it is difficult to stop the scrolling at precisely the right spot. Fortunately, other means are available for reviewing display listings that have multiple pages. For directory listings, use the P parameter to list files a page at a time with the DIR command. For other displays, use the MORE command. (The DIR command is discussed in Chapter 6. The MORE command and DOS filters are discussed in Chapter 14.)

Occasionally it is necessary to warm boot DOS to reload the nucleus. The Ctrl-Alt-Del sequence accomplishes this task. This sequence should be used with caution, because when it is invoked, all information in memory is lost. If something has gone awry when using a program, you should first attempt to recover by using control sequences and commands associated with that software. You should also use Ctrl-C to halt the execution of the program. If the keyboard gets "hung up" so that you get no response when typing, a warm boot may be necessary to make the computer operational again.

At times, a warm boot is a necessary and a normal part of an operating sequence. For example, when you make changes to the CONFIG.SYS file or to your AUTOEXEC.BAT file, it is necesary to reboot, because these two files are normally read only during the power-on process or during the warm-boot process. Therefore, a change to CONFIG.SYS (to add a device such as a mouse) or a change to AUTOEXEC.BAT (to modify the PATH command) requires a warm boot in order to have DOS recognize these modifications to the system. (The CONFIG.SYS and AUTOEXEC.BAT files are covered in Chapter 21.)

SINGLE-KEY SEQUENCES

Most of the other keyboard controls listed in Table 2.1. are single-key sequences. Several of these toggle the keyboard into certain modes. The better keyboards have lights that indicate mode status.

The Caps Lock key puts the alphabetic part of the keyboard in either uppercase or lowercase mode. If Caps Lock is on and the indicator is lit, you can press any alphabetic key to produce that letter as a capital letter. If you press Caps Lock again, the keyboard is toggled back to lowercase mode, the indicator light goes off and all alphabetic characters you type are lowercase. The Num Lock or Num key operates the same way for the numeric keypad on the keyboard. If the Num Lock light is on, pressing the keypad keys produces numbers. If Num Lock is off, the 2, 4, 6, and 8 keys act as cursor control keys rather than numeric keys. The better keyboards have separate keys for cursor control. If your keyboard has separate keys for cursor control, it is recommended that these keys be used for all cursor movement.

The Ins key is used to toggle the keyboard into and out of insert mode. Normally, upon booting the computer, the keyboard is in typeover mode. Any characters typed will overlay characters already in the keyboard buffer. Pressing the Ins key once puts the keyboard into insert mode. Now when characters are typed, the characters are inserted into the character string in the keyboard buffer, and characters already there are pushed to the right. Learning to use this typeover/insert feature is very useful for correcting typing errors. A little practice with this key, in combination with the function key sequences discussed below, will increase your proficiency at the keyboard.

DOS uses the Esc key to cancel a command that is in the keyboard buffer. Use this key when you want to delete everything from the buffer to start over again. When this key is pressed, it produces a backslash character on the screen. Press the Enter key to bring the DOS prompt back to the screen.

The Del and Backspace keys accomplish similar functions. The Backspace key is used to backspace over information displayed on the screen while deleting it. If you want to backtrack without deleting the information, use the Left Arrow cursor key to move the cursor without deleting the characters. The Delete (Del) key deletes a character at the cursor position. Both visible characters as well as nonvisible characters can be deleted. (An example of a nonvisible character is a space or a return.) The Del key also causes all characters to the right of the deleted character to be moved one space to the left. The Del key can be used to delete characters from the middle of a string, command, or other data entry.

Many of these key sequences work with application software as well as with DOS. Some are replaced by sequences that are used for the application program. When you learn to use an application software package, be aware of its control key sequences. The DOS function key sequences may still work, or they may be replaced by a different sequence used by the application software program.

The Function keys F1, F2, F3, and F4 can be used with the DOS editor EDLIN and will perform the same functions within EDLIN as they do with DOS. Likewise, Ins, Del, and Backspace will work with EDLIN just as they do with DOS.

For example, let's compare some key functions in DOS to those in the popular word processing software package WordPerfect. The Ins, Del, and Backspace keys work with WordPerfect in much the same way as in DOS. DOS places the keyboard in typeover mode when the computer is booted. Typed characters replace or "type over" characters already in the keyboard buffer. WordPerfect places the keyboard in insert mode. Therefore, typed characters are inserted into the text, rather than typing over the text. The function key sequences, however, for F1, F2, F3, F4 and so on, do not have the same functions. They are replaced by word processing function key sequences for WordPerfect.

THE DOSKEY COMMAND

One of the new features added with the release of DOS Version 5 is the DOSKEY command. DOSKEY provides two basic features to simplify and enhance the use of DOS. DOSKEY maintains a file of commands previously entered for recall, modification, or execution. DOSKEY can also record sequences of keystrokes that can be used to create keyboard macros. In general, you will want to include DOSKEY as part of your AUTOEXEC.BAT file so that its features are available every time you turn on the computer. DOSKEY can also be started from the command line by typing its name. To execute DOSKEY, type the sequence shown below:

```
C:\> DOSKEY /bufsize=256
```

This command will install DOSKEY with a 256-byte buffer for saving commands typed at the keyboard. A 256-byte buffer will be adequate for most command sequences. To see how DOSKEY works, type the following sequence of commands:

```
C:\>cls
C:\>date
C:\>time
C:\>ver
C:\>vol
C:\>prompt $p$g
C:\>path
C:\>dir
```

After typing each command, press the Enter key. As these commands are entered, DOS prompts for the date and time. Just press the Enter key. You have now entered eight commands. Without the help of DOSKEY the only command available (i.e., stored in the keyboard buffer) would be the last command (dir). With DOSKEY, however, all the commands are available for recall.

To retrieve all eight commands, press the F7 function key. DOSKEY now displays the entire sequence on the screen

```
C:\>
1: cls
2: date
3: time
4: ver
5: vol
6: prompt $p$g
7: path
8: dir
C:\>
```

In addition to displaying the entire sequence, DOS numbers commands so you can recall them by line number without retyping. Press the Up Arrow key, and DOS displays the last command, DIR. If Up Arrow is pressed again, DIR is replaced by the command PATH. Down Arrow has just the opposite effect of Up Arrow.

To request a specific command by line number, use the F9 function key. For example, to request the VOL command, press function key F9. DOSKEY will display the message:

```
C:\>Line number: _
```

Type the number **5** to request the VOL command and DOS displays:

```
C:\>vol
```

Page Up moves to the top of the list and recalls the first command in the stored list (CLS). Page Down moves to the bottom of the list and recalls the last command entered (DIR). To clear the buffer and delete the entire list, use the Alt-F7 key sequence (where F7 refers to function key F7).

Table 2.2 describes the functions performed by various keys when you use the DOSKEY command. These keys combined with the three function key sequences F7, F9, and Alt-F7, implement the capabilities of DOSKEY. For a more detailed explanation of DOSKEY, along with several installation features and the implementation of its macro capabilities, refer to Chapter 15 on Input/Output Control.

TABLE 2.2 **DOSKEY Control and Editing Sequences**

Key Sequence	Function
Up Arrow [↑]	Displays the previous command in the list based on the command pointer.
Down Arrow [↓]	Displays the next command in the list based on the command pointer.
Left Arrow [←]	Moves the cursor one character to the left from its current position.
Right Arrow [→]	Moves the cursor one character to the right from its current position.
Page Up	Moves the command pointer to the top of the list and displays the first command.
Page Down	Moves the command pointer to the bottom and displays the last command.
Ctrl-[←]	Moves the cursor one word to the left.
Ctrl-[→]	Moves the cursor one word to the right.
Home	Moves the cursor to the beginning of the command.
End	Moves the cursor to the end of the command.
Ctrl-Home	Deletes all characters from the current cursor position to the beginning of the command.
Ctrl-End	Deletes all characters from the cursor location to the end of the command.
Ins	Puts the keyboard into insert mode so that characters are added at the current cursor position.
Del	Deletes characters at the current cursor location; the cursor remains in its current position.
Esc	Erases the command currently displayed.

The use of DOSKEY, along with the use of the function keys F1, F2, and F3, will dramatically improve your speed at the keyboard, as well as significantly reduce typing errors. Spend a little time learning to use these two very valuable features if you have upgraded your system to DOS Version 5. If you haven't upgraded to Version 5, DOSKEY, coupled with several other features unique to this version, is a strong reason to upgrade.

FUNCTION KEY SEQUENCES

In addition to providing hardware control functions through keyboard sequences, DOS also provides function key sequences that can increase your speed and skills at the keyboard. The sequences explained below work not only at the DOS command line, but also with other programs such as the DOS line editor EDLIN. If you learn to use these function key sequences, your speed and skills at the keyboard will increase. An added benefit is that you cut down on the number of characters typed, thereby reducing the probability of making typing errors. A few hours spent now learning to use the DOS function keys will save many hours in the future. Even unskilled typists can increase their efficiency by using function key sequences.

TABLE 2.3 DOS Function Key Sequences

F1	Recalls one character from the keyboard buffer each time it's depressed.
F2 *x*	Displays all characters up to the first occurrence of the character (represented by *x*) typed from the keyboard buffer.
F3	Recalls all characters from the buffer or the remaining characters in the buffer.
F4 *x*	Deletes all characters in the keyboard buffer up to but not including the character (*x*) pressed.
F5	Accepts the line edited as the current buffer line.
F6	Generates an EOF (End of File) character (Ctrl-Z) when pressed.
F7	Recalls to the screen the entire list of commands in DOSKEY's command buffer.
Alt-F7	Deletes all the commands from DOSKEY's command buffer and leaves it empty.
F9	Displays the message "Line Number" and allows a specific command to be recalled from the DOSKEY command buffer, based on its line number.

Function keys F7, Alt-F7, and F9 are activated by the execution of the DOSKEY command. The rest are activated when DOS is booted. A few examples will illustrate how to use these function key sequences. Once these examples are understood, you can then practice any time you're typing at the DOS command line. From the DOS prompt, type the following:

```
C:\> CHKDSK C:
```

The CHKDSK program executes and provides the standard CHKDSK report. The keyboard buffer is a 132-character memory that contains the last command typed. The F1 function key recalls the previous command, one character at a time. Now press the **F1** function key three times. Each time F1 is pressed, a single character from the previous command is recalled. Pressing F1 three times recalls in sequence the C, the H, and the K characters from the CHKDSK C: command stored in the keyboard buffer memory. Now press **F3.** The rest of the previous command (DSK C:) is recalled. What now appears on your screen is the previous command in full, CHKDSK C:. Press **Enter** to execute the CHKDSK command again.

Now press **F3.** The entire command from the keyboard buffer is recalled. Press **Enter** to execute the command again. As you can see, F3 recalls either the entire command or the remainder of the command from the keyboard buffer. In the first example, F3 recalled the remainder of the command from the buffer memory. In the second example, it recalled the entire command from the keyboard buffer.

Now let's look at the F2 and F4 function keys and how these work with the keyboard buffer. Pressing either of these keys alone does nothing. In both cases you must press another key in addition to the function key. The command CHKDSK C: is still stored in the keyboard buffer. Press the function key **F2** and then press the **K** key on the keyboard. The F2 function key recalls the previous command up to but not including the first occurrence of the character pressed. Because the K character was the character you typed, the CH characters (up to but not including the K) from the previous command are recalled. Now press the **F3** key to recall the rest of the command. Then press **Enter** to execute the command.

The F4 function key works just the opposite way from the F2 function key. To see how, press the **F4** function key followed by the **K** key. Now press the **F3** function key. The CH characters have been deleted from the command CHKDSK C:. Press the **Enter** key. You should receive the message "Bad Command or File Name" because there is no command KDSK C:. The F4 function key will probably have limited applications as you use DOS, whereas F2 will find many applications when you wish to modify the fields in a command. Let's illustrate through just one example.

Enter the CHKDSK command as you did before, but this time to check Drive A on your computer:

```
C:\> CHKDSK A:
```

Press the **F2** key now followed by **A.** The command is recalled up to but not including the A. Now type **C:** and press the **Enter** key. By using the F2 function key and typing a single character you were able to modify a command. Now press **F2** again followed by **C.** Then press **A:** and then the **Enter** key again to check Drive A. The DOS F2 function key has many uses: copying files, building directory structures, and so on. F4 is more limited in its applications.

Practice using these function keys, including those associated with DOSKEY, which we discussed earlier. Once you've developed some proficiency, you will find the use of these keys extremely valuable.

FLOPPY DISKETTES

Figure 2.3 shows a 5 1/4-inch floppy diskette, with the major parts identified.

The label shown may or may not be present on your diskette. For major brands of diskettes, the label normally appears in the upper lefthand corner of the protective jacket. The write-protect notch is shown on the right edge of the disk. When it is uncovered, as shown in the picture, the diskette is in read/write mode. In this mode data can be read from and written to the diskette. To place the diskette in read-only mode, (so that no additional data can be stored on it) cover the notch with a protective tab supplied with the diskette. The opening for the disk drive spindle is shown along with the diskette hub. The index hole is shown on the right next to the spindle hole. If the diskette is turned within the sleeve, a

FIGURE 2.3 Major parts of a 5 1/4-inch Diskette

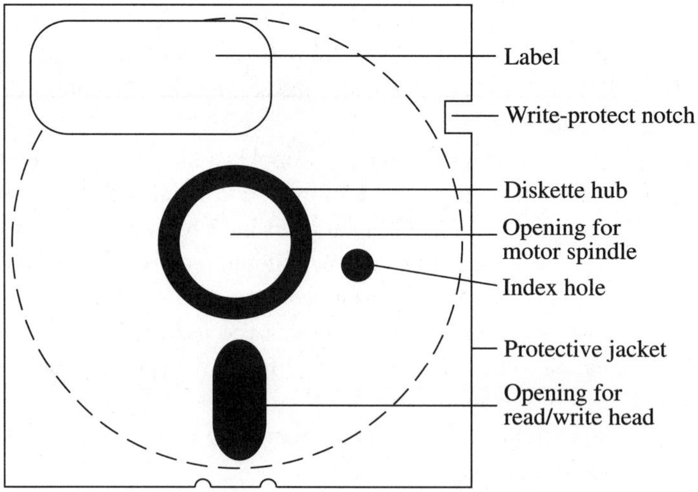

hole in the diskette media itself will line up with the index hole in the sleeve. If there is only one hole in the diskette it is a soft-sectored diskette. If it has several holes, the diskette is a hard-sectored diskette. Most diskettes for personal computers are soft-sectored. The sectoring on the diskette is established by the software formatting routine (FORMAT). The opening for the read/write head is shown at the bottom of the figure. This area of the diskette should be protected from dust and dirt as much as possible. When not in use, the diskette should be housed in its protective sleeve or jacket.

Figure 2.4 shows the major parts of a 3 1/2-inch floppy diskette.

The label shown may or may not be present on the diskette. The write-protect notch is shown in the lower righthand corner of the figure. When covered, the disk is in read/write mode. This is just the opposite of the 5 1/4-inch disks. In this mode, data can be read from and written to the diskette. To place the diskette in read-only mode, slide the plastic piece to open the notch. With this notch hole open, no data can be written to the diskette. Notice the opening on the back for the disk drive motor spindle. The shutter part of the diskette is shown at the top. This shutter slides left and right and is spring-loaded. In its normal position, the shutter is closed and protects the opening for the read/write head from dust and

FIGURE 2.4 Major parts of a 3 1/2-inch Diskette

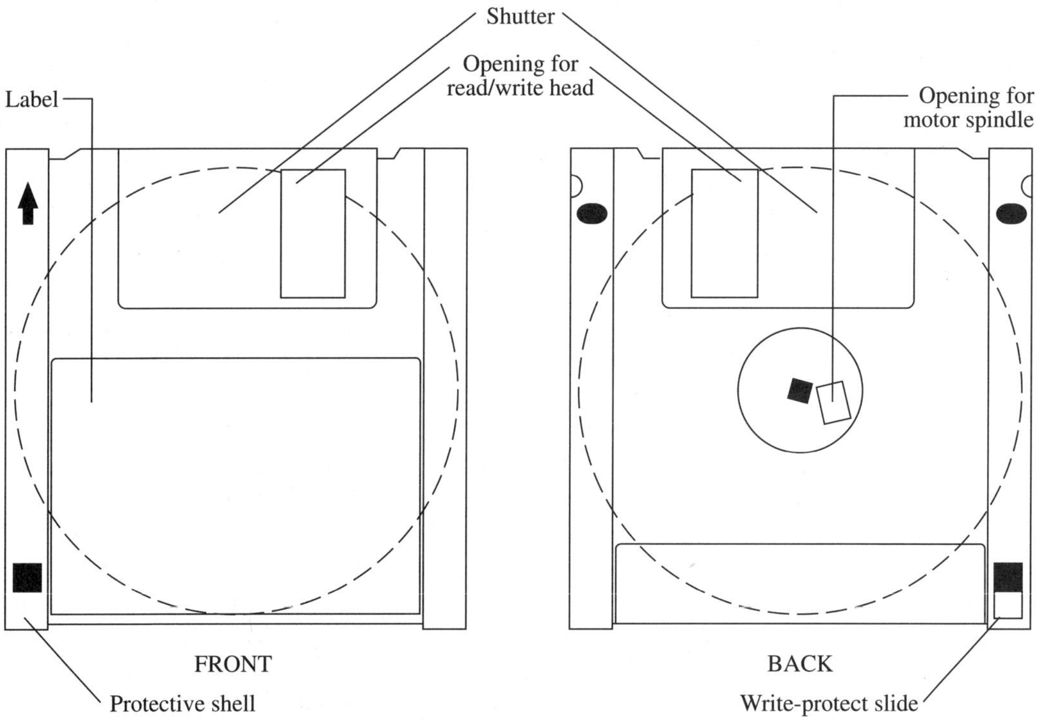

dirt. When the diskette is inserted in the drive, this shutter will slide open to expose the media to the read/write head of the drive. This area of the diskette should be protected from dust and dirt as much as possible. The spring-loaded shutter will normally do this automatically.

FILENAMES AND FILE EXTENSIONS

You can create files using DOS or by using application software programs. Regardless of what program creates the files, you can use DOS to manage and manipulate the files. For this reason, files that are created must obey the DOS file-naming conventions. A file specification under DOS consists of two parts: a **filename,** which is required, and a **file extension,** which is optional. Filenames may be one to eight characters in length. File extensions may be one to three characters in length. Table 2.4 shows all the characters that may be used in a filename or in a file extension; it also shows characters that are *not* permitted.

TABLE 2.4 **Characters in DOS File Specifications**

Valid Characters	**Invalid Characters**
■ Any alphabetic character	■ A space
■ Any numeric character	■ Special characters ^ * + = [ ] : ; " \ , . ? / < >
■ Special characters ! @ # $ % & ( ) - _ { } ' ` ~	

As you scan this table, a little thought shows why some characters may not be used in a filename or its extension. The backslash (\) character is used in addressing files; the asterisk (*) and the question mark (?) are wildcard characters that can be used in file addressing. DOS uses the dollar sign ($) in the extension to indicate an incomplete file. The character that can cause great difficulty when creating filenames is the space character. Although DOS does not allow a filename to contain a space, many application programs allow a filename to be created containing a space. When this happens, you then have a file that cannot be addressed, copied, or moved by DOS. This problem is a fairly common one. If this happens, use the Rename (REN) command (see Chapter 7) to change the name to one that does not contain the space character.

The problem when using special characters in filenames is remembering which of the special characters are valid characters and which are invalid. In general, the safest course of action in naming all files, whether through DOS or through application software, is to follow the few simple rules outlined in Table 2.5. You can violate these rules as long as you use valid characters. These rules are simple, easy to learn, and easy to remember.

TABLE 2.5 Rules for File Specifications

- Use structured filenames as much as possible so that it is easy to remember the contents of the file.
- Use only alphabetic and numeric characters in a filename.
- Start each filename with an alphabetic character
- Avoid the use of all special characters in filenames.

By following these simple rules, you avoid many of the problems found when naming files. You avoid addressing problems when using drive and path names along with filenames to address files. You avoid problems when using wildcard characters such as the asterisk and the question mark to address groups of files. Finally, by using structured filenames, it becomes easy to copy and manipulate groups of like files.

Some examples of structured filenames will give an idea of how you can use the name of a file to remember its contents. When writing letters or memos, begin the filename with the characters LET (if it is a letter) or MEM (if it is a memo). Use the next three characters to indicate to whom the letter or memo is addressed. For example, a letter to James R. Smith becomes LETJRS. Finally, use the last two characters to indicate the number of the correspondence, so the first letter becomes 1 or 01, the second letter is 2 or 02, and so on. Thus, the second letter to James R. Smith becomes a file with a filename LETJRS2 or LETJRS02. In scanning the files in a directory or on a diskette containing correspondence, it is easy to find all the letters to James R. Smith. It is also easy to copy or back up all letters by using structured filenames.

Be careful when giving extension names to files. Most application software packages use extensions to denote the types of files that are being created. Lotus 1-2-3 adds the file extension WK1 or WK3 to any spreadsheet file created. dBASE adds file extensions to each file created by dBASE: database files are given the extension DBF, database index files have an extension NDX, database reports are denoted by an extension RPT, and so on. If creating a file with an application software package, it is best to only use the filename. Leave the extension field to the application software.

SYSTEM DEFAULTS

System defaults are features built into the hardware and software that make the computer work in a certain way. These features are usually designed to make the computer easy to use. There are many such defaults built into your personal computer. This section will not attempt to discuss them all. Rather, the purpose of mentioning them early in the book is to make the user aware of assumptions that the computer makes when you turn the power on, when you type a command, and when you address a file. As you learn DOS and learn how to use its many features and commands, keep system defaults in mind. It will make you a more sophisticated user of your computer.

One example of a system default is built into the power-on procedure. During the power-on process, DOS looks for two files in the root directory. These two files are CONFIG.SYS and AUTOEXEC.BAT. If it finds these two files, DOS reads them and processes the information. It then uses that information to set up your computer for use. But suppose DOS doesn't find either of these files. Does the user get an error message indicating that the files are missing? Does the computer fail to boot? The answer to both questions is No. Instead, DOS uses some system default values for what *would* have been in the CONFIG.SYS and AUTOEXEC.BAT files so that your computer still boots successfully. In the case of CONFIG.SYS, default values are set for the BREAK parameter and for the BUFFERS and FILES parameters. These may not be the values needed to use a specific piece of software, but the computer still works and the boot process is still successful. Likewise, even though no AUTOEXEC.BAT file exists, DOS processes a default AUTOEXEC.BAT file. With no AUTOEXEC.BAT file in the root directory, DOS will request the user to enter both Date and Time information so that files can be correctly date- and time-stamped. Then DOS displays the default disk drive for your computer, along with the DOS prompt character—the greater-than sign (>).

Another example of system defaults occurs any time the user types a command. If the command is an external command and there is no AUTOEXEC.BAT file, DOS makes some assumptions about where to look to find that command. The user can override these assumptions in any one of several ways. What does DOS assume when an external command is typed at the DOS prompt? Without any other instructions, DOS automatically looks for the executable file on the default drive and in the default or current directory. If the user gets the message "Bad Command or Filename," it does not mean that the executable program does not exist. It only means that the file is not in the default directory on the default drive. Change the default drive and/or the default directory to correspond to the place where the executable file is stored (for example, change from the A drive to the C drive) and the external program will execute.

Finally, what does DOS assume when addressing a file? For example, where does DOS look when the user copies a file if the file is not fully addressed? Without addressing information (the drive and the directory where the file is located), DOS looks in the default directory on the default drive.

These are but a few examples of system defaults built into your computer. Keep the idea of system defaults in mind the next time a command doesn't work, or when the command works incorrectly. Consider system defaults the next time you lose a file. One of the reasons may be that DOS made an assumption (i.e., used a system default) in the absence of specific information from you.

We'll discuss system defaults throughout this book so that you become keenly aware of many of the system defaults built into your computer. A sophisticated user of DOS can use the concept of system defaults to advantage when executing DOS commands and when using application software. Just as DOS has many system defaults built into its structure, application software packages have defaults built into their programs and installation processes. These defaults are vital to the correct installation and successful use of application software, just as they are to DOS.

INPUT/OUTPUT REDIRECTION

DOS provides a method for input or output to be redirected to a device other than the one normally used by a specific command. The input and output redirection symbols are the less-than sign (<) for input and the greater-than sign (>) for output. Input redirection is not used extensively. As you learn to use DOS, you'll use input redirection primarily when using the DOS filter commands (Chapter 14).

Output redirection, however, is used extensively when using DOS. It has many applications, one of which is described below. The DIR command normally displays the directory listing to the display screen or monitor. Suppose, however, that you need a hard copy of the directory listing, perhaps for documentation purposes, or to help you reorganize a diskette or a directory. DOS provides a very simple method for getting hard-copy information when using the DIR command. Just redirect the output to the default printer. The first example below shows the normal method for getting a listing of the directory of the diskette in Drive A. The second example shows output redirection to get a hard copy on the default printer. Output redirection has many uses, and it is very easy to implement.

`C:\> DIR A:`	The output of the directory listing goes to the display screen.
`C:\> DIR A: > PRN`	The output directory listing in this case is redirected to the printer because of the redirection symbol (>) and the default printer code PRN.

Output redirection can also be used to append information to a file. The double output-redirection symbol (>>) is used to append information to an existing file. To send a directory to a file named DIRECTRY use the command shown below.

`C:\> DIR C:\ > DIRECTRY`	The output of the directory listing goes to a file named DIRECTRY on Drive C.

To append a subdirectory listing to this file, you would enter the following:

`C:\> DIR \WP51 >> DIRECTRY`	The output directory listing for the directory \WP51 is now added to the end of the file DIRECTRY.

QUESTIONS AND PROBLEMS

1. What is the meaning of the term *keyboard control sequence?* Give an example of such a sequence and how you might use it.
2. What function is performed by the F3 function key when used in connection with DOS?
3. What three keys perform no function by themselves, but instead must be used in combination with one or more other keys to perform operational command sequences in DOS?
4. What are some of the features found on an enhanced keyboard as compared to the standard IBM-style keyboard?
5. What is the keyboard buffer? How many characters or bytes of information can the keyboard buffer hold when filled to capacity?
6. What control key sequence performs a warm boot under DOS? When might a warm boot be performed as part of a normal operating sequence?
7. What does the write-protect notch on a diskette do? How do you determine when a 5 1/4-inch diskette is read-only? When a 3 1/2-inch diskette is read-only?
8. What are the special characters used to represent wildcards when addressing a group of files?
9. What are some advantages of using structured filenames to name similar groups of files?
10. Give an example of a system default associated with the cold boot or power-on process.
11. What is the default directory used by DOS when executing an external command file?
12. What is the default device used by DOS to display output and error messages while executing a command?
13. What symbol is used to override the default output device if a user wants to obtain hard-copy output via a command to the system printer?

CHAPTER 3

COMMANDS AND COMMAND GROUPS

INTRODUCTION

As the power of microcomputers has increased and as software packages have become more sophisticated, operating systems in general, and DOS in particular, have taken on added importance. Whether it is DOS, UNIX, DR DOS, or several other operating systems, they have all been required to increase their power and sophistication, due to the increase in computer power, the availability of larger disk drives, and the need for more RAM. Microsoft Corporation has responded to these demands by steadily improving DOS's features and capabilities. A glance back at Table 1.1 in Chapter 1 gives some insight into the tremendous increase in DOS capability in the last 10 years. Will DOS be replaced in popularity by another operating system in 1995 or in the year 2000? No one can be sure of the answer to that question. We *can* be sure, however, that operating systems will only increase in importance as microcomputers continue to increase in power and sophistication.

For these reasons it is important that today's user of microcomputers understands the power available through the operating system. This text concentrates on DOS, but we can use DOS as a window to understanding operating systems in general. With this understanding, the user gains knowledge that can be applied to understanding other operating systems and their functions, whether this be a network system such as Novell or another operating system such as OS/2, or UNIX, or the Macintosh System 7 operating system for that matter. While the primary purpose of this text is to teach DOS, a secondary purpose is to teach the basic functions and capabilities that are provided by most operating systems.

COMMAND GROUPS

This text is organized around the major tasks and functions provided by DOS. This is the concept behind command groups, and how the commands are presented in this text. Command groups bring together DOS commands, based on the major functions they perform within the context of the operating system. The two basic groups are internal commands (Part II of this book), and external commands (Part III). Within each group commands are organized by function. For example, all the internal commands that have to do with directory management are grouped together and discussed in Chapter 6; external commands for directory management are presented in Chapter 10. File management commands that are internal are discussed in Chapter 7; external file management commands are discussed in Chapter 12.

In general, commands that are simple and use no or few parameters are internal. Internal DOS commands are the commands stored within the DOS command processor COMMAND.COM. Commands that are complicated and use many parameters are always external. External files will generally require in excess of 10,000 bytes of hard drive space.

The major DOS functions include disk management, directory management, file management, I/O control, and so on. Within each of the major functions, the commands are discussed from the most-used to the least-used. In general, this order is also from the most important commands to the least important within that group.

You will gain an understanding of DOS and the major functions for your computer by sampling a few commands from within each group. How and where you use your computer (for example, whether you use it within the United States only or internationally) will determine what DOS commands you need to understand. There are some DOS commands you may never use. If you don't need these commands, your use and application of your computer and its software is in no way diminished. Your need for DOS, its functions, and its commands depends on you. Learn the commands and functions you need. Don't worry if you never learn to use the EXE2BIN command or the CTTY command if those functions don't affect your work. Build your understanding and knowledge in areas that are most useful to you.

Table 3.1 shows the DOS command groups for both internal and external commands. These command groups give an insight into the major management functions DOS performs on your computer.

TABLE 3.1 DOS Command Groups

Command Group	Internal	External
Disk management	X	X
Directory management	X	X
File management	X	X
Memory management		X
System control	X	X
Filter		X
I/0 control		X
Device control		X
Utilities		X

Your version of DOS may vary slightly, depending on the version you use. If you have a compatible operating system with an emulator, the emulator will normally be an external command file.

The commands for PC-DOS Version 5 are shown in Table 3.2. These commands are identified as to internal, external, configuration, and batch file commands.

TABLE 3.2 **Command Types for PC-DOS Version 5**

Internal	External		Configuration	Batch File
	APPEND	EXE		
	ASSIGN	COM		
	ATTRIB	EXE		
	BACKUP	EXE		
	BASIC	COM		
	BASICA	EXE		
			BREAK	
			BUFFERS	
				CALL
CD				
	CHKDSK	EXE		
CLS				
	COMMAND	COM		
	COMP	EXE		
COPY				
			COUNTRY	
CTTY				
DATE				
	DEBUG	EXE		
DEL				
			DEVICE	
DIR				
	DISKCOMP	COM		
	DISKCOPY	COM		
	DOSKEY	COM		
			DRIVPARM	
				ECHO
	EDIT	COM		
	EDLIN	EXE		
	EMM386	EXE		
	EXE2BIN	EXE		
ERASE				
	EXPAND	EXE		
	FASTOPEN	EXE		
			FCBS	
	FC	EXE		

continued

TABLE 3.2 Command Types for PC-DOS Version 5

Internal	External		Configuration	Batch File
	FDISK	EXE		
			FILES	
	FILESYS	EXE		
	FIND	EXE		
				FOR
	FORMAT	COM		
				GOTO
	GRAFTABL	COM		
	GRAPHICS	COM		
	HELP	EXE		
				IF
				IF EXIST
				IF ERROR-LEVEL
				IF NOT
				IF NOT EXIST
				IF NOT ERROR-LEVEL
	IFSFUNC	EXE		
			INSTALL	
	JOIN	EXE		
	KEYB	COM		
	KEYBxx	COM		
				LABEL
	LABEL	COM		
			LASTDRIVE	
MD				
	MEM	EXE		
	MIRROR	COM		
	MODE	COM		
	MORE	COM		
	NLSFUNC	EXE		
PATH				
				PAUSE

continued

TABLE 3.2 Command Types for PC-DOS Version 5

Internal	External		Configuration	Batch File
	PRINT	EXE		
PROMPT				
RD				
	RECOVER	EXE		
				REM
REN				
	REPLACE	EXE		
	RESTORE	EXE		
	SELECT	EXE		
SET				
	SETVER	EXE		
	SHARE	EXE		
			SHELL	
	SHELLB	COM		
	SHELLC	EXE		
				SHIFT
	SORT	EXE		
			STACKS	
	SUBST	EXE		
			SWITCHES	
	SYS	COM		
TIME				
	TREE	COM		
TYPE				
	UNDELETE	EXE		
	UNFORMAT	EXE		
VER				
VERIFY				
VOL				
	XCOPY	EXE		

QUESTIONS AND PROBLEMS

1. Give some examples of major functions performed by DOS.
2. Why is the FORMAT command included as part of the operating system rather than made a part of an application software package such as WordPerfect, Lotus 1-2-3, or dBASE?
3. What program keeps track of the storage space on the hard drive of your computer?
4. How can a user identify all the internal commands available as part of a given version of DOS?
5. How can a user identify all the external commands available as part of the version of DOS that is installed on the hard drive of their computer system?
6. What extension is used to denote that a command is a configuration command?
7. Where are the programs associated with internal commands stored in the DOS operating system?
8. What is the meaning of the letters *DOS* when referring to the operating system for a personal computer?
9. What are some advantages of storing DOS on a hard drive rather than on a floppy diskette when operating a personal computer?
10. What extensions are used to denote that a program supplied as an external file with DOS is an executable program?

CHAPTER 4

INTRODUCTORY COMMANDS

INTRODUCTION

Several basic commands, from several command groups, are needed to get started with the DOS operating system. Each of these commands will be discussed in depth in the chapter that handles that command group, but a few basic skills are necessary to begin to use and understand DOS. This chapter provides a quick introduction to a few commands that will help you understand the capabilities of DOS. These commands are covered in depth in Part II of the book (if they are internal) or Part III of the book (if they are external). These introductory commands include:

HELP
FORMAT
CHKDSK
PROMPT
DIR
DISKCOPY
COPY

Each command, when entered at the DOS prompt, consists of several parts. All parts need not be entered, depending upon the reason for typing the command. At a minimum, only the command itself must be entered. The general format for all commands is:

```
C:\> COMMAND <Field1> <Field2> /Parameter > Device
```

COMMAND is the name of the command such as DIR, COPY, CHKDSK, and so on. If this is typed incorrectly, the message "Bad Command or Filename" will be issued by DOS. *Fields* are information that indicate what the DOS command should operate on, such as a directory name or a group of files. An example of a field is \WP51 to indicate the \WP51 directory for WordPerfect. *Parameters* or *switches* are always preceded by a forward slash (/) and modify the command in some way. For example, the /W parameter for the DIR command indicates that the report should be in wide mode. Commands normally display all results on their default *device,* namely the display screen (CON). Error messages and reports can be redirected, however, to another device. If the redirection symbol (>) is used, then a device name must be indicated such as COM1, PRN, etc. Information can also be redirected to a disk drive such as C: or A:. If so, then a filename must also be given. To redirect output to a disk, for example, the device might be C:TEMPFILE.

THE HELP (HELP) COMMAND

The HELP command is new with Version 5 of DOS. However, this command is not "the answer to all your prayers" if you are just learning DOS. HELP does not display a detailed explanation of each command and how to use it; rather, it provides a brief (maximum of one page) summary display of information about the specified command. It also displays a list of parameters or switches associated with that command, and the meaning or function associated with those parameters.

HELP is particularly useful when using switches such as /P, /O, and /B with the DIR command, for example. HELP does not tell how or when to use a command. Error messages are not explained. Furthermore, some commands are not covered by HELP; in this case you will receive the message "Help not available for this command." Other commands may refer you to your reference manual. For example, the message received after typing HELP RECOVER says "Consult your User's Guide before using the RECOVER command "

To use the HELP command, type the word HELP followed by the name of the command at the DOS prompt, or type the command followed by a question mark, as shown in the example below, which shows how to get help with the command DISKCOPY. Enter at the DOS prompt:

`C:\>` **`HELP DISKCOPY`** or **`DISKCOPY /?`**

A maximum one-page display of information about DISKCOPY, including the parameters or switches associated with the command, will be displayed. For DISKCOPY the HELP command display is:

```
Copies the contents of one floppy disk to another.
DISKCOPY [drive1: [drive2:]] [/1] [/V]
/1 Copies only the first side of the disk.
/V Verifies that the information is copied correctly.

The two floppy disks must be the same type.
You may specify the same drive for drive1 and drive2.
```

THE FORMAT (FORMAT) COMMAND

The FORMAT command is used to prepare any diskette so that it can store files of information. In addition to formatting the diskette, the FORMAT command can also prepare a diskette so that it can boot the operating system. The FORMAT command permits selective formatting so that a diskette will be compatible across a range of computer systems and floppy disk drives.

The first time you format a diskette on a floppy drive, you can learn the default format of the drive itself. The default format could be 720 KB or 1.44 MB capacity for a 3 1/2-inch drive, or 360 KB or 1.2 MB for a 5 1/4-inch drive. To format a diskette on your floppy drive, insert a high-density diskette in the drive; at the DOS prompt, type the following:

```
C:\> FORMAT d:
```

where d: is either A: for Drive A or B: for Drive B.

In response, the FORMAT.COM file will be loaded into memory from the hard drive and executed. You will then receive a message to load a diskette into Drive A or Drive B and to press Enter. Follow the instructions on the screen. The FORMAT program will display the cylinders and read/write heads being addressed as it formats the diskette. The final message displayed on the screen will indicate how many tracks are used on each side of the disk: either 40 tracks for 360 KB diskettes or 80 tracks for any of the other formats.

If, in formatting the high-density diskette, a message "Invalid media" is received, use a double-density diskette in place of the high-density one. The "Invalid media" message normally indicates that the diskette is incompatible with the disk drive.

When the diskette is formatted, it will display a disk capacity of one of the four types shown below:

- 5 1/4-inch DSDD 362,496 bytes
- 5 1/4-inch DSHD 1,213,952 bytes
- 3 1/2-inch DSDD 730,112 bytes
- 3 1/2-inch DSHD 1,457,664 bytes

It is important to know the default formatting capacity of your floppy drive because it determines the type of diskette that you should purchase—either double-density (DD) or high-density (HD). For an IBM-AT or AT-compatible computer with a 5 1/4-inch drive, buy high-density (HD) rather than double-density (DD) diskettes to take full advantage of the maximum capacity of the disk drive. Likewise, for a 3 1/2-inch drive, note whether the drive formats diskettes at the 1.45 MB capacity level or at 730 KB. If the drive capacity is 1.45 MB, buy high-density diskettes to take maximum advantage of the capability of the disk drive.

In addition to formatting the disk so that it can store files, the FORMAT command can also build a diskette with the DOS kernel or nucleus stored on it. In other words, the FORMAT command can build diskettes that will boot the computer. Note, however, that only Drive A can be used as a boot drive for diskettes. Personal computers, in general, are not designed to boot from a diskette drive other than Drive A.

To format a bootable system disk, load a diskette into the floppy drive and at the DOS prompt, use the format command shown below:

```
C:\> FORMAT A:/S
```

Now use the directory (DIR) command to check the space available on the disk; note that the difference between the space originally available on the disk and the size of the COMMAND.COM file leaves a large block of space unaccounted for. A diskette built as a system disk contains two hidden files along with the COMMAND.COM processor. When viewed with DIR, only the COMMAND.COM file will show up on the file listing. To see the hidden files on the disk use the Check Disk (CHKDSK) command. In addition to formatting the diskette in the default format as a bootable system disk, the FORMAT command allows the diskette to be formatted in a variety of ways depending on specific requirements. One example illustrates the point. If a 3 1/2-inch diskette is used on a number of different computers, you may need to format the diskette as double density or 730 KB. Diskettes formatted at 730 KB can be read by high-density drives as well as double-density drives, but double-density drives cannot read high-density diskettes. So, if a diskette must be used on both double-density and high-density drives, format the diskette as double-density, so you can use it on either system without worrying about the capacity of the individual disk drive. It is also important to note that software is normally distributed on double-density diskettes; these diskettes can then be read by either double-density or high-density drives when the software is installed.

To format a disk as a double-density diskette, use the formatting parameters to override the default format of the disk drive. The first example below formats 3 1/2-inch, high-density diskette in a high density drive at double-density capacity. The second example illustrates a high-density 5 1/4-inch diskette formatted as a double-density diskette in a high-density drive. For the 3 1/2-inch diskette type the following:

```
C:\> FORMAT A: /N:9/T:80
```

A 1.45 MB diskette will now have a data capacity of only 730,112 bytes. (730 KB)

For the 5 1/4-inch disk type the following:

```
C:\> FORMAT A:/4
```

A 1.2 MB diskette will now have a data capacity of only 362,496 bytes (360 KB).

To gain compatibility, we must sacrifice the higher storage capacity of the diskette. In the case of the 1.45 MB diskette, we lose half of the disk's potential data capacity. In the case of the 1.2 MB diskette, we sacrifice almost 70 percent of the disk's storage capacity.

The above examples illustrate the basic capabilities of the FORMAT command. For more detailed information on the full range of parameters that can be used with FORMAT, refer to Chapter 9 on Disk Management (External Commands).

THE CHECK DISK (CHKDSK) COMMAND

The Check Disk (CHKDSK) command provides capabilities for checking the space utilization of a diskette. It also provides information on the internal memory of your computer, including the size of the memory and the amount of free space available. The space used in RAM is that consumed by the DOS nucleus, including device drivers and other programs, and data space allocated as a result of information and commands contained in your CONFIG.SYS and AUTOEXEC.BAT files. DOS processes the information in these files during the boot process.

A sample CHKDSK command along with the report it generates is shown below. The report shown is in three parts. The first part provides information on a 20 MB hard disk and the information stored on it.

```
C:\> CHKDSK C:

21135360 bytes total disk space
   53248 bytes in 3 hidden files
   38912 bytes in 16 directories
14256128 bytes in 474 user files
   10240 bytes in bad sectors
 6787072 bytes available on disk

    2048 bytes in each allocation unit
   10337 total allocation units on disk
    1704 available allocation units on disk

  655360 bytes total memory
  491904 bytes free
```

The first line shows the total amount of data space available on the disk. The space the system uses for the FAT table, the system directory, and so forth, is not included in the first line of the report. This hard disk has a data capacity of 21,135,360 bytes. The second line of the report shows the amount of space used by hidden files. Because a hard disk is usually bootable, you can expect to have at least two hidden files on the disk. One of these is the DOS I/O Manager and the second is the DOS File Manager. If there is a third hidden file, it will normally be the Volume Label on the disk. (Other hidden files may be present, depending on the applications installed on the disk and the way the drive has been set up.) The third line of the report shows the number of directories, in addition to the root directory, that are present on the disk, and the amount of disk space they require.

The fourth line shows the total number of bytes consumed by all the user files on the disk. These are the files that show up when you execute the DIR command. There are a total of 474 user files on the disk in addition to the three hidden files.

The fifth line of the report may or may not be present. On a hard disk report it shows up quite frequently. On a report for a floppy disk there should not be a bad sector line in the report. Floppy diskettes are normally certified to be error free. On this report there are 10,240 bytes of space on the hard drive that have been flagged by DOS as "bad." DOS has made them unavailable for use by setting certain codes in the FAT table. Finally, there is 6.787 MB of space still available on this disk for use. In other words, approximately 70 percent of the space on the hard disk has already been utilized.

The second part of the report provides information on how space will be used on the hard drive. This disk has been formatted to use a minimum of 2048 bytes of space each time a file is created. An allocation unit for this disk consists of four sectors (4 × 512 = 2048). This disk has a total of 10,337 allocation units, each of which is 2048 bytes in size. There are 1704 allocation units remaining on the drive.

The third part of the report provides information on the computer's internal memory or RAM. This computer would normally be said to contain 640K of RAM, with each 1K of RAM equivalent to 1024 bytes of memory, so the actual number of bytes on a 640K computer is 655,360 bytes (640 × 1024 = 655,360 bytes). The DOS nucleus and related parts of the operating system have consumed 163,456 bytes. The remainder of RAM (491,904 bytes) is free to use for application software and the associated data that may be generated.

CHKDSK can be used with a number of parameters. To see the hidden files on the disk, use the /V parameter with CHKDSK. For more detail on the use and application of CHKDSK, see Chapter 9 on Disk Management (External Commands).

THE PROMPT (PROMPT) COMMAND

The Prompt (PROMPT) command sets the DOS system prompt. If the prompt is not set specifically by the user, DOS displays the default prompt, which is the default drive letter followed by the greater-than (>) sign. DOS provides a great deal of flexibility in setting the system prompt. In many cases you will want to tailor the system prompt to specific needs or to specific circumstances; for example, you could set up a batch file menu system in which you could use a string prompt such as "Enter Selection" with the menu.

As mentioned earlier, DOS uses many default values when you enter a command. One of the primary defaults DOS uses in addressing files is the default or current directory. Therefore, it is desirable to have the default directory as well as the default drive displayed as part of the standard DOS prompt. To have DOS display the default directory as well as the default drive, enter the following command:

PROMPT pg

DOS will now display both directory and drive information. If the current directory is the root directory, then the prompt will include a Backslash (\). To make this prompt change permanent, this command should be included in the AUTOEXEC.BAT file stored in the root directory on the hard drive.

Chapter 8 discusses the PROMPT command in much greater detail. It also includes the use of many other character combinations ($d, $n, $h, and so on) and a discussion on using alphabetic strings in the prompt.

THE DIRECTORY (DIR) COMMAND

The Directory (DIR) command is probably the most frequently used DOS command. The DIR command displays the contents of any disk and directory combination. The DIR command provides a listing of the user files in the specified directory. Hidden files are not shown in the directory listing.

The DIR command makes certain assumptions (system defaults) if the drive and directory are not specified as part of the command. Several examples will illustrate how DOS handles the DIR command.

1. C:\> **DIR /W**
2. C: > **DIR \WP50**
3. C:\> **DIR A:\DOS330**

In the first example, only DIR was typed at the DOS prompt along with the /W parameter. Since no drive or directory was specified, DOS uses the system defaults to decide what directory information to provide. The directory listing provided is for the default drive—in this case, the C drive, as shown by the DOS prompt, and the default directory—in this case, the root directory, sometimes referred to as the Backslash (\) directory. So, if the user does not specify a drive or directory, DOS reports on the default directory for the default drive. Both of these are normally displayed as part of the DOS prompt. Including the switch /W produces a wide listing with only the filename and extension included. The date and time of file creation or update, along with the file size, are not shown for each file.

In the second example, a directory was included as part of the command. The \WP50 directory was part of the DOS command line. DOS has a directory specified so it looks on the default drive (C:) to find a listing for the \WP50 directory. If there is a \WP50 directory on drive C, DOS will provide a directory listing for it. In the first example, no mistake was possible since DOS always knows the default drive and the default directory on that drive. In the second example, it is possible that \WP50 might not exist on the default drive. If not, DOS would supply the message "File not found." DOS will not indicate that an incorrect directory name has been specified.

In the third example, the command line specifies both a drive (A:) and a directory (\DOS330), along with the command. This command requests a directory listing for Drive A instead of C. Assuming that there is a \DOS330 directory on the diskette in Drive A, DOS will provide the listing for this drive-and-directory combination.

The DIR command can also be used to list a file or group of files on a drive-directory combination. The following is an example:

```
C:\> DIR A:\DOS330\*.COM
```

This command line asks for a listing of only the files that have a COM extension. The *.COM is a wildcard that specifies any file with a COM extension. Thus, this directory listing will be for Drive A, the \DOS330 directory, but for only those files having a COM extension. Files having the extension EXE or SYS, or any other extension, will not be shown in the directory listing. For more information on the DIR command, see Chapter 6 on Directory Management.

THE DISKCOPY (DISKCOPY) COMMAND

The Diskcopy (DISKCOPY) command makes a sector-by-sector copy of the contents of a source diskette onto a target diskette. The source and target diskettes must be of similar format in order to make a duplication. Thus a 720 KB diskette of 3 1/2-inch size cannot be duplicated onto a 1.2 MB diskette that is 5 1/4 inches in size. The DISKCOPY program does just what the name implies. It makes an exact duplicate, track for track and sector for sector, of a source disk copied on to a target diskette.

In many versions of DOS, the DISKCOPY program will format the target disk if it is not already formatted. While this capability is included in DOS versions after 3.10, the duplication process is not always reliable. Therefore, it is recommended that you format all target diskettes before using DISKCOPY. If DISKCOPY is used with unformatted disks, then use DISKCOMP (discussed in Chapter 9) after DISKCOPY to check that the duplication was successful. If an error message indicates that the DISKCOPY was unsuccessful with an unformatted diskette, try DISKCOPY again after first formatting the target diskette.

To avoid accidentally destroying programs or data, it is always advisable to use working copies of any master software disks rather than the master itself. The DISKCOPY program can reproduce this working copy from the master. DISKCOPY can produce copies by copying from one floppy drive to a second floppy drive on dual-drive systems. The floppy drives must be of similar format, however. To make duplicates on single-drive systems, the source and target drive letters will be the same. In this case, DISKCOPY will prompt you to load the source and target diskettes at the appropriate time.

Whenever duplicating diskettes, it is recommended that the source diskette be write-protected to prevent the accidental copying of a blank diskette over the source disk. Diskettes are discussed in Chapter 2 and the method for write-protecting both 5 1/4- and 3 1/2-inch diskettes is explained there.

THE COPY (COPY) COMMAND

The COPY command is used to copy a single file or a group of files from one hardware device to another. These devices are addressed through their device name. For instance, the console display screen is addressed as CON, the printer as PRN, and the first floppy disk drive is addressed as A:. In copying files, the COPY command expects a FROM field followed by a TO field. In essence, you copy a file *from* a device *to* another device. The source is the file or group of files residing on the device from which they will be copied. The target is typically the destination or place where the files copied will reside. DOS allows you to address the source files directly using a drive letter and a pathname. Likewise, the target or destination for the file(s) to be copied can be directly addressed.

If the source or target group of files is *not* directly addressed, DOS makes assumptions about the drive and path or directory address. If the drive letter is not specified, DOS assumes the default drive. This assumption is made for both the source (or FROM field) and the target (or TO field). Likewise, if the path is not specified, DOS assumes the default directory for the path (i.e., the current directory).

The COPY command is one of the most frequently used of all DOS commands. When employed with wildcard characters, COPY can accomplish a large number of file management functions in seconds. COPY is particularly useful when installing large software application programs and when setting up directories of data files. Learn to use COPY in all of its many forms. The COPY command is discussed in detail, with a wide variety of examples, in Chapter 7 on File Management.

A few examples will illustrate the capabilities of the COPY command:

FROM Field	TO Field
1. C:\> **COPY FILE1.TXT**	**A:**
2. C:\> **COPY A:*.***	**C:\WP51**
3. C:\> **COPY A:*.COM**	**C:\DOS500 /V**

In the first example, a single file named FILE1.TXT is copied to the diskette in Drive A. Since a drive and directory are not specified as part of the

FROM field, DOS expects to find the file FILE1.TXT on Drive C in the root directory. In the second example, all the files (*.*) on Drive A are copied to Drive C. The files will be placed in the specified directory \WP51. In the third example, files are copied from Drive A to Drive C. All the files with a COM extension on Drive A are sent to the \DOS500 directory on Drive C. Since the /V parameter was specified, DOS will verify that the copying of all these files is correct and that no errors occurred during the copy process.

This concludes a brief introduction to some of the most used DOS commands. For more detail refer to Part II of the text for internal commands and Part III of the text for external commands.

QUESTIONS AND PROBLEMS

1. What is the purpose of the HELP command? Can it be used to obtain help for all commands?
2. What format will result when formatting a diskette if the FORMAT command does not include any parameters or switches?
3. Can the contents of a diskette that is formatted as double density be duplicated onto a diskette that has previously been formatted as high density?
4. What information is not displayed about a file if the /W parameter is used with the DIR command?
5. What form of the FORMAT command must be used to create a system diskette that can be used to boot the computer from a diskette mounted in Drive A?
6. What information must be included with the DIR command to obtain a listing for a specified directory?
7. What command can be used to display information about space utilization and space available on a disk or diskette?
8. What command is used to display the current directory name as part of the DOS prompt?
9. What file or group of files will not be copied from a source directory to a target directory when using the COPY command?
10. What command will display information about the amount of space lost from bad sectors on a hard drive?
11. What parameter or switch is used with a command in order to invoke help with that command?
12. What command is used to duplicate a diskette, where the source and target diskettes are mounted in the same drive?

13. What will be the format of a target diskette if the source diskette being duplicated is double-sided, double-density?
14. What wildcard characters can be used with the COPY command when copying files?

PART II

DOS INTERNAL COMMANDS

CHAPTER 5

DISK MANAGEMENT (INTERNAL COMMANDS)

INTRODUCTION

To manage the files on your disks, whether hard disks or floppy diskettes, requires familiarity with several internal commands. In order to manage the files on a disk, DOS stores information in its system directory area that records key information about the file. Among this information is the filename, the file extension, the size of the file, the attribute byte, and so on. The DOS system directory area, coupled with the FAT table, is how DOS keeps track of all the pieces of a file. The internal commands used by DOS to manage disks include:

DATE
TIME
VOL
Drive selection (A:, B:, C:, etc.)

LAYOUT OF A DISK

How does DOS organize a disk, and then manage the files stored on the disk? In order for DOS to store information on a disk, the disk must first be formatted. The FORMAT command, discussed briefly in Chapter 4, is covered in more detail in Chapter 9. During formatting, DOS divides the disk into two fundamental areas: a *system area* that is used for managing the files on the disk, and a *data area* that is used to store the actual files. This data area becomes the root directory for the disk; in essence, the FORMAT command creates the root directory for any disk. The system area is then subdivided into three areas: the boot area, the FAT table area, and the system directory area.

We can illustrate this organization using a 5 1/4-inch double-sided double-density diskette as an example. These are sometimes referred to as 360 KB diskettes. This diskette, when formatted in the default format, contains 40 tracks on each side for a total of 80 tracks. Each track contains nine sectors, and each sector has a storage capacity of 512 bytes. The total capacity of the diskette is then 80 × 9 × 512 bytes or a total of 368,640 bytes. This 368,640-byte area is distributed over 720 sectors (80 × 9) on the diskette, and the sectors are addressed as 1 through 720.

Why, when we format a diskette of this type, does it show a capacity of only 362,496 bytes? The reason is that DOS consumes a total of 12 sectors for the system area and allocates the remaining 708 sectors for the data area. The total data area on the diskette is then 708 × 512 bytes, for a total of 362,496 bytes. The system area totals 6,144 bytes (12 × 512 bytes).

The system area is subdivided into three areas: a boot area of one sector, a FAT table area of four sectors, and a system directory area of seven sectors. Why does a 360 KB diskette have a maximum capacity of 112 entries? Each file or subdirectory entry on the disk takes 32 bytes. There are seven sectors devoted to the system directory area. Each of the seven directory sectors can hold information on a total of 16 files or directory entries (32 × 16 = 512 bytes). Because seven sectors are allocated to this area, it can hold 112 entries (7 × 16 = 112).

Table 5.1 shows similar information for other diskette formats. Information is included for both 5 1/4-and 3 1/2-inch diskettes.

Table 5.1 shows the various formats available under DOS for diskettes along with the diskette capacities for each of the formats. The 5 1/4-inch diskettes can accommodate both single-sided and double-sided formats. Single-sided diskettes are rarely used because the data capacity is so restricted. Most floppy disk drives found in today's microcomputers are of the double-sided variety and have two read/write heads. In addition to showing the total capacity of the disk in bytes, Table 5.1 also shows the number of bytes allocated to the system area and the data area for each type of diskette. The numbers in parentheses represent the number of sectors allocated to each of the areas as well as the total number of sectors on the diskette.

TABLE 5.1 Diskette Capacity Chart

Size	No. of Sides	Tracks per Side	Sectors per Track	Total Capacity*	Data Capacity*	System Area Capacity*
5 1/4″	1	40	8	163,840 (320)	160,256 (313)	3,584 (7)
5 1/4″	1	40	9	184,320 (360)	179,712 (351)	4,608 (9)
5 1/4″	2	40	8	327,680 (640)	322,560 (630)	5,120 (10)
5 1/4″	2	40	9	368,640 (720)	362,496 (708)	6,144 (12)
3 1/2″	2	80	9	737,280 (1440)	730,112 (1426)	7,168 (14)
5 1/4″	2	80	15	1,228,800 (2400)	1,213,952 (2371)	14,848 (29)
3 1/2″	2	80	18	1,474,560 (2880)	1,457,664 (2847)	16,896 (33)

*Capacity figures are in bytes. Numbers in parentheses indicate number of sectors.

For example, a 5 1/4-inch double-sided double-density diskette has a total capacity of 368,640 bytes and contains 720 sectors. Of these 368,640 bytes, 6,144 bytes are allocated to the system area, and 362,496 bytes to the data area. Of the 720 sectors on the diskette, 12 are allocated to the system area, and 708 are in the data area.

THE DATE (DATE) COMMAND

The DATE command is used to set your computer's system date. It is not absolutely necessary to set the system date at boot time. If you do not set the system date, the computer uses the default date stored when the computer was initially set up. However, if the system date is not entered at boot time, then every file created on your computer will have the default date. This will make file management extremely cumbersome when the BACKUP command is used and when you track file updates later.

The system date can be set automatically through your hardware. Many users find this well worth the cost. If you choose to use this method, you need a clock card, which will automatically keep track of the system date. The clock card contains a small battery that operates the clock and thus keeps track of the date when the computer is turned off. Your computer may have come with a clock card. If your screen shows the correct date every time you turn on your computer, then it has a clock card installed. In that case the date will be correct as long as the battery is good. (You can expect four or five years of life for a typical battery.)

The form of the DATE command is shown below:

DATE ***<mm-dd-yy>***

□ EXAMPLES

1. C:\> **DATE**
2. C:\> **DATE 10-27-93**

1. C:\> **DATE** In the first example, the command is entered with no date information. The system responds with the date and stops to allow the entry of a new system date. If the date is correct, the user need only press Enter or Return. If the date is not correct, the user should enter the correct date. The date can be entered with the year typed in four digits (1993, for example), or the year entry may be abbreviated by typing the last two digits only (in this case, 93).
2. C:\> **DATE 10-27-93** In the second example, the command was entered along with the new date information. DOS changes the system date stored in the nucleus to the date just entered—in this case, October 27, 1993.

THE TIME (TIME) COMMAND

The TIME command is used to set your computer's system time. It is not necessary to set the system time when you boot the computer, but if you do not, the computer uses the default time stored when the computer was initially set up. Also, if the system time is not entered at boot time, every file created on your computer will have the same time, which will prevent you from managing your files effectively.

The system time can be set automatically along with the date using a clock card. The clock card will control both automatically. If your screen shows the correct time every time you turn the computer on, it has a clock card installed. In that case, the time will be correct as long as the battery is good.

The form of the TIME command is:

TIME <*hh:mm*> <*:ss*> <*.xx*>

□ EXAMPLES

1. C:\> **TIME**
2. C:\> **TIME 10:23**
3. C:\> **TIME 15:45:40**

1. C:\> **TIME** When the TIME command is entered, the computer system displays the current time and waits for the user to enter a new time. The entry of the TIME command and the computer's response are shown below:

```
C:\> TIME

Current time is 9:13:42.40
Enter new time:
```

   If the time is correct, the user need only press the Enter or Return key to return to the prompt. If the time is not correct, you should enter the correct time.

2. C:\> **TIME 10:23** In Example 2 the TIME command was entered along with the time in hours, and minutes. Time is always entered in the military time (24-hour) format. This time would represent 10:23 AM.
3. C:\> **TIME 15:45:40** In Example 3 the TIME command was entered along with the time in hours, minutes, and seconds. The hours value is greater than 12, so the time is past 12:00 noon. This time represents 3:45 and 40 seconds, or approximately 3:46 PM.

THE VOLUME (VOL) COMMAND

The Volume (VOL) command is used to display a disk's volume label. The volume label uniquely labels the individual disk or diskette and can help identify its content. The volume label may be up to 11 characters, which may be alphanumeric and may contain certain special characters.

The volume label is encoded magnetically on the disk, and is typically entered at the time a disk is formatted for use. After formatting is complete, the FORMAT routine will ask for a volume label. The volume label should reflect the kind of information that will be stored on the disk. (The volume label can also be placed on the disk using the LABEL program that is part of DOS.) The format of the VOL command is shown below:

VOL <*drive*>

□ **EXAMPLES**

1. C:\> **VOL**
2. C:\> **VOL A:**
3. C:\> **VOL C:**

1. C:\> **VOL** In Example 1 the VOL command is issued with no other information. DOS responds by displaying the volume label on the default drive. In this case the volume label is displayed for Drive C.
2. C:\> **VOL A:** In Example 2 the VOL command is given, along with the drive specification. DOS responds with the volume label of Drive A. If the diskette in Drive A does not have a label, DOS responds, "Volume in Drive A has no label."
3. C:\> **VOL C:** In Example 3 the VOL command is given, along with the drive specification. DOS responds with the Volume label of the default drive—Drive C. If the diskette in Drive C does not have a label, DOS responds, "Volume in Drive C has no label." This example produces the same result as Example 1 above.

THE DRIVE SELECTION (D:) COMMAND

The Drive Selection (D:) command allows the user to change the default disk drive. DOS normally displays the default disk drive as part of its prompt. That drive is the disk that DOS will use when searching for external files to be executed. Normally the default drive will be the disk that contains the programs that are executed. Typically, for a single-user hard drive system, the default drive is C. If the system contains only floppy disk drives, the default drive is normally Drive A.

There are occasions, however, when you'll want to change the default drive. In order to do so, issue a drive selection command. The form of the command is shown below (where *D* represents the letter of the drive you want to make the default drive.) Note that the command may be either uppercase or lowercase, but must be followed by a colon.

D:

□ EXAMPLES

1. `C:\>` **`A:`**
2. `A:\>` **`B:`**
3. `B:\LESSON>` **`C:`**
4. `C:\>`

1. `C:\>` **`A:`** The default drive is Drive C in the first example. The command to change drives is given by typing A followed by a colon. DOS changes the default drive to A. The prompt then displays A as the default drive.
2. `A:\>` **`B:`** In the second example the default drive is Drive A. The command to change to drive B is given by typing B followed by a colon. In response, DOS changes the default drive to B. The prompt in the third example then displays B as the default drive. Note that the prompt in Example 3 also displays \LESSON as the default directory rather than the root directory. That is because the default directory on Drive B had been previously set to \LESSON. When the change drive command is issued to change to Drive B, the prompt then shows that the default directory on Drive B was \LESSON. Remember that DOS displays only the default directory on the default drive as part of its prompt. The default directories on any other drives are not displayed.
3. `B:\LESSON>` **`C:`** In Example 3 the default drive is Drive B. The change drive command is given by typing C followed by a colon to change the default drive back to hard drive C. In response, DOS changes the default drive to C. The prompt then displays C as the default drive (C:\>), shown in Example 4. Note that the default directory is now the backslash or root directory on C. The default directory on Drive B remains \LESSON, but the prompt does not display it now. The prompt displays only the default directory of the default drive. The default drive has been changed to C and the default directory for C is the root directory. The prompt in Example 4 confirms this.

QUESTIONS AND PROBLEMS

1. What is the total storage capacity of a 3 1/2-inch diskette that is formatted as a high-density disk?
2. For the diskette formatted in Question 1 above, how many bytes are available for file storage? How many bytes are used by the system area on the disk?
3. What are the three major components of information stored in the system area on a diskette?
4. How many sectors are formatted on each track on a high-density 5 1/4-inch diskette? On a high-density 3 1/2-inch diskette?

5. What is the advantage in having a clock card installed on your personal computer?
6. Why is it recommended that all files be date- and time-stamped when they are created or updated?
7. What uses can be made of the volume label on a diskette?
8. What does the term *default drive* mean?
9. What does the term *default directory* mean? Is this the same as the current directory?
10. When might you want to make the default drive a drive other than the hard drive on your system?

CHAPTER 6

DIRECTORY MANAGEMENT (INTERNAL COMMANDS)

INTRODUCTION

DOS uses a number of internal commands to create and manage the directories on a disk. The directory structure allows a disk to be divided into a number of separate areas, regardless of whether the disk is a floppy diskette or a hard disk. Subdirectories are used relatively infrequently on 360 KB floppy diskettes. Most users use subdirectory structures for hard drives because it is important to subdivide the large megabyte capacity of the hard drive into sections so the files can be effectively managed. This is far less important and perhaps even unnecessary on a 360 KB diskette, which has a maximum capacity of only 112 entries.

As floppy diskette capacity has increased and continues to do so, subdirectory structures will be used more frequently with floppy diskettes as well as hard disks. We will, in all likelihood, see floppy diskette capacity in the 3 1/2-inch size of 4 MB or more in the not too distant future. Even 1.45 MB capacity frequently merits a subdirectory structure for effective file management reasons. Furthermore, optical floppies of 20 MB or more are now available in the 3 1/2-inch size.

The commands used to create and manage directory structures on a disk are shown below:

MD
RD
CD
DIR

A typical directory structure is shown in Figure 6.1. This is a sample directory structure similar to what might be found on many hard disks with a few applications installed.

FIGURE 6.1 Sample directory structure

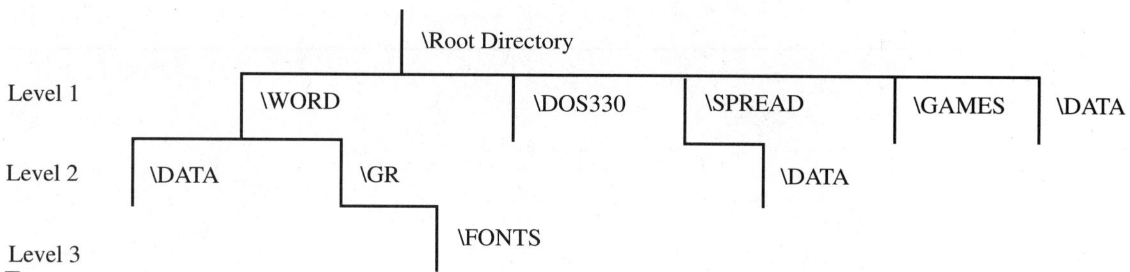

TERMINOLOGY

When discussing directories and directory structures, a number of terms are used regularly:

1. *Directory:* A directory is an area set up on the disk to hold a related group of files. This term is sometimes also used interchangeably with the term *subdirectory,* (see below). When a directory is addressed, the name of the directory or subdirectory is usually preceded by a backslash (\). Thus, we refer to the WORD directory as \WORD.
2. *Root directory:* The beginning or first directory that DOS creates in order to manage any disk is the root directory. The root directory, sometimes referred to as the backslash (\) directory, is created whenever a disk is formatted. The directory structure created on any disk begins with the root directory. The first level of directories directly below the root directory (\WORD, \SPREAD, \DOS330, \GAMES in Figure 6.1) are referred to as *subdirectories* of the root (see below).
3. *Subdirectory:* A directory may also be referred to as a subdirectory. When referred to in this way it is a subdirectory of the directory just above it. The directory shown as \DATA in Figure 6.1 is a subdirectory of \SPREAD. This directory shown as \DATA is actually addressed as \SPREAD\DATA to distinguish it from the \DATA directory that is a subdirectory of \WORD. That \DATA directory is addressed as \WORD\DATA.
4. *Default directory:* Each disk has a default directory. This is the directory that typically shows as part of the DOS prompt if that drive is the default or current drive. If a file is not specifically addressed, DOS saves it to the default directory on that disk.
5. *Current directory:* The current directory is frequently used as another term for the default directory. This is the first directory DOS searches when executing an external command. It is also the directory DOS searches when looking for a file if the user addresses the file only by name and extension.
6. *Pathname:* A pathname is an addressing technique. The path is the directory path that must be followed to find a file in a specific directory. For example, a file named HELVET.14P is stored in the \FONTS directory in Figure 6.1. The pathname for this file is \WORD\GR\FONTS. Starting from the root directory (\) the user would trace the directory structure \WORD to \GR to \FONTS to get to this file. If this file were stored on the hard drive (Drive C), the file would be addressed as C:\WORD\GR\FONTS\HELVET.14P. The drive address is C:, the pathname is \WORD\GR\FONTS, the filename is HELVET, and the extension is 14P.

THE MAKE DIRECTORY (MKDIR OR MD) COMMAND

The Make Directory (MKDIR or MD) command is used to create a directory entry. (Usually the shorter command form MD is used, rather than the longer form MKDIR.) The primary purpose of creating directories is to provide a place to store related files, such as all the data files associated with an application software program. Today's disk drives store 1,000 to 2,000 or more files. To manage these files requires a directory structure that allows related groups of files to be stored in the same directory. When you build a directory structure, always build it from the root directory down. A directory name can be one to eight characters in length. It is not recommended that directory names have extensions. When naming directories, it is recommended that only alphanumeric characters be used. The examples below illustrate several examples of alphanumeric naming. Directory names should always start with an alphabetic character rather than a numeric character. The format of the Make Directory command is:

MD <*drive*> <*path*>

□ **EXAMPLES**

1. C:\> **MD \WORD**
2. C:\> **MD \WORD\DATA**
3. C:\> **MD C:\SPREAD**
4. C:\> **MD A:\LETTER91**
5. C:\> **MD C:\SPREAD\DATA**
6. C:\> **MD C:\DATA**

1. C:\> **MD \WORD** Based on the DOS prompt, the default drive is C and the default directory is the root or backslash (\) directory. In this example, DOS creates a directory named WORD. Because the drive was not specified, DOS creates this directory on the default drive C. The directory \WORD is a subdirectory of the root directory.
2. C:\> **MD \WORD\DATA** In the second example DOS creates a directory \WORD\DATA. This directory is on the default drive. The \WORD\DATA directory is a subdirectory of the \WORD directory; it is not the same as the \DATA directory. If it were termed the \DATA directory, there would be no way to distinguish among the three DATA directories \WORD\DATA, \SPREAD\DATA, and \DATA (see Figure 6.1). To avoid confusion, a directory is always known by its full name, so in this example the directory name is \WORD\DATA.
3. C:\> **MD C:\SPREAD** In this example DOS creates a directory called \SPREAD on the specified drive, C. Just like \WORD, the directory \SPREAD is a subdirectory of the root directory. The WORD directory and the SPREAD directory are on the same level because they are both subdirectories of the root. (Refer to Figure 6.1 for a diagram showing the different levels).
4. C:\> **MD A:\LETTER91** In the fourth example a directory named \LETTER91 is created on Drive A, which is normally the first floppy diskette drive on the computer. The LETTER91 directory is a subdirectory of the root direc-

tory on the particular diskette that is currently in Drive A. The directory was placed on Drive A because the command addressed the drive as part of the command. Thus, the command overrides the default drive value that would have otherwise been used.

5. C:\> **MD C:\SPREAD\DATA** In this example another DATA directory is created. The directory, named \SPREAD\DATA, is a subdirectory of \SPREAD. This directory may sometimes be referred to as the DATA directory, but the real name of the directory is \SPREAD\DATA. If it is referred to as the DATA directory, the user is using a shorthand notation to refer to the directory as a subdirectory of \SPREAD. The directory's full name must always be used when you address it. The full name of the directory is \SPREAD\DATA, which tells DOS the path that must be followed, starting at the root directory, to reach this directory.
6. C:\> **MD C:\DATA** In this last example DOS creates a directory named DATA. This directory, a subdirectory of the root directory, is on the same level as the SPREAD and the WORD directories. It is addressed as the \DATA directory.

This group of examples illustrates the diversity of uses of the MD command. A directory can be created on any drive or diskette. Before you can create a directory, its parent directory must already exist. Thus, the \WORD\DATA directory cannot be created before the \WORD directory. In creating a directory structure you must create directories from the top down; in other words, you must start from the root directory and work "down" the tree. In the examples above, note that the \WORD directory was created before the \WORD\DATA directory. Likewise, the \SPREAD directory was created before the \SPREAD\DATA directory.

THE REMOVE DIRECTORY (RMDIR OR RD) COMMAND

The Remove Directory (RMDIR or RD) command is used to remove a directory from a disk drive. The command has two forms as shown above, but the short form RD is normally used. In order to remove a directory from a drive, the directory must first be empty. That means that the directory cannot contain files of any kind, including hidden files or subdirectories. If an application creates hidden files and stores them in a directory, those files must be first unhidden and then removed before the directory can be removed.) (A variety of utility programs are available to remove the hide bit of the attribute byte so that the file will be visible and can be removed.) With DOS 5, the ATTRIB command can be used to unhide a file. (See Chapter 12.) Neither can the directory contain any subdirectories. A subdirectory is empty when the only entries shown are the dot (.) and the double-dot (..) directory entries. An example of a directory that is empty is shown below:

```
Directory of C:\TEMP
.          < DIR >     1-11-91 8:05p
..         < DIR >     1-11-91 8:05p
2 Files  678350 bytes free
```

When removing a directory, make sure that the directory to be removed is *not* the default directory. The safe way to remove directories is to do so where the default directory is the root directory, as shown in the examples below. It is not required that the default directory be the root directory. It is required, however, that the directory to be removed *not* be the current or default directory. Thus if the default directory was the \WORD directory, it would be possible to remove the \WORD\DATA directory, but it would not be possible to remove the \WORD directory. In order to remove the \WORD directory the user would have to change to the root directory. The format of the Remove Directory command is:

RD *<drive>* *<path>*

□ EXAMPLES

1. C:\> **RD \WORD\DATA**
2. C:\> **RD \WORD**
3. C:\> **RD C:\SPREAD\DATA**
4. C:\> **RD C:\SPREAD**
5. C:\> **RD A:\LETTER91**
6. C:\> **RD \DATA**

The examples shown here remove the directory structure created earlier with the Make Directory command. Note that, although directory structures are created from the root directory down, directory structures are removed from the bottom up. Thus, in the examples above, the \SPREAD\DATA and \WORD\DATA directories are removed before the \SPREAD and \WORD directories. This is because a directory may not be removed unless it is empty. Note also that the root directory on a disk cannot be removed. The root directory is created when a disk is formatted, and not with the MD command. Because the default directory can never be removed, it is not possible to remove the root directory. DOS allows directories to be removed only if they were first created with the Make Directory command.

1. C:\> **RD \WORD\DATA** In the first example above the \WORD\DATA directory is removed. Because a drive letter was not specified, DOS assumes that the directory to be removed is on the default drive (Drive C).
2. C:\> **RD \WORD** In the second example the \WORD directory is removed. Remember that a directory must be empty to be removed. The subdirectory \WORD\DATA of the \WORD directory was removed in the first example, so the \WORD directory may now be removed. A drive letter was not specified, so DOS assumes the default drive.

3. C:\> **RD C:\SPREAD\DATA** In this example the drive directory combination is fully specified. The \SPREAD\DATA directory is removed from Drive C, as specified.
4. C:\> **RD C:\SPREAD** In the next example \SPREAD directory is removed on Drive C as specified. The subdirectory \SPREAD\DATA was removed in the previous step.
5. C:\> **RD A:\LETTER91** In the fifth example a directory on a drive other than the default drive is removed. In order to remove the \LETTER91 directory from Drive A, the user must specify both the drive and the directory. In this case the LETTER91 directory on Drive A is removed. Any directory can be removed on any drive as long as you specify both the drive and the directory.
6. C:\> **RD \DATA** In the last example the \DATA directory is removed from Drive C. The drive was not specified in this case, so DOS again assumes the default drive (Drive C).

THE CHANGE DIRECTORY (CHDIR OR CD) COMMAND

Change Directory (CHDIR or CD) is the command used to change the default or current directory. (Usually, the shorter command form CD is used rather than the longer form CHDIR.) It allows the user to change from one directory to another on any drive. Changing the directory on a drive with the CD command changes the default directory on that drive. DOS keeps track of the default directory on every disk or diskette on your system. On the default drive, DOS will display the default directory if the DOS prompt is set up to display the directory as part of the prompt. The user can use the Prompt command PROMPT PG to display the default directory. If the DIR command is used without referring to a specific directory, DOS displays the directory listing for the current directory on the appropriate disk drive. The format of the Change Directory command is shown below:

CD *<drive> <path>*

□ **EXAMPLES**

1. C:\> **CD \WORD**
2. C:\WORD> **CD \WORD\DATA**
3. C:\WORD\DATA> **CD C:\SPREAD**
4. C:\SPREAD> **CD **
5. C:\> **CD A:\LETTER91**
6. C:\> **CD C:\SPREAD\DATA**
7. C:\SPREAD\DATA > **CD ..**
8. C:\SPREAD> **CD **
9. C:\> **CD A:**

1. **C:\> CD \WORD** In the first example, the default directory is changed to the \WORD directory. In this case the change is on the default drive C, because the drive was not specified. In the next line (Example 2) the DOS prompt displays that the default directory is now the \WORD directory on the default drive (Drive C).
2. **C:\WORD> CD \WORD\DATA** In the second example, the default directory is changed to the \WORD\DATA directory on Drive C because no drive was specified. The computer displays the appropriate DOS prompt in the next example.
3. **C:\WORD\DATA> CD C:\SPREAD** In this example, both the drive and the directory are specified. The default directory on Drive C is now changed to the \SPREAD directory.
4. **C:\SPREAD> CD ** In this example, the default directory is changed to the root (backslash) directory. The DOS prompt in Example 5 displays the default drive as C and the default directory as the root directory.
5. **C:\> CD A:\LETTER91** In Example 5 the default directory has been changed on the floppy disk drive. This is a nondefault drive (Drive A). The fact that this change has been made is not readily visible because the DOS prompt displays the default directory for only the default drive. Nevertheless, the default directory on Drive A is now \LETTER91.
6. **C:\> CD C:\SPREAD\DATA** In this example, the default directory on Drive C has now been changed to \SPREAD\DATA. We have jumped from the root directory down two levels to the \SPREAD\DATA directory. Through the CD command, DOS provides the capability to jump from one directory to another, regardless of the level. It is not necessary to step down the directory levels one by one to get to a directory at the second or third level. In the next example, the DOS prompt displays this as the default directory.
7. **C:\SPREAD\DATA> CD..** Here the double-dot (..) directory symbol is used with the CD command. The directory \SPREAD\DATA is a subdirectory of \SPREAD. (Refer to Figure 6.1 for the directory diagram.) The \SPREAD directory is referred to as the *parent directory* of \SPREAD\DATA. The double-dot (..) symbol refers to the parent directory (\SPREAD). Likewise, the root directory is the parent directory of \SPREAD. In this example, the CD command causes the default directory to be changed from \SPREAD\DATA to \SPREAD.
8. **C:\SPREAD> CD ** In Example 8 the default directory is changed to the root directory. The DOS prompt C:\> now displays the root as the default directory. In the CD command, the root directory (\) was part of the command and the directory was specifically addressed. We could also have typed the command in as CD .. because the parent directory of \SPREAD is the root directory.

9. **C:\> CD A:** The DOS prompt displays the results of the command issued in Example 8. This form of the Change Directory command requests that the default directory for the diskette in Drive A be displayed. DOS will display a directory name for the diskette in Drive A such as \LETTER 91. (See Example 5.) In many cases, the directory name that will be displayed for a diskette will be the root directory.

THE DIRECTORY (DIR) COMMAND AND ITS VARIATIONS

The Directory (DIR) command is used to examine information about specific files or to display information about the contents of a specific directory on a specified disk drive. DIR is one of the most used commands in the DOS repertoire. The command has many variations as illustrated in the examples below. The directory listing normally includes all user files and all directories that are part of the specified directory. The directory listing does not include any hidden files or hidden directories. Therefore, the DOS hidden files that are part of the nucleus and reside in the root directory will not be displayed. The DIR command can also be used to display a single file or a group of files based on the specific file specification that is entered.

The DIR command examines information in the system directory area on the disk and supplies that information to the user via the directory report. If no parameters are specified, the report scrolls across the screen in normal format until all entries are displayed. This may result in a multipage report with only the last page still displayed on the screen. There are two parameters associated with the command in all versions of DOS up to Version 5. DOS Version 5 introduced several new parameters that substantially expand the capability of the DIR command. The first parameter (/P) causes the report to be displayed one page at a time. This allows a multipage report to be reviewed page by page. The second parameter (/W) changes the report format to wide mode. In wide mode, the directory entries are displayed in five columns across, but the size, date, and time associated with each directory entry are not displayed. Figure 6.2 illustrates a directory report in normal format. Figure 6.3 shows the same report in wide format.

The form of the DIR command is shown below:

```
DIR <drive> <directory><file spec> /P /W /S /B /L
/A:<attribute> /O:<sort order>
```

<*drive*> is the disk drive of the directory that is to be displayed. *<Drive>* is optional. If it is not specified, DOS displays a directory from the default drive.

<*directory*> is the directory or subdirectory whose file list is to be displayed. *<Directory>* is an optional field. If it is not specified, DOS displays the file list from the default or current directory.

```
Volume in drive C has no label
Volume Serial Number is 1750-6B27
Directory of C:\DCTEMP

                       <DIR>         10-16-93        11:47a
                       <DIR>         10-16-93        11:47a
SITE                            658109-04-93        11:55a
DCINTRO                         959209-04-93        11:10a
CONCLUS                         511109-20-93        11:55a
PROBLEMS                       1952809-04-93        11:21a
REGS                            516409-04-93        10:45a
CONTENTS                        132609-04-93         7:54p
GOALS                           139709-04-93         7:45p
ASSESSME                        110809-05-93         2:49p
CHARACTE                        908709-09-93        12:26p
STORMPRO                        457509-11-93         3:23p
DCC          911               1042209-16-93        11:32a
DCB          911               1259309-12-93         2:08p
BMP                            6603109-16-93         1:35p
NEEDS                           622809-18-93         2:16p
HYDROL                          626809-18-93         2:16p
DCBIB1                         9305309-20-93        11:24a
ACKNOW                          371609-20-93        12:59p
RECOMMEN                        418409-20-93         1:06p
CREAT        OPT               1175509-20-93        12:16p
STORMWAT     BIB               1304108-05-93         1:54p
DCBIB1       COM               6949307-22-93         2:44p
             23 files(s)          360253 bytes
                                 6852608 bytes free
```

FIGURE 6.2 Sample directory report in normal format

<file spec> is the name of the file for which information is to be displayed. *<file spec>* is an optional field. It can be a single file or a group of files. Wildcards, including ? and *, may be used in this field.

/P displays the directory list one page at a time. Successive screens of information are displayed by striking any key to scroll to the next screen display.

/W displays the file list in wide mode. This parameter causes only the filename and extension fields to be displayed. Directory names will not be distinguishable from files without an extension except under Version 5. Under

```
Volume in drive C has no label
Volume Serial Number is 1750-6B27
Directory of C:\DCTEMP

[.]             [..]            SITE            DCINTRO
PROBLEMS        REGS            CONTENTS        GOALS
CHARACTE        STORMPRO        DCC.991         DCB.991
NEEDS           HYDROL          DCBIB1          ACKNOW
CREAT.OPT       STORMWAT.BIB    DCBIB1.COM
        23 file(s)          360253 bytes
                            6852608 bytes free
```

FIGURE 6.3 Sample directory report in wide format

Version 5 directory names are placed in square brackets; filenames are displayed as text only.

Note: All parameters other than /P and /W are unique to Version 5 of DOS. Only /P and /W work in DOS versions prior to Version 5.

/S displays every file in all subdirectories that match the <*file spec*> given. DOS identifies each subdirectory where the file is stored before displaying the directory entry.

/B displays the names of files and subdirectories, but includes no heading information or summary information.

/L displays the directory entries in lowercase.

/A:<*attribute*> displays the entries for files associated with the attribute specified. Attributes can be specified by H for hidden files, S for system files such as the DOS hidden files, A for the archive attribute, R for read-only files, and D to display only the names of directories.

/O: <*sort order*> specifies the order in which all of the directory entries should be sorted. Entries are normally sorted in ascending order. To reverse the order or for descending order, use a hyphen in front of the character. The <*sort order*> characters, which can be typed in either uppercase or lowercase, are as follows:

- D sorts in date order from the earliest date to the most recent date.
- E sorts in alphabetic order by extension name.
- G sorts directories listed as a group before the files.

- N sorts entries by filename in alphabetic order.
- S sorts by the size of the file from smallest to largest.

□ **EXAMPLES**

1. C:\> **DIR**
2. C:\> **DIR \DOS330 /O:N /P**
3. C:\> **DIR A:\LETTERS**
4. C:\> **DIR *.EXE**
5. C:\> **DIR \DOS330*.COM /W**
6. C:\> **DIR *.**
7. C:\> **DIR A:COMMAND.COM**
8. C:\DOS330> **DIR ..**

1. C:\> **DIR** In the first example, the Directory command is issued with no drive or directory specification. DOS uses its defaults to determine the information to be displayed. Because no drive was specified, the default drive—Drive C—is used. No directory was specified, so DOS selects the default directory (\). In response to this command, DOS displays information about the contents of the root directory on Drive C. If the information is longer than one page, the information scrolls across the screen until the report completes. The first page of a sample DIR report is shown in Figure 6.4.
2. C:\> **DIR \DOS330 /O:N /P** In Example 2 the directory \DOS330 is specified, along with two parameters, O:N and P. No drive is specified. DOS will display a directory report for the \DOS330 directory for Drive C in page format. Because /O:N was specified for the sort order, the displayed files will be sorted in alphabetic order by filename. /O is a new parameter with Version 5 and only valid with that version.
3. C:\> **DIR A:\LETTERS** In this example, both a drive and a directory are specified. No parameter is specified. The report will be for the \LETTERS directory for Drive A.
4. C:\> **DIR *.EXE** In Example 4 the directory command does not specify a drive or a directory. It does, however, specify a group of files. This directory report will include all files with an EXE extension for the default drive and directory (C:\), because no drive or directory was specified. Files with an EXE extension will be listed.
5. C:\> **DIR \DOS330*.COM /W** In Example 5 the directory report will include all files with a COM extension in the \DOS330 directory on the default drive (Drive C). The report will be displayed in wide format, similar to the report shown in Figure 6.3.
6. C:\> **DIR *.** In Example 6 the report specification is for all files that do not have an extension, because no character is specified after the period. No

```
Volume in drive C has no label
Volume Serial Number is 1750-6B27
Directory of C:\

COMMAND  COM      47845  04-09-93   5:00a
SNSI     SYS       1678  03-17-87  12:00p
AUTOEXEC BAK         92  07-16-93   8:47a
COUNTRY  SYS      11285  03-17-87  12:00p
CONFIG   SYS        183  10-16-93   1:25p
DOS330        <DIR>      10-16-93  11:47a
CRTEND        <DIR>      10-16-93  11:47a
DCTEMP        <DIR>      10-16-93  11:47a
DCCW          <DIR>      10-16-93  11:48a
123           <DIR>      10-16-93  11:49a
MACLINK       <DIR>      10-16-93  11:51a
DCDBASE       <DIR>      10-16-93  11:51a
MCWORKS       <DIR>      10-16-93  11:52a
ASCTEXT       <DIR>      10-16-93  11:55a
ACGRAM        <DIR>      10-16-93  11:55a
WP51A         <DIR>      10-16-93  11:56a
XTALK1        <DIR>      10-16-93  12:02p
TEXTFINL      <DIR>      10-16-93  12:03p
TEXTSUB       <DIR>      10-16-93  12:03p
Press any key to continue . . .
```

FIGURE 6.4 Directory display report for root directory

drive or directory is specified, so DOS will report on the root directory on Drive C. The root directory normally has a limited number of files, but does contain the first-level directory listing for all the major application directories on the system. When you specify *. the DIR command will display all entries that do not have an extension. This list is normally a listing of the directory names in the root directory. A sample directory listing based on this example is shown in Figure 6.5.

7. `C:\>` **`DIR A:COMMAND.COM`** In this example a specific file is specified on floppy disk Drive A. Because no directory is specified, the default directory on Drive A will be used. The report will be a single-line display of information about the COMMAND.COM file.

8. `C:\DOS330>` **`DIR ..`** In this last example, the parent directory is specified by the double dot (..). The DOS prompt displays the default directory as \DOS330, so DOS will display a directory report for the parent directory of \DOS330. The parent directory of \DOS330 is the root directory (\). The resulting directory report is for the root directory of Drive C.

```
Volume in drive C has no label
Volume Serial Number is 1750-6B27
Directory of C:\

DOS330          <DIR>          10-16-93      11:47a
CRTEND          <DIR>          10-16-93      11:47a
DCTEMP          <DIR>          10-16-93      11:47a
DCCW            <DIR>          10-16-93      11:48a
123             <DIR>          10-16-93      11:49a
MACLINK         <DIR>          10-16-93      11:51a
CCDBASE         <DIR>          10-16-93      11:51a
MCWORKS         <DIR>          10-16-93      11:52a
ASCTEXT         <DIR>          10-16-93      11:55a
ACGRAM          <DIR>          10-16-93      11:55a
WP51A           <DIR>          10-16-93      11:56a
XTALK1          <DIR>          10-16-93      12:02p
TEXTFINL        <DIR>          10-16-93      12:03p
TEXTSUB         <DIR>          10-16-93      12:03p
TEXTWRK1        <DIR>          10-16-93      12:04p
TEXTWRK2        <DIR>          10-16-93      12:04p
DOSBOOK         <DIR>          10-16-93      12:04p
TOOLS           <DIR>          10-16-93      12:04p
TEMPLL          <DIR>          10-16-93      12:14p
MOUSE           <DIR>          10-16-93       2:04p
          20 file(s)                  0 bytes
                               6852608 bytes free
```

FIGURE 6.5 Directory listing for command DIR *.

COMMON MISTAKES

1. `C:\>` **`MD \WORD\DATA`**
2. `C:\>` **`MD C:DATA`**
3. `C:\>` **`RD \WORD`**
4. `A:\>` **`RD \SPREAD\DATA`**
5. `C:\>` **`CD \DATA`**
6. `C:\WORD\DATA>` **`CD ..`**
7. `C:\>` **`CD A:\LETTER91`**
8. `A:\>` **`DIR \DOS330 /P`**

1. `C:\>` **`MD \WORD\DATA`** A subdirectory of \WORD cannot be created unless the \WORD directory has first been created. When you create directories, the first-level directories must be created before any subdirectories below them can

be created. Use MD to create \WORD. Then MD \WORD\DATA will execute correctly.

2. C:\> **MD C:DATA** The MD command cannot fully address the directory being created. If a DATA directory is to be created as a subdirectory of the root directory, then it should be fully addressed. The command should be typed MD C:\DATA, using the Backslash character as part of the address of the DATA directory.
3. C:\> **RD \WORD** To be removed, a directory must be empty of all files as well as any subdirectories it may contain. Use the RD command to get rid of any subdirectories of \WORD. Then use the DEL command to delete any files in the directory before removing it.
4. A:\> **RD \SPREAD\DATA** The directory structure associated with \SPREAD is on Drive C, not Drive A. This RD command will assume that the directory structure is on the default drive (Drive A). To remove the directory \SPREAD\DATA on Drive C while at this prompt, you must fully address the directory. Use the command RD C:\SPREAD\DATA.
5. C:\> **CD DATA** When you address a directory without the Backslash, only directories directly above and below the default directory can be addressed. To change to the DATA directory associated with \SPREAD, the prompt must be C:\SPREAD>.
6. C:\WORD\DATA> **CD ..** The double-dot symbol addresses the parent directory of the current directory. This CD command will cause the default directory to be the \WORD directory. If your intent is to change to the root directory, you must address it directly using the command CD \.
7. C:\> **CD A:\LETTER91** This command changes the default directory on Drive A to the \LETTER91 directory. However, it does not make it the current directory. To make \LETTER91 the current directory, change to Drive A by entering A:.
8. A:\> **DIR \DOS330 /P** The default prompt displays Drive A. The \DOS330 directory is on Drive C. To display the \DOS330 directory, you must fully address it. Use the command DIR C:\DOS330 /P to see the contents of the \DOS330 directory on Drive C.

QUESTIONS AND PROBLEMS

1. What directories must first be created in order to create a directory named \WORD\GR\FONTS?
2. Write the command to display only the directory entries that are found in the root directory.

3. What are the conditions that must be true in order to remove a directory from a disk?
4. What directory is addressed when the double-dot (..) symbol is used to refer to a directory?
5. What command would be used to change the default directory on the non-default drive?
6. Write the command or commands to change into the \TEXT directory on Drive A when the default drive is Drive C.
7. What information is displayed about each file when the /W parameter is used with the DIR command?
8. What pathname should be used to address a file stored in the \SPREAD\DATA directory on Drive A?
9. What directory is addressed when the single-dot (.) symbol is used to refer to a directory?
10. Write a series of commands that will allow you to remove all the files and directories associated with the directory structure \WORD\GR\FONTS.
11. How can you find all occurrences of a given filename on a disk, along with the directory name in which they are stored?
12. What command or commands can be used to display a list of subdirectories of a named directory?
13. What command is used to display a list of files in alphabetic order by filename?
14. Give an example of two hidden files normally found in the root directory.
15. What command or commands can be used to display a list of hidden files in the root directory of your hard drive?

CHAPTER 7

FILE MANAGEMENT (INTERNAL COMMANDS)

INTRODUCTION

One of the most important functions performed by any operating system is file management. Regardless of the problem solved, software regularly creates files as it performs its functions. These files then need to be named, stored, and managed in a systematic way. DOS uses a variety of commands, both internal and external, to perform this function. This chapter concentrates on the internal file management commands stored in the DOS command processor, COMMAND.COM. (For a discussion of the external commands associated with file management, see Chapter 12.)

The internal commands discussed in this chapter are:

COPY
DEL or ERASE
REN
TYPE
VERIFY

TERMINOLOGY

The following terms relate to file management:

1. *Executable file:* An **executable file** is simply a program. DOS determines if a file is executable by examining the file's extension. Executable program files are those that have either a COM or an EXE extension. A file with an extension BAT is also executable, though it normally contains the names of several programs to be executed.
2. *Formatted data file:* Application programs such as spreadsheets, word processors, and database managers create various kinds of files that are associated with that application. These files, called formatted data files, typically contain control characters that are used to format these files for display and output purposes. The application software is needed to extract data from these types of files.
3. *ASCII text file:* An **ASCII text file** is one that only contains ASCII text characters. A batch file is an example of an ASCII text file. These files normally contain alphabetic, numeric, and punctuation characters. An ASCII text file can be displayed on the screen using the DOS TYPE command.
4. *Wildcard character:* DOS recognizes two wildcard characters that can be used when addressing a file. The asterisk (*) is used to represent part or all of either a filename or a file extension. The question mark (?) is used to address a single character in either a filename or a file extension.

THE COPY (COPY) COMMAND

The COPY command is a very powerful command used to copy a single file or a group of files from one location to another. When used with wildcards, the COPY command allows literally hundreds of files to be copied with a single command.

To copy files, DOS deals with hardware devices connected to the computer. These devices are addressed through their device names. For example, the console display screen is addressed as CON, the printer as PRN, and the first floppy diskette drive as A:. In copying files, the COPY command expects a FROM field followed by a TO field. In essence, you copy a file from a device to another device. Two forms of the COPY command are shown and discussed below.

1. **COPY *<source>* /A /B *<target>* /A /B /V**
2. **COPY *<source>* /A /B + *<source>* *<target>* /A /B /V**

In each example, *<source>* is the file or group of files to be copied. *<Target>* is the place where the files copied will reside. DOS makes extensive use of defaults when copying files. Remember that you always copy a file or group of files FROM somewhere TO somewhere. In addressing the source files, DOS allows you to address the files directly using a drive letter and a pathname. Likewise, the target for the file(s) to be copied can be directly addressed.

If the source or target group of files is not directly addressed, DOS makes assumptions about the drive and path or directory address. If the drive letter is not specified, DOS assumes the default drive. This assumption is made for both the source or FROM field and the target or TO field. Likewise, if the path is not specified, DOS assumes the default directory for the path. Most uses of the COPY command will use the first form shown above.

Files can be combined during the copy process by using the second form of the command shown above. Files are combined by using the plus (+) sign, which indicates that the files are to be combined.

Three parameters are associated with the COPY command. These parameters are described below:

1. **/A** The /A parameter tells DOS to treat the file as an ASCII text file. If the /A is used with the source file and files are to be combined, DOS treats all source files as ASCII text files. If /A is used with the target file, DOS treats the target file as an ASCII text file.
2. **/B** The /B parameter tells DOS to treat the file as a binary file. The same rules apply to the treatment of combined files and target files as for the /A parameter.
3. **/V** The /V parameter tells DOS to verify that the COPY command executed correctly with no errors. If the /V parameter is used, DOS verifies that the new file is identical to the old file. If key files are copied, or if wildcard characters

are used to copy a group of files, the /V parameter can be used to ensure the accuracy of the copy.

EXAMPLES

			FROM Field	TO Field
1.	C:\>	**COPY**	**FILE1.COM**	**A:**
2.	C:\>	**COPY**	**FILE1.COM**	**A:\MEMO\FILEM.COM**
3.	C:\>	**COPY**	**\DOS330\SORT.EXE**	**A:\DOS**
4.	C:\>	**COPY**	**A:\DOS\FIND.EXE**	**C:\DOS330**
5.	C:\>	**COPY**	**A:\DOS*.***	**B: /V**
6.	C:\>	**COPY**	**C:\DOS*.12?**	**C:\TEMP**
7.	C:\>	**COPY**	**\DOS\DISK*.COM**	
8.	C:\>	**COPY**	**\BATCH\MENU.BAT**	**PRN**
9.	C:\>	**COPY**	**TEXT1 /A + TEXT2**	**TEXT3 /A**

These examples show a wide variety of applications of the COPY command. Note that in each case there is a source or FROM field followed by a target or TO field. Note also that when a file or group of files is addressed, no spaces are left in either the FROM field or the TO field. The fields in our examples are clearly separated to delineate the FROM and the TO fields. In typing a typical command line for the COPY command, however, it is only necessary that a single blank space separate the FROM and TO fields, as shown below. In Example 4 the file FIND.EXE is addressed on Drive A in the \DOS directory as A:\DOS\FIND.EXE. There are no blank spaces between the drive letter (A) and EXE in the extension field.

1. C:\> **COPY FILE1.COM A:** In the first example, FILE1.COM is the file to be copied. Because no drive or directory information is supplied with the command line for the FROM field, DOS uses the default drive (C) and the default directory (\) as the place where it looks to find the file. This file is copied to Drive A and goes into the default directory on that drive. Note also that no filename or extension was used in naming the file on the destination drive. Therefore, DOS gives the file the same name, FILE1.COM, as it had on the source drive.
2. C:\> **COPY FILE1.COM A:\MEMO\FILEM.COM** In this example, the file FILE1.COM is copied to the \MEMO directory on Drive A and renamed FILEM.COM. This example shows that a file can not only be copied from one device to another device, but it can also be renamed as part of the copy process. If the file is not renamed, DOS gives the file the same name and the same extension it had on the source device. In this example FILE1.COM on Drive C becomes FILEM.COM on Drive A.
3. C:\> **COPY \DOS330\SORT.EXE A:\DOS** In the Example 3, a file SORT.EXE is copied from the \DOS330 directory on the default drive to the

\DOS directory on Drive A. The file is given the same name and extension it had on the source device.

4. **C:\> COPY A:\DOS\FIND.EXE C:\DOS330** In this example, a file FIND.EXE is copied from the \DOS directory on Drive A. The file is copied to the \DOS330 directory on the hard drive, Drive C.
5. **C:\> COPY A:\DOS*.* B: /V** In this example, we illustrate the use of wildcard characters. All files with any extension in the \DOS directory on Drive A are copied to Drive B. These files retain the same name and extension they had on Drive A, and they are placed in the default directory on Drive B. Because the V parameter is used with the TO field, DOS will verify that all files are copied correctly.
6. **C:\> COPY C:\DOS*.12? C:\TEMP** In this example, we illustrate the use of the ? wildcard character. Files are copied from the \DOS directory on Drive C. Every file with an extension whose first two characters are 12 are copied. The files are copied to the \TEMP directory on Drive C.
7. **C:\> COPY \DOS\DISK*.COM** In this example, the wildcard character asterisk (*) is used to indicate part of a field rather than the entire filename field. Files whose names begin with the characters DISK, have any characters for the last four in the filename, and have an extension COM are copied from the \DOS directory on Drive C. Note that no TO field is specified. The field is left blank. Since this field is missing, DOS relies on its defaults. The files are copied to the default directory on the default drive. Therefore, the files are copied to the root (\) directory on Drive C.
8. **C:\> COPY \BATCH\MENU.BAT PRN** This example illustrates the use of a device name in the target field. A single file MENU.BAT is copied from the \BATCH directory on the default drive. The file is sent to the system printer, known by its device name as PRN, and will be printed. This file will be readable when printed because a batch file is an ASCII text file.
9. **C:\> COPY TEXT1 /A + TEXT2 TEXT3 /A** The last example illustrates the use of the /A parameter as well as the idea of combining files. Two files TEXT1 and TEXT2 are copied from the default directory and the default drive. The two files are combined into a single file and placed in the default directory on the default drive with the name TEXT3. The first /A parameter after TEXT1 tells DOS to treat the source files TEXT1 and TEXT2 as ASCII text files. The second /A parameter after TEXT3 tells DOS to make the target file an ASCII text file also.

THE DELETE (DEL) OR ERASE (ERASE) COMMAND

The Delete command has two forms. Although either form can be used, in most cases the short form (DEL) rather than ERASE is used simply because it involves less typing. DEL or ERASE is used to delete a file or set of files from a disk or diskette. DEL does not physically remove the file from the disk. Instead, it modifies the filename in the system directory area. Basically, the area that the file uses on the disk is flagged as available for use the next time DOS needs some space for another file.

Programs such as Norton Utilities as well as the DOS UNDELETE command use this feature of DOS to recover files that have been deleted. So, if you accidentally delete a file or a group of files, remember this very important fact: the files are still on the disk. They are no longer directly accessible because DOS has modified the filename and flagged the data area for reuse. If you need to recover these files, use UNDELETE (Chapter 9) or software such as Norton Utilities. A file or portion of a file is physically gone only when DOS reuses the data area by writing another file over the data area of the file flagged for deletion.

The format of the DEL command is as follows:

DEL *<file spec>* /P

<file spec> is an optional drive and path, and must include the filename and extension (if any) of each file to be deleted. The /P parameter prompts you to enter a Y or N for each file selected for deletion.

The Delete command supports the use of both wildcard characters; the ? and *. As a result, groups of files and entire directories can be deleted with a single command. As with other commands discussed earlier, DOS makes assumptions about the default drive and the default directory if the file or files to be deleted are not fully addressed. Thus, when using wildcard characters to delete groups of files, make sure that the files to be deleted are, in fact, the ones you want to remove from the disk. It is recommended that files be fully addressed when using the wildcard notation *.* to mean delete "all files with any extension." While a file utility may allow you to recover the files accidentally deleted, you may spend considerable time recovering what it took seconds to delete. A planned and systematic backup procedure also offers protection from accidental deletion.

While you may think it will never happen to you, take the advice of experienced users. *Back up critical data regularly.* Sooner or later you too will delete an entire directory of files by accident. When it happens you will be glad you took a few extra minutes to back up the data. When using the DEL command with wildcards, take an extra 15 seconds to make sure that the command line was typed correctly. Get in the habit of always fully addressing groups of files when using the DEL command. If you do delete files by accident, use UNDELETE or a file recovery utility before you copy anything else to the disk.

The /P parameter can be used with some versions of DOS to have DOS prompt you for confirmation before a file is deleted. In most cases it is not necessary to use /P, but there are cases where the use of wildcards coupled with /P becomes extremely useful for selectively deleting files.

□ **EXAMPLES**

1. C:\> **DEL FILE1**
2. C:\> **DEL \MEMO\FILE1.DOC**
3. C:\> **DEL A:\MEMO\FILE1.DOC**
4. C:\> **DEL A:*.DOC**
5. C:\> **DEL C:\DOS330*.***
6. C:\> **DEL \WP50\MEMOS\FILE1.***
7. C:\> **DEL FILE?.* /P**

1. C:\> **DEL FILE1** In the first example, a file named FILE1 is deleted from the disk. No extension was used in addressing the file, so this file had only a filename. No drive or directory was specified, so DOS deletes this file from the root directory on Drive C.

2. C:\> **DEL \MEMO\FILE1.DOC** In Example 2, a file named FILE1.DOC is deleted from the default drive (C) in the directory \MEMO. In this case a directory was specified.

3. C:\> **DEL A:\MEMO\FILE1.DOC** In Example 3, the file FILE1.DOC is deleted. In this case both the drive (A:) and the directory (\MEMO) were specified. No defaults are used in this case, since both the drive and the directory were specified when addressing the file.

4. C:\> **DEL A:*.DOC** In this example, a group of files are to be deleted, since the wildcard character * is used. All files with the extension DOC are to be deleted. The files are in the default directory on Drive A.

5. C:\> **DEL C:\DOS330*.*** In this example, wildcards are used to specify both the filename and the extension. All files with any extension (*.*) are deleted from the \DOS330 directory on Drive C.

6. C:\> **DEL \WP50\MEMOS\FILE1.*** In Example 6 all copies of a file named FILE1 having any extension are to be deleted. The directory was specified (\WP50\MEMOS) but not the drive, so these files will be deleted from the directory \WP50\MEMOS on Drive C (the default drive).

7. C:\> **DEL FILE?.* /P** In the last example, the wildcard character ? is used along with the DOS parameter /P. DOS will delete any file beginning with the characters FILE and having any character as the fifth character of the filename. These files can have any extension. DOS will prompt for each file before deleting it, because the prompt parameter /P was used as part of the command line.

The Delete command (DEL) is a powerful DOS command. It can remove hundreds of files in seconds from a directory. Because it is so powerful, a little caution is in order when using it. Be careful when using wildcard characters to delete groups of files. It is recommended that files be fully addressed with both the drive letter and the directory name when using wildcard characters. With some versions of DOS, the prompt parameter (/P) can be used, as it prompts for confirmation before deleting the file. The prompt character can be used with wildcard character addressing to selectively delete a group of files. Finally, remember that the file is not physically removed from the disk. DOS merely flags the area occupied by the file so that it can be reused. It also modifies the first character of the filename, replacing it with a special control character. If a file is accidentally deleted, it can be fully recovered using either UNDELETE with DOS 5 or a file utility program such as Norton Utilities.

THE RENAME (REN) COMMAND

The Rename (REN) command renames a single file or a group of files. When renaming files only the name in the system directory area is changed. Thus, a file must remain in the directory in which it currently resides. It cannot be physically moved to another directory using REN. If you want to rename a file and move it to a different directory, use the COPY command discussed earlier in this chapter. When renaming a file, the new filename may not be the same as that of any other file currently in the same directory. When addressing the file, only the old name may be addressed with a drive letter and a pathname. The format of the Rename command is:

```
REN <oldname> <newname>
```

□ EXAMPLES

	Old Name	New Name
1.	C:\> **REN FILE1**	**FILE1.TXT**
2.	C:\> **REN FILE90.WP4**	**FILE91.WP5**
3.	C:\> **REN \MEMO\FILE89**	**FILE90**
4.	C:\> **REN A:\MEMO\FILE1**	**FILE91.WP5**
5.	C:\> **REN FILE*.TXT**	**LETR*.TXT**
6.	C:\> **REN *.TXT**	***.DOC**
7.	C:\> **REN *.***	**TX*.***

1. C:\> **REN FILE1 FILE1.TXT** In the first example, a file named FILE1 without any extension is renamed. The new filename is the same as the old filename. An extension has been added so that the file is now addressed as FILE1.TXT. The file is now known by its new name, which includes both a filename and an extension. This file must reside in the default directory on the default drive since no addressing was used. DOS assumes the default directory (\) and the default drive (C) in looking for this file.
2. C:\> **REN FILE90.WP4 FILE91.WP5** In Example 2, a file named

FILE90.WP4 has both its name and its extension changed. The filename is now FILE91; the extension is WP5.

3. **`C:\> REN \MEMO\FILE89 FILE90`** In Example 3, the file named FILE89 with no extension is addressed via the directory \MEMO. DOS looks for this file on the default drive (C) in the \MEMO directory. The filename is changed to FILE90.
4. **`C:\> REN A:\MEMO\FILE1 FILE91.WP5`** In Example 4, the file is fully addressed in the \MEMO directory on Drive A. The filename FILE1 is now changed to FILE91 and the extension WP5 is added.
5. **`C:\> REN FILE*.TXT LETR*.TXT`** Example 5 illustrates the use of wildcard characters to address a group of files. A group of files that begin with the first four characters FILE and have an extension TXT are renamed. These files will now begin with the first four characters LETR and will retain their extension of TXT.
6. **`C:\> REN *.TXT *.DOC`** In Example 6, all the files with TXT extensions will be renamed. These files will retain the same names, but will now have an extension of DOC.
7. **`C:\> REN *.* TX*.*`** In Example 7, all files in the default directory on the default drive are to be renamed. These files will now begin with the first two characters TX, will retain in their names the remaining six characters, and will have the same extension.

Note in each of the cases described above, the second field in the command has no addressing information. The <*newname*> field contains only a filename and an extension if appropriate. No directory name or drive letter appears in the <*newname*> field. DOS does not permit the file to be moved to another directory or to another drive when using the REN command. For this reason DOS does not permit any addressing information in the <*newname*> field. The filename field can be changed in any way. The file extension field can be changed in any way. A file extension can be added to a filename so the file is now known by a name field and an extension field. Wildcard characters can be used to change the name of a group of files with one single REN command.

THE TYPE (TYPE) COMMAND

The TYPE command is normally used to display ASCII text files on the display screen. The file is displayed character by character and line by line until DOS reaches the end of the file. If the file contains too many lines to fit on the screen, DOS scrolls the display until it reaches the end of the file. The form of the command is:

```
TYPE <filename>
```

A typical application of TYPE might be the display of a batch file on the display screen. ASCII text files may contain alphabetic characters, numeric characters, and typical punctuation characters. Program files such as files with an EXE or COM extension are not ASCII text files. There is no rule against using program files with the TYPE command, but a COM or EXE extension file will not display correctly. The screen display will contain unintelligible characters and the computer will beep occasionally if these are used with the TYPE command.

Likewise, files prepared by a word processing program such as Wordstar or WordPerfect or spreadsheet or database files cannot be displayed correctly with the TYPE command. The reason is that these application-software-prepared files typically contain control characters, such as soft carriage returns and bolding characters, that are used to format the document. The TYPE command cannot handle these control characters. Although the display may be more readable with some of these files as compared with COM or EXE files, the computer will still beep occasionally and will not display the file in a correct format.

It is best to use the TYPE command with files that you know are ASCII text files. The most common example of known ASCII text files are batch files that have the extension BAT or documentation files, usually having an extension DOC.

□ EXAMPLES

1. `C:\>` **`TYPE LETJXD01.TXT`**
2. `C:\>` **`TYPE \LET90\LETLRL1.TXT`**
3. `C:\>` **`TYPE A:\LETTER\LETMASTR.DOC`**
4. `C:\>` **`TYPE A:LETJXD01.TXT > PRN`**

1. `C:\>` **`TYPE LETJXD01.TXT`** In the first example, a file LETJXD01.TXT is displayed on the display monitor. The file is not specifically addressed, so DOS looks for the file in the default directory on the default drive. DOS expects to find this file on Drive C in the root directory.
2. `C:\>` **`TYPE \LET90\LETLRL1.TXT`** In this example, a file LETLRL1.TXT is copied from the \LET90 directory on Drive C and displayed on the display screen. In this case the default directory was overridden because a specific directory was included to address the file.
3. `C:\>` **`TYPE A:\LETTER\LETMASTR.DOC`** In Example 3 a file named LETMASTR.DOC is copied from the \LETTER directory on Drive A and displayed on the monitor. In this case the file was copied from the floppy drive to the display screen.
4. `C:\>` **`TYPE A:LETJXD01.TXT > PRN`** In this example the command line has indicated that the default device for displaying the file is to be overridden. If no device is specified, the TYPE command uses the display monitor as

the display device. Here, redirection (the use of the > symbol) indicates that the file is to be redirected to the system printer, so the file will not appear on the display screen. Instead the file LETJXD01.TXT is printed on the printer.

THE VERIFY (VERIFY) COMMAND

The VERIFY command turns the DOS Verify feature on or off. The Verify feature is a check feature that can be used whenever files are copied. If this feature is used, DOS confirms that data is correctly written to disk when a file is copied. (It is similar to the /V parameter of the COPY command.) The format of the VERIFY command is:

VERIFY *<status>*

EXAMPLES

1. `C:\> VERIFY on`
2. `C:\> VERIFY off`
3. `C:\> VERIFY`

The default value or *status* for VERIFY is off. Therefore, when copying files, DOS does not confirm or check to see that the data is copied correctly. It is recommended that VERIFY normally be left off because DOS normally copies files correctly. If there is a particular need to verify file copying, use the /V parameter with the COPY command.

1. `C:\>VERIFY on` In the first example, VERIFY is turned on. Now, when using the COPY command, DOS will confirm that the files have been correctly copied. If the VERIFY feature is on, file copying takes longer because DOS checks to see that the file or files are correctly transferred.
2. `C:\> VERIFY off` In Example 2 the VERIFY feature is turned off, or returned to its default value. Once turned off, it remains off until turned back on again.
3. `C:\> VERIFY` In this example, the command is typed without the *status* field. In this case, DOS will respond with the status of the Verify feature. Based on the examples above, VERIFY is now off, so DOS would respond:

```
VERIFY is off
```

If VERIFY had been turned on, DOS would have responded:

```
VERIFY is on
```

COMMON MISTAKES

Shown below are some common mistakes encountered when using these commands. Some mistakes generate error messages such as "A file cannot be copied on to itself." Many mistakes, however, cause execution errors. The user gets no message when the command executes. The problem, for example, may be that a group of files are copied into the wrong directory. The mistakes are discussed and explained below.

1. C:\> **COPY FILE1.COM**
2. C:\> **COPY A:\DOS\DISKCOPY*.* B:**
3. C:\> **COPY C:\DOS*.* C: \TEMP**
4. C:\> **DEL \MEMO**
5. C:\> **DEL \WP50\MEMOS\FILE1.*.***
6. C:\> **TYPE LETJXD01.WP5**
7. C:\> **TYPE A:AUTOEXEC.BAT < PRN**
8. C:\> **REN \MEMO\FILE89 \MEMO\FILE90**
9. C:\> **REN A:\MEMO\FILE1 C:\MEMO\FILE91.WP5**
10. C:\> **VER**

1. C:\> **COPY FILE1.COM** The COPY command copies a file or group of files from one place to another. When both the FROM and TO fields are not specified, DOS uses its defaults to determine where to look for the file(s) and where to put them. Because no drive or directory information is specified in this example, DOS looks for the FILE1.COM file on Drive C in the root directory. The TO field is not specified, so DOS tries to copy the file to Drive C in the root directory. This example would generate the error message, "File cannot be copied on to itself." If DOS executed this command, it would copy FILE1.COM from the root directory on Drive C to the root directory on Drive C and give the file the same name. This would copy FILE1.COM onto itself, and that is the reason for the error message. This command will not be executed.

2. C:\> **COPY A:\DOS\DISKCOPY*.* B:** Filenames can be a maximum of eight characters. DISKCOPY is already eight characters, so the first asterisk is not appropriate. An error message "Invalid path or filename" will be issued. The asterisk or question-mark wildcard character can be used only as part of the filename if the filename specification is seven characters or less. To copy the file DISKCOPY with any extension use the file specification DISKCOPY.*.

3. C:\> **COPY C:\DOS*.* C: \TEMP** The COPY command should normally specify a FROM field and a TO field. Three fields, as shown in this example, are not appropriate. An error message "Invalid number of parameters," meaning invalid number of fields, will be issued in this case. If the files are to be copied into the \TEMP directory on Drive C, the space must be eliminated between C: and \TEMP. The TO field should be typed as C:\TEMP, without the space.

4. `C:\>` **`DEL \MEMO`** This DEL command will attempt to delete the file MEMO from the root directory. The intent was to delete all files in the \MEMO directory. To do that, specify DEL \MEMO*.*. This change to the command deletes all files with any extension in the \MEMO directory.

5. `C:\>` **`DEL \WP50\MEMOS\FILE1.*.*`** In this example the specification of the files to be deleted is incorrect. The correct specification could be FILE1.* or FILE1*.*. Even though you may not have two periods in the file specification, DOS assumes that the meaning is FILE1, with any extension. No error message is issued, despite the fact that there is clearly an error in the way the command was typed. This example illustrates how undesirable results can occur when you make a mistake in typing a command. It is particularly important to check your typing whenever the wildcard asterisk (*) is used in deleting files. Despite the error, each copy of FILE1 with any extension will be deleted from the \WP50\MEMOS directory.

6. `C:\>` **`TYPE LETJXD01.WP5`** The TYPE command is intended for use with text files. The file referenced here, LETJXD01, is a WordPerfect file. The TYPE command will display the file on the console display, but it will not be correctly formatted because the TYPE command cannot handle the WordPerfect formatting characters. The TYPE command should normally be used to display text-only files such as batch files.

7. `C:\>` **`TYPE A:AUTOEXEC.BAT < PRN`** In this example a batch file is to be displayed to the printer. A file with a BAT extension is a text file. To display the file on the standard system printer use the greater-than (>) sign, not the less-than sign (<).

8. `C:\>` **`REN \MEMO\FILE89 \MEMO\FILE90`** The Rename command can be used to rename a file. It may not, however, be used to move the file from one disk to another or from one directory to another. In order to prevent this, DOS does not allow any addressing information to be part of the second or *newname* field. The *newname* field should contain only the new filename FILE90.

9. `C:\>` **`REN A:\MEMO\FILE1 C:\MEMO\FILE91.WP5`** When renaming a file or group of files, you can add an extension as part of the new name. No addressing information, however, can be part of the *<newname>* field. Here the characters C:\MEMO must be eliminated from the *<newname>* field. If the intent was to rename the file and to move it from Drive A to Drive C, the COPY command should have been used.

10. `C:\>` **`VER`** VER is the shorthand notation for the Version command, not the Verify command. This command will produce a message telling what version of DOS is installed on the computer. To determine the status of VERIFY, the full command name must be typed. Because that was the intent here, this command should have been typed as VERIFY to determine the status of VERIFY, either off or on.

QUESTIONS AND PROBLEMS

1. What types of files can be displayed correctly with the TYPE command?
2. Can the Rename command be used to rename a directory as well as a file?
3. What is the purpose of the VERIFY command?
4. Can the COPY command be used to copy groups of files from more than one directory, such as a directory structure, using a single command?
5. What parameters are associated with the COPY command and what is the meaning or effect of each parameter?
6. What types of files are deleted when the Delete command is used with the file specification *.*?
7. Can the Rename command be used to change the name of the file as well as the extension?
8. How can the COPY command be used to rename a file while copying it from one disk to another?
9. A total of 10 files are stored in your root directory. Two of these are hidden files. How many files will be copied to a floppy diskette if you use the file specification *.* to address the files while copying them?
10. Can the Delete command be used to delete both the files in a directory and the directory itself?

CHAPTER 8

SYSTEM CONTROL (INTERNAL COMMANDS)

INTRODUCTION

DOS uses a number of commands for controlling the system. Some of these commands are used to display information. This information is also used to maintain control of the system. An example is the DOS version number. DOS uses the VER command to display the version number of the system installed on the computer. The version number is also used to ensure that external commands executed are consistent with the version of the DOS command processor (COMMAND.COM) stored in RAM.

For example, if the DOS version installed is DOS 3.30, the computer displays that information when the VER command is executed. The version information displayed is extracted from a data area within COMMAND.COM.

Suppose that the CHKDSK command from DOS Version 4.01 is executed on this system. DOS notes that the version number in the CHKDSK.COM file (4.01) is different from the version number stored in COMMAND.COM (3.30). DOS issues an error message, "Incorrect DOS Version." This indicates that the CHKDSK program is from a different version of DOS. The commands executed under DOS must be consistent with the DOS nucleus that is loaded at boot time.

The commands used for system control are:

CLS
VER
PROMPT
PATH
SET
CTTY

THE CLEAR SCREEN (CLS) COMMAND

The Clear Screen (CLS) command clears the existing information from the display screen. After clearing the screen, the cursor is returned to the upper left corner of the screen. There are no parameters associated with the CLS command. The format of the Clear Screen command is:

CLS

THE VERSION (VER) COMMAND

DOS uses the Version (VER) command to display the DOS version number of the system installed on your computer. This version number ensures that external commands that are executed are consistent with the DOS nucleus stored in RAM.

As we have seen, if the DOS version installed on your system is DOS 3.30, the VER command will cause this information to be displayed. The information displayed about the version is extracted from COMMAND.COM. There are no parameters associated with the VER command. The format of the Version command is:

```
VER
```

THE PROMPT (PROMPT) COMMAND

The PROMPT command helps tailor the DOS prompt to your individual needs. PROMPT defines the format of the system prompt. The default DOS prompt is normally displayed as the current drive letter followed by a greater-than sign (>). This drive letter will normally be the drive letter associated with the hard drive.

The system prompt can be changed to include any character that DOS can display, along with system information if that is desired. Examples of system information include date, time, and the current directory, or combinations of these. The prompt can also include a text string, as shown in the examples below. The format of the PROMPT command is:

```
PROMPT <string>
```

The <*string*> portion is optional. If included, it defines the new DOS prompt. A PROMPT command will normally be part of the AUTOEXEC.BAT file and thus sets the prompt when the computer is first powered up or any time it is rebooted. The DOS prompt can also be tailored to display system information by including a series of codes shown in Table 8.1. Each code is actually a two-character string. The first character of the string is always the dollar ($) sign. If any character other than those listed in Table 8.1 follows the first dollar sign in the prompt string, DOS ignores both characters. If the PROMPT command is entered without any string, DOS resets the system prompt to the standard or default version. A single code may be used, but a sequence of several codes is also permissible, as illustrated in the examples below.

□ EXAMPLES

1. `C:\> PROMPT Enter a Command $g`
2. `C> PROMPT $p $g`
3. `C:\> PROMPT $t $g`
4. `C:\> PROMPT $d$_$t$_$p$g`
5. `C:\> PROMPT $t$h$h$h$h$h$h$_$p$g`
6. `C:\> PROMPT`

TABLE 8.1 **Prompt Control Strings**

Code	Information Displayed
$b	Vertical bar (|)
$d	The system date
$e	Escape character
$g	Greater-than sign (>)
$h	Backspace (which erases the previous character)
$l	Less-than sign (<)
$n	The current disk drive
$p	The current directory and the current drive
$q	Equal sign (=)
$t	The system time
$v	The DOS version number
$_	Start a new line (underscore)
$$	Dollar sign ($)

1. `C:\>` **`PROMPT Enter a Command $g`** This example of the PROMPT command will change the DOS prompt to a pure text prompt. The default disk drive letter as well as the default directory will no longer be shown. The new DOS prompt will appear as the text string **Enter a Command** followed by the greater-than sign. The cursor will immediately follow the greater-than sign.
2. `C>` **`PROMPT $p $g`** In this example, the default prompt is shown as the drive letter followed by the greater-than sign. The Prompt command is followed by a set of codes, which are described in Table 8.1. The $p code will cause the default drive and the default directory to appear. The $g code will cause the greater-than sign to appear. The two codes are separated by a space, so in this prompt there will be a space between the directory name and the greater-than sign. If the default drive were D and the default directory \WP50, the new prompt would display as

   ```
   D:\WP50 >
   ```

3. `C:\>` **`PROMPT $t $g`** In this example, the prompt is changed to display the current time along with the greater-than sign. This type of DOS prompt would help you keep track of time if you have an appointment. Every time the new prompt is displayed, the current time will be displayed. The time is displayed in hours, minutes, seconds, and hundredths of seconds. If only hours and minutes are desired in the time display, you can use the $h code to limit the display to only hours and minutes. See Example 5 below for a way to limit the time to hours and minutes.

4. `C:\>` **`PROMPT $d$_$t$_$p$g`** This example produces a multiline prompt as opposed to a single-line prompt. In effect, the underscore character generates a Return after the display of the date ($d) and after the display of the time ($t). In this example the prompt is displayed as a three-line prompt; the current date appears on the first line, the current time appears on the second line, and the default drive, default directory, and greater-than sign appear on the third line. For example:

```
Wed 9-11-1993
13:27:32.58
C:\WP50>
```

5. `C:\>` **`PROMPT $t$h$h$h$h$h$h$_$p$g`** This PROMPT command uses the $h code to backspace over characters that are to be eliminated as part of the DOS prompt display. The $t code will display the time in hours, minutes, seconds, and hundredths of seconds. A display of time in the default mode was illustrated in the previous example. Normally, a display in hours and minutes is sufficient. To eliminate all the characters except hours and minutes requires that six characters be eliminated from the normal time display. In the previous example, the characters :32.58, which represent seconds and hundredths of seconds, would be eliminated—a total of six characters, including the colon and decimal point. Therefore, the prompt command in this example includes $t followed by six $h codes to tailor the time display. The remainder of the string includes $_ to skip to the next line, plus the pg codes to generate the default drive, default directory, and greater-than sign. This DOS prompt example will generate a two-line DOS prompt such as:

```
10:32
C:\LOTUS>
```

6. `C:\>` **`PROMPT`** The DOS prompt can be reset to the default DOS prompt at any time. Issuing the PROMPT command with no string following the command performs the reset. The above example shows a PROMPT command to reset the DOS prompt to its default value. The normal default prompt will display the default drive and the greater-than sign only. Most users find a prompt that includes the default drive, the current directory, and the greater-than sign in the display of the prompt to be the most useful. This display for Drive C and the root directory would appear as:

```
C:\>
```

The PROMPT command allows the DOS prompt to be tailored to a wide range of display situations, including menu systems, command-line systems, and the like. Control codes allow date, time, disk drive, directory, and other information to be displayed. More sophisticated PROMPT applications can also be included by using Escape code sequences to control color and text display modes. It is recommended that a PROMPT command be included in the AUTOEXEC.BAT file. A good starting point is the command **PROMPT pg.**

THE PATH (PATH) COMMAND

The PATH command sets the path or paths that DOS will search when trying to execute a command. When executing any command, DOS always searches in the current directory on the default drive to find the command (program) to execute. In searching for the program to execute, DOS looks only for files that have an extension field of COM, EXE, or BAT, based on the command that has been typed. For instance, if the user types the command FORMAT and then executes it by pressing the Enter key, DOS looks in the current directory on the default drive for a file that has the name FORMAT.COM, FORMAT.EXE, or FORMAT.BAT. If it finds a file with one of these names, that file is loaded and executed. If a file named FORMAT.TXT is in the directory, it will not be executed. Why not? The file did not have an extension that indicates that it is an executable program. DOS considers only files having an extension COM, EXE, or BAT as executable. Therefore, the FORMAT.TXT file is not considered an executable file.

The format of the PATH command is:

PATH *<drive>* *<directory>* ;

Normally, if the PATH command is not used, only the current directory is searched in order to execute a program. In many cases it is important that the current directory be set prior to executing a program. If the WordPerfect program for WordPerfect 5.0 is to be executed, for instance, the user should have set the default directory as \WP50 prior to executing the WP.EXE file. In the absence of any other paths being set, DOS issues the error message "Bad Command or File Name" if it does not find an executable file in the current directory.

In many other cases, however, it is desirable to have a set of directories that will be searched when a command is typed. For example, DOS programs are normally stored in their own directory, such as \DOS500. The FORMAT.COM file would normally be stored in the DOS directory. If \DOS500 is part of the search path, a user who wants to format a floppy disk need not change to the DOS directory every time a diskette is to be formatted . In order to avoid having to change to the DOS directory, just add the DOS directory to the path with the PATH command.

```
C:\> PATH C:\DOS500
```

By doing this, the user has told DOS to always search the \DOS500 directory in addition to the current directory before issuing the error message "Bad Command or File Name."

It is desirable to establish the path or paths to be part of the search process at boot time. Therefore, the PATH command is another command that should be part of the AUTOEXEC.BAT file, similar to the PROMPT command.

It is not recommended that application directories be included as part of a PATH command set up during the boot process. This is a fairly common practice, but it can lead to problems. For example, a lab used to teach several different word processing applications might have installed WordPerfect 5.0 in a \WP50 directory, WordPerfect 5.1 in a \WP51 directory, and Multimate in an \MM directory. All three of these software packages use the same name for the executable file: WP.EXE. Assume the PATH command is set up in the AUTOEXEC.BAT file as shown below:

```
PATH C:\;C:\DOS500;C:\WP50;C:\WP51;C:\MM
```

What application will be executed when the user types WP at the DOS prompt, when the prompt is C:\>? DOS searches the path and executes WordPerfect Version 5.0. Version 5.0 is executed because it occurs in the PATH command (C:\WP50) before either Multimate or Version 5.1 of WordPerfect. The only way to execute Version 5.1 of WordPerfect or Multimate is to change into their associated directory. However, if we change the path command to:

```
PATH C:\;C:\DOS500;C:\MM;C:\WP50;C:\WP51
```

Multimate becomes the word processor that executes because it is placed first on the path. The problem arises because all three software packages use the same name for the executable file: WP.EXE. This situation is not that uncommon on a system used to demonstrate lots of software, such as one at a software retailer, or in a computer lab that supports a wide variety of computer software courses.

The problem can also arise on a computer used for business or personal work. Assume a software package is upgraded. Two versions of the same software now exist in two different directories, perhaps because you want to keep the old version while learning to use the new version. Which directory should be first on the path? You have to make a choice.

If you choose to violate this rule and put application directories on the path, at least be aware of the problems that can arise. One solution that works well and avoids the problem is to create a batch directory \BATCH. The PATH command in AUTOEXEC.BAT might then be:

```
PATH C:\;C:\DOS500;C:\UTIL;C:\BATCH
```

Application software can now be executed using batch files, and all the batch files can be stored in the \BATCH directory. To handle our problem with the three word processing packages, just use three different batch files. The batch file for WordPerfect 5.0 might be WP50.BAT, the batch file for WordPerfect 5.1 might be WP51.BAT, and the one for Multimate might be WPMM.BAT. Each batch file is now unique to its software. Including the \BATCH directory on the path solves the access problem. (See Chapter 19 for more information on the use and application of batch files.)

□ **EXAMPLES**

1. C:\WP50> **PATH C:\;C:\DOS401**
2. C:\UTIL> **PATH C:\;C:\MENUD;C:\DOS330;C:\UTIL**
3. A:\> **PATH C:\;C:\DOS330;C:\WP51;C:\LOTUS**
4. C:\> **PATH ;**
5. C:\> **PATH**

1. C:\WP50> **PATH C:\;C:\DOS401** This example modifies the path to include both the root directory on Drive C and the DOS directory \DOS401, also on Drive C. When specifying a path, it is recommended that the specification always include a drive and a directory combination, not just the directory. If only the directory is specified, DOS searches the named directory on the default drive. Frequently that may be a floppy drive if data is being stored on a floppy diskette, for example. In this example the system has been set to search the root directory as well as the DOS401 directory, in addition to the default directory, for any commands that are executed. This execution of the PATH command modifies any previous path that may have been set, even one set in the AUTOEXEC.BAT file. If a command is now issued, the default directory will be searched, followed by the root directory, followed then by the \DOS401 directory. If the command issued is not found in any of these directories, a "Bad Command or Filename" error message will be issued.
2. C:\UTIL> **PATH C:\;C:\MENUD;C:\DOS330;C:\UTIL** In this example, the path has been modified to include a total of four directories. The order of search for a command to execute is the order in which the directories are specified in the PATH command. This PATH command specifies that order as the root directory followed by the \MENUD directory followed by the \DOS330 directory and finally by the \UTIL directory. This might be a typical path specification for a system with a menu installed, and one that includes some DOS utilities stored in the \UTIL directory. Note that once the path in this example is set, a command issued from this prompt will actually search the \UTIL directory first. This is because DOS always searches the current directory first, and in this case the current directory is \UTIL. It only searches other directories based on the path setting after first determining that the command to be issued is not in the current directory. The order of search once this path had been set would be \UTIL followed by the root directory (\) followed by the other directories as set by the PATH command above.
3. A:\> **PATH C:\;C:\DOS330;C:\WP51;C:\LOTUS** In this example,

the PATH command includes two application directories: \WP51 and \LOTUS. These directories would normally contain the WordPerfect 5.1 application software in \WP51 and the Lotus 1-2-3 software in the \LOTUS directory. Based on this path specification, the order of search is the root directory followed by the \DOS330 directory followed by the \WP51 directory followed by the \LOTUS directory on Drive C. Note that the system would have first searched the root directory on Drive A because that is the current drive and directory in the DOS prompt. In general, it is not recommended that application directories such as \WP51 and \LOTUS be included in a path set in the AUTOEXEC.BAT file. The reason is that most applications require that the user be in the application directory before executing an application program such as WordPerfect. For that reason it is recommended that a PATH command contain only the DOS directory (such as \DOS330), menu directories, and a utility directory (such as \UTIL).

4. `C:\>` **PATH ;** In this example, the previous path setting has been deleted. Executing the PATH command followed by a semicolon deletes the previous path setting.
5. `C:\>` **PATH** In this last example, no path is set, because no string was entered following the PATH command. In this case the user is requesting that the system display the current path setting. If no path has been set, the system will respond with the message "No Path." If a path has been set, the system will display the current path setting. This execution of the PATH command displays the path setting only; it does not modify the path setting.

THE SET (SET) COMMAND

The SET command creates, changes, displays, or deletes a value assigned to an environmental variable. It can also be used to define replaceable parameters that are used with batch files. Examples of variable names and some sample values are shown in Table 8.2.

The variable COMSPEC is the command specification variable. It tells DOS where to find the control program that is loaded at boot time, as well as the

TABLE 8.2 Environmental Variables

Name	Value
COMSPEC	C:\COMMAND.COM
PATH	C:\;C:\DOS330;C:\UTIL
PROMPT	PG

name of the file. COMMAND.COM is the name of the file that is loaded during a cold or a warm boot. This variable is stored in an area of memory called the *environment.* Likewise, when a path is set, either by the AUTOEXEC.BAT file or by the user issuing the DOS PATH command, the value of this variable is also stored in the environment.

DOS stores key variables used in controlling the system in the environment. The normal environment has room to store 160 bytes of information. The COMSPEC variable as well as the PATH and PROMPT values are stored in this area. Other variables can be created.

The format of the SET command is:

SET <*string*>

□ EXAMPLES

1. C:\> **SET Drive = C:**
2. C:\> **SET PROMPT = $P**
3. C:\> **SET PROMPT =**
4. C:\> **SET**

1. C:\> **SET Drive = C:** The SET command can be used to create a new environmental variable. In this example, a variable named Drive is created and defined as equal to C:. This variable can then be referenced in a batch file by enclosing the variable name between percent (%) symbols. To reference the variable Drive in a batch file, refer to it as %Drive%.
2. C:\> **SET PROMPT = $P** The value of the variables for both PATH and PROMPT are stored in the environment. These values can be changed by either issuing the appropriate command or by using the SET command. Thus the value for the prompt can be changed with the SET command, as in this example that defines its value as $P. This could also be accomplished by issuing a PROMPT command and defining the value as $P, such as **PROMPT $P.**
3. C:\> **SET PROMPT =** An environmental variable can be deleted. To do this, use the SET command along with the name of the variable, followed by an equals sign. In this example the variable PROMPT will be deleted from the environment. The DOS prompt will return to its system default value, which consists of a drive letter followed by the greater-than sign.
4. C:\> **SET** In this example, the SET command is used to display the names of all environmental variables as well as their values. The command is issued by itself, with no string following the command. A typical display resulting from the SET command might be:

```
COMSPEC=C:\COMMAND.COM
PROMPT=$P$G
PATH=C:\;C:\DOS330
```

THE CHANGE CONSOLE DEVICE (CTTY) COMMAND

The CTTY command specifies the device to be used for standard input and standard output. The device assigned must be able to handle both input and output information. The normal device for standard input and output is the console (CON). Standard input for CON is the computer keyboard; standard output for CON is the display screen or monitor.

The format of the CTTY command is:

CTTY *<device>*

<device> is the name of the device to be assigned. Other devices that might be used for standard input and output are COM1 and AUX. Remote operation of your computer could be accomplished using the CTTY command to assign the COM1 port as the standard input and output device. Input would then be received via the computer's modem, and output would be redirected back to the controlling system via the modem. If a device other than a standard DOS system device is specified, the device driver software must be available to DOS on the system, and a DEVICE command must be included in the CONFIG.SYS file at boot time.

EXAMPLES

1. C:\> **CTTY COM1**
2. C:\> **CTTY CON**

1. C:\> **CTTY COM1** This CTTY command assigns standard input and output to the computer's COM1 port. The system now expects commands to be issued from a remote system via a modem connected to this port. Output from the execution of any command, such as command output or error messages will be directed to COM1 also.
2. C:\> **CTTY CON** The CTTY command in this example has been used to set standard input and output back to the local system via the console device. This is the normal setup for a personal computer, with commands issued via the keyboard and messages and error information displayed on the computer display.

COMMON MISTAKES

Shown below are some common mistakes encountered when using these commands. Some mistakes generate error messages. Many mistakes, however, cause execution errors, but generate no messages.

1. C:\> **CLR**
2. C:\> **VER 4.01**

3. `C:\> PROMPT $s $g`
4. `C:\> PROMPT $p >`
5. `C:\> PATH C:\;C:\DOS401:C:\MENUD`
6. `C:\> CTTY PRN`

1. `C:\> CLR` The command to clear the screen is CLS. Because CLR is not a DOS command, the user gets the message "Bad Command or Filename."
2. `C:\> VER 4.01` The VER command has no parameters or string fields associated with it. In this example, DOS ignores the 4.01 part of the command and issues a message indicating the version number that is part of the COMMAND.COM file. If DOS 4.01 is installed, the message will indicate that. If some other version is installed, DOS will indicate the actual version that is installed. To upgrade from one version of DOS to another requires you to follow a several-step procedure. The VER command requests that DOS indicate what version is installed; it cannot be used to do an upgrade.
3. `C:\> PROMPT $s $g` The PROMPT command has a specified list of codes that can be issued as two-digit codes using the dollar sign (See Table 8.1). The $s part of this command is invalid. DOS will ignore the $s part of this command and interpret only the $g part of the command. DOS will display no error message telling the user that $s is an invalid code.
4. `C:\> PROMPT $p >` This example of the PROMPT command contains the greater-than sign as part of the string. If the greater-than sign is to be part of the DOS prompt, the $g code must be used as part of the command. In this example the user will receive an error message "File creation error." The greater-than sign as part of the command indicates that the output is to be redirected to another device.
5. `C:\> PATH C:\;C:\DOS401:C:\MENUD` In this example, part of the PATH command is correct and the system will function correctly. The problem is that a colon (:) instead of a semicolon (;) was entered after DOS401. As a result, the last drive directory combination—C:\MENUD—will be ignored. DOS issues no error message indicating that a mistake was made in entering the command. This command can be corrected by replacing the colon following DOS401 with a semicolon.
6. `C:\> CTTY PRN` The CTTY command can be changed from CON to another device. The device selected, however, must be capable of both input and output. The standard system printer (PRN) is only an output device, and thus cannot be used. DOS issues no error message indicating that PRN is an output device only. The user loses control of the keyboard if the above command is entered. To regain control of the keyboard, reboot the computer using the Ctrl-Alt-Del warm-boot procedure.

QUESTIONS AND PROBLEMS

1. Where is the cursor positioned after a CLS command is issued?
2. How do you determine what version of DOS is installed on your computer?
3. Why is the version of DOS installed important to the operation of a personal computer?
4. What command is used to tailor the display of directory, drive, and other information at the command line?
5. How can a directory be added to the list of directories to be searched for executing a command issued at the command line?
6. How can a user at a remote location be given access to and control of your personal computer?
7. Give a list of commands that affect information stored in the DOS environment.
8. What commands discussed in this chapter would most likely be found in an AUTOEXEC.BAT file?
9. What are the typical directories that would normally be part of a PATH command in an AUTOEXEC.BAT file? Why?
10. Why is it important to specify both drive and directory as part of an entry in a PATH command?

PART III

DOS EXTERNAL COMMANDS

CHAPTER 9

DISK MANAGEMENT (EXTERNAL COMMANDS)

INTRODUCTION

To manage disk files, whether on hard disks or floppy diskettes, requires a number of external commands. In order to manage the files on a disk, DOS stores information in its system directory area that records key information about each file. Among this information is the filename, the file extension, the size of each file, the attribute byte, and the date and time the file was created or last modified. The system directory area, coupled with the FAT table, allows DOS to keep track of all the pieces of a file. The external commands used by DOS to perform disk management include:

FORMAT
CHKDSK
DISKCOPY
DISKCOMP
LABEL
FDISK
FASTOPEN
MIRROR
UNDELETE
UNFORMAT
RECOVER

In addition to these DOS commands, several useful DOS utility packages that supplement the functions provided by DOS are available. Two of the most popular include Norton Utilities and PC Tools. You may want to examine these two software packages as well as others so that you have a full array of software support for your system. Version 5.00 of DOS incorporates several functions previously found in utility software. In fact, three of these programs (MIRROR, UNDELETE, and UNFORMAT) were licensed from Central Point Software.

THE FORMAT (FORMAT) COMMAND

The FORMAT command is used to prepare any disk so that it can store files. In addition to formatting the disk, the FORMAT command can also be used to prepare a disk so that it can boot the operating system. The FORMAT command also permits selective formatting so that a floppy diskette will be compatible across a range of computer systems and floppy diskette drives. The composition of the FORMAT command is:

FORMAT *<drive>* /B /Q /U /S /1 /4 /8 /N:*<sectors>* /T:*<tracks>* /F:*<size>* /V:*<label>*

`<drive>` is the letter of the drive containing the disk to be formatted, followed by a colon.

`/B` formats a disk and reserves space for the DOS hidden files. The hidden files may then be loaded into this reserved space using the DOS Transfer System (SYS) command.

`/Q` performs a quick reformat of an already formatted disk. DOS essentially cleans the disk of previously stored information so that the full data storage area is available. The disk has the same storage capacity as the original disk. DOS does not check for bad sectors or unusable areas on a quick-reformatted disk. This feature is new with Version 5.00.

`/U` performs a format of the disk, destroying all previously stored information. If the /U parameter is used, DOS cannot recover the contents of the disk using the UNFORMAT command.

`/S` creates a bootable system disk. This parameter results in the hidden files being loaded into the proper area on the disk, followed by copying the COMMAND.COM file to the disk. A disk containing the two hidden files along with COMMAND.COM is frequently referred to as a *system disk* or a *bootable system disk.*

`/1` results in only one side of a 5 1/4-inch diskette being formatted, even if the diskette has been loaded into a double-sided disk drive.

`/4` results in a diskette being formatted as a double-density diskette when formatted using a high-density 1.2 MB 5 1/4-inch drive. Diskettes formatted as double-density in a high-density drive frequently do not work reliably when used in a double-density 360 KB disk drive. The /4 parameter is used with 5 1/4-inch drives only.

`/8` results in a 5 1/4-inch diskette with eight sectors allocated per track rather than the standard nine sectors per track.

`/N:<sectors>` specifies the number of sectors per track that should be used in the formatting process. If you specify /N, you must also specify /T when formatting. (Refer to the diskette capacity table in Appendix B for more information on diskette capacities.)

`/T` specifies the number of tracks to be used during the format process. If you specify /T, you must also specify /N. (Refer to Appendix B for information on diskette capacities.)

`/F:<size>` specifies, in kilobytes, the capacity to be formatted on the diskette. The parameter /F can be used in place of /N and /T. Valid entries for /F include 160, 180, 320, 360, 720, 1200, 1440, and 2880.

`/V:<label>` specifies the volume label that will be assigned to the formatted disk.

The first time you format a diskette on your floppy drive, use that experience to learn the default format of the drive. Depending on the type of disk drive, the default format will probably be 720 KB or 1.44 MB capacity (for a 3 1/2-inch drive) or 360 KB or 1.2 MB (for a 5 1/4-inch drive). To format a diskette, place a the diskette in the floppy drive and at the DOS prompt type the following:

```
C:\> FORMAT d:
```

Where *d*: is the drive letter of the disk to be formatted. This will typically be A: or B: on most systems.

The FORMAT.COM file will be loaded into memory from your hard drive and executed. You will receive a message to load a diskette into the disk drive and then to strike the Enter key. Follow the instructions on the screen. The FORMAT program will display the cylinders and read/write heads being addressed as it formats the diskette. If you watch this process you can learn how many tracks are used on each side of the diskette. There will be either 40 tracks (in the case of the 360 KB diskettes) or 80 tracks (in the case of any of the other formats).

When your diskette is formatted, it will display one of the capacities shown below:

5 1/4-inch DSDD:	362,496 bytes
5 1/4-inch DSHD:	1,213,952 bytes
3 1/2-inch DSDD:	730,112 bytes
3 1/2-inch DSHD:	1,457,664 bytes

It is important to know the default formatting capacity of the floppy drive, because it determines the type of diskette you should buy. If you own an IBM-AT or AT-compatible computer and the disk drive is of the 5 1/4-inch variety, purchase high-density rather than double-density diskettes to take full advantage of the maximum capacity of the drive. Likewise, if the drive is a 3 1/2-inch drive you need to know whether the drive formats diskettes at the 1.44 MB capacity level or at 720 KB. If the drive capacity is 1.44 MB, purchase high-density diskettes to take advantage of the storage capacity of the drive.

In addition to formatting a diskette so that it can store files, the FORMAT command can also build a diskette with the DOS kernel or nucleus stored on it. These diskettes are referred to as system diskettes and can be used to boot the computer when loaded in Drive A.

To format a bootable system disk, load a diskette into Drive A and use the FORMAT command below to load the DOS kernel on the diskette:

```
C:\> FORMAT A: /S
```

Use the DIR command to check the space on the diskette once the format process is complete. Note that the difference between the space originally available on the diskette and the size of the COMMAND.COM file leaves a block of space missing. As you learned earlier, a diskette built to be bootable has two hidden files loaded on the diskette, along with the COMMAND.COM processor. When viewed with the DIR command, only the COMMAND.COM file will show up on the directory listing. To see the hidden files along with the user files, use the CHKDSK command.

In addition to formatting the disk in the default format or as a bootable system disk, the FORMAT command allows the diskette to be formatted in a variety of ways, depending on specific requirements. For example, if a 3 /2-inch diskette is needed for use on a variety of computers, you may need to format the diskettes as double-density (720 KB) diskettes. The reason is that high-density drives can read double-density diskettes, but double-density drives cannot read high-density diskettes. So, if you will be using diskettes at home and at work or in other situations where you are unsure of the disk drive capacity, format the high-density diskettes as double-density so the diskettes can be used on either system. Also, note when buying software that the installation diskettes supplied are always double-density in format. Software installation diskettes are supplied in this format because they will work on any system.

To format a diskette as a double-density diskette, use the formatting parameters to override the default format of the disk drive. The first example below formats a high-density 3 1/2-inch diskette in a high-density drive as a double-density diskette. The second example formats a high-density 5 1/4-inch diskette in a high-density drive as a double-density diskette.

For a 3 1/2-inch diskette type, the following; where d: is the drive letter:

```
C:\> FORMAT d:/N:9/T:80
```

The 1.44 MB diskette will now have a data capacity of only 730,112 bytes.

For a 5 1/4-inch diskette type the following, where d: is the drive letter:

```
C:\> FORMAT d:/4
```

The 1.2 MB diskette will now have a data capacity of only 362,496 bytes.

To gain this compatibility, you sacrifice the higher capacity of the diskettes. In the case of the 1.44 MB diskette, half of the diskette's data capacity has been sacrificed. In the case of the 1.2 MB diskette, almost 70 percent of the diskette's potential storage capacity has been lost.

□ EXAMPLES

1. `A:\> FORMAT C:/S`
2. `C:\> FORMAT A:/S/V`
3. `C:\> FORMAT A:/Q`
4. `C:\> FORMAT B:/S/N:9/T:80`
5. `C:\> FORMAT A:/4`
6. `C:\> FORMAT A:/F:720`

1. `A:\> FORMAT C:/S` In this example, Drive C, which is normally the hard drive, is formatted as a bootable system disk. The /S parameter indicates that the DOS system nucleus is to be loaded at the conclusion of the format process. **Be very careful when using this command. You are about to wipe out all information on your hard drive!** It is extremely unlikely that you will ever use

this form of the FORMAT command. Only if your system is new or your hard drive has been repaired are you likely to use it.

2. `C:\>` **`FORMAT A:/S/V`** In this example a diskette in the first floppy drive (Drive A) will be formatted. Two parameters, /S and /V, have been specified. The diskette will have the DOS nucleus loaded onto it and the system will prompt for a volume label to be specified.
3. `C:\>` **`FORMAT A:/Q`** The diskette in Drive A will be quick-reformatted based on its previous format parameters. The diskette must have been previously formatted. All information stored on the disk will be deleted so that the full data capacity will be available. The disk will not be checked for bad sectors or unusable areas.
4. `C:\>` **`FORMAT B:/S/N:9/T:80`** In this example the diskette in Drive B will be formatted as a system diskette. The parameter specifications for /N and /T indicate that the diskette should be formatted with 80 tracks and 9 sectors per track. These are the parameters for a double-density, 3 1/2-inch diskette.
5. `C:\>` **`FORMAT A:/4`** The format specification in this example is for a 360 KB format of a 5 1/4-inch diskette in a 1.2 MB drive. The /4 parameter is only used in high-density 1.2 MB drives when a diskette is to be formatted in double-density 360 KB format.
6. `C:\>` **`FORMAT A:/F:720`** In this example the size parameter is used to specify the format specification rather than the track and sector parameters /N and /T. Drive A must be a 3 1/2-inch drive. The diskette will be formatted as a double-density diskette.

THE CHECK DISK (CHKDSK) COMMAND

The Check Disk (CHKDSK) command provides capabilities for checking the space utilization of a diskette. It also provides information on the internal memory of the computer, including the size of the memory components as well as the amount of free space available. The space used in RAM is that consumed by the DOS nucleus, including device drivers and other programs, and data space allocated as a result of information and commands contained in the CONFIG.SYS and AUTOEXEC.BAT files. DOS processes the information in these files during the boot process. The format of the Check Disk command is:

```
CHKDSK <drive> <filename> /V /F
```

<*drive*> is the letter of the drive that contains the disk to be checked, followed by a colon. If no drive letter is specified DOS checks the current or default drive.

<*filename*> specifies the file(s) to be checked for noncontiguous sectors. The <*filename*> field is optional and normally not specified.

/V specifies that the full pathname and filename of each file and directory on the disk should be displayed. When /V is specified, the display will include hidden filenames as well as volume labels as part of the display in addition to the user files.

/F specifies that DOS should analyze the disk being checked for file allocation errors. If the program finds any allocation errors, you are provided the opportunity to recover the lost space on the disk by responding "Y" (for Yes) to the message. Files recovered during the recovery process are given the name FILE*nnnn* where *nnnn* is a sequence number. Files recovered are grouped by clusters and chains and are placed in the root directory on the disk. All files recovered have the extension CHK.

A sample CHKDSK command along with the report it generates is shown below. The report shown is in three parts. The first part provides information on a 20 MB hard disk and the information stored on it.

```
C: \> CHKDSK C:

21135360 bytes total disk space
   53248 bytes in 3 hidden files
   38912 bytes in 16 directories
14256128 bytes in 474 user files
   10240 bytes in bad sectors
 6787072 bytes available on disk

    2048 bytes in each allocation unit
   10337 total allocation units on disk
    1704 available allocation units on disk

  655360 bytes total memory
  491904 bytes free
```

The first line above shows the total amount of data space available on the disk. The space the system uses for the FAT table, the system directory, and so on is not included in the first line of the report. This hard disk has a data capacity of 21,135,360 bytes. The second line of the report shows the amount of space used by hidden files. Because a hard disk is usually bootable, you can expect to have at least two hidden files on the disk. One of these is the DOS I/O Manager and the second is the DOS File Manager. If there is a third hidden file, it will normally be the volume label on the disk. (Other hidden files may be present, depending on the applications installed on the disk and the way the drive has been set up.)

The third line of the report shows the number of directories, in addition to the root directory, that are present on the disk, and the amount of disk space they require. The fourth line shows the total number of bytes consumed by all the user files on the disk. These are the files that show up when the DIR command is executed. In this example, there are a total of 474 user files on the disk in addition to the 3 hidden files.

The fifth line of the report may or may not be present. On a hard disk report it shows up quite frequently. On a report for a floppy disk there should not be a bad sector line in the report. Floppy diskettes are normally certified to be error-free. This report shows a total of 10,240 bytes of space on the hard drive that have been flagged by DOS as "bad." DOS has made them unavailable for use by setting a code in the FAT table. Finally, the sixth line tells us there is 6.787 MB of space still available on this disk for use. In other words, approximately 70 percent of the space on the hard disk has already been utilized.

The second part of the report provides information on how space will be used on the hard drive. This disk has been formatted to use a minimum of 2048 bytes of space each time a file is created. An allocation unit for this disk consists of four sectors ($4 \times 512 = 2048$). This disk has a total 10,337 allocation units, each of which is 2048 bytes in size. There are 1704 allocation units remaining on the drive.

The third part of the report provides information on the computer's internal memory or RAM. This computer would normally be said to contain 640K of RAM, with each 1K of RAM equivalent to 1024 bytes of memory, so the actual number of bytes on a 640K computer is 655,360 bytes ($640 \times 1024 = 655{,}360$ bytes). The DOS nucleus and related parts of the operating system have consumed 163,456 bytes. The remainder of RAM (491,904 bytes) is free to use for application software and the associated data that may be generated.

□ EXAMPLES

1. `C:\>` **`CHKDSK`**
2. `C:\>` **`CHKDSK C:/V > PRN`**
3. `C:\>` **`CHKDSK A:`**
4. `C:\>` **`CHKDSK B:/F`**

1. `C:\>` **`CHKDSK`** In this example, the CHKDSK command has been given but no fields are specified and no parameters used. DOS uses its default values and does a standard check of the hard disk for Drive C.
2. `C:\>` **`CHKDSK C:/V > PRN`** A check is done on Drive C, but the /V parameter has been specified. The report will contain a complete listing of all files and directories for the disk, along with the standard CHKDSK summary report. The entire report will be listed on the standard system printer because the command indicates that the report is to be redirected from the display unit to the printer. The file listing will include hidden files and any volume label present.
3. `C:\>` **`CHKDSK A:`** A check is performed on the diskette in Drive A. This type of check is normally done on a diskette to find out how much space is left on it and how the space is utilized. It is also used to determine if a diskette is a bootable system diskette, since bootable disks must have two hidden files allocated. The space allocation for the hidden files will show up in the CHKDSK summary report.

4. **C:\> CHKDSK B:/F** In this example, the check is done on the diskette in Drive B. The /F parameter has been used so that any space lost due to file allocation errors can be recovered. If the space is to be recovered, reply "Y" to the question about file recovery. Files recovered will be placed in the root directory of the disk in Drive B, with filenames FILE*nnnn* (where *nnnn* is a sequence number). Each file will have an extension CHK. To delete the files, delete all files with the extension CHK by issuing the command **DEL B:*.CHK.**

THE DISK COPY (DISKCOPY) COMMAND

The Disk Copy (DISKCOPY) command makes a sector-by-sector copy of a source diskette onto a target diskette. The source and target diskettes must be of similar format in order to make a duplicate. Thus, a 3 1/2-inch 720 KB diskette cannot be duplicated onto a 5 1/4-inch 1.2 MB diskette. Neither can a 3 1/2-inch 720 KB diskette be duplicated onto a 3 1/2-inch 1.44 MB diskette. The DISKCOPY program does just what the name implies. It makes an exact duplicate—track for track and sector for sector. The format of the DISKCOPY command is:

DISKCOPY *<source>* *<target>* /1

<source> is the letter of the drive where the source diskette will be loaded, followed by a colon.

<target> is the letter of the drive that will contain the diskette that is the target disk, followed by a colon.

/1 is a parameter that indicates that only a single side of the diskette is to be copied, even if the diskette is double-sided. This parameter is only used with single-sided diskettes.

In many versions of DOS, the DISKCOPY program will format the target disk if it is not already formatted. Although this capability is included in DOS versions after 3.10, the duplication process is not always reliable when it is necessary to format the diskette while copying. Therefore, it is recommended that you format all diskettes before using DISKCOPY. If you do DISKCOPY files onto unformatted disks, it is recommended that you use DISKCOMP (see next heading) after DISKCOPY to check the duplication for accuracy.

It is always advisable to use working copies of any master software disks rather than the master itself. The DISKCOPY program can reproduce this working copy from the master supplied with commercial software. DISKCOPY can produce copies by copying from one floppy drive to a second floppy drive on dual-drive systems. The floppy drives, however, must be of similar format. To make duplicates on single-drive systems, the source and target drive letters will be the same. In this case, DISKCOPY will prompt you to load the source and target diskettes at the appropriate times during the copy process.

Whenever duplicating diskettes, make sure that the source diskette is write-protected. This will prevent the accidental copying of a blank disk over the source disk. Chapter 2 discusses the method for write-protecting both 5 1/4- and 3 1/2-inch diskettes.

□ EXAMPLES

1. `C:\>` **`DISKCOPY A: B:`**
2. `C:\>` **`DISKCOPY A: A:`**
3. `A:\>` **`DISKCOPY`**
4. `C:\>` **`DISKCOPY A:`**
5. `C:\>` **`DISKCOPY B: B:/1`**

1. `C:\>` **`DISKCOPY A: B:`** The DISKCOPY command is used to duplicate the contents of a diskette in Drive A onto a diskette in Drive B. The two drives must use the same size and format diskettes, either 5 1/4- or 3 1/2-inches. The source diskette should be in Drive A and the target diskette should be in Drive B. Both sides of the diskettes will be duplicated because no parameter was specified.
2. `C:\>` **`DISKCOPY A: A:`** In this example the contents of the diskette in Drive A are duplicated onto another diskette in Drive A. First, the program will prompt you to load the source diskette into Drive A. The information will be copied from the diskette into RAM. The program will then prompt you to load the target diskette into Drive A and the information will be copied from RAM onto the target diskette. The system will continue to prompt for loading the source and target diskettes in turn until all information has been copied from the source to the target.
3. `A:\>` **`DISKCOPY`** In this example the DISKCOPY command is issued but no drive is specified. DOS uses its defaults. Because the DOS prompt indicates that A is the default drive, the source and target diskettes should be loaded on Drive A. DOS will prompt you to load the source and target diskettes in turn. For some versions of DOS, an error message will be given because no drive letter was specified.
4. `C:\>` **`DISKCOPY A:`** This DISKCOPY will be for diskettes loaded into Drive A. Both the source and target diskettes must be loaded into Drive A. Both sides of the diskettes will be copied in the duplication process.
5. `C:\>` **`DISKCOPY B: B:/1`** In this example a diskette loaded in Drive B will be duplicated onto a target diskette loaded in Drive B. The system will prompt you to load the source and target diskettes in turn. Only the first side of the diskette will be copied.

THE DISK COMPARE (DISKCOMP) COMMAND

The DISKCOMP command is used to compare two diskettes to see if their contents are identical. When comparing two diskettes, they must not only be the same physical size, but they must also be of similar format. The DISKCOMP command is generally used after the DISKCOPY command to ensure that a diskette duplicated with DISKCOPY is in fact identical to the original. The format of the DISKCOMP command is:

DISKCOMP <*source*> <*target*> /1/8

<*source*> is the letter of the diskette drive that will be used as the source or original diskette. All comparisons are made to the source disk, which is the master for comparison purposes.

<*target*> is the letter of the diskette drive that will contain the target diskette. Information from the target or second diskette is compared to the source diskette.

/1 indicates that only the first side of the diskettes are to be compared, even though the diskettes may be double-sided. The /1 parameter is intended for use only with diskettes that are single-sided.

/8 If the /8 parameter is used, only the first eight sectors of each track on the diskette are compared, even though the diskette may have more than eight sectors per track. The /8 parameter is intended for use with diskettes that have eight sectors per track.

Remember that when using DISKCOPY and DISKCOMP, a diskette with bad information on it or damaged sectors will also be duplicated, just as will a "good" diskette. Using DISKCOMP does not guarantee that a diskette is good. It only guarantees that it is identical to the original or source diskette.

If the two diskettes are not identical, a list of differences will be provided on the display screen.

Many computer systems today have a mix of disk drives. For example, Drive A may be a 3 1/2-inch drive, and Drive B a 5 1/4-inch drive or vice versa. When making comparisons in which only one drive of a given size is available, the source and the target drives may be the same letter. The DISKCOMP program will then prompt you to load the source and target diskettes in turn. Just follow the instructions on the screen when making the comparison.

DISKCOMP is a sector-for-sector, track-for-track comparison of two diskettes that have similar formats. It cannot be used to compare two diskettes that are of different sizes or have different formats. DISKCOMP does not verify the accuracy of the data on the diskette. Neither can DISKCOMP be used to tell if a diskette has bad sectors or is otherwise damaged in any way.

□ **EXAMPLES**

1. C:\> **DISKCOMP A: B:**
2. C:\> **DISKCOMP A: A:**
3. C:\> **DISKCOMP A:**
4. C:\> **DISKCOMP A: A: /1**
5. C:\> **DISKCOMP B: B: /8**

1. C:\> **DISKCOMP A: B:** In this example the contents of a diskette in Drive A will be compared to a diskette in Drive B. The diskettes must be of the same physical size and format. Any differences will be noted in a report to the display. If the diskettes are identical, a message indicating such will be issued.
2. C:\> **DISKCOMP A: A:** A disk compare is done on two diskettes alternately loaded into Drive A. The system will prompt for the loading of the two diskettes, since only a single drive is used. The report will indicate any differences between the first and the second diskettes.
3. C:\> **DISKCOMP A:** In this example a disk compare is done on a source diskette and a target diskette that are loaded alternately into Drive A. The system prompts for the loading of the first and then the second diskette. Any differences will be listed on the display screen.
4. C:\> **DISKCOMP A: A: /1** A DISKCOMP is done in this example using Drive A, but only one side of the disk is compared, even if the disk is double-sided. The system prompts for the loading of the two diskettes.
5. C:\> **DISKCOMP B: B: /8** In this example two diskettes will be compared using Drive B. Only the first eight sectors of the diskette will be compared even if the diskettes have nine sectors. Both sides of the diskettes will be compared. The differences, if any, will be listed on the display screen.

THE LABEL (LABEL) COMMAND

The LABEL command assigns or manipulates the volume label on a disk. Labels can be assigned to fixed disks as well as diskettes. The LABEL command can be used to display the volume label of a disk, to assign a new label to a disk, to change the existing label on a disk, and to delete the label from a disk. The label can be up to 11 characters in length, and once assigned, is stored in the filename and file extension fields in the system directory area of the disk. The volume label is treated just like any other file entry when stored; however, no space for storing a file is actually used on the disk. Spaces are permitted in volume labels, whereas they are not permitted as part of a filename. When the volume label is stored, the volume bit in the attribute byte is set to 1 to indicate that the entry is a volume label.

Volume labels can be used to identify the owner of a disk or the type of information stored on it. To display the volume label on a disk, use the Volume command (VOL). The format of the LABEL command is:

LABEL *<drive>* *<newlabel>*

<drive> is the disk drive in which the disk's volume label is to be affected.

<newlabel> is the volume label that is to be assigned to the disk in the addressed drive.

□ **EXAMPLES**

1. C:\> **LABEL A:**
2. C:\> **LABEL B:Ferguson**
3. C:\> **LABEL A:Client List**
4. A:\> **LABEL**

1. C:\> **LABEL A:** The LABEL command is used here to request the display of the volume label for Drive A. Since the *<newlabel>* field was not specified, DOS does not assign a label, but instead displays the existing volume label. DOS will then ask if a new label is to be assigned. If a new label is assigned, it will replace the existing label on the disk. If no label is typed, DOS asks whether the current label is to be deleted. Responding "Y" will result in the current label being deleted from the disk. If you want to delete the volume label from a disk rather than replace it with a new label, use this form of the command.
2. C:\> **LABEL B:Ferguson** The label *Ferguson* is given to the diskette mounted in Drive B. This label replaces whatever label is currently on the diskette in Drive B.
3. C:\> **LABEL A:Client List** The label *Client List* is given to the diskette mounted in Drive A. The label with a space between the two words is valid, because a space is a valid character in a volume label. The label, including the space, is exactly 11 characters long, which is the maximum length allowed for a volume label.
4. A:\> **LABEL** The LABEL command is given without any of the optional field information. DOS displays the label for the diskette in Drive A and asks if a new label is to be assigned. A new label can be entered or the current label can be deleted.

THE FIXED DISK (FDISK) COMMAND

The Fixed Disk (FDISK) program is used to prepare a fixed or hard disk for use with DOS. If the hard drive already contains information when you want to execute FDISK, be sure to back up the hard drive first. The use of FDISK will result in the loss of all information stored on the hard drive. FDISK is a menu-driven program. It allows you to do the following in building a hard drive:

- Create DOS partitions that can be independently addressed on the hard drive.
- Select an active partition from which DOS will be started.
- Set up logical drives that can be independently addressed as though they were separate physical drives.
- Display partition information about a hard disk that has already been prepared for use.

The format of the FDISK command is:

```
FDISK
```

No parameters or fields are associated with the FDISK command. FDISK can be used only with a hard disk.

There are several terms that must be understood in order to understand the menu selection options associated with FDISK.

1. *Active partition.* This is the partition from which you start DOS in order to boot your computer. To start DOS from the fixed disk, the primary DOS partition must also be the active partition.
2. *Cylinder.* A measure of the amount of space that is available on a fixed disk. When displaying information about partitions, FDISK displays the total number of cylinders available on the fixed disk as well as the range of cylinder addresses. A cylinder is comprised of the tracks that can be addressed when the disk access arm is in a fixed position, with the read/write heads positioned over the surface of the disk. If a given fixed disk has six read/write heads, positioning the heads on a cylinder would give access to six tracks on the disk. Figures 9.1 and 9.2 illustrate the parts of a fixed disk. FDISK allows the fixed disk to be divided into partitions based on a specified number of cylinders or on the basis of a percentage of the disk. If you do not know how many cylinders are on your hard drive, use the percentage method. To find out the number of cylinders, format the disk and watch the cylinder addresses until the disk is formatted. The supplier of your computer or hard drive may also be able to provide this information. Cylinder addresses start with cylinder 0 and end with the highest cylinder address for the disk being used.
3. *Logical drive.* A portion of a DOS partition that is used as though it were a separate disk drive. It is termed a **logical drive** because DOS treats that part of the disk as though it were a separate disk drive. It is also addressed with a separate drive letter such as D or E, depending on the drive letter assigned.
4. *Partition.* A portion of a fixed disk. A fixed disk can be divided into one or two partitions. The primary DOS partition is the one from which DOS is started when the computer's power is turned on. The second DOS partition is

referred to as the extended DOS partition. The extended DOS partition can be divided into logical drive units.

5. *Track.* A concentric circle on a disk that can store information. Tracks are divided into sectors so that DOS can address pieces of a track when storing information. Figure 9.2 illustrates how a disk is subdivided. The basic units used in subdividing a disk are the same for a fixed disk and for a floppy diskette.

FIGURE 9.1 Parts of a fixed disk.

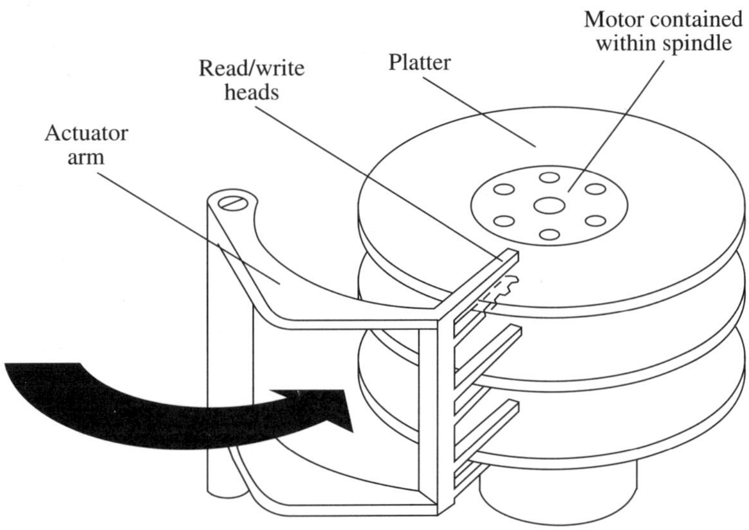

FIGURE 9.2 Tracks and sectors.

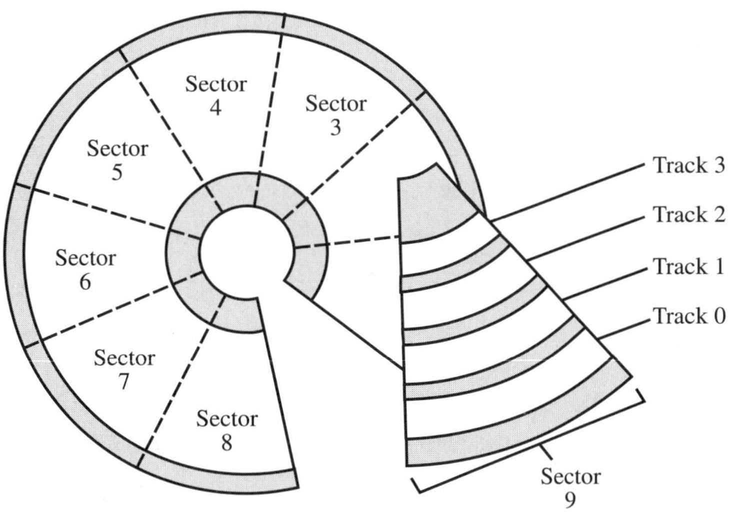

THE FAST OPEN (FASTOPEN) COMMAND

The FASTOPEN command is used to speed up the accessing of information from files on a fixed disk. FASTOPEN results in DOS maintaining a list of disk storage locations of subdirectories and files that have been used during the current session. When it executes FASTOPEN, DOS first checks in memory before searching the disk whenever it is requested to find a file or a subdirectory. If the file has already been used, its disk location is stored in memory. DOS then goes directly to the storage location on the disk instead of searching the disk for the file. The format of the FASTOPEN command is:

```
FASTOPEN <drive> = <files> /X
```

<*drive*> is the drive letter of the fixed disk whose files and subdirectories you want DOS to track, followed by a colon. The drive letter must be the letter for a fixed disk.

<*files*> is the number of file and subdirectory locations DOS will keep in memory. Up to 999 files can be specified. If the number of files is not specified, DOS keeps track of the last 34 files that have been addressed. Each file to be tracked requires approximately 50 bytes of internal memory for storing the associated file information. Using FASTOPEN reduces the amount of internal memory available for application program storage.

/X tells DOS to keep the FASTOPEN-related information in expanded memory rather than RAM, if the computer has expanded memory.

The FASTOPEN command can be entered only once during a session. FASTOPEN is essentially a DOS setup command. It can noticeably speed up file access and cut down on the wear and tear on the hard drive. The command can be entered at the DOS prompt, as part of a batch file, or as a command in AUTOEXEC.BAT or in CONFIG.SYS. Beginning with Version 4 of DOS, you can include FASTOPEN as part of the CONFIG.SYS file by using the INSTALL command.

Because FASTOPEN can be used only once, it is recommended that it be included in CONFIG.SYS if you use Version 4 or Version 5 of DOS. If you use Version 3.3, make FASTOPEN part of the AUTOEXEC.BAT file.

□ EXAMPLES

1. `C:\>` **`FASTOPEN C:=20`**
2. `C:\>` **`FASTOPEN C:=50`**
3. **`INSTALL=C:\DOS400\FASTOPEN.EXE C:30`**
4. **`INSTALL=C:\DOS500\FASTOPEN.EXE C:50 /X`**

1. `C:\> FASTOPEN C:=20` In this example the FASTOPEN command is issued to keep track of the last 20 files and subdirectories used on Drive C. DOS will provide storage to keep track of this information in internal memory in order to speed disk access when searching for information.
2. `C:\> FASTOPEN C:=50` In this example the FASTOPEN command has been issued to increase the number of entries to 50 files and subdirectories used on Drive C. DOS will provide storage to keep track of this information in internal memory in order to speed disk access.
3. `INSTALL=C:\DOS400\FASTOPEN.EXE C:30` Under Version 4 or later of DOS, the INSTALL command can be used to issue a FASTOPEN command in the CONFIG. SYS. file as part of the boot process. When you use INSTALL, the location of the FASTOPEN command must be identified. In this example, the FASTOPEN command is located in the \DOS400 directory on Drive C. As a result of this command, the number of files and subdirectories tracked in memory will be 30.
4. `INSTALL=C:\DOS500\FASTOPEN.EXE C:50 /X` In this example the INSTALL procedure is again part of the CONFIG.SYS file. FASTOPEN is identified as being stored in the \DOS500 directory on Drive C. DOS will track up to a total of 50 files and subdirectories, but will keep the information in expanded memory rather than RAM memory because the /X parameter was included as part of the command. This frees up additional RAM for use by the application program and any data space needed for other files.

THE MIRROR (MIRROR) COMMAND

One of the valuable features added to DOS in Version 5.00 is the ability to recover deleted files. This capability was previously available only through the use of utility software such as Norton Utilities, PC Tools, and similar packages. Version 5.00 of DOS added both a file-recovery feature through the UNDELETE command and a disk-recovery feature through UNFORMAT.

When files are deleted from a disk, they are not physically removed from the disk. Instead, the file entry in the directory table is altered to indicate that the space occupied by the deleted file is now free for storing another file. The file-recovery feature in DOS Version 5.00 is activated using the MIRROR command and a feature called *delete tracking*. As files are deleted from the disk, information about their storage locations is saved in a file named PCTRACKR.DEL. The UNDELETE command then uses this tracking data to restore the file, *as long as a subsequently saved file has not overwritten that same space.*

The format of the MIRROR command is:

MIRROR *<drive>* /T*<drive>*-*<files>* /PARTN /1 /U

<drive> is the disk drive whose file and directory information is to be recorded, followed by a colon. A read-only file named MIRROR.FIL is created for storing the necessary file-tracking data.

/T*<drive>*-*<files>* activates the delete-tracking feature of MIRROR. *<Drive>* is the letter of the drive on which MIRROR will track deleted files. If the *<files>* parameter is specified, it must be preceded by a hyphen (-). *<Files>* is the maximum number of deleted files to be tracked. It can be a number between 1 and 999. A Terminate and Stay Resident (TSR) routine is loaded to record information about deleted files.

/PARTN specifies that partition information associated with a fixed disk should be saved. Partition information about a hard drive must be saved to a floppy diskette; MIRROR will prompt for the drive letter on which to save the partition data. The data is stored in a file on diskette named PARTNSAV.FIL.

/1 specifies that only a single copy of the file MIRROR.FIL is to be saved. If not specified, the MIRROR program checks for previous versions of MIRROR.FIL. If a previous version is found, the old version is renamed MIRROR.BAK before a new MIRROR.FIL file is created.

/U specifies that delete tracking is to be deactivated. This does not destroy information previously stored about files deleted. It only turns off the feature so that files deleted subsequently will not be tracked.

When installing the delete-tracking feature with MIRROR, DOS will assign the number of files to be tracked if the *<files>* parameter described above is not stated as a number. The number assigned by DOS as a default value is based on the size of the diskette or fixed disk. Table 9.1 shows the default values for the *<files>* parameter when a value is not assigned.

TABLE 9.1 MIRROR File with Delete Tracking

Disk Size	Number of Files	Approximate Size of PCTRACKR.DEL
360 KB	25	5 KB
720 KB	50	9 KB
1.2 MB	75	14 KB
1.44 MB	75	14 KB
< 20 MB fixed	101	18 KB
32 MB fixed	202	36 KB
> 32 MB fixed	303	55 KB

□ **EXAMPLES**

1. `C:\> MIRROR`
2. `C:\> MIRROR C: D:`
3. `C:\> MIRROR /PARTN`
4. `C:\> MIRROR /Tc-500 /Ta`
5. `C:\> MIRROR /u`

1. **`C:\> MIRROR`** The MIRROR command is entered with no other information. Mirror assumes that disk storage information should be saved for the fixed disk (Drive C) and activates delete tracking. All deleted files will be tracked and the associated disk storage information saved. The maximum number of files tracked will be based on the size of the fixed disk, as described in Table 9.1.
2. **`C:\> MIRROR C: D:`** File tracking is activated for both Drive C and Drive D because both are specified. The number of files tracked for each is based on the size of the respective fixed disks. You should also save partition information on a floppy diskette using the /PARTN parameter, as shown in Example 3 below.
3. **`C:\> MIRROR /PARTN`** Using the /PARTN parameter results in MIRROR saving information about the partition table on a floppy diskette. MIRROR will prompt you to load a floppy diskette into Drive A, because no drive was specified. After saving the required data MIRROR responds with the message "Successful."
4. **`C:\> MIRROR /Tc-500 /Ta`** Delete file tracking is activated by MIRROR for both Drive C and Drive A because the /T parameter is specified for both drives. The file allocation table for Drive C will also be recorded. The maximum number of files tracked for Drive C will be 500 because the number was stated as part of the command. For Drive A, the maximum number of deleted files tracked will be based on the disk size.
5. **`C:\> MIRROR /u`** The delete tracking TSR program will be unloaded from RAM and delete tracking will be deactivated. If other memory-resident TSRs were loaded after MIRROR, delete tracking cannot be unloaded. Delete tracking will, however, be disabled.

THE UNDELETE (UNDELETE) COMMAND

UNDELETE is a command new to DOS Version 5. It can be used to recover a file intact, so long as the space used by the deleted file has not been overwritten by a new file. Files written to disk are frequently stored as a set of consecutive pieces that are placed in different places on the disk. The pieces are usually not stored in consecutive clusters or allocation units. The ability of UNDELETE to recover a complete file is dependent upon its ability to find all the pieces of the file, regardless of how they may be scattered about the disk. If a link between two pieces of a file is lost or damaged, DOS reaches a dead end in terms of recovery. In this case only a part of a deleted file will be recoverable.

UNDELETE can be used on its own with DOS or with the delete tracking feature activated by the MIRROR command. Delete tracking, in general, will produce more successful results. It is recommended that delete tracking be installed on your hard drive. It can also be installed for floppy diskettes that contain critical information.

The format of the UNDELETE command is:

UNDELETE <*filename*> /DT /DOS /ALL /LIST

<*filename*> is the name of the file or files that are to be recovered. Both a drive letter and a pathname can be specified as part of addressing the file or files. Wildcards are permissible. If no filename is given, UNDELETE assumes that all deleted files in the current directory on the default drive are to be recovered.

/DT specifies that delete tracking installed by MIRROR is to be used to recover the file or files. If multiple files are to be recovered, UNDELETE will prompt you before restoring each file.

/DOS specifies that information recorded by DOS for deleted files should be used to recover the deleted file or files. UNDELETE will still prompt for confirmation before restoring each file. If delete tracking is not installed, DOS assumes this parameter as a default for the recovery process.

/ALL specifies that all deleted files should be restored, and that it is not necessary for DOS to prompt for confirmation during the process.

/LIST specifies that a list of files that can be restored should be displayed, but that the undelete process should not be initiated. To restore the files, reissue the UNDELETE command without the /LIST parameter.

□ EXAMPLES

1. C:\> **UNDELETE A:\FILE1.TXT**
2. C:\> **UNDELETE B:\TEXT /LIST**
3. C:\> **UNDELETE A:*.* /DT**
4. C:\> **UNDELETE B:*.TXT /DOS /ALL**

1. C:\> **UNDELETE A:\FILE1.TXT** The file FILE1.TXT on the diskette in Drive A was accidentally deleted. The UNDELETE command tries to recover the file. No parameters are specified, so DOS will use the delete tracking file. DOS assumes /DT as a default if it is not specified. A message will indicate if all clusters can be recovered, and DOS will prompt with a message "Undelete (Y/N)?" Respond "Y" if the file is to be restored.
2. C:\> **UNDELETE B:\TEXT /LIST** This command will list all the files

that have been deleted from the \TEXT directory on the diskette in Drive B. Unrecoverable files are marked. No file recovery is attempted when the /LIST parameter is specified.

3. `C:\>` **`UNDELETE A:\*.* /DT`** Delete tracking (/DT) will be used to recover all files that have been deleted from the root directory on the diskette in Drive A. DOS will prompt for confirmation before attempting to recover each file.
4. `C:\>` **`UNDELETE B:\*.TXT /DOS /ALL`** Files that have been deleted with a TXT extension on the diskette in Drive B will be scanned for recovery. The /DOS parameter is specified so DOS will use information recorded by the operating system and not delete tracking to attempt recovery. DOS will prompt for confirmation before attempting to recover each file. DOS will also ask that the first character of each filename be supplied, because the first character was modified when the file was deleted.

THE UNFORMAT (UNFORMAT) COMMAND

The UNFORMAT command is new with Version 5 of DOS. It can be used to recover the contents of a fixed disk or diskette that has accidentally been reformatted. UNFORMAT will *not* recover a disk or diskette that has been formatted using the /U (unconditional format) parameter. UNFORMAT has the greatest chance for doing a complete recovery if the MIRROR command has been used. Consider including the MIRROR command in the AUTOEXEC.BAT file.

UNFORMAT can recover both partitioned and nonpartitioned disks. To recover partitioned fixed disks, partition table information must have been recorded. UNFORMAT is designed for disaster avoidance after an accidental reformat. It should not be part of normal operating procedures. Disk recovery is best effected through good backup procedures, particularly with the large hard drives that are part of today's systems. Invest some time and effort in installing a good set of backup procedures for all files that are critical to your operation. Good utility software such as Norton Utilities, PC Tools, Mace Utilities, and others also deserve consideration.

The form of the Unformat (UNFORMAT) command is:

`UNFORMAT` ***`<drive>`*** **`/J /L /P /U /TEST /PARTN`**

`<drive>` is the letter of the drive that contains the disk to be unformatted, followed by a colon. *<Drive>* can be either a diskette or a fixed disk, but it cannot be a network drive.

`/J` specifies that disk recovery should be done using information recorded by the MIRROR command. UNFORMAT will try to verify that the disk can be unformatted, but it does not attempt actual recovery. Use the /J parameter to check a disk for possible recovery.

/L can be used by itself or in conjunction with the /PARTN switch discussed below. When used with the /PARTN parameter, UNFORMAT displays information about the partition table of the current drive. The size of the partition table is shown in megabytes, based on 512-byte sectors. When /L is used without / PARTN, UNFORMAT searches the disk and lists all files and directories found as part of the root directory. In general, UNFORMAT cannot recover files that have been fragmented. UNFORMAT will prompt for specification of whether files are to be recovered, truncated, or deleted.

/P specifies that the UNFORMAT command should send all its messages to the print device PRN or LPT1. This option provides hard copy of the state of a reformatted or otherwise damaged disk or diskette.

/U specifies that rebuilding of a disk should be done with the information recorded by DOS rather than that recorded by the MIRROR program. Use the /U parameter if MIRROR tracking was not used with the disk or diskette to be recovered.

/TEST specifies that the disk in <*drive*> should be tested for recovery but should not use files recorded by the MIRROR command. The disk specified will be checked, but no actual recovery will be attempted.

/PARTN specifies that a damaged partition table should be restored on the fixed disk. Use of this parameter requires that the MIRROR command was in effect and that a file PARTNSAV.FIL exists as a result of using the /PARTN parameter with MIRROR.

□ EXAMPLES

1. A:\> **UNFORMAT C: /J**
2. C:\> **UNFORMAT /PARTN**
3. C:\> **UNFORMAT A: /TEST**
4. A:\> **UNFORMAT C: /L /PARTN**
5. A:\> **UNFORMAT C:**
6. A:\> **UNFORMAT C: /U**

1. A:\> **UNFORMAT C: /J** UNFORMAT will check the fixed disk using MIRROR information to see if the disk can be restored. No unformatting will take place, because the /J parameter was used. The test is done using a system startup diskette mounted in Drive A. The system should be booted from Drive A. To unformat the fixed disk execute the UNFORMAT command without the /J parameter.
2. C:\> **UNFORMAT /PARTN** This example will rebuild a partition table associated with the fixed disk (Drive C). This command should be used when a single disk has been divided into logical components (partitions) such as Drives C, D, and E.
3. C:\> **UNFORMAT A: /TEST** The UNFORMAT program will check on a

reformatted diskette mounted in Drive A. With the /TEST parameter, UNFORMAT performs its examination of the damaged diskette, without using the MIRROR file information. The diskette will not be unformatted, only examined and tested. To unformat the diskette, execute the command without the /TEST parameter.

4. `A:\>` **`UNFORMAT C: /L /PARTN`** The partition table in the specified Drive C will be displayed without attempting to unformat the disk or rebuild the partition table. UNFORMAT uses information stored in PARTNSAV.FIL. To actually rebuild the table for a damaged disk, drop the use of the /L parameter and re-execute the UNFORMAT command.
5. `A:\>` **`UNFORMAT C:`** This command will unformat the hard disk (Drive C) using information saved by the MIRROR command. A system startup diskette is used in Drive A in order to perform this operation.
6. `A:\>` **`UNFORMAT C: /U`** UNFORMAT will attempt to unformat the hard drive using information recorded by DOS. In this example the UNFORMAT operation is attempted without using any information recorded by the MIRROR program.

THE RECOVER (RECOVER) COMMAND

The RECOVER command attempts to rebuild files from a disk that has damaged sectors or a damaged directory. The recovered file is assigned a sequenced filename with an extension of REC and is placed in the root directory. When DOS uses RECOVER to rebuild a damaged directory, the original directory is erased. The format of the RECOVER command is:

RECOVER *<filespec>*

<filespec> can be either a drive letter followed by a colon or a filename, depending upon the type of recovery to be attempted.

Depending upon the problem with the disk and the type of damage to files or directories, **the RECOVER command can trash the hard drive on your system.** Because of the potential damage that can be done to a hard drive, **THE USE OF RECOVER IS NOT RECOMMENDED**. If you have damaged files on a disk, use one of the utilities designed for this purpose instead, such as PC Tools, Mace Utilities, or Norton Utilities.

If RECOVER must be used to rebuild a damaged file or disk, confine its use to floppy diskettes. Refrain from using RECOVER with a fixed disk. Using RECOVER to try to rebuild anything other than individual files you suspect are damaged is dangerous and should be used with extreme caution.

EXAMPLES

1. `C:\DATA>` **`RECOVER FILE1.TXT`**

2. C:\> **RECOVER B:**

1. C:\DATA> **RECOVER FILE1.TXT** The file FILE1.TXT is reconstructed and stored in the current directory \DATA as FILE0001.REC. Damaged sectors are excluded during the recovery process. The recovered file may need editing. To edit the file, use the program you originally used to create the file.

2. C:\> **RECOVER B:** In this example the directory information on Drive B is recovered into a single file and the directory of Drive B is destroyed. The information in the file will include as much of the information in the directory as could be recovered. This form of the command should be used only if the directory is indeed damaged and considered unusable.

COMMON MISTAKES

1. C:\> **FORMAT**
2. C:\> **FORMAT C:**
3. C:\> **FORMAT A:/N:9/T:80/F:1440**
4. C:\> **DISKCOPY**
5. C:\> **DISKCOPY A:**
6. C:\> **DISKCOMP C:*.COM A:**
7. C:\> **FDISK A:**
8. C:\> **CHKDSK**
9. C:\> **RECOVER**

1. C:\> **FORMAT** The FORMAT command has been specified but no drive letter was specified. Some versions of DOS will attempt to format the hard drive. Normally the hard drive should not be formatted because doing so will cause all information on the hard disk to be lost. It is always best to specify a drive letter when using the FORMAT command.

2. C:\> **FORMAT C:** In this example the FORMAT command specifies formatting the hard drive. This is a technically correct command; however, formatting the hard drive should normally include the /S parameter because the hard drive should be a bootable disk. Either specify the correct floppy drive letter or include the /S parameter if indeed the hard drive is to be formatted.

3. C:\> **FORMAT A:/N:9/T:80/F:1440** In this example the diskette in Drive A is to be formatted based on the parameters specified. The problem is that the values for /N and /T are in conflict with the /F parameter's value. When using these parameters, use /N and /T together, or /F, but not both. /N:9 and /T:80 specify a double-density format of a 3 1/2-in diskette, which gives a 720 KB format. The /F:1440 parameter specifies a high-density diskette format of 1.44 MB. These two specifications are contradictory. Select one or the other.

4. C:\> **DISKCOPY** The DISKCOPY command duplicates a copy of a floppy diskette. In this example no floppy drive is specified. When using this com-

mand, specify the source and target drive letters, such as DISKCOPY A: B: if your system has two drives of identical format and size. Otherwise, the drive letters should be identical.

5. `C:\> DISKCOPY A:` In this example only the source drive is specified; the target drive is not. Some versions of DOS will accept this command, while others will issue an error message. When using DISKCOPY, specify both the source and target drives, even if they are the same drive letter, to avoid the error message. To duplicate a diskette in A, type DISKCOPY A: A:.
6. `C:\> DISKCOMP C:*.COM A:` The DISKCOMP command compares the contents of two diskettes to determine if they are identical. This command cannot compare the hard drive or portions of the hard drive to a diskette. Neither can it compare files from the hard drive to those of a diskette. To compare files, use the Compare (COMP) command. The only valid parameters for the DISKCOMP command are floppy drive letters such as A: or B:.
7. `C:\> FDISK A:` The FDISK command is used to partition a hard drive, not a floppy drive such as Drive A. A floppy drive cannot be partitioned. Use the FDISK command without any drive letter when partitioning your hard disk or setting up logical drives. The FDISK command has no fields or parameters.
8. `C:\> CHKDSK` This is a valid command as long as the command is to be exercised against the default drive. To perform a check disk against a floppy drive, specify the drive letter, such as A:. If files are to be recovered because of the "Lost clusters and chains" error message, the /F parameter must be specified.
9. `C:\> RECOVER` The RECOVER command has been specified, but no filename or drive letter has been specified. This is a very dangerous command and potentially even more dangerous if a mistake is made. Use RECOVER with great care. To recover damaged and lost files, use one of the better utility packages instead of RECOVER.

QUESTIONS AND PROBLEMS

1. How can lost clusters and chains of data be recovered from a disk? What is the name of the file sequence created by the command, and where are they placed on the disk?
2. How can you determine the default format capability of a floppy disk drive?
3. What command and parameters should be used to create a bootable floppy system diskette?
4. Can a floppy diskette be duplicated if the user's system contains only a single floppy disk drive?

5. What file on your system will normally contain the FASTOPEN command for setting some default parameters on your system?
6. What are some of the dangers of using the RECOVER command to recover damaged files on the hard disk?
7. How is the DISKCOPY command different from the COPY command in terms of its general capabilities and functions?
8. What precautions should you take before using the FDISK command with your hard disk drive?
9. How can you determine the names of any hidden files that are stored on your disk?
10. How might you use the LABEL command to advantage with a large group of diskettes containing similar information?
11. What command is used to install the delete tracking feature in DOS Version 5.00? What file is used to install this feature as part of the setup of your system?
12. How is partition information saved for a fixed disk?
13. What is the value of building a system startup diskette so that your system can be booted from Drive A rather than from the fixed disk?
14. What does DOS do to a file when the file is deleted from the disk?
15. What command and parameters are used when recovering accidentally deleted files if delete tracking is not installed?
16. What is a fragmented file and how can it be recovered if you accidentally delete it?
17. What command and parameters are used to test for recovery a diskette that has been accidentally reformatted?
18. What command is used to install delete tracking on your hard drive and track up to 500 deleted files? What are the approximate space requirements to save the information associated with tracking 500 deleted files?

CHAPTER 10

DIRECTORY MANAGEMENT (EXTERNAL COMMANDS)

INTRODUCTION

DOS uses a number of commands to create and manage the directories on a disk. This directory structure allows a disk to be divided into a number of separate areas, regardless of whether the disk is a floppy diskette or a hard disk. Subdirectories have been used relatively infrequently on 360 KB floppy disks. Subdirectory structures are used regularly for hard drives because it is important to subdivide the large megabyte capacity of the hard drive into sections. This is far less important and perhaps even unnecessary on a 360 KB floppy disk, which has a maximum capacity of only 112 entries.

As floppy disk capacity has increased and continues to increase, subdirectory structures will be used more frequently with them as well as with hard disks. In all likelihood, we will see 3 1/2-inch floppy disk capacity of 3 to 4 MB or more in the not too distant future. Optical floppies promise storage capacities in the 20 to 100 MB range. Even a 1.44 MB diskette capacity frequently merits a subdirectory structure for effective file management.

The external commands used to create and manage directory structures on a hard disk or diskette are:

TREE
SUBST

THE TREE (TREE) COMMAND

The TREE command is used to display the structure or organization of a disk or an individual directory on the disk. The command can be used to display the directory organization only; alternatively, it can be used to display all the user files associated with the directory structure, in addition to the directory structure itself. The format of the TREE command is:

TREE *<drive>* *<path>* /F /A

<drive> is the letter of the disk drive to be displayed followed by a colon.

<path> is the pathname for the specified directory that is to be displayed.

/F displays the list of files in each directory and subdirectory, in addition to the directory structure.

/A specifies that an alternative character set be used to draw the tree diagram so that it can be printed using printers that do not support the IBM extended character set.

The TREE command shows how the disk drive or a part of the disk drive is organized. To see the organization of the entire disk, specify the root directory as the *<path>* parameter, along with the drive letter. The TREE command does not tell how much space is consumed by an individual directory on the drive. The list of files rather than just the directory structure can be displayed using the /F parameter. If no files are displayed when the /F parameter is used, the directory exists, but the directory itself is empty.

□ **EXAMPLES**

1. `C:\>` **`TREE`**
2. `C:\>` **`TREE A:\TEXT`**
3. `C:\>` **`TREE C:\WP50\GR /F`**
4. `C:\>` **`TREE B: /A > PRN`**

1. `C:\>` **`TREE`** In this example, the TREE command is issued, but no drive or directory is specified. The tree displayed will be of the default drive and directory, in this case the root directory of Drive C. Since the root directory is used, the structure will be for the entire directory structure of Drive C.
2. `C:\>` **`TREE A:\TEXT`** In this example, the directory structure to be displayed will be for the \TEXT directory on Drive A and all of its subdirectories. Other subdirectories of the root directory on Drive A will be ignored.
3. `C:\>` **`TREE C:\WP50\GR /F`** In this example, the /F parameter has been specified as part of the command. This display will include a listing of all files in the directory \WP50\GR on Drive C and any other subdirectories of the specified directory \WP50\GR, along with their files.
4. `C:\>` **`TREE B:\ /A > PRN`** In response to this command, a directory listing for the entire structure of Drive B will be displayed on the printer, since the output has been redirected to that device using the greater-than sign. The /A parameter has been specified so that the printer listing will use the alternate character set in place of the line drawing characters to depict the tree structure.

THE SUBSTITUTE (SUBST) COMMAND

The Substitute (SUBST) command instructs DOS to treat a subdirectory as though it were a disk drive. This command will normally be used in conjunction with special application programs. Some application programs recognize disk drives, but do not recognize pathnames. As a result, they are unable to address files outside the default directory. The SUBST command provides an alternative method for addressing the files the application must access.

The format of the Substitute command is:

`SUBST` ***`<drive> <pathname>`*** **`/D`**

`<drive>` is the drive letter followed by a colon that will be substituted for the path.

<pathname> is the path to the subdirectory the user wishes to address. It may include both a drive letter and a directory path.

/D deletes a substitution and returns the drive to its original meaning or leaves it unassigned.

The drive letter cannot be the current drive. Normally the drive letters used with the Substitute command are other than physical drives on the system. Instead, they are logical drives. The user can provide access to additional logical drives by using the LASTDRIVE command as part of the CONFIG.SYS file.

Typically, the highest drive letter on a stand-alone PC is Drive C. Three additional logical drives can be provided by including a LASTDRIVE=F command in the CONFIG.SYS file. The user now has access to three logical drives: Drive D, Drive E, and Drive F. Drive F is the highest drive letter that can be used on this system.

Substitutions are drive/pathname combinations. If two different directories are to be linked to drives, two different drive letters must be used. Drive D could be linked to one directory and Drive E to a different directory. To delete a substitution, specify the drive letter and the pathname, followed by the /D parameter.

□ **EXAMPLES**

1. `C:\>` **`SUBST D: C:\WP50\TEXT`**
2. `C:\>` **`SUBST E: A:\LOTUS\DATA\PROJECT1`**
3. `C:\>` **`SUBST E: A:\LOTUS\DATA\PROJECT1 /D`**
4. `C:\>` **`SUBST`**

1. `C:\>` **`SUBST D: C:\WP50\TEXT`** In this example, Drive D is being substituted for the \WP50\TEXT directory on Drive C. Copying a file to Drive D, for example, will result in the file being placed in the \WP50\TEXT directory on Drive C. Drive D must have been made available as a logical drive via the LASTDRIVE command in the CONFIG.SYS file. The system must also have been booted so that this statement is read as part of the boot process.
2. `C:\>` **`SUBST E: A:\LOTUS\DATA\PROJECT1`** This use of the Substitute command assigns logical Drive E in place of the directory \LOTUS\DATA\PROJECT1 on Drive A. One of the advantages of the Substitute command is that it shortens the length of commands that must be typed when referring to long directory names. Instead of referencing the drive and directory as A:\LOTUS\DATA\PROJECT1 to address a file, just address it as E:, along with the filename.
3. `C:\>` **`SUBST E: A:\LOTUS\DATA\PROJECT1 /D`** To delete a substitution once it is made requires the use of the /D parameter. Here, the substitution made in Example 2 above using logical Drive E is canceled. The SUBST command is entered, followed by the /D parameter.

4. `C:\>` **SUBST** The substitutions in effect at any time can be displayed by typing the SUBST command without any strings or parameters. Based on the other examples entered here, DOS would indicate that there was one substitution in effect:

```
D: => C:\WP50\TEXT
```

COMMON MISTAKES

Shown below are some common mistakes encountered when using directory management commands. Some mistakes generate error messages. Many mistakes, however, cause execution errors, but generate no messages. Some sample mistakes are illustrated below.

1. `C:\>` **TREE/F A:**
2. `C:\>` **TREE C:\WP51 /V**
3. `C:\>` **SUBST C: \WP51\GR\FONTS**
4. `C:\>` **SUBST A: A:\LOTUS\DATA**
5. `C:\>` **SUBST X: C:\WP51\GR**

1. `C:\>` **TREE/F A:** The TREE command is issued for floppy Drive A. In the case of many commands, the parameters may follow either the command or the fields. In the case of the TREE command, the / F parameter cannot precede the drive letter; it must follow it. The correct form of this command is TREE A:/F. When executed correctly, the directory listing will be displayed for the diskette in Drive A as well as a listing of all user files in each directory on the diskette.
2. `C:\>` **TREE C:\WP51 /V** The TREE command can be issued for an entire drive or for a directory, along with its subdirectories on that drive. In this case the tree display would be for the \WP51 directory on Drive C. The parameter /V is a parameter for the CHKDSK command, not for the TREE command. To see only the directory structure, do not use any parameters. To see all the files within each directory, use the /F parameter, not /V, with the TREE command. To see hidden files use CHKDSK /V.
3. `C:\>` **SUBST C: \WP51\GR\FONTS** The Substitute command cannot be used with the current drive, so the drive letter cannot be C. Typically the drive specification letter is a logical drive on the system, not a physical drive letter. On a typical system logical drive letters might be D or E, where the hard drive is Drive C.
4. `C:\>` **SUBST A: A:\LOTUS\DATA** When specifying a drive letter with the Substitute command, use a logical drive letter rather than a physical drive letter. Drive A cannot be substituted for the directory \LOTUS\DATA on Drive A. Instead, use D or E, so the command might be SUBST E:

A:\LOTUS\DATA. The LASTDRIVE command must also specify E in this example as part of the CONFIG.SYS file.

5. `C:\> SUBST X: C:\WP51\GR` It is correct to use Drive X in the SUBST command as long as the LASTDRIVE command in the CONFIG.SYS file specifies Drive X or higher. Normally the LASTDRIVE command will specify F, H, or a similar letter lower in the alphabet. Specifying H as the Lastdrive in CONFIG.SYS would typically give the user access to Drives D, E, F, G, and H as logical drives. In normal situations, four to six logical drives are adequate. Only use a high letter such as X if you have set the CONFIG.SYS file to accommodate that high a Lastdrive parameter.

QUESTIONS AND PROBLEMS

1. What are some advantages of using the Substitute (SUBST) command when dealing with long pathnames?
2. Why should the Substitute command always substitute a logical drive for a directory rather than using a physical drive letter?
3. What is the purpose of the /A parameter when used with the TREE command?
4. When using the /F parameter with the TREE command, a listing of the files in the directories will also be given. What files, if any, are not shown as part of the TREE listing?
5. It is frequently suggested that commands such as SUBST and ASSIGN be used only in batch files so that they can be canceled at the end of the batch file. Why is this suggestion made?
6. How might the TREE command be used to document your system?
7. What information will be displayed in a listing by the command TREE C:\WP51?
8. What information will be displayed in a listing by the command TREE C:\WP50 /F > PRN?

CHAPTER 11

THE DOS TEXT EDITORS (EXTERNAL COMMANDS)

INTRODUCTION

Since it was first released as an operating system, DOS has supplied a **text editor.** The original editor was a line-editing program named EDLIN. With the release of Version 5.00, you can now select from two different editors. These include the original line editor—EDLIN, and a new full-screen editor—EDIT. Both provide line-editing capabilities, since both require that each line of information be terminated by pressing the Enter key. Those familiar with EDLIN may wish to continue using it for writing batch files and editing simple text files. For new DOS users, EDIT will probably be the better choice, because of its Help features, as well as its full-screen editing and menu bar command capabilities.

This chapter describes both programs. It also provides a sample file creation and editing session for each editor. If you are new to DOS, skip to the section on EDIT. The Help features will make learning the EDIT program relatively painless. If you are knowledgeable about EDLIN, consider staying with what you know. The typical session on EDIT, described later in this chapter, can provide a quick introduction to EDIT. Select the program best suited to your needs for simple line and text editing. Both provide essentially the same features and capabilities.

THE LINE EDITOR: EDLIN

EDLIN is a text editor supplied as part of DOS. Its primary use is for building batch files. Batch files expand the power of the DOS operating system by providing a method for automating certain procedures. This chapter concentrates on EDLIN and EDIT and the various commands that are part of these programs. (The subject of batch files is discussed in Chapter 19.)

EDLIN, in addition to being a text editor, is a line editor. It is not a full-screen editor. When files are created or displayed, the program automatically assigns a line number to each line. The user can then modify or display the file by referring to these line numbers. The line numbers are not part of the actual file. Instead, they are a programming technique to provide access to each line of the file.

A simple illustration demonstrates the basic capabilities of EDLIN. We will first create a simple batch file of 12 lines using EDLIN. The EDLIN commands used in this example are Insert (I), Page (P), End (E), and Quit (Q). We will then check the file visually for accuracy and save it.

When creating a file with EDLIN, the file is named at the time EDLIN is executed. EDLIN checks first to see if a file by that name already exists. If it does, EDLIN retrieves it for editing. If the file does not exist, EDLIN displays a message, "New File" and then displays its prompt character. The command prompt for EDLIN is the asterisk (*).

To begin the text session, type EDLIN, followed by the filename. The name of the demonstration file is AUTO1.BAT, so you would type:

```
C:\> EDLIN AUTO1.BAT

New File
*
```

EDLIN has two fundamental modes of operation. These are *command mode* and *insert mode.* The default mode is command mode. When in command mode, the asterisk is displayed, followed by the cursor. Any valid EDLIN command may be entered when in command mode.

The second mode of operation for EDLIN is insert mode, sometimes also referred to as *input mode.* In this mode, EDLIN displays a line number, followed by a colon. This mode is used to create a file or to insert changes into a file. In order to create the file for AUTO1.BAT, use insert mode.

The session below shows the creation of the AUTO1.BAT file using insert mode. The line number is automatically generated by EDLIN. At the end of each line, press the Enter key. The asterisk displayed after the colon on each line is not the EDLIN prompt character. It is the *line pointer.* In insert mode, EDLIN displays the line pointer, indicating that this is the current line. In command mode, EDLIN keeps track of the line pointer; the line pointer always points to the current line. If a command is entered and no line number is referenced, EDLIN executes that command at the current line.

In later sessions, we'll illustrate how the line pointer works in command mode. For now, accept that an asterisk will be displayed after the colon on each line in insert mode. EDLIN will generate the next line number in the sequence. Once the file is created, the key sequence Ctrl-C will be used to change to command mode. Type the following:

```
*1i <Enter>
 1:*echo off
 2:*REM
 3:*REM This is a sample file for booting the computer.
 4:*REM To boot automatically rename the file AUTOEXEC.BAT
 5:*REM
 6:*DATE
 7:*TIME
 8:*VER
```

```
 9:*PROMPT $p $g
10:*PATH C:\;C:\DOS330
11:*CLS
12:*DIR
13:*Ctrl-C
*
```

A 12-line batch file has been created. Line 13 is not part of the file because insert mode was terminated by entering the Ctrl-C key sequence. Note that when exiting back to command mode, EDLIN displays the asterisk prompt, showing that the session is now in command mode again. The file contains all the commands that were entered on each line. The line numbers, along with the colon and the line pointer (*), are also not part of the file.

To display the file and check it for accuracy, use the Page (p) command. Following the display, the End Edit (e) command is issued. The End command terminates the EDLIN session and saves the file on disk. The new file AUTO1.BAT is now on disk in the default directory on the default drive.

```
*1p <Enter>

 1: echo off
 2: REM
 3: REM This is a sample file for booting the computer.
 4: REM To boot automatically rename the file AUTOEXEC.BAT
 5: REM
 6: DATE
 7: TIME
 8: VER
 9: PROMPT $p $g
10: PATH C:\;C:\DOS330
11: CLS
12:*DIR

*e <Enter>
```

As illustrated in the example session above, EDLIN commands can be issued at the EDLIN prompt (*) to perform various operations. EDLIN commands are single-character commands issued along with line designations to edit a file.

EDLIN recognizes a number of symbolic references when executing a command and manipulating a file. Reference will frequently be made to the current line or the line pointer. The line pointer or current line can be seen by displaying the file or by just typing "l" for List. The current line is the line displaying the asterisk symbol (*) after the line number reference and the colon. The symbolic references are as follows:

.	A period refers to the current line.
#	The pound sign refers to the line after the last line in the file. In effect, # refers to the EOF (end of file) mark in the file.
+ or –	Specifies the number of lines up or down relative to the current line. +5 means five lines past the current line pointer.

The commands are discussed below in groups, organized from the most useful to the least useful. Later versions of DOS have continued to support some EDLIN commands, but because of the increases in hardware capacities such as RAM, some EDLIN commands have limited or little usefulness on today's systems. The first group of commands (End, Insert, List, Page, and Quit) are basic to the use of EDLIN. If you use EDLIN you will use one or more of these commands in every session. The second group (Copy, Delete, Edit, Move, and Transfer) are used extensively to edit existing files. These too will see extensive use if EDLIN is used on a regular basis.

The last two groups have more limited usefulness. The third group (Replace and Search) may be used if you have occasion to use search and replace to edit text files. Because EDLIN is normally used to create small ASCII text files such as batch files, these commands have limited usefulness. If used with text files other than command (batch) files, these two commands might help to do searches within a file. The last group (Append and Write) has almost no application on today's systems. These commands had limited application when memory was much smaller and to create large text files. Today, a word processing package or a full-screen text editor is more likely to be used when working with large text files. It is safe to say that most microcomputer users will rarely use the EDLIN commands in either Group C or Group D. Should the occasion arise where these are needed, refer to the appropriate section for the format of commands in these two groups.

EDLIN COMMANDS: GROUP A

This group of commands consists of End Edit, Insert, List, Page and Quit. These commands are frequently used with Edlin.

End Edit (E or e) The End Edit command writes the file currently in memory to disk and ends the editing session. If an existing file is being edited, EDLIN changes the extension on the existing file to BAK as part of the process of ending the session. If there is insufficient room on the disk to save the file, EDLIN writes as much of the file as it can to the disk and adds the extension $$$. A "Disk Full" message will be displayed. The part of the file that cannot be saved to disk will be lost. In this case the existing file will not be given the extension BAK.

The last line of the file should end with a carriage return (Enter). If it does not, EDLIN will add a carriage return when it ends the editing session. The last character in the file should be a Ctrl-Z or end-of-file character. If it is not, EDLIN adds a Ctrl-Z to the end of the file when it ends the edit.

The End Edit command is issued at the EDLIN prompt, as shown below. EDLIN commands can be typed in uppercase (E) or lowercase (e).

```
*e
```

Insert (i) The Insert command puts EDLIN in insert or input mode rather than command mode. In input mode, EDLIN displays a line number, followed by a colon as the prompt rather than the asterisk (*) prompt. As each line is entered (followed by pressing the Enter key), DOS prompts with the next line number. This sequence continues until input mode is terminated. To terminate input mode, enter Ctrl-C and the EDLIN command mode prompt (*) will be displayed.

Control characters such as Ctrl-G can be entered as part of a file. To do this, first press Ctrl-V followed by the uppercase letter that is to be entered. To enter a Ctrl-G sequence to make the computer beep, type Ctrl-V followed by G.

Escape sequences can also be entered into files for controlling external devices such as the printer. To place Escape sequences in a file, press Ctrl-V followed by a left bracket ([ ).

An insert or input session can be initiated at the EDLIN prompt as shown:

```
*Ni
```

where *N* is the line number in front of which lines are to be inserted. To insert lines at the beginning of the file, type **1i.** To insert lines at the end of the file type **#i.** To insert lines in front of line 10, type **10i.**

List (l) The List command displays a group of lines centered about the current line or the range of lines specified in the command. The List command is issued at the EDLIN prompt as shown:

```
* <from>,<to>l
```

Entering the *<from>* and *<to>* range is optional. If the range is entered, EDLIN displays the range of lines specified up to the end of the file. If the range is not specified, EDLIN displays 23 lines centered about the current line. If the file is less than 23 lines long, EDLIN will display the entire file on the screen.

Page (p) The Page command displays up to one full screen of lines on the computer display. It also alters the line pointer so that it points to the last line displayed. The Page command provides the ability to page through a file screen by screen, because it keeps track of the line pointer. To page through a file specify **1p** as the first Page command. Then just issue a **p** to view subsequent screens until the entire file has been displayed. The form of the Page command is:

```
* <from>,<to>p
```

Entering the *<from>* and *<to>* range is optional. If the range is entered, EDLIN displays the range of lines specified up to the end of the file. If the range is not specified, EDLIN displays 23 lines, beginning with the line after the current line pointer. If the file is less than 23 lines long, EDLIN will display the complete file.

Quit (q) The Quit command terminates an EDLIN session without saving any changes to disk. EDLIN will prompt to verify that the session is to be aborted by issuing a message, "Abort edit (Y/N)?" If you respond "Y," the session is aborted and no changes are saved. If the file is already on disk it remains unaltered. If no file yet exists on disk, nothing is saved. Responding "N" to the abort-edit message results in EDLIN returning back to the EDLIN prompt; the file remains in memory. The editing session on the file can then continue. The form of the Quit command is:

```
*q
```

□ EXAMPLES

1. ***e**
2. ***1i**
3. ***10i**
4. ***#i**
5. ***l**
6. ***1,#l**
7. ***1p**
8. ***10,25p**
9. ***p**
10. ***q**

1. ***e** This EDLIN command will terminate an edit session. The file will be saved under the name given it when EDLIN was first executed. If a pathname was specified, the file is saved in the specified directory and on the specified disk. If a previous version of the file already exists in this directory, that version will have its extension changed to BAK.
2. ***1i** The Insert command will place EDLIN in insert mode instead of command mode. Line number 1 followed by a colon will be displayed so that new lines can be created in the existing file. To return to command mode, issue a Ctrl-C. After each line is typed, press the Enter key to terminate that line and display the next sequential line number.
3. ***10i** An Insert command is issued indicating that lines are to be inserted in

front of line 10 of the existing file. The line number 10 will be displayed, followed by a colon. New lines can now be typed that will be inserted between lines 10 and 11 of the existing file in memory.

4. **`*#i`** The Insert command is issued for lines to be inserted at the end of the file. Lines will be inserted in front of the end-of-file mark of the existing file. EDLIN will generate a line number that is one greater than the last line of the existing file.
5. **`*l`** The List command lists the existing file centered about the current line pointer. The group of lines listed depends on the position of the current line pointer. The current line will be displayed in the center of the screen, with 11 lines above that line displayed at the top of the screen and 11 lines below the current line displayed at the bottom of the screen.
6. **`*1,#l`** The range of lines to be displayed here is specified along with the command. The file will be displayed from line 1 to the last line of the file. If the file is more than 23 lines long, the lines will scroll across the screen until the last 23 lines are displayed.
7. **`*1p`** Only the beginning *(from)* field is entered along with the Page command. The file will be displayed, beginning with line 1. Up to 23 lines will be displayed on the screen. The line pointer is adjusted to line 23 or the end of the file so that additional pages can be displayed with the Page command.
8. **`*10,25p`** A range of lines are to be displayed, beginning with line 10. Lines 10 through 25 will be displayed. The line pointer will be moved to line 26 or the line past the last line in the file, if the file is less than 25 lines long.
9. **`*p`** Only the Page command is given and no range is specified. Up to one page of lines will be displayed, beginning with the current line. The line pointer will be moved one line past the last line displayed on the screen.
10. **`*q`** The EDLIN editing session will be terminated without saving the current file being edited. EDLIN will prompt with a message to confirm that you want to abort the edit.

EDLIN Commands: Group B

The second group of commands is also commonly used. Many are used in creating and editing files based on an already existing file or files. This group of commands includes Copy, Delete, Line Edit, Move, and Transfer. Each is described and used in an example.

Copy (c) The Copy command copies a block of lines from one location to another during an EDLIN session. The command works like most other implementations of a Copy command, with one exception; that exception can prove to be extremely useful in certain applications. The EDLIN Copy command can duplicate the block of lines to be copied as many times as necessary, specified by the *<count>* variable. Thus a 10-line block, when copied, can produce a 100- or 200-line block at the specified destination if the entered command indicates that the original 10-block group of lines is to be duplicated 10 or 20 times. The format of the Copy command is:

```
* <from>,<to>,<target>,<count>c
```

Delete (d) The Delete command can delete a single line or a group of lines from the file being edited. When lines are deleted, the line after the last line deleted becomes the current line. The *<from>* and *<to>* fields are optional. If no line number is specified, EDLIN deletes the current line, based on the line pointer. The number in the *<to>* field must always be greater than the number in the *<from>* field. The *<from>* and *<to>* fields should always be specified unless only the current line is to be deleted. EDLIN renumbers the file after deleting lines, so lines after those deleted will have new line numbers. The format of the Delete command is:

```
* <from>,<to>d
```

Line Edit (*n*) The Line Edit command is implemented by typing a line number (*n*). No character is used to implement the command. To edit a particular line, type the line number, followed by pressing the Enter key. The contents of that line will be displayed followed by the same line number and a colon. If the line is to be changed, enter the appropriate characters, followed by the Enter key. The new characters replace the old line. The F1 function key can be used to recall part of the line if only a portion of the old line is to be changed. The Line Edit command causes the line being edited to become the current line after the edit is complete. The format of the Line Edit command is:

`* <line number>` or `.` for the current line

Move (m) The EDLIN Move command moves a single line or group of lines from one place to another within the file. The lines are extracted from their existing location within the file and placed in their new location. The lines in the file are renumbered after the move. Because the lines are merely moved from one place to another in the existing file, the file does not change size; it is merely re-arranged. The first line moved becomes the new current line. The *<to>* field must be equal to or greater than the *<from>* field. The format of the Move command is:

```
* <from>,<to>,<target>m
```

Transfer (t) The Transfer command incorporates another file into the file being edited. The file to be merged into the existing file is specified as part of the *<filename>* field. If the file is not addressed, it must be in the current directory.

Normal addressing techniques can be used as part of the <*filename*> field, including specifying both drive letter and path. The <*target*> field specifies the line in the existing file where the specified file will be placed. The merged file will be placed in front of the line number specified in the <*target*> field. If no <*target*> field is specified, EDLIN assumes the current line. The format of the Transfer command is:

```
* <target>t<filename>
```

□ EXAMPLES

1. ***10,15,5c**
2. ***20,#,1c**
3. ***1,10,#,5c**
4. ***20d**
5. ***11,#d**
6. ***8**
7. ***10,15,6m**
8. ***15,#,1m**
9. ***1tAUTOEXEC.BAT**
10. ***#tC:\MENUD\START.BAT**

1. ***10,15,5c** In this example lines 10 through 15 inclusive are duplicated and copied into the file. They are placed before line 5. The set of six lines also remain in their original place in the file. The file is renumbered after the Copy command is executed. After the copy, the file has now increased by six lines.
2. ***20,#,1c** The group of lines beginning at line 20 through the last line in the file are duplicated and placed in front of line 1 in the file. This group of lines is now at the beginning of the file as well as at the end of the file. How many lines are moved depends upon the length of the file. The last line number is unknown since it was referenced by the # symbol.
3. ***1,10,#,5c** The group of 10 lines, beginning at line 1, will be copied to the end of the file. The group of lines will be duplicated five times before the copy destination, so this file will increase by a total of 50 lines.
4. ***20d** The Delete command is used to delete a single line: line 20 in the file. In deleting a single line, it is not necessary to specify a range. The remaining lines in the file will be renumbered.
5. ***11,#d** A group of lines will be deleted. The lines deleted begin at line 11 and go through the last line in the file. After EDLIN executes this Delete, the file will contain 10 lines.

6. ***8** To edit a line, only the line number need be specified. Here, for example, line 8 will be displayed so that the line can be edited. After editing the line, new line 8 will replace the old line 8.
7. ***10,15,6m** Lines 10 through 15 will be extracted from their position in the file and moved as a group in front of line 6. The file will be renumbered. The file does not get any larger as a result of a Move command. Lines are merely moved from one place to another within the file.
8. ***15,#,1m** Lines 15 through the last line in the file will be moved to the beginning of the file. The file will be renumbered.
9. ***1tAUTOEXEC.BAT** The Transfer command is used to merge the AUTOEXEC.BAT file into the current file in front of line 1. No addressing information is specified, so the AUTOEXEC.BAT file must be in the current directory on the current or default drive.
10. ***#tC:\MENUD\START.BAT** A file named START.BAT is merged into the existing file and placed at the end of the existing file because the # was specified. START.BAT is addressed based on its location on the disk. EDLIN will look for START.BAT on Drive C in the \MENUD directory.

EDLIN COMMANDS: GROUP C

This group of commands will be used infrequently. The functions described here are also found in most database management software. These commands can be useful if a database manager is not available. The commands described in this group are Replace and Search. Remember that these are EDLIN commands and can be used only with files that can be edited by EDLIN.

Replace (r) The Replace command replaces one character string with another character string in one or more lines of the file. EDLIN displays the line or lines that have been changed. The form of the Replace command is:

```
*<from>,<to>?r<string1>Ctrl-Z<string2>
```

<from> is the line number of the first line in which the string is to be replaced. If you don't enter a *<from>* value, EDLIN begins with the line following the current line.

<to> is the number of the last line in which the string should be replaced. If *<to>* is omitted, EDLIN searches to the last line in the file. The line number specified in the *<to>* field should be equal to or greater than the line number specified in the *<from>* field.

? specifies that EDLIN should prompt for confirmation before making the replacement. EDLIN displays the line and prompts with a "OK?" To make the change, reply "Y" to the question; otherwise, reply "N" if the change is not to be made.

<string1> is the string in the file that is to be replaced when found. Type the string exactly as it appears in the file using uppercase and lowercase letters as necessary.

<string2> is the new replacement string. Ctrl-Z should be used to separate the *<string1>* and *<string2>* fields.

Search (s) The EDLIN Search command searches for a specified character string, then stops when the string is found. The line containing the string is displayed, and made the current line by setting the line pointer. The search can also be set to prompt for confirmation so that the search can be continued if there is more than one occurrence of the string in the file. If the string is not found in the file, a message "Not Found" is displayed. The format of the Search command is:

```
*<from>,<to>?s<string>
```

<from> is the line number of the first line to be searched. If you don't enter a *<from>* line number, EDLIN begins with the line following the current line.

<to> is the number of the last line to be searched. If *<to>* is omitted, EDLIN searches to the last line in the file. The line number specified in the *<to>* field should be equal to or greater than the line number specified in the *<from>* field.

? specifies that EDLIN should prompt for confirmation before ending the search. EDLIN displays the line and prompts with "OK?" To continue the search, reply "Y" to the question; otherwise, reply "N".

<string> is the string in the file that is to be searched for. Type the string exactly as it appears in the file, using uppercase and lowercase letters as necessary. If another command follows the Search command when commands are concatenated, follow the string with a Ctrl-Z before typing the next command.

□ **EXAMPLES**

1. ***10,50rWill<Ctrl-Z>William**
2. *** ,50rWill<Ctrl-Z>William**
3. ***1,#?rApartment<Ctrl-Z>Apt.**
4. *** ,#?rApartment<Ctrl-Z>Apt.**
5. ***1,#sconsultant**
6. ***10,#?sMgr**

1. ***10,50rWill<Ctrl-Z>William** The file should be searched beginning at line 10 through line 50 for the string *Will*. All occurrences of the string Will should be replaced by the string *William.*
2. *** ,50rWill<Ctrl-Z>William** The file will be searched beginning at the next line number after the current line, because the *<from>* field was not

specified. If the line pointer is at the top of the file, the search will begin at line 2, not line 1. EDLIN will search through line 50, and every occurrence of the string *Will* will be replaced with the string *William.*

3. **`*1,#?rApartment<Ctrl-Z>Apt.`** In this example the question mark (?) indicates that EDLIN should provide prompting. The search for the string *Apartment* begins at line 1 and continues to the end of the file. EDLIN will prompt for replacement of each occurrence of the string *Apartment.* If the answer given is "Y," *Apartment* is replaced with *Apt.,* as specified.
4. **`*  ,#?rApartment<Ctrl-Z>Apt.`** The search will begin at the next line after the current line number, because the *<from>* field is not specified. In each case EDLIN will prompt to replace the string *Apartment* with the abbreviation *Apt.* The replacement is made if you answer "Y" to the prompt; if you answer "N," the substitution of the new string is not made.
5. **`*1,#sconsultant`** The Search command in this example begins at line 1 and proceeds to the end of the file. The search is made for the first occurrence of the string *consultant.*
6. **`*10,#?sMgr`** The search in this example begins at line 10 and proceeds to the end of the file. The search occurs with prompting; because the ? was used, the search will continue until terminated. EDLIN will then set the line pointer to be equal to the line where the search was terminated.

EDLIN COMMANDS: GROUP D

The final group of commands was originally developed for early systems with very limited memory capabilities. These commands, including Append and Write, will find little use on today's computers.

Append (a) The Append command reads additional lines from disk to the end of the file being edited. It is used when a file is larger than 75 percent of the available memory. If available memory is full, you must use the Write command (see below) to write a block of lines from memory to disk to make room for the additional lines to be appended. The form of the Append command is:

```
*<lines>a
```

`<lines>` is an optional field and indicates the number of lines to be appended to the end of the file in memory. If the number of lines is not specified, EDLIN appends lines to the file until memory is 75 percent full.

Write (w) The Write command writes lines from the beginning of the file being edited to disk under the filename assigned when EDLIN was first executed. By writing lines out of memory, EDLIN makes room in memory for appending lines or for inserting additional lines in the file. The form of the Write command is:

***<lines>w**

<lines> specifies the number of lines to write to disk. If *<lines>* is not specified, EDLIN writes enough lines to disk until available memory is only 25 percent full. If memory is less than 25 percent full, EDLIN ignores the Write command.

□ **EXAMPLES**

1. ***100a**
2. ***a**
3. ***200w**
4. ***w**

1. ***100a** The user is at the EDLIN prompt. This command instructs EDLIN to append 100 lines to the file by reading them from the existing file on disk.
2. ***a** The optional field *<lines>* is not used. The command instructs EDLIN to append lines to the file in memory from the existing file on disk. Lines will be appended until internal memory is 75 percent full.
3. ***200w** Lines from the existing file in memory are to be written to the file on disk. EDLIN will write 200 lines to disk, beginning with the first line of the file.
4. ***w** The number of lines to be written to disk is not specified. EDLIN writes lines to disk until memory is 25 percent utilized. If memory is less than 25 percent full at the time the command is given, EDLIN will ignore the command.

THE FULL-SCREEN EDITOR: EDIT

Beginning with Version 5, DOS supplies two text editors as part of the operating system. EDIT is a text editor just like EDLIN. However, EDIT differs substantially from EDLIN in the way it is used. EDIT also differs in some basic requirements and in how both the program and files are manipulated.

EDIT requires that the QBASIC.EXE file be available in order to start the program. Normally, QBASIC.EXE will be in the DOS directory; therefore it will be on the path established by the AUTOEXEC.BAT file. If EDIT is started without access to QBASIC.EXE, a message "Cannot find QBASIC.EXE file" will be displayed.

EDIT is a full-screen editor so far as cursor movement is concerned, but it is not a full-screen editor in the same sense as most word processors. EDIT requires that the Enter key be pressed at the end of every line. In this sense, EDIT is a line editor, just like EDLIN.

EDIT does not require that a file be named when it is started. The name for a new file can be supplied at the time the file is saved. EDIT does not create a

BAK file as EDLIN does. If a file is edited and saved in EDIT, the new copy replaces the old copy, and the old copy is lost. EDIT can be used from the keyboard using function and control keys, along with menus, or it can be used with a mouse.

To start EDIT, just enter the command at the DOS prompt as shown:

```
C:\> EDIT
```

DOS will load the EDIT program and display the opening screen. Press the Enter key to get to the HELP: Survival Guide screen, shown in Figure 11.1. The EDIT screens are similar to the DOS Shell display screens. The menu bar is displayed across the top of the display. Control-key sequences are shown at the bottom of the screen. Information about the subject of the menu appears on the screen. The screen can be partitioned into two pieces to include information and a window for entering data; or the entire screen can be used for information or the data entry window. The F6 function key, along with the Esc key, provides control over the windowing option.

FIGURE 11.1 HELP: Survival Guide screen for the EDIT text editor.

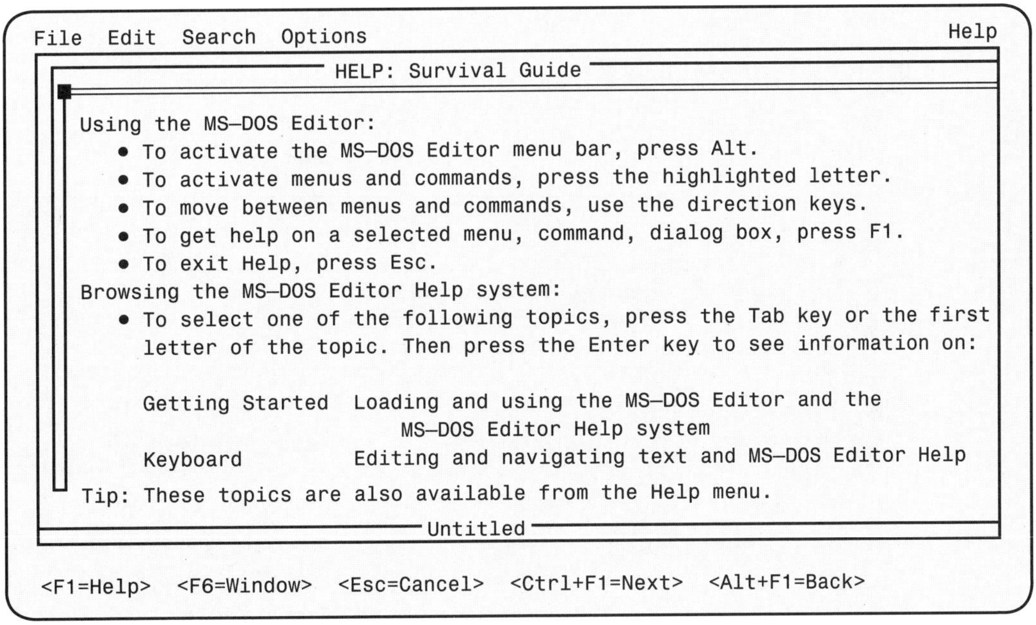

CURSOR CONTROL AND FUNCTION KEYS FOR EDIT

The cursor-control key sequences for EDIT are defined in Table 11.1; the function key sequences are shown in Table 11.2. These two tables provide basic information for editing data in a file and for using the Help and Window features. Information lines may be greater than 80 characters, but in general, it is best to limit most lines of information to the size of the screen. Remember that EDIT has no soft carriage return feature built into the software. A line of information is only terminated by pressing the Enter key.

TABLE 11.1 Cursor Control Movements in EDIT

Key	Cursor Movement (Move to:)
Left Arrow [←]	Previous character
Right Arrow [→]	Next character
Up Arrow [↑]	Previous line
Down Arrow [↓]	Next line
Home	First nonblank character in the line
End	Last character in the line
Ctrl-[←]	Beginning of previous word
Ctrl-[→]	Beginning of next word
Ctrl-Home	Beginning of the document
Ctrl-End	End of the document
Ctrl-Enter	Beginning of the next line

TABLE 11.2 Function Key Control in EDIT

Key	Description	Effect
F1	Help	Display the HELP screen
F6	Window	Toggle between the EDIT window and the HELP window
Ctrl-F1	Next	Display next HELP page
Alt-F1	Back	Display previous HELP page
Esc	Cancel	Close HELP, return to EDIT
Alt	Menu Bar	Move to menu bar

THE EDIT COMMAND

The format of the EDIT command is shown below:

```
C:\> EDIT <filename> /B /G /H /NOHI
```

<*filename*> is the name of the existing file to be edited. If <*filename*> is omitted, no file is loaded into memory. A name can be assigned to a file after it is prepared with EDIT, unlike the line editor EDLIN.

/B starts EDIT in monochrome mode if a color monitor is present.

/G uses the quickest screen updating with a CGA adapter.

/H tells EDIT to display the maximum number of lines possible on the monitor.

/NOHI enables the use of eight-color monitors. The default value for color is 16 colors.

Associated with the EDIT command are five menus, along with their associated pull-down options. The purpose of each menu is briefly summarized in Table 11.3. For more detail, use the Help features built into EDIT. Help is available with each of the menus described in Table 11.3.

TABLE 11.3 Menus for the EDIT Program

Menu	Description
HELP	Located at the right corner of the screen, it provides access to online help. The Getting Started command provides guidance on using this menu and its features.
OPTION	Controls the screen for access to online help features. The Display command provides control of the screen features.
FILE	Provides file management functions, including opening, saving, and printing files. The Exit command is used to quit EDIT.
EDIT	Provides file edit capabilities, including cut, copy, and paste functions. The cut and copy features use a temporary clipboard to save text for later pasting.
SEARCH	Used to search a document for a character string, beginning at the current cursor position. Upper- and lowercase can be ignored if desired.

A Typical EDIT Session

The session below describes a typical EDIT session. A file is first created and then saved to disk to store a permanent copy. Later, the file is recalled, then edited, printed to retain a hard copy, and saved in final form. The EDIT session is ended when the file is complete. The file created in this session is a simple batch file that executes the WordPerfect WP.EXE file. Upon exiting from the WordPerfect session, the files created are saved to a floppy diskette.

To begin the session, execute the DOS full-screen editor:

```
C:\> edit
```

The beginning menu screen is displayed, saying "Welcome to the MS-DOS Editor" and "Press Enter to see the Survival Guide." This screen is shown in Figure 11.2. Press **Enter** to see the Survival Guide screen shown in Figure 11.3.

Press function key **F1** to initiate the data entry mode, and then press function key **F6** to move the cursor into the data entry window in the middle of the screen. The meaning of the function keys is displayed at the bottom of each menu screen. The cursor is now positioned at the top left corner of the data entry window. The screen display is shown in Figure 11.4.

Begin entering commands as shown below and press the **Enter** key at the end of each line. Continue typing, even if you make mistakes, until the entire file has been entered. If your lines do not fit on the screen, EDIT will scroll lines out of view so that the currently typed characters can always be seen.

```
@ ECHO off
C:
CD\wp51\data
C:\wp51\wp
CLS
ECHO:
ECHO Load Backup Diskette into Drive A
ECHO:
ECHO:
DIR a: /P
```

Once you've entered the entire file, the cursor should display just below the last command typed. Now save the file so that a permanent copy is retained on disk. To save the file, press the **Alt** key. Pressing the Alt key activates the menu bar at the top of the screen. Use the **Down Arrow** key to move the highlighted area down to the **Save** command. Press the **Enter** key. A dialog box is then presented so that a filename can be entered. The screen will appear as shown in Figure 11.5.

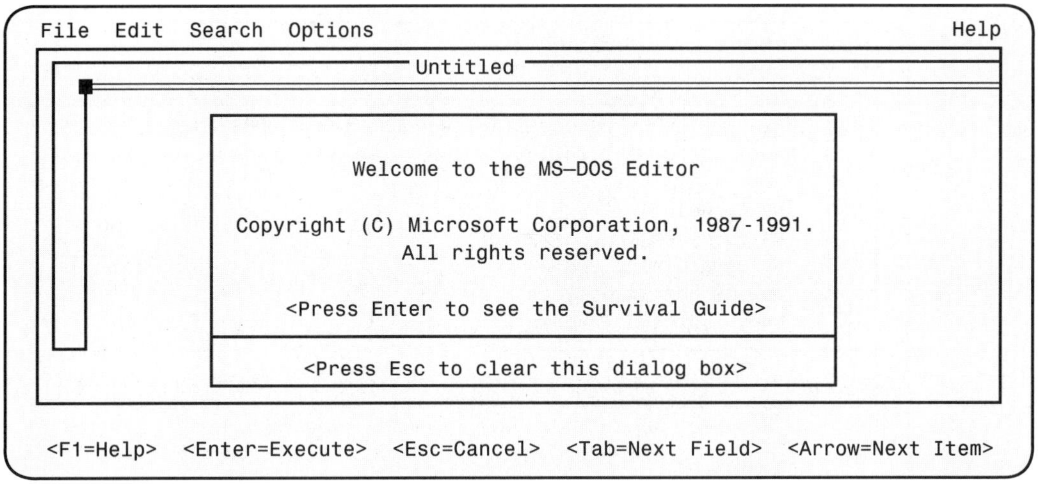

FIGURE 11.2 Welcome screen for MS-DOS EDIT program.

FIGURE 11.3 HELP: Survival Guide screen for the EDIT text editor.

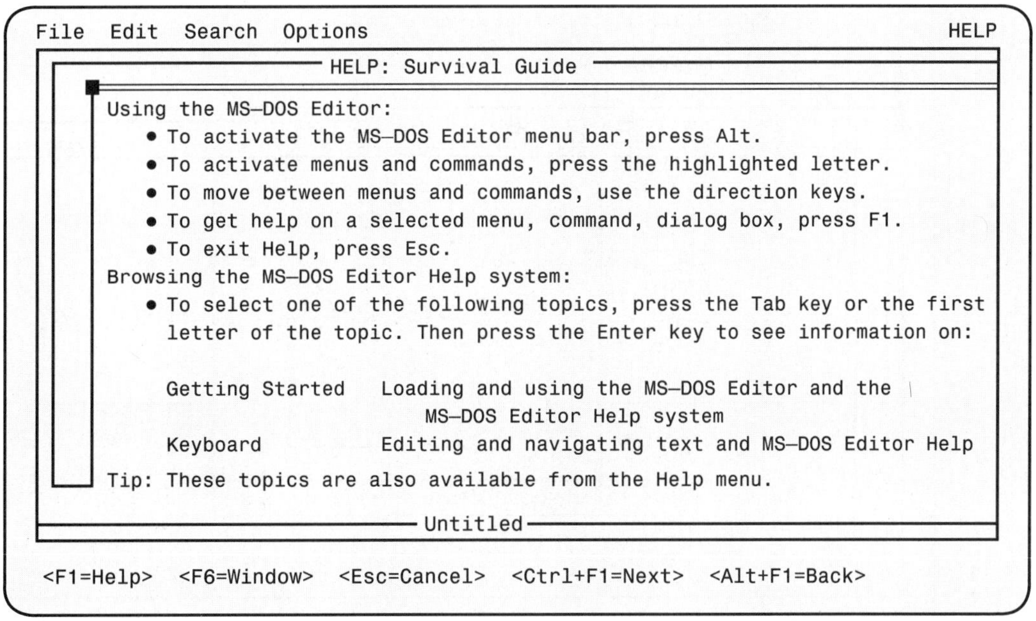

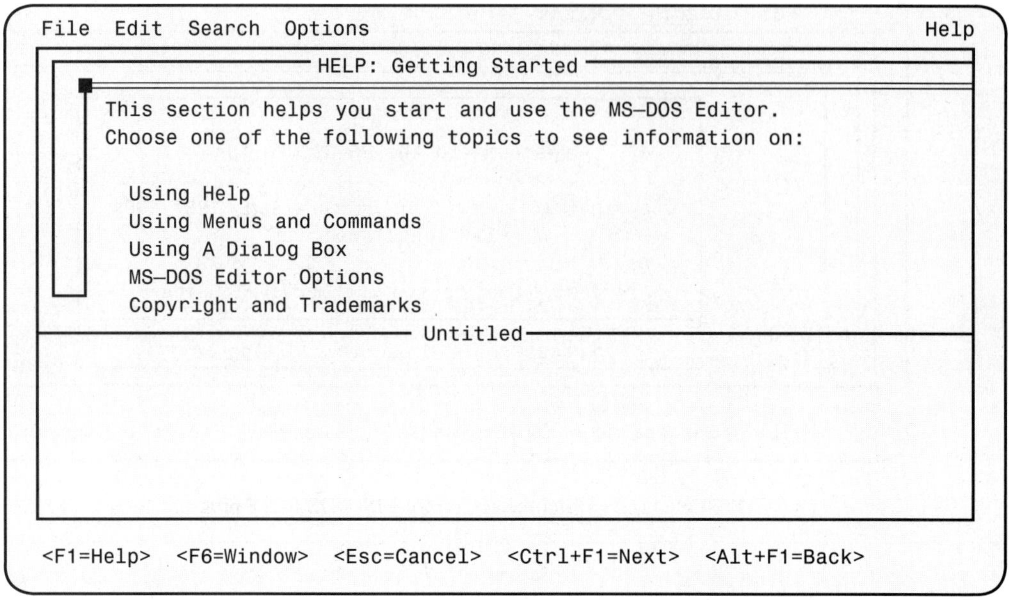

FIGURE 11.4 HELP: Getting Started screen with data entry window.

FIGURE 11.5 File menu screen with dialog box.

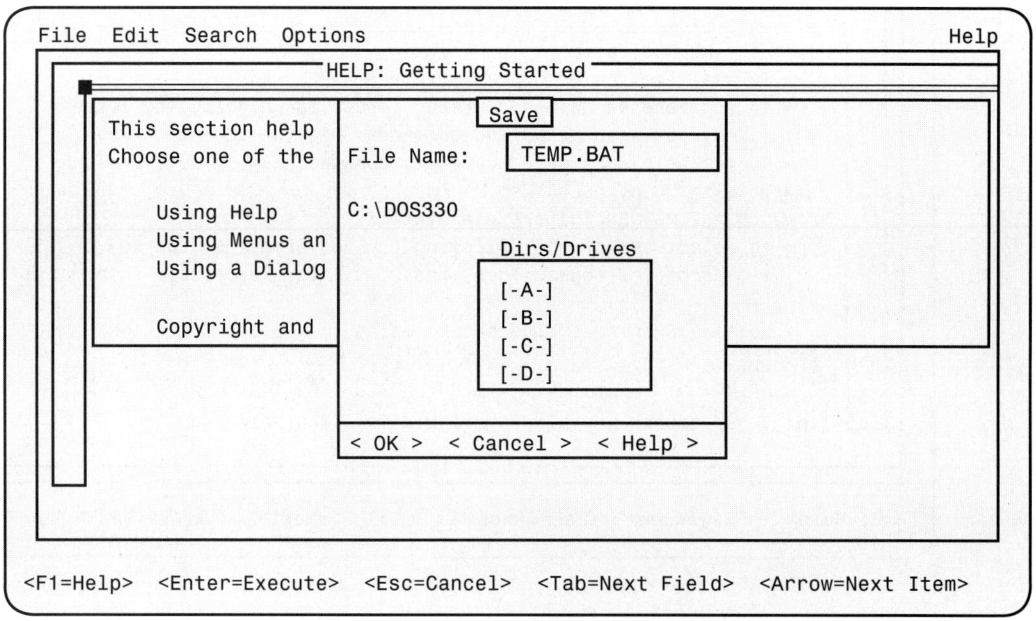

Enter the filename **TEMP.BAT** and press **Enter**. The file is now saved to disk in the current directory.

Now, use the **Up Arrow** key to move the cursor to the top of the file. Examine each of the commands for accuracy. Correct any mistakes by typing over the incorrect characters. The arrow keys can be used to move about the file, just like you do with your word processor. When all mistakes are corrected, the file can be saved using the procedure described earlier.

Press the **Alt** key again to activate the menu bar. Use the **Down Arrow** key to highlight the **Exit** command, and press **Enter** to end the EDIT session. The first part of the EDIT session is now complete and you have saved a file to disk.

To edit the file in a second EDIT session, restart EDIT using one of two methods described next. The first method executes the editor, opens the file, and places you directly in the EDIT session. To initiate this type of session, enter the following command at the DOS prompt:

```
C:\> edit temp.bat
```

The screen display shown in Figure 11.6 will appear on the screen. Note that the filename now appears at the top of the data entry window.

FIGURE 11.6 File menu with TEMP.BAT opened.

```
File  Edit  Search  Options                                    Help
                  HELP: Getting Started
  This section helps you start and use the MS-DOS Editor.
  Choose one of the following topics to see information on:
     Using Help
     Using Menus and Commands
     Using A Dialog Box
     MS-DOS Editor Options
     Copyright and Trademarks
                        TEMP.BAT
C:
CD\WP51\data
C:\wp51\wp
CLS
ECHO
ECHO  Load Backup Diskette into Drive A
ECHO:
ECHO:
DIR a: /P

MS-DOS Editor  <F1=Help>  Press ALT to activate menus      N 00001:001
```

With the second restart method, EDIT is again initiated, but no filename is given. Press **Enter** and then function key **F1** to start the session, as you did earlier. Then use the **Alt** key to activate the menu bar, and the **Down Arrow** key to highlight the **Open** command. Press **Enter** to get to the dialog box and type the filename **TEMP.BAT.** Press **Enter** after entering the filename in the dialog box. The file now appears in the data entry window area. Figures 11.7 and 11.8 show the menu bar highlighted for the Open command, then the dialog box with the filename TEMP.BAT entered.

FIGURE 11.7 File menu bar for opening a file.

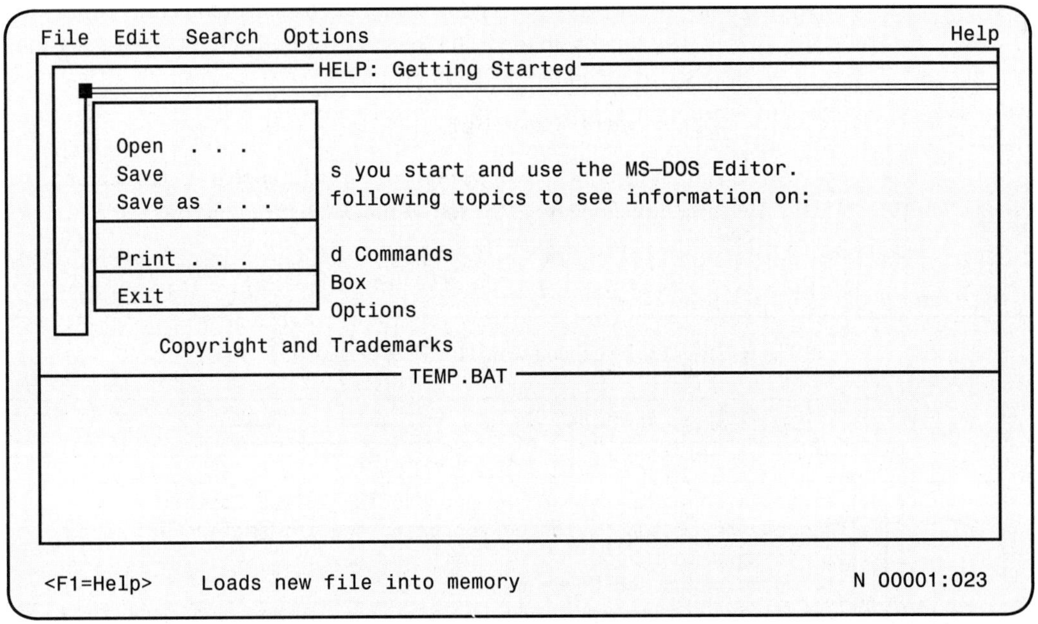

Now make two corrections to the file. Two commands will be added that first pause the execution of the batch file, then copy all the files in the named directory to a floppy diskette to be mounted in Drive A. Using the COPY command, this diskette will provide backup for the files created and stored on the hard drive. The two additional commands are:

PAUSE and **COPY C:\wp51\data*.* A:**

These will be entered as shown in the new file listing shown below.

```
ECHO off
C:
CD \wp51\data
C: \wp51\wp
```

```
CLS
ECHO:
ECHO Load Backup Diskette into Drive A
ECHO:
ECHO:
PAUSE
COPY C:\wp51\data\*.* A:\
DIR a: /P
```

FIGURE 11.8 Dialog box display for opening a file.

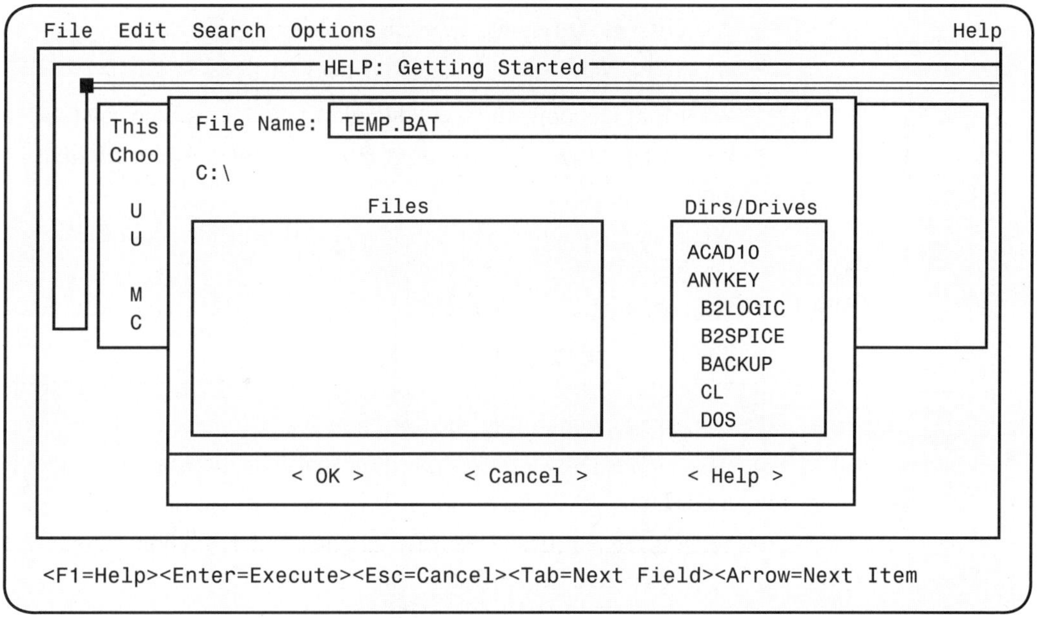

Use the **Down Arrow** key to move the cursor to the DIR a: /P command and press **Enter twice** to create two blank lines above it. Press the **Up Arrow twice.** Now type the two additional commands shown above. At the end of each command, do not press the Enter key. Instead, use the arrow keys to move to the next line. Again, use the arrow keys to move to the top of the file. Then use Down Arrow to move down the file. Make sure each command is correct. When complete, the file is ready to be saved in final form.

Use the **Alt** key to activate the menu bar. Highlight the **Save** command and press **Enter** to save the new copy of the file. Now use the **Alt** key again to activate the menu bar. Select **Print** from the File menu to print a copy of the file on your printer. The file has now been saved in final form as TEMP.BAT. No BAK extension file is created as with the EDLIN editor. A hard copy of the file has also been created on the printer. Activate the menu bar one last time with the **Alt** key. Select **Exit** with the Down Arrow key and press **Enter** to end the session.

EDIT is easy to use and easy to learn. When questions arise, turn to the HELP menus using the F1 function key. To see more HELP, use Ctrl-F1 and Alt-F1 to page forward or backward through the HELP screens, as shown at the bottom of the screen.

QUESTIONS AND PROBLEMS

1. What is the meaning of the # sign when it is used with a file being edited in EDLIN?
2. What two modes characterize file operations in EDLIN?
3. What types of files can be edited using EDLIN?
4. What EDLIN command is used to view a file one screen at a time?
5. What EDLIN command is used to display line 20 in a file that is 50 lines long?
6. What happens to the existing file on a disk when the edited file is saved during the exit process of EDLIN?
7. What EDLIN command can be used to duplicate an entire file to produce a total of 20 copies of the file?
8. What character is added to a command to get EDLIN to prompt for an answer in a Search or Replace operation?
9. What command is used to exit from EDLIN's insert mode back to command mode?
10. What is the purpose of the EDLIN line pointer and how can you tell what is the current line in the file?
11. What are some differences between EDIT and EDLIN as text editors? Which program is supported by DOS versions prior to Version 5?
12. What function key is used to activate the HELP feature in EDIT?
13. What function key is used to activate the EDIT data entry window and place the program in data entry mode?
14. What key is used to end each line of data entry in either the EDLIN or EDIT text editors?
15. What control-key sequences are used to move to the beginning and to the end of a document in the EDIT program?

CHAPTER 12

FILE MANAGEMENT (EXTERNAL COMMANDS)

INTRODUCTION

One of the most important functions performed by any operating system is file management. Regardless of the problem to be solved, software regularly creates files as it performs its functions. These files then must be named, stored, and managed in a systematic way. DOS uses a variety of commands, both internal and external, to perform this function. This chapter concentrates on the external file management commands stored in the DOS directory on your hard drive. For a discussion of the internal commands associated with file management, see Chapter 7.

The external commands discussed in this chapter are:

COMP
FC
ATTRIB
BACKUP
RESTORE
XCOPY
REPLACE
EXPAND
APPEND

THE COMPARE (COMP) COMMAND

The Compare (COMP) command compares two individual files or two sets of files, byte by byte. Up to 10 differences in the files are reported. The hexadecimal value of the differences in the files, counting from the beginning of the file, are reported. Reporting can also be done in other forms by specifying one of several switches associated with COMP. The normal application of the COMP command is to determine whether two files are identical. The format of the COMP command is:

COMP *<file1>* *<file2>* /A /C /D /L /N=*nnn*

<file1> is the name of the file that will be used as the basis for the comparison. The file can be addressed with a drive and a pathname if the file is not in the current directory. Wildcard characters can be used to specify a group of files. A file specification of *.* specifies all the files in the addressed directory.

<file2> is the name of the second file or group of files that will be compared to *<file1>*. A drive and path can be used to address *<file2>* just as with *<file1>*. Wildcard characters can also be used to address a group of files.

/A translates the numbers into characters using the ASCII coding system.

/C specifies that differences resulting from upper- or lowercase coding of characters should be ignored.

/D displays differences that are found in decimal rather than hexadecimal form.

/L displays the line number where the difference was found. This specification might be useful in comparing two copies of programming files.

/N=nnn specifies the number of lines *(nnn)* of the files that should be compared.

The parameters used with the COMP command specify the type of comparison to be done between two files or groups of files. Many of the options are useful to programmers in comparing two different versions of a program, or in specifying that a file comparison be limited to a given number of lines of a program using the /N parameter.

□ EXAMPLES

1. `C:\>` **`COMP report.doc customer.txt`**
2. `C:\>` **`COMP report.doc a:customer.txt`**
3. `C:\>` **`COMP acctlist a:\DATA\number.txt`**
4. `C:\>` **`COMP C:\CUST\*.* A:\ > PRN`**
5. `C:\>` **`COMP C:\PROGF\PROG1.SCR \PROGF\PROG2.SCR /N=50`**

1. `C:\>` **`COMP report.doc customer.txt`** In this example, two files are to be compared. No addressing information is given, so both files must exist in the root directory on Drive C; these are the defaults. The file customer.txt will be compared to the file report.doc. Any differences, or the fact that they are identical, will be reported to the display monitor.
2. `C:\>` **`COMP report.doc a:customer.txt`** A file named customer.txt from Drive A will be compared to a file named report.doc from the root directory of Drive C. The report will indicate how customer.txt differs from report.doc, if it does.
3. `C:\>` **`COMP acctlist a:\DATA\number.txt`** A file named number.txt from the \DATA directory on Drive A will be compared to a file acctlist on Drive C in the root directory. This example illustrates how files can be addressed when doing a file comparison. There is no need to copy the files into the same directory. When comparing two files, just use standard addressing techniques to access them wherever they are located.
4. `C:\>` **`COMP C:\CUST\*.* A:\ > PRN`** In this example, all the files in the \CUST directory on Drive C will be compared to their counterparts on Drive A. DOS will access the first file in \CUST, then search Drive A for a file of similar name. DOS will then compare the two files and report on the status of the comparison. DOS will then access the second file from \CUST and repeat

the process. This will continue until DOS has tried to compare every file in \CUST on Drive C to its counterpart in the root directory on Drive A. Redirection has been used to send the report to the printer. This hard copy will make it easier to see which files compare and which do not.

5. `C:\>` **`COMP C:\PROGF\PROG1.SCR \PROGF\PROG2.SCR /N=50`**
Two files are to be compared from the \PROGF directory on Drive C. The /N=50 parameter indicates that only the first 50 lines of the two files PROG1.SCR and PROG2.SCR are to be compared.

THE FILE COMPARISON (FC) COMMAND

The File Comparison (FC) command compares two files and displays a list of differences on standard output. On IBM-compatible computers, the FC command is similar to the COMP command. The FC command can be used to compare either text files or program files with COM or EXE extensions. Files can be compared line by line, as in the case of program files, or byte by byte, as in the case of text or other data type files. The format of the FC command is as follows. Note that the parameters *precede* the filenames rather than following them, as in other commands.

`FC /A /B /C /L /LB`*`n`*` /N /`*`nn`*` /T /W `*`<file1> <file2>`*

/A specifies that the file comparison report should be abbreviated. In the abbreviated report, only the beginning and ending lines of each group of mismatches are shown.

/B specifies that the files are to be compared byte by byte. When you specify /B, no other parameters may be used.

/C specifies that upper- and lowercase should be ignored when comparing text.

/L specifies that the files should be compared line by line. This is the default for all files except those with EXE, COM, BIN, SYS, OBJ, or LIB extensions.

/LB*n* specifies the size of the internal buffer. The default is 100 lines.

/N instructs DOS to include line numbers in the display resulting from the comparison of two ASCII files.

/nn specifies how many lines must match in order to realign the comparison when comparing ASCII files. This must be a value between 1 and 9; the default in most cases is 2.

/T instructs DOS to compare tab stops as literal characters rather than as a series of spaces.

/W prompts DOS to ignore any spaces or tabs before, after, or in the center of text.

□ **EXAMPLES**

1. C:\> **FC \DATA\REPORT.TXT A:REPORT.DOC**
2. C:\> **FC /B \WP51\DATA\MEMFXD01 B:MEMFXD99.TXT**
3. C:\> **FC /L /N AUTOEXEC.BAT A:AUTO1.BAT**
4. C:\> **FC /B D:DOCUMENT.TXT B:DOCUMENT.001**
5. C:\> **FC /B \DOS400\INIT.COM A:FORMAT.COM**

1. C:\> **FC \DATA\REPORT.TXT A:REPORT.DOC** A file comparison will compare the file REPORT.DOC on Drive A to the file REPORT.TXT in the \DATA directory on Drive C. Differences will be reported to the display screen.
2. C:\> **FC /B \WP51\DATA\MEMFXD01 B:MEMFXD99.TXT** In this example, two files will be compared on a byte-by-byte basis, because /B was specified. Note that the parameter precedes the two filenames in the command, rather than following the filename fields, as is normally the case. The file MEMFXD99.TXT will be compared to the file MEMFXD01 that resides in the \WP51\DATA directory on Drive C.
3. C:\> **FC /L /N AUTOEXEC.BAT A:AUTO1.BAT** The two files in this example will be compared as ASCII text files because the /L parameter was included in the command. Line numbers will be included in the comparison report because /N is specified. The file AUTO1.BAT will be compared to AUTOEXEC.BAT. The comparison program assumes that AUTOEXEC.BAT resides in the root directory on Drive C since no addressing information is given.
4. C:\> **FC /B D:DOCUMENT.TXT B:DOCUMENT.001** A file DOCUMENT.001 on Drive B will be compared to a file DOCUMENT.TXT on a byte-by-byte basis, because the /B parameter is included in the command. The file DOCUMENT.TXT is found in the root directory on Drive D.
5. C:\> **FC /B \DOS400\INIT.COM A:FORMAT.COM** A command file FORMAT.COM from Drive A is compared to a command file INIT.COM in the \DOS400 directory on Drive C. The two files are compared byte by byte.

THE DISPLAY OR CHANGE FILE ATTRIBUTES (ATTRIB) COMMAND

The Display or Change File Attributes (ATTRIB) command displays the status of the read-only and archive bits in the attribute byte of a file. In DOS Version 5.00, this list has been expanded to include the hide and system bits. The ATTRIB command can also be used to change the status of these bits for a particular file. Thus, read-only protection can be removed from a file that is read-only. A file can be hidden by turning on the hide bit so that the filename will not display when the DIR command is used. Likewise, a file's archive bit can be turned off, along with its system bit, using the ATTRIB command.

First you must understand the meaning of each of these bits and how they relate to the status of a file. When a file is created or when an existing file is modified, the archive bit of the file is set to one (turned on). The archive bit is 1 of the eight bits of the **attribute byte**. An attribute byte is associated with every file and stores the status for that particular file. The attribute byte is also used to store information about directory names and volume labels. Therefore, the attribute byte is associated with every entry in every directory on every disk. (For more information on the attribute byte, refer to "File Attributes" in Appendix B.)

When the archive bit is set to on, it means that the file has just been created or modified. The bit remains on, under normal conditions, until the file is backed up using the BACKUP command. When a file is backed up, a duplicate of that file, which includes information about its path, is copied to a backup diskette or some other backup media. During the backup process, the BACKUP command sets the archive bit to off or zero for the file on the hard disk. The archive bit being off means (1) the file has been backed up so a copy exists if it must be restored for any reason, and (2) the file on the hard disk has not been modified since the last backup.

If the file is modified, DOS will turn the archive bit on again, indicating that the file has been modified since the last backup. If the ATTRIB command is used to display the status of the files on a disk and any files display without the A appearing next to their name, these files have been backed up and they have not been modified since the last backup.

Another bit that is part of the attribute byte is the read-only bit. When this bit is set to on, it means that the associated file is a read-only file. In other words, that file can be read and executed if it is a command file, but it cannot be overwritten with the COPY command. The file is protected from accidental modification. A file that is read-only, meaning it can only be read, will normally be an executable program file that you want to protect. However, it could also be a key data file.

The ATTRIB command can display the status of these various bits in the attribute byte. If the letters R and A display next to a filename, it means that the file is read-only and the archive bit is on. Similarly, S and H indicate that a file is a system file and that it is hidden. Other combinations are possible also.

The hide bit results in a file being hidden so that it will not display with the normal directory listing of files. The DOS operating system uses two hidden files as part of its normal file management and input/output operations. Some application software uses hidden files as part of a copy protection scheme. Hiding files provides a degree of system protection. It also makes invisible certain files and directories that you may not want displayed.

The **system bit** is normally reserved by DOS for use with certain operating- system files. It is a bit that will normally only be used by programmers in building application software programs. DOS Version 5.00 makes this bit available to all users through the ATTRIB command. Normally the IO.SYS and MSDOS.SYS or COM files are set as both system files and hidden files. Few other files on your system will be coded with both these bits on.

The ATTRIB command can also be used to modify the status of these four bits. In versions prior to 5, only the R and A bits can be modified. If the bit is turned on, you can use the ATTRIB command to turn the bit off. Likewise, if the bit is turned off, you can use the ATTRIB command to turn the bit on. Use extreme caution in modifying the system bit for any file, particularly one associated with either DOS or other packaged software. The format of the ATTRIB command for Version 5 is as follows. (Note that versions prior to DOS 5 only support +R −R +A −A.)

ATTRIB +R -R +A -A +H -H +S -S <*filename*> /S

+R indicates that the read-only bit is to be turned on.

-R indicates that the read-only bit is to be turned off.

+A specifies that the archive bit is to be turned on.

-A specifies that the archive bit is to be turned off.

+H indicates that the hide bit is to be turned on.

-H indicates that the hide bit is to be turned off.

+S specifies that the system bit is to be turned on.

-S specifies that the system bit is to be turned off.

<*filename*> is the file or files that are to be affected by the attribute command.

/S specifies that all of the files in any existing subdirectories of <*filename*> are to be affected as well.

□ EXAMPLES

1. C:\> **ATTRIB +R AUTOEXEC.BAT**
2. C:\> **ATTRIB +A C:\LOTUS\DATA*.WK1**
3. C:\> **ATTRIB -R CONFIG.SYS**
4. C:\> **ATTRIB C:*.***
5. C:\> **ATTRIB +R +H CONFIG.SYS**
6. C:\> **ATTRIB -H AUTOEXEC.BAT**

1. C:\> **ATTRIB +R AUTOEXEC.BAT** The AUTOEXEC.BAT file will be made a read-only file because +R was indicated as part of the command line.
2. C:\> **ATTRIB +A C:\LOTUS\DATA*.WK1** In this example all the files with a .WK1 extension in the \LOTUS\DATA directory will have their archive bit set to on. This, in effect, indicates that all these files have been modified since their last backup.

3. `C:\> ATTRIB -R CONFIG.SYS` The CONFIG.SYS file will have its read-only bit set to off. This would be required if you wanted to modify CONFIG.SYS using EDLIN or EDIT. After completing the modifications and saving the new version, use ATTRIB with the +R parameter to make the new version a read-only file.
4. `C:\> ATTRIB C:\*.*` All of the files in the root directory on Drive C will have their attributes displayed. The files will be displayed on the monitor, with each filename preceded by an R and an A if these two attributes are on. If the attributes associated with a filename are off, the R and A will not display. An example of the display is shown below.

```
             C:\DATA\REPORT1
A            C:\DATA\REPORT2
       R     C:\DATA\REPORT3
A      R     C:\DATA\REPORT4
             C:\DATA\REPORT5
```

5. `C:\> ATTRIB +R +H CONFIG.SYS` The ATTRIB command is used to protect the CONFIG.SYS file from accidentally being modified by setting both the read-only bit on (+R) as well as hiding the file using +H. CONFIG.SYS cannot accidentally be modified. If CONFIG.SYS is to be updated later, these two bits will have to be set off using –R and –H at the time the file is to be updated.
6. `C:\> ATTRIB -H AUTOEXEC.BAT` The ATTRIB command is used to unhide the AUTOEXEC.BAT file. With the hide bit turned on, the AUTOEXEC.BAT file will not display in a directory listing of the root directory. Setting the hide bit to off with the –H control means that AUTOEXEC.BAT will now display as one of the files in the root directory.

THE BACK UP FILES (BACKUP) COMMAND

The Back Up Files (BACKUP) command makes a copy of a file or files to protect against the loss of data. Files may be backed up from any type of disk. BACKUP is more than just another DOS command. It is a command that can save you many hours of time. BACKUP should be part of your planning when you consider performing any of the following actions:

- Updating data on the hard drive with an application program
- Upgrading software to a new version
- Experimenting with new software
- Running routine operations, such as general ledger accounting or payroll, on a cyclical basis

For these reasons and many others it is important to learn to use BACKUP and its many features. A few hours spent now to thoroughly understand this command will save countless hours later on when something goes wrong, and something going wrong does not always mean hardware failure. More often than not the loss of data is caused by a typing mistake or a software error on the part of the user. Any regular DOS user will tell you, "I've lost a lot more data due to my mistakes and software problems than I've ever lost because of failure of my hard drive or the failure of a disk."

While learning the BACKUP command, also learn its companion command, the RESTORE command (see below.) Used judiciously and with a little planning, they will save countless hours in data restoration or system rebuilding. They are not easy to learn; each has many parameters. They can be used in a wide variety of ways, so begin by learning their fundamental uses. When some of their special capabilities are needed don't depend upon your memory. Open this book, look up the command, and double-check your typing before pressing the Enter key. The format of the BACKUP command is:

```
BACKUP <path><filename> <drive> /A /S /M /F:<size>
/D:<date> /T:<time> /L:<logfile>
```

<*path*><*filename*> specifies the file or files that are to be backed up. A drive letter followed by a colon must be specified. A pathname can be included. The filename can be a single file or a set of files specified by using wildcard characters.

<*drive*> is the letter of the drive followed by a colon that will contain the backup disk. In early versions of DOS, the disk must be formatted before starting a backup procedure. It is highly recommended that enough diskettes be formatted to hold the backup files before beginning the backup process.

/A specifies that the backup files will be added to an existing backup disk. If /A is not used, DOS issues a warning message that the target disk's contents will be destroyed in the backup process. If /A is not used, the backup disk should be a formatted blank disk or a formatted disk that no longer contains information of any value.

/S specifies that the files to be backed up should include all subdirectories contained in the specified pathname.

/M specifies that only files that have been modified since they were last backed up should be included in the current backup process.

/F:<*size*> instructs DOS to check the target disk and format it if necessary. If you specify /F, the current command path must include the drive/directory combination containing the file FORMAT.COM. The size is specified in kilobytes. Valid entries for <*size*> include 160, 180, 320, 360, 720, 1200, 1440, and 2880. Size can be specified in a variety of ways such as 1440, 1440K, 1440KB, 1.44, 1.44M, and 1.44MB.

/D:<*date*> specifies that the files to be included in the backup should be only files modified since the date specified. Specify the date just as you would when entering data for the DATE command.

/T:<*time*> specifies that the files to be included in the backup should be those which have been modified since the <*time*> on the <*date*> that was specified. Enter the <*time*> just as you would for the TIME command.

/L:<*logfile*> creates on the source drive a logfile that contains the date and time of the backup, the pathname and filename of each file that is backed up, and the backup number that DOS assigns to the disks on which the files are backed up. Information is added to the logfile with each backup, creating a history file of backups. If no name is specified for the logfile, DOS will assign the name BACKUP.LOG.

When DOS backs up files using the BACKUP command, every byte on each backup diskette is used if multiple diskettes are required. The only diskette that may have free space will be the last one. In addition, each backup diskette is given a number. DOS prompts for succeeding diskettes if additional space is needed to complete the backup operation. DOS also numbers the diskettes in sequential order so that it can check for the sequence number when doing a restore. DOS will split files into pieces if necessary when doing the backup in order to fully utilize all space on the disk. Files will be reassembled correctly during the restore process. DOS displays the name of each file as the backup proceeds. If a file is split and has pieces residing on each disk, DOS will display the name for each disk as it proceeds.

Prepare and format diskettes before backing up the hard drive. Most backups require multiple diskettes. Since several diskettes are required, you need a method for estimating the number of backup diskettes required. To estimate that number requires two pieces of information. First, determine the space available on the diskettes to be used for backup. This will be the basic storage capacity of the diskette. If using 31/2-inch diskettes, it will be 730K or 1.457M bytes. If using 51/4-inch diskettes, it will be the corresponding numbers for high-density and double-density diskettes. Second, estimate the size of the files to be backed up. If the entire hard drive is to be backed up, use the CHKDSK command to find the total space required. If backing up an entire directory, there are several utilities, such as PC Tools, that will tell you the space consumed by all files in a single directory or series of directories.

With these two numbers, an estimate of the number of diskettes required for the backup can be made. The example below illustrates the calculation based on a CHKDSK report from the hard drive. This example assumes you are backing up the files onto 3 1/2-inch, high-density diskettes.

A high-density 3 1/2-inch diskette holds 1,457,664 bytes of data. A sample CHKDSK report will illustrate:

```
21135360   bytes total disk space
   53248   bytes in 3 hidden files
   38912   bytes in 16 directories
14256128   bytes in 474 user files
   10240   bytes in bad sectors
 6787072   bytes available on disk

  655360   bytes total memory
  491904   bytes free
```

From the above information, you can calculate the total space used on the diskette by files that will be backed up. If the entire hard drive is backed up, the backed-up files will include the hidden files, the directory information, and the user files. The total space is then (53,248 + 38,912 + 14,256,128) bytes. The bad sectors will not be included in the backup. Therefore, the total space required is 14,348,288 bytes. An estimate of the number of diskettes needed can be obtained using the formula:

Diskettes Needed = (*Total File Space/ Diskette Capacity*) + 1

A backup diskette includes a small control file normally requiring a few hundred bytes, plus a much larger backup file containing all the backup data. In calculating the diskettes required for the total file space, adding one more diskette compensates for the space required by the small control file on each backup diskette. In the example above, the calculation would yield a result as follows:

Diskettes Needed = (14,348,288/1,457,664) + 1
= 9.84 + 1 = 10.84 = 11 diskettes

Based on these estimates, a total of 11 high-density diskettes should be formatted for doing the backup of the entire hard disk. In the case of double-density, 3 1/2-inch diskettes, the total space estimate would be divided by 730,112 bytes. Doing a similar calculation using double-density diskettes would yield an estimate of 21 diskettes.

EXAMPLES

1. `C:\> BACKUP C:\ACCOUNT\CHACCTS.DAT A:/A`
2. `C:\> BACKUP C:\ACCOUNT\*.DAT A:`
3. `C:\> BACKUP C:\ACCOUNT\*.* A:/S`
4. `C:\> BACKUP C:\*.* B:/S`
5. `C:\> BACKUP C:\ACCOUNT\*.* A:/S/M/A`
6. `C:\> BACKUP C:\ACCOUNT\*.* A:/D:09-30-93/S/A`
7. `C:\> BACKUP C:\WP51\*.* B:/S/L`
8. `C:\> BACKUP C:\LOTUS\DATA\*.WK1 B:/F/L`

1. `C:\> BACKUP C:\ACCOUNT\CHACCTS.DAT A:/A` In this example, a file named CHACCTS.DAT is backed up from the \ACCOUNT directory on Drive C. The file will be backed up to a backup diskette loaded in Drive A, and because the /A parameter is specified, the file will be added to an existing backup diskette.
2. `C:\> BACKUP C:\ACCOUNT\*.DAT A:` In this example, all the files with the extension DAT in the directory \ACCOUNT on Drive C will be backed up to the diskette in Drive A. No parameters are specified, so DOS will issue a warning message that all information on the target diskette will be lost. The user should make sure that the diskette to be used is blank or one with data that can be written over by the BACKUP program. All data currently on the disk will be overwritten by the files associated with the file specification *.DAT.
3. `C:\> BACKUP C:\ACCOUNT\*.* A:/S` Here, all the files in the directory \ACCOUNT on Drive C will be backed up to the diskette in Drive A. The backed-up files will include not only the files in \ACCOUNT, but also all the files in all subdirectories of \ACCOUNT, because the /S parameter is specified. The warning message that all information on the target disk will be lost will also be issued because the backed up files will overwrite any previous information on the target diskettes.
4. `C:\> BACKUP C:\*.* B:/S` In this example all files with any extension from the root directory on Drive C will be backed up to Drive B. Because the /S parameter was specified all subdirectories of the root directory will also be backed up. This specification starts with the root directory and specifies all subdirectories of the root directory, so this is the BACKUP command to back up the entire hard disk drive, Drive C.
5. `C:\> BACKUP C:\ACCOUNT\*.* A:/S/M/A` Files from the \ACCOUNT directory and all its subdirectories will be backed up in this example. Though the specification is *.* for the backup, the /M parameter indicates that only files modified since the last backup should be sent to the backup disk. This backup, in essence, represents an update to a previous backup. As such, the /A parameter is also specified, indicating that the files backed up should be added to the backup diskette. The BACKUP program will issue a message telling the user to load the last backup diskette into Drive A. Load the last backup diskette from the previous backup of the \ACCOUNT directory and its subdirectories.
6. `C:\> BACKUP C:\ACCOUNT\*.* A:/D:09-30-93/S/A` Here, files from the \ACCOUNT directory and all its subdirectories will be backed up. The specification is *.* for the backup, but the /D parameter indicates that only files modified since the backup done on 09-30-93 should be included. Therefore,

this backup is an update to the backup of 09-30-93. The /A parameter is also specified, indicating that the files backed up should be added to the backup diskette. The BACKUP program will issue a message telling the user to load the last backup diskette into Drive A. Load the last backup diskette from the backup of 09-30-93 for the \ACCOUNT directory and its subdirectories.

7. `C:\>` **`BACKUP C:\WP51\*.* B:/S/L`** This backup is for the \WP51 directory and all its subdirectories, as indicated by the /S parameter. The backup will be done to diskettes loaded into Drive B. The /L parameter is indicated, but no filename specified. A logfile will be created on the hard drive with the default filename BACKUP.LOG.
8. `C:\>` **`BACKUP C:\LOTUS\DATA\*.WK1 B:/F/L`** In this example, all the worksheet files with the extension WK1 are to be backed up from the directory \LOTUS\DATA. This backup will be done to Drive B. The /F parameter is specified, indicating that the diskettes should be formatted if they are not already formatted. These diskettes would be formatted based on the default format of Drive B. A logfile named BACKUP.LOG will be created on Drive C and will include basic history information about the backup.

The last example illustrates the use of the /F parameter. It is generally not recommended that /F be used except in emergency situations. Most of these emergencies can be avoided if you make an estimate of the number of backup diskettes needed before the backup is done. Three problems may arise if diskette formatting is required during the backup process:

First, the diskettes cannot be formatted based on setting the density of the diskettes. If you plan to be able to use the backup diskettes across a range of systems, you may need to make sure that the diskettes are double-density rather than high-density in capacity. This flexibility is lost when formatting during backup because format parameters cannot be specified as part of the backup process.

Second, a problem with a diskette may be encountered during the format process. For example, bad sectors might be indicated. If this kind of problem is encountered, the backup process may have to be aborted. If that is the case, the whole process will have to be reinitiated after the problem with the diskette is resolved. This can be quite time-consuming in an entire hard disk backup, which could require 30 to 45 minutes, depending on the size of the hard disk. It is particularly frustrating to be on diskette 30 and suddenly have a problem. Starting over means all the time spent doing the backup to 30 diskettes was wasted.

Finally, without an estimate of the number of diskettes required, you may not have enough diskettes to complete the backup. You must then scramble around to get some more diskettes, or abort the process and reinitiate it another time. In the case of backups done as part of a software installation or testing process, this can be particularly annoying.

THE RESTORE BACKED UP FILES (RESTORE) COMMAND

The RESTORE command copies files that were backed up with the BACKUP command from a single or a series of backup diskettes. It places the files specified into the same directory in which they were originally located. Thus, files backed up from the \WP51 directory will be placed back into a \WP51 directory. The fundamental idea behind the RESTORE command is to restore individual files, a directory, or an entire disk into the same condition that existed when the backup was made. RESTORE can be used with data files, program files, or both. The BACKUP and RESTORE commands are a companion set. When using BACKUP to back up a set of files, you should also think in terms of the companion RESTORE command that will restore your system to its previous state. In many cases a particular set of backup diskettes will never be used. If you never suffer a loss of data, or have a hardware failure, or experience a software problem, you may not need the backup diskettes. On the other hand, if any of these problems do occur, you will treasure the set of backup disks that will save countless hours of file recreation or software installation time.

For these reasons and many others, the RESTORE command is one of the most important DOS commands. A few hours spent now to thoroughly understand this command will save you countless hours later when something goes wrong. The RESTORE command has many parameters, just as does BACKUP. The command can also be used in a variety of ways.

One example will illustrate this point. When doing the backup, you may decide to back up your entire hard disk. Doing this may generate a series of 20 to 30 diskettes. Later on, in deleting some files, you might accidentally delete all the files in the \LOTUS directory. No problem; just use RESTORE to restore the \LOTUS directory only, and you are back in business. The RESTORE command will search the backup diskettes for the \LOTUS directory and all the files associated with this directory as well as all its subdirectories. The RESTORE command selects only those files that you need to put you back in operation. Learn the fundamental uses of the RESTORE command. When you need some special capability of the command, don't depend upon your memory. Get out the book, look up the command, and implement the operation. In cases where regular or frequent backups are required, such as with accounting files, implement both BACKUP and RESTORE via batch files. These are two commands for which batch files are extremely valuable. (Refer to Chapter 19 for more information on and examples of batch file applications.)

The format of the RESTORE command is:

```
RESTORE <drive> <path><filename> /S /P /M /N /D
/B:<date> /A:<date> /E:<time> /L:<time>
```

<drive> is the letter of the disk drive that will contain the backup disk or series of disks from which files will be restored, followed by a colon.

<path><filename> specifies the file or files that are to be restored. A drive letter followed by a colon must be specified. A pathname can be included. The filename can be a single file or a set of files including those specified using wildcard characters.

/S specifies that the backup files should be restored to the specified subdirectory as well as all subdirectories of that specified directory.

/P specifies that DOS should prompt you before restoring a hidden file, a read-only file, or a file that has been modified since the last backup.

/M specifies that only files that have changed since the last backup should be restored.

/N specifies that only files that do not exist on the target disk should be restored.

/D displays all the files on the backup diskettes that match the specified *<filename>*.

/B:<date> specifies that only files created or changed since the specified *<date>* should be restored.

/A:<date> specifies that only files created or changed on or after the specified *<date>* should be restored.

/E:<time> specifies that only files created or changed at or earlier than the specified *<time>* should be restored.

/L:<time> specifies that only files created or changed later than the specified *<time>* should be restored.

DOS prompts for succeeding diskettes if additional disks are needed to complete the restore operation. DOS will check to ensure the diskettes are loaded in sequential order. DOS will reassemble files that have been split between two diskettes when it does the restore. DOS displays the name of each file as the restore proceeds.

It is not always necessary to start with the first diskette when performing a restore. If restoring a group of files from a directory structure that begins on diskette 6, such as the \WP51 directory, it is possible to start the restore beginning with diskette 6. Just insert diskette 6 and press the Enter key at the "insert diskette 1" message. DOS will prompt that it is not diskette 1. Press Enter and ignore the message. The restore will proceed with files beginning with those for the \WP51 directory from the sixth diskette in the sequence.

□ **EXAMPLES**

1. `C:\>` **`RESTORE A: C:\ACCOUNT\CHACCTS.DAT`**
2. `C:\>` **`RESTORE A: C:\ACCOUNT\*.DAT`**
3. `C:\>` **`RESTORE A: C:\ACCOUNT\*.* /S`**

4. C:\> **RESTORE B: C:*.* /S**
5. C:\> **RESTORE B: D:\ACCOUNT*.* /S/M/P**
6. C:\> **RESTORE A: C:\ACCOUNT*.* /A:09-30-93/S**
7. C:\> **RESTORE B: C:\WP51*.* /S**
8. C:\> **RESTORE A: C:\LOTUS\DATA*.WK1 /N**

1. C:\> **RESTORE A: C:\ACCOUNT\CHACCTS.DAT** In our first example, a single file named CHACCTS.DAT will be restored from a backup diskette mounted in Drive A. The file will restored to the directory \ACCOUNT on Drive C. If no pathname is specified, the file is restored to the current directory.
2. C:\> **RESTORE A: C:\ACCOUNT*.DAT** In this example, a group of files with the extension DAT are restored from Drive A. The files are restored to the directory \ACCOUNT on Drive C.
3. C:\> **RESTORE A: C:\ACCOUNT*.* /S** The file specification in this example is *.*. All the files in the directory \ACCOUNT will be restored. All files in all subdirectories of \ACCOUNT will also be restored, since the /S parameter is specified. The files will be restored to Drive C from Drive A.
4. C:\> **RESTORE B: C:*.* /S** This command is an example of restoring all the files to the hard drive. The file specification is *.*, and the directory specification is the root directory of Drive C. The /S parameter specifies that all subdirectories of the root directory should also be restored. The backup diskettes will be mounted in Drive B.
5. C:\> **RESTORE B: D:\ACCOUNT*.* /S/M/P** In this example, three parameters—/S, /M, and /P—are specified with the restore being done from Drive B. The files specified are all files with any extension, noting that the /M parameter will modify this specification. Files will be restored to the directory \ACCOUNT on Drive D. All subdirectories of the \ACCOUNT directory will be restored since the /S parameter was specified. The /M parameter specifies that only files modified since the last backup should be restored; the system should prompt you before doing the restore on each file that has been modified, since the /P parameter was included as part of the command line.
6. C:\> **RESTORE A: C:\ACCOUNT*.* /A:09-30-93/S** In the next example, all files with any extension are to be restored, but only those files that were modified after the date 09-30-93. The restore will be done for the directory \ACCOUNT and all its subdirectory structure. The files are restored from the diskettes in floppy drive A.
7. C:\> **RESTORE B: C:\WP51*.* /S** This example is typical of restoring an application program as well as any data files that might be stored in subdirectories of its main directory. All of the files in the directory \WP51 and all its subdirectories are to be restored from diskettes mounted in Drive B. All

subdirectories of \WP51 are included in the restore since the /S parameter is specified.

8. `C:\> RESTORE A: C:\LOTUS\DATA\*.WK1 /N` In our last example files are to be restored from Drive A to the directory \LOTUS\DATA on Drive C. Only worksheet files with the extension WK1 will be restored. Since the /N parameter is specified, only files that do not already exist on Drive C will be included in the restore.

THE COPY FILES AND DIRECTORIES (XCOPY) COMMAND

The XCOPY command functions in many ways just like the COPY command. This command, along with COPY and REPLACE, forms a companion set. Most everyone learns to use COPY, but many never learn the unique capabilities of XCOPY and REPLACE. Take time to learn all three.

The XCOPY command is very powerful. It copies files just like the COPY command. However, the XCOPY command can do much more, because it can deal with entire subdirectory structures. In copying a directory structure, XCOPY not only copies all the files in the directory structure on the source drive, it also creates any necessary directories on the target drive as part of the copy process. Since most application programs consist of an entire directory structure, rather than just a single directory, XCOPY is the ideal command for copying these directory structures from one place to another.

XCOPY is a command with a large number of parameters. The basic operations can be learned without much difficulty, but this is another command that often requires referring to the book when employing its more complicated features. Remember that any copy operation has two basic fields: a FROM field, which is the source, and a TO field, which is the target.

The format of the XCOPY command is:

XCOPY <*source*> <*target*> /A /D:<*date*> /E /M /P /S /V /W

<*source*> is the name of the file or group of files that are to be copied. <*Source*> must be specified and can include only a drive letter if an entire disk is to be copied.

<*target*> specifies the disk onto which all the files are to be copied. The target can be any combination of a drive letter, a pathname, and a filename specification, including an extension.

/A specifies that only files for which the archive bit is on in the attribute byte should be included in the copy. The attribute byte is left unchanged.

/D:<*date*> specifies that the copy should include only those files for which the date specification is the same or later than the <*date*> specified.

/E specifies that subdirectories should be created on the target, even if they are empty on the source. Normally XCOPY automatically creates any necessary directories as part of the copy process. However, it does not create a subdirectory on the target if the companion directory on the source is empty. If the /E parameter is specified, every directory that exists on the source will be created on the target, even if the directory on the source drive is empty.

/M specifies that only files for which the archive bit is on in the attribute byte should be copied. These archive bits will be turned off on the target if the /M parameter is specified.

/P specifies that the user should be prompted before each file is copied from the source to the target. The user can select which files should be part of the copy process by using this parameter.

/S specifies that all subdirectories of the source specification should be included in the copy. If only a drive letter is specified as the source, the entire disk will be included in the copy.

/V specifies that the copy process should include verification to ensure that the files on the target drive will be identical to those on the source.

/W specifies that the system should wait and prompt the user before initiating the copy process. By using the /W parameter, the user can mount the correct diskette and then initiate the copy process by pressing any key.

□ EXAMPLES

1. C:\> **XCOPY \WP51*.DAT A:/S**
2. C:\> **XCOPY A:*.* C:\DATA /S/V**
3. C:\> **XCOPY B:*.* C:\LOTUS\DATA /S/E**
4. C:\> **XCOPY D:\MKT*.* /D:09-30-93 /P**
5. C:\> **XCOPY C:\WP50*.* D:\WP51 /S/E**
6. C:\> **XCOPY A:*.* B:\ /S/E/V/W**

1. C:\> **XCOPY \WP51*.DAT A:/S** In this example, all the files with the extension DAT will be copied from the \WP51 directory on Drive C to Drive A. Since the /S parameter is specified, the program will not only copy files from the \WP51 directory, but also all subdirectories of \WP51.
2. C:\> **XCOPY A:*.* C:\DATA /S/V** In this example, all the files on Drive A from the root directory are to be copied to the \DATA directory on Drive C. Since the /S parameter is specified, all subdirectories of the root directory on Drive A will also be copied. Since the /V parameter is specified, XCOPY will verify that the files on the target drive match the files on the source drive.
3. C:\> **XCOPY B:*.* C:\LOTUS\DATA /S/E** In this example, all the files on Drive B in the root directory will be copied on Drive C. The files will be placed in the \LOTUS\DATA directory. Since /S is specified, any subdirec-

tories of the root directory on Drive B will also be transferred to Drive C and will become subdirectories of \LOTUS\DATA. If any subdirectories on Drive B are empty, no files will be copied. However, XCOPY will build a subdirectory of the same name on Drive C since the /E parameter was specified.

4. `C:\> XCOPY D:\MKT\*.* /D:09-30-93 /P` In this example, all the files from the \MKT directory on Drive D will be copied to the root directory on Drive C. Files are transferred to Drive C as the default, since no target drive was specified. The files transferred will be those for which the date is on or after 9-30-93. The /P parameter is specified, so XCOPY will prompt the user for verification before copying each file.
5. `C:\> XCOPY C:\WP50\*.* D:\WP51 /S/E` In this example, all the files associated with an application directory \WP50 will be transferred to a new directory \WP51. This might be the case when an application is upgraded to a new version. The \WP50 directory is on Drive C and the \WP51 directory is on Drive D. All subdirectories of \WP50 will be copied, and XCOPY will build a similar subdirectory structure for \WP51. If any empty subdirectories are associated with \WP50, there will be no files to copy; however, the subdirectory will still be created under \WP51.
6. `C:\> XCOPY A:\*.* B:\ /S/E/V/W` In our last example all the files from a diskette in Drive A will be copied to a diskette in Drive B. The entire subdirectory structure from Drive A will be transferred, since the /S and the /E parameters were specified. XCOPY will verify that the files on the target drive are identical to those on the source drive, since /V was specified. The program will wait and provide a prompt for loading the appropriate diskettes since the /W parameter was part of the command.

THE REPLACE OR ADD FILES (REPLACE) COMMAND

The REPLACE command is the last of the three commands associated with the copy function. REPLACE is primarily intended to replace documents on a specified target drive. It is the only one of the three copy commands that can replace or overwrite read-only files. REPLACE has several unique features that complement COPY and XCOPY. REPLACE uses many of the same parameters that XCOPY provides. It can handle entire subdirectory structures, just as can XCOPY. It also provides for adding files to a target disk without replacing files that already exist on the target. Many of the features of REPLACE are useful when doing updates to application software or to data files.

The format of the REPLACE command is:

```
REPLACE <source> <target> /A /P /R /S /U /W
```

<source> is the name of the file or group of files that are to be copied. *<Source>* must be specified and can include only a drive letter if the entire contents of a disk is to be copied.

<target> specifies the disk to which all the files are to be copied. The target can be any combination of a drive letter, a pathname, and a filename specification, including an extension.

/A specifies that files should be added to the target drive. The only files copied are those on the source drive that do not exist on the target drive. This allows files to be copied to a target drive without replacing files that already exist there. If /A is not specified, files existing on the source will also be copied to the target.

/P specifies that the user should be prompted before each file is copied from the source to the target. The user can select which files should be part of the copy process by using this parameter.

/R specifies that read-only files on the target should be replaced. If /R is not specified, read-only files are left intact.

/S specifies that all subdirectories of the source specification should be included in the copy. If only a drive letter is specified as the source, the entire disk will be included in the copy.

/U replaces files on the target that are older than their counterparts on the source. If /U is specified, all other files are ignored during the copy process.

/W specifies that the system should wait and prompt before initiating the copy process. By using the /W parameter, the user can mount the correct diskette and begin the copy process by pressing any key.

□ EXAMPLES

1. C:\> **REPLACE \WP50*.TXT A:/S**
2. C:\> **REPLACE A:*.* C:\LOTUS /S /R**
3. C:\> **REPLACE B:*.* C:\LOTUS\DATA /A**
4. C:\> **REPLACE D:\MKT*.* /P**
5. C:\> **REPLACE C:\WP50*.* D:\WP51 /U**
6. C:\> **REPLACE A:*.* B:\ /S /W**

1. C:\> **REPLACE \WP50*.TXT A:/S** In our first example, all the files with TXT extensions will be copied from the \WP50 directory on Drive C to the current directory on Drive A. The /S parameter is specified, so all subdirectories of \WP50 will be copied, and a similar set of directories will be created on Drive A.

2. C:\> **REPLACE A:*.* C:\LOTUS /S /R** Here, all of the files on Drive A will be copied to the \LOTUS directory on Drive C. Since the /S parameter is specified, all subdirectories of Drive A will also be transferred, and a similar set of directories will be created as a subdirectory under \LOTUS. The /R parameter is specified, so the replace will be only for read-only files on the target drive.

3. `C:\> REPLACE B:\*.* C:\LOTUS\DATA /A` In this example, all the files in the root directory on Drive B will be copied to the \LOTUS\DATA directory on Drive C. The /A parameter is specified, so the only files copied will be those that do not exist on the target drive.
4. `C:\> REPLACE D:\MKT\*.* /P` In this example, the files in the \MKT directory on Drive D will be copied to the default drive, since no target information was specified. The transfer will be to the root directory of Drive C. The user will be prompted for each file before the copy takes place since /P is specified.
5. `C:\> REPLACE C:\WP50\*.* D:\WP51 /U` In the next example, the files in the \WP50 directory on Drive C will be copied to the \WP51 directory on Drive D. /U is specified, so only files on the target directory that are older than their counterparts on the source directory will be replaced.
6. `C:\> REPLACE A:\*.* B:\ /S /W` This example illustrates the transfer of files from one diskette to another. All the files in the root directory on Drive A, as well as all subdirectories of the root, will be transferred to Drive B. The /W parameter will result in a prompt to the user so that the proper diskettes can be inserted in each drive.

THE EXPAND COMPRESSED DOS FILES (EXPAND) COMMAND

Beginning with Version 5.00 of DOS, the operating system files are supplied on diskette in compressed form. Compressed files are coded with an extension containing the underscore character, such as CHKDSK.CO_. In compressed form, these files cannot be copied to the hard drive and used directly. Instead, they must first be expanded. The EXPAND command is supplied with Version 5.00 so that any of these files can be expanded when they are to be added to your fixed disk. Wildcards are not permitted with EXPAND. Each file must be separately addressed, so files must be expanded on a file-by-file basis.

If you are upgrading to Version 5.00, there is no need to use EXPAND. The installation process invoked by typing INSTALL will take care of the file expansion and upgrade process automatically. EXPAND is used to add files to the hard drive from the Version 5.00 installation disks. This might occur as a result of a hardware upgrade made to the system. Before the upgrade, some of the Version 5.00 files may have been left off the hard drive since they were not used (such as RAMDRIVE or EMM386). To now add these to the hard drive, the files must be accessed from the Version 5.00 upgrade diskette, then expanded and placed in the DOS directory on the hard drive.

The example below illustrates the form of the EXPAND command. First, find the appropriate files on the various upgrade diskettes using the command:

```
C:\> TYPE A:PACKING.LST > PRN
```

This command provides a hard copy of the list of files. To expand the SMARTDRV file, enter the command:

```
C:\> EXPAND A:SMARTDRV.SY_ C:\DOS500\SMARTDRV.SYS
```

The compressed file from the upgrade diskette will be expanded and installed in the \DOS500 directory on the hard drive. Note that the file extension changed from SY_ to SYS. Some changes of this type may necessitate changes to CONFIG.SYS and AUTOEXEC.BAT in order to make these device drivers part of the installed system. In cases such as these, reboot the system to complete installation so that the device drivers are read as part of processing the commands in CONFIG.SYS and AUTOEXEC.BAT. If either of these files has been protected using the ATTRIB command, remove the protection before performing the installation. Then add the protection after the installation is complete and working.

THE DEFINE A DATA PATH (APPEND) COMMAND

The APPEND command does for data files what the PATH command does for command files. When APPEND is executed, a set of drive-directory combinations are specified so that DOS will search a directory other than the current directory for a data file. The format of the APPEND command is:

APPEND /E /X or **/X:off /path:on (off) <*path*>;**

/E specifies that the data path should be part of the DOS environment. /E may only be specified the first time APPEND is executed. /E will normally be used when APPEND is included in the AUTOEXEC.BAT file as part of the boot process. A second APPEND must be issued to establish the search path.

/X specifies that DOS should search for command files as well as data files in the appended directories, beginning with Version 4. In Version 3.3, the /X parameter merely makes the data path available to other DOS commands.

/X:off specifies that DOS should not search the appended directories for command files.

/path:on (off) tells DOS if the search should include the appended directories for a file if the filename is not preceded by a drive letter and/or a path. /Path:on tells DOS to include the drive letter and/or pathname; /path:off tells DOS not to include them. The default value in Version 4 is /path:on.

<*path*> is the name of the directory to be added to the path. When you specify <*path*>, it is recommended that the path be a drive-directory combination. When you specify more than one path, separate the pathnames with a semicolon.

□ EXAMPLES

1. `C:\> APPEND C:\DATA;A: /E`
2. `C:\> APPEND /X:on`
3. `C:\> APPEND \WP51\DATA;\LOTUS\DATA`
4. `C:\> APPEND`
5. `C:\> APPEND ;`

1. `C:\> APPEND C:\DATA;A: /E` In this example, the directory \DATA will be added to the data path search; it will also be made part of the DOS environment since the /E parameter was specified. If you wish to view the contents of the DOS environment use the SET command.
2. `C:\> APPEND /X:on` In the next example, when the /X parameter is used with :on, DOS searches the specified directories for command files as well as data files. Any previously appended data paths will now also be searched for command files.
3. `C:\> APPEND \WP51\DATA;\LOTUS\DATA` In this example, the two directories \WP51\DATA and \LOTUS\DATA are made part of the search path when DOS looks for data files. No drive is specified, so DOS assumes that the directories are on Drive C, the default drive.
4. `C:\> APPEND` Appended directories can be displayed using the APPEND command. This example, the use of APPEND without fields or parameters, will cause DOS to display a list of directories that are part of the appended data directories.
5. `C:\> APPEND ;` Directories can be made part of the data path search; they can also be removed from the search path. In this example, the directories currently part of the APPEND search will be removed, since the command is followed by a semicolon (;).

■ COMMON MISTAKES

Shown below are some common mistakes encountered when using these commands. Some mistakes generate error messages. Many mistakes, however, cause execution errors, but generate no messages. Some sample mistakes are illustrated below.

1. `C:\> COMP C:*.TXT`
2. `C:\> BACKUP C:\ A:/S`
3. `C:\> BACKUP C:\WP51\*.* B:`
4. `C:\> BACKUP C:\ A:/A`
5. `C:\> XCOPY C:\LOTUS\*.* D:\123 /E`
6. `C:\> REPLACE C:\WP51\*.WP4 A:\*.WP5 /S`
7. `C:\> RESTORE A: C:\WP51\*.*`
8. `C:\> RESTORE B:*.* C:\DATA /S`
9. `C:\> ATTRIB -H CONFIG.SYS`

1. C:\> **COMP C:*.TXT** COMP compares two files or sets of files. In this example the second file has not been specified. In some versions of DOS you will be prompted for the second file or set of files. Normally both files or sets of files should be specified.
2. C:\> **BACKUP C:\ A:/S** BACKUP requires that a set of files be specified as part of the source information. The root directory of Drive C has been specified, but not the file or group of files. If the entire hard drive is to be backed up, the specification should be C:*.*; otherwise, specify the group of files intended, such as *.BAT or some other group. The /S parameter indicates all subdirectories of the root will be included, so the file will probably be specified using wildcards.
3. C:\> **BACKUP C:\WP51*.* B:** BACKUP is often used to back up an entire application program, such as WordPerfect or Lotus 1-2-3. Normally these applications contain subdirectory structures of the main application directory, such as \WP51\GR or \WP51\TUTOR. When backing up the application, you should use the /S parameter so that all subdirectories of the specified directory, in this case \WP51, are included. Specify the target field as B:/S.
4. C:\> **BACKUP C:\ A:/A** In this example, the drive and directory to be backed up are specified, but not the group of files. The /A parameter specifies that files be added to the backup diskettes. The source specification must include a file specification. An example of a correct specification would be C:*.*.
5. C:\> **XCOPY C:\LOTUS*.* D:\123 /E** XCOPY can copy a group of files from one subdirectory to another, but can also copy the entire subdirectory structure. When copying a directory structure, it also creates any subdirectories needed as long as the subdirectory structure on the source contains at least one file. If /E is specified, XCOPY creates a companion subdirectory on the target, even if that subdirectory on the source is empty. If the /E parameter is specified, you must also specify /S. In this example, the correct target specification is D:\123 /S/E.
6. C:\> **REPLACE C:\WP51*.WP4 A:*.WP5 /S** When executing REPLACE, specify the set of files to be copied as part of the source specification. In this example, that set of files is specified as *.WP4. The target specification can contain a drive letter and a path. It may not contain a file or set of files. The correct target specification can only be A:\; it cannot contain the file specification *.WP5.
7. C:\> **RESTORE A: C:\WP51*.*** When restoring application directories such as the \WP51 directory for WordPerfect, there will normally be a subdirectory structure associated with the application directory. However, as specified here, only the files in \WP51 would be restored; any subdirectories of

\WP51 would be ignored. Normally the specification for restoring an application will include the /S parameter, indicating that all subdirectories should also be included in the RESTORE operation.

8. `C:\> RESTORE B:*.* C:\DATA /S` The source specification for the RESTORE command should only contain a drive letter, not the file specification. The target specification includes the file or group of files to be restored. The fields in this command should be changed to RESTORE B: C:\DATA*.* /S.

9. `C:\> ATTRIB -H CONFIG.SYS` The ATTRIB command in versions before DOS 5 can only change or display two of the bits in the attribute byte: the archive bit and the read-only bit. It cannot change the hide bit. Therefore, the –H field is invalid as specified in this example unless using Version 5. To change the hide bit, acquire a set of DOS utilities that provide access to it or upgrade to Version 5.

QUESTIONS AND PROBLEMS

1. Which directories will be backed up if the /S parameter is specified with the BACKUP command and the pathname specifies \WP51?
2. Can the COPY or XCOPY commands be used to extract files from a backup disk to place them in a specified subdirectory on the hard drive?
3. What command should be issued to back up the entire hard drive that is addressed as Drive C?
4. What information from the attribute byte can be displayed using the ATTRIB command?
5. How can a selective group of files with the extension WK1 be restored from backup diskettes if the backup diskettes represent a backup of the entire hard drive?
6. What command allows files that are read-only to be overwritten on a hard drive? Are any special parameters required in order to perform the overwrite of these read-only files?
7. Can selective files be restored to the hard drive from a set of backup disks even though all files were backed up using the file spec *.*?
8. Can the COMPARE command be used to compare all the files in a directory to another set of files in a different directory? Must the two groups of files in different directories be identical in number?
9. What is the difference in function between XCOPY and DISKCOPY when copying sets of files involving more than one directory?

10. What happens to the archive bit in the attribute byte when a file is backed up to diskette?
11. Write a command or commands that will make the CONFIG.SYS file read-only and hide the file in the root directory.
12. Write a command or commands to install the HIMEM.SYS and SMARTDRV.SYS files from the DOS Version 5.00 installation disks onto the hard drive in the \DOS500 directory.
13. Write a command to compare the first 100 lines of two program files.
14. Write a command that will display a group of files and indicate whether a backup copy of those files has been made.
15. Write a command to restore the Lotus directory, including all its subdirectories, from a set of backup disks that contain all the files from the hard drive. Files should be restored into the \LOTUS22 directory.

CHAPTER 13

SYSTEM CONTROL (EXTERNAL COMMANDS)

INTRODUCTION

One of the functions performed by any operating system is *system control.* DOS provides two commands for performing system control operations. The first of these is SYS, a command for accessing and upgrading the two hidden files associated with the nucleus of DOS. The SYS command is used if you wish to upgrade your version of DOS, from Version 2.10 to Version 3.30 for example. The hidden files are normally never accessed directly by the user, since they are hidden and require a program that can address them. The use of the SYS command is but one step in a multistep process for upgrading from one version of DOS to another.

The second command, the SHARE command, is used when files are to be shared on a networked system. For those using their personal computer as a stand-alone machine, the SHARE command will never be used. It is discussed here only briefly since the focus of this book is the single-user system and the application of DOS to single-user system problems. Network problems in a multiuser system involving file sharing are normally handled by a network administrator.

The external commands discussed in this chapter are:

SYS
SHARE

THE TRANSFER SYSTEM FILES (SYS) COMMAND

The nucleus of DOS (DOS kernel) is composed of three files. These consist of a control program (COMMAND.COM) that normally resides in the root directory as a user file, and two hidden files, also in the root directory. The two hidden files are named IBMBIO.COM and IBMDOS.COM on IBM PC-DOS systems and IO.SYS and MSDOS.SYS on IBM-compatible MS-DOS systems. In order to perform a power-on sequence—either a cold boot or a warm boot—a set of these hidden files must be present. Furthermore, they must be consistent with the COMMAND.COM processor. In other words, the three files must be from the same version of DOS. You may not mix a DOS 3.30 COMMAND.COM processor with a set of hidden files from DOS 4.01, for example. If this is done, DOS will issue an error message at boot time, indicating that the three files are not from the same version of DOS. The message issued is "Incorrect DOS Version."

Table 13.1 shows the size of the files associated with various versions of PC-DOS. Since only COMMAND.COM is directly visible when a DIR command is issued, it is the only one for which the file size is readily visible.

To see the size of the two hidden files requires a program that can view hidden files on a disk. One such program is Norton Utilities. (For more information on installing DOS on a hard drive, see Appendices C, D, and E.) The format of the SYS command is:

```
SYS <source> <drive>
```

<source> specifies where the system files will be found that are to be copied. Both a drive letter and a directory name can be specified. If they are not specified, DOS copies from the current drive and directory.

<drive> specifies the drive followed by a colon where the system files are to be loaded.

TABLE 13.1 DOS Control Program Information Table

DOS Version	Filename	Size of File
1.0	COMMAND.COM	3231
	IBMBIO.COM	1920
	IBMDOS.COM	6400
1.1	COMMAND.COM	4959
	IBMBIO.COM	1920
	IBMDOS.COM	6400
2.0	COMMAND.COM	17664
	IBMBIO.COM	4608
	IBMDOS.COM	17152
2.1	COMMAND.COM	17792
	IBMBIO.COM	4736
	IBMDOS.COM	17024
3.0	COMMAND.COM	22042
	IBMBIO.COM	8964
	IBMDOS.COM	27920
3.1	COMMAND.COM	23210
	IBMBIO.COM	9564
	IBMDOS.COM	27760
3.2	COMMAND.COM	23791
	IBMBIO.COM	16389
	IBMDOS.COM	28477
3.3	COMMAND.COM	25307
	IBMBIO.COM	22100
	IBMDOS.COM	30159
4.0	COMMAND.COM	37888
	IBMBIO.COM	32810
	IBMDOS.COM	35984
5.0	COMMAND.COM	47845
	IBMBIO.COM	33430
	IBMDOS.COM	37394

The SYS command requires that space for the hidden files already be allocated on the disk that is to receive them. In the case of a system upgrade, that allocation has already been made. Before Version 5, the SYS command will not copy COMMAND.COM. The COMMAND.COM file must be copied with the COPY command in order to complete the transfer of the nucleus when doing a DOS upgrade.

□ **EXAMPLES**

1. A:\> **SYS A:\ C:**
2. A:\> **SYS C:**

1. A:\> **SYS A:\ C:** In the first example, the system has been booted from Drive A with a startup disk for the new version of DOS. The SYS.COM file must be on Drive A in order to execute the system transfer. Executing the SYS command transfers the two hidden files from Drive A to Drive C. This completes the first part of the upgrade procedure. Use the COPY command to transfer COMMAND.COM for the new version from Drive A to Drive C. Drive C will then be a bootable hard drive.
2. A:\> **SYS C:** In this example, only the target drive is specified, not the source drive. DOS assumes that the system transfer will be from the current directory on the current drive. System files are transferred from Drive A as the current drive to Drive C. Again, in versions before Version 5, you must use the COPY command to transfer COMMAND.COM to Drive C to make the transfer of all files associated with the nucleus consistent.

THE SHARE (SHARE) COMMAND

The SHARE command allows files to be shared by several programs on a networked system. If you have a single-user computer, you will not need the SHARE command. If your system is part of a network but file sharing is not necessary, the SHARE command will not be required.

The SHARE command is used only on networked systems that require file sharing. Networks of this sort are normally administered by someone assigned as the network administrator or system administrator. If your system has this requirement, talk with the administrator about sign-on and setup procedures related to file sharing and the use of the SHARE command.

The format of the SHARE command is:

SHARE </f:*space*> </l:*locks*>

Executing the SHARE program will install file-locking and file-sharing capabilities on your system. The SHARE program is installed by including a line in your CONFIG.SYS file similar to the following:

INSTALL=<*drive*><*path*>SHARE.EXE</F:*space*></L:*locks*>

<*drive*><*path*> specifies the drive (followed by a colon) and directory where the SHARE.EXE file is located.

</F:*space*> allocates file space for the storage area used to record file-sharing information. The default value is 2048 bytes.

</L:*locks*> sets the number of files that can be locked at any one time. The default value is 20 files.

Allocating space for file sharing requires space to record the path and filename of the file to be shared. On a hard disk system this will mean storing the drive letter, pathname, and filename of the file. This is the information required when a file is fully addressed when you copy it from one place to another. A typical file, which includes the drive letter, the directory name where it is located, and the name of the file, including the extension, will be 20 to 30 characters in length. A reasonable estimate for the file-sharing space required for each file is 25 bytes per filename to be shared. Sharing 50 files will require an estimated 1250 bytes of storage be specified with the /F parameter.

File locking is required when files are being accessed and should be locked to prevent other programs from accessing them. In accounting applications, as many as 20 to 30 files or more may be in use at one time, depending upon the number of terminals in operation and the number of accounting applications active at any one time. It would not be unusual for general ledger, payroll, accounts receivable, and accounts payable applications to be active in a typical day at a small company. Consult your network administrator when selecting values for both the /F and /L parameters in a multiterminal situation.

□ EXAMPLES

1. **INSTALL=C:\DOS330\SHARE.EXE /F:2048 /L:20**
2. **INSTALL=C:\DOS401\SHARE.EXE**
3. **INSTALL=C:\DOS401\SHARE.EXE /F:3072 /L:30**

1. **INSTALL=C:\DOS330\SHARE.EXE /F:2048 /L:20** In our first example, the INSTALL command should be one line in the CONFIG.SYS file that is read and executed at boot time. The SHARE.EXE file is found on Drive C in the \DOS330 directory. File locking for a maximum of 20 files is specified, and 2048 bytes are allocated for file-sharing storage space.
2. **INSTALL=C:\DOS401\SHARE.EXE** Here, the INSTALL command specifies the path for executing the SHARE command as part of the boot process in CONFIG.SYS. No parameters are specified, so the default values are in effect. File-sharing space will be 2048 bytes, with a default value for file locking of 20 files.

3. **INSTALL=C:\DOS401\SHARE.EXE /F:3072 /L:30** This INSTALL command should be one line in the CONFIG.SYS file that is read and executed at boot time. The SHARE.EXE file is found on Drive C in the \DOS401 directory. File locking for a maximum of 30 files is specified, and 3072 bytes are allocated for file-sharing storage space.

COMMON MISTAKES

Shown below are some common mistakes encountered when using these commands. Some mistakes generate error messages. Many mistakes, however, cause execution errors, but generate no messages. Some sample mistakes are illustrated below.

1. **INSTALL=SHARE.EXE**
2. **INSTALL=C:\SHARE.EXE**
3. C:\> **SYS**
4. C:\> **SYS C:**

1. **INSTALL=SHARE.EXE** The INSTALL command is included as part of the CONFIG.SYS file, but no path has been specified for locating and executing the SHARE command. The SHARE.EXE filename should be preceded by a drive letter and a pathname specifying the location of the SHARE.EXE file. If the SHARE.EXE file cannot be located, it will not be executed as part of the boot process during the power-on or warm boot procedure.
2. **INSTALL=C:\SHARE.EXE** The INSTALL command includes a drive letter and specifies the root directory as part of the path. The SHARE.EXE file is typically stored in the DOS directory, along with the rest of the DOS external commands. Since the SHARE.EXE file is not in the root directory, it will not be executed.
3. C:\> **SYS** The SYS command is specified for execution, but a destination drive is not specified. Likewise, the SYS command is executed from Drive C. Typically in a DOS upgrade the default drive should be Drive A, not Drive C.
4. C:\> **SYS C:** The SYS command is specified with a destination drive; however, the default drive is Drive C, not Drive A. An upgrade will be done from Drive C to Drive C, which accomplishes nothing. To upgrade the system hidden files, execute the SYS command with a default prompt of Drive A after first booting from Drive A with an upgrade system disk.

QUESTIONS AND PROBLEMS

1. Which files that are part of DOS are transferred by the SYS command?
2. What label or name is given to files copied by the SYS command?

3. Which files make up the DOS kernel or nucleus?
4. Why must the files for the DOS kernel all be from the same version of DOS?
5. How is the command processor file different from the other files that make up the DOS kernel?
6. How many bytes will be allocated for file sharing when the SHARE.EXE program is installed if the /F parameter is not specified?
7. What is the reason that files may be locked on a networked system?
8. In doing a system upgrade, what version of the operating system should be used to boot the computer that is being upgraded?
9. In doing a system upgrade from a floppy disk, what type of diskette must be in Drive A in order to accomplish the upgrade?
10. What are the default values of the /F and /L parameters associated with the SHARE command?
11. In what directory would you normally expect to find the SHARE.EXE file?
12. What files must be transferred to the hard drive in order to do a complete system upgrade to a new version of DOS?

CHAPTER 14

FILTER COMMANDS (EXTERNAL COMMANDS)

INTRODUCTION

Filter commands have several unique features. These features allow commands to be used as single commands, or in conjunction with other DOS commands. An example perhaps best illustrates the use of a filter command in conjunction with another DOS command.

A directory listing for the WordPerfect directory is to be displayed which contains a long list of files. If displayed using just the DIR command, the files will be listed based on their order on the disk. To help scan the list of files in search of a particular file, the listing can be displayed in alphabetic order. To do this, issue the DIR command in conjunction with the filter command SORT, as shown below:

```
C:\> DIR C:\WP51 ¦ SORT
```

The files contained in the \WP51 directory will be listed in alphabetic order by filename, making it much easier to scan the list for a particular file. (The double-bar symbol (¦) is usually found on the same key as the Backslash key.)

If this list of files is lengthy, it may also scroll by so fast that you won't have time to note a file of interest at the beginning of the list. To allow the list to be scanned in a controlled manner, type the following sequence of commands, which adds the MORE filter command to the sequence:

```
C:\> DIR C:\WP51 ¦ SORT ¦ MORE
```

The MORE command now causes the display of the listing to stop at the end of the first page of the listing. Pressing the Spacebar or any key causes the second page of the listing to display; pressing any key again causes the third page to display, and so forth.

The filter commands discussed in this chapter are:

MORE
SORT
FIND

Filter commands are all external commands in DOS. Filter commands have several special features that are common to all of them. These special features give these commands unique capabilities. To better understand these unique qualities let's look at what happens when the following command sequence is executed using the filter commands SORT and MORE.

```
C:\> DIR C:\WP51 ¦ SORT ¦ MORE
```

This command sequence requests that DOS execute a set of three commands, one after the other. Two of the commands are external files residing on the hard disk,

SORT and MORE, and one of the commands is an internal program (DIR) that is part of COMMAND.COM. DOS will process each of these commands one at a time. The sequence of events will be as follows:

1. The DIR command will be executed. The listing of files will be for the \WP51 directory on Drive C. The listing will be in the order that the files were found on the disk within this directory. This listing would normally be sent to the display screen. Instead, the directory listing is copied to Drive C as a temporary output file. The double bar (¦) indicates that another command is to be executed.
2. Because the DIR command is "chained" via the double-bar symbol to the SORT command, DOS searches for and loads an external file, SORT.EXE, into memory. It passes control to the SORT command and tells the SORT command that its input is a temporary file on Drive C. The SORT command executes, reads the temporary file, and begins sorting the directory listing from this input file. Again, the output from the sort would normally go to the display screen. Because the SORT command is chained via the double-bar symbol to another command, DOS instead writes the sorted directory listing to Drive C as another temporary file. The double-bar symbol following the SORT command again indicates that another command is to be executed.
3. The SORT command is chained via the double-bar symbol to the MORE command, so DOS searches for and loads an external file, MORE.COM, into memory. It passes control to the MORE command and tells the MORE command that its input is a temporary file on Drive C. The MORE command executes, reads the temporary file, and begins organizing the directory listing from this input file into a series of page displays. The output from the MORE command would normally go to the display screen. Because the MORE command is the last command in the sequence and is not chained to any other command, the output is sent to the display screen as the standard output device.

It is important to realize that for each occurrence of the double-bar symbol, a temporary file will be written to disk. Therefore, there must be sufficient space on the disk to accommodate the temporary file. The temporary file is always written to the default drive and directory. In the examples shown here, these temporary files went to the root directory of Drive C. Normally there is sufficient space on a hard drive to accommodate the temporary file or files. In cases where these files are written to a floppy drive, such as Drive A, there may not be sufficient space to accommodate the temporary file or files. In such cases the command will not execute and a message "Insufficient disk space" will be issued.

By using the double bar as a chaining symbol between commands, a sequence of commands is executed, one after the other. This example also illustrates some of the special features associated with the two filter commands SORT and MORE. These special features are:

- A filter command can receive its input from a temporary file, as was the case with the SORT command in this example.
- A filter command can be chained to another command. It can be chained to another DOS command and receive input from that command; it can also be chained to another DOS filter command and send its output to disk as a temporary file so that another command can read that temporary file as input. In the example above, the MORE command received its input from the SORT command.
- All DOS commands, including filter commands, write their output automatically to disk as a temporary file if DOS detects that the command is chained to a filter command.
- Finally, the temporary files written to the default drive, usually Drive C, are only temporary. DOS will automatically delete the temporary files once the sequence has been executed and the temporary files are no longer needed.

Filter commands add an extra dimension of flexibility to DOS. They can also be used with actual files on the disk; their use is not confined solely to use with other DOS commands. Thus, the SORT command can be used to sort a wide variety of files based on a character's position within each record. An accounting file could be sorted on the description field or the account number field, for example. The examples associated with each command below illustrate the diversity of uses for each of the filter commands.

THE MORE (MORE) COMMAND

The MORE command displays a file listing in page format, one screen at a time. The MORE command provides the same type of paging control that the /P parameter does when used with the DIR command. The DIR command is the only command that provides a paging parameter to control the output listing. All other commands send their output to the screen, one line after the other. If the output listing happens to be three pages in length, the listing just scrolls on the screen. With the speed of today's 80386 and 80486 processor chips, the listing whips across the screen at a speed that makes it impossible to read. No other command other than DIR provides a paging parameter to control the display. Instead, the MORE command can be chained to any command if control of the output listing in page format is desired.

The MORE command can be used in a chaining sequence, or it can be used by itself to read a file and display it in paged format. If a file is to be read as an input file and then formatted for output in a series of displays, the less-than (<) symbol is used to read the input file. In the example below, the INSTALL.BAT file is to be read by the MORE command, then displayed a page at a time. The command line would appear as:

```
C:\> MORE < INSTALL.BAT
```

The format of the MORE command is:

MORE < *<filename>*

<filename> is an optional field. It is the file that is to be displayed in a paged format. If *<filename>* is used it must be preceded by a less-than symbol (<), indicating that the file is an input file to the MORE command.

□ **EXAMPLES**

1. C:\> **MORE < AUTOEXEC.BAT**
2. C:\> **TYPE AUTOEXEC.BAT ¦ MORE**
3. C:\> **DIR ¦ MORE**

1. C:\> **MORE < AUTOEXEC.BAT** In this example, the MORE command is used to display the file AUTOEXEC.BAT, one page at a time. The AUTOEXEC.BAT file will be read as an input file and set up in page format. MORE will then display the file one page at a time, pausing after displaying a page so that each page can be reviewed as needed. Striking any key will cause the next page to be displayed until you reach the end of the document or file.
2. C:\> **TYPE AUTOEXEC.BAT ¦ MORE** This example is identical in function to the previous example. Using the TYPE command to display the file is much less efficient, however, because two commands (TYPE and MORE) are executed rather than only the MORE command. In this example, the TYPE command reads the AUTOEXEC.BAT file. Because TYPE is chained to the MORE command, a temporary file is written to disk for input to MORE. The MORE command is then loaded and executed. MORE reads the temporary file created by TYPE from disk. MORE formats the file for display one page at a time, and then sends it to the monitor for display. When displaying files in paged format, it is recommended that the MORE command be used directly with the file, as shown in Example 1.
3. C:\> **DIR ¦ MORE** In this example, the internal command DIR is chained to the filter command MORE. The directory listing is developed for the root directory on Drive C, because that is the default. This output file is written to disk and then read by the MORE command. The directory listing is then displayed in page format, stopping at the end of each page. Subsequent pages can be displayed by pressing the Spacebar or any other key.

THE SORT (SORT) COMMAND

The SORT command is used to arrange the records in a file based on the binary code representation for particular characters. Records can be sorted in either ascending or descending order. They can also be sorted based on a particular column or position in the record. SORT can be used in conjunction with files created by DOS commands, but it is not restricted to use only with DOS-created files. Files created by accounting programs, database programs, and others can also be processed by SORT if they need to be reorganized. The format of the SORT command is:

SORT /R /+*<column>* < *<filename>*

/R causes the file to be sorted in reverse order or descending order rather than ascending order. The default value is a sort in ascending order.

/+*<column>* specifies the particular column that will be used as the basis for the sort. The default column, if none is specified, is column 1. *<Column>* is equivalent to a character's position within the record.

<filename> is an optional field. It is the file that is to be sorted if the file was not generated by a previous command. If *<filename>* is used, it must be preceded by a less-than symbol (<) indicating that the file is an input file to the SORT command.

□ EXAMPLES

1. C:\> **SORT < DATAB.TXT**
2. C:\> **SORT/+15 < ACCTFILE**
3. C:\> **DIR ¦ SORT/R**
4. C:\> **DIR ¦ SORT/R/+14 > PRN**

1. C:\> **SORT < DATAB.TXT** A file DATAB.TXT is read as an input file by the SORT command and arranged in ascending alphabetic order. The records will be rearranged based on the character in position 1 or column 1 of each record. The sort is based on the default parameters, because no parameters were specified as part of the command. The sorted output file is sent to the display for viewing.
2. C:\> **SORT/+15 < ACCTFILE** A file ACCTFILE is read as an input file by the SORT command and arranged in ascending alphabetic order. The records will be rearranged based on the character in position 15 of each record. The sorted output file is sent to the display for viewing.
3. C:\> **DIR ¦ SORT/R** The DIR command is chained to the SORT command by the double-bar symbol. The output of the DIR command is sent to the disk as a temporary file. That file is then read by the SORT command and sorted in descending order, because the R parameter is specified. The sort will be based on filename, because the filename field begins in column 1 of each record. Filenames that begin with *z* or characters at the end of the alphabet will appear first in the display listing, and filenames beginning with *a* or characters at the beginning of the alphabet will appear at the end of the list.
4. C:\> **DIR ¦ SORT/R/+14 > PRN** The DIR command is chained to the SORT command by the double-bar symbol. The output of the DIR command is

sent to the disk as a temporary file. That file is then read by the SORT command and sorted in descending order, because the /R parameter is specified. The sort will be based on the size field of the directory listing, because the Size field begins in column 14 of each record. The files will be sorted in descending order by size. The sorted output file will be sent to the printer rather than the display, because the command specifies that the output be redirected to the PRN output device.

THE FIND COMMAND

The FIND command is used to search a file or files based on a search string, and select those records for display that meet the search criteria. The search can be based on the occurrence of the string within the records of the file; it can also be based on the nonoccurrence of the string in each record of the file. The format of the FIND command is:

FIND /V /N /C /I <*"string"*> < <*filename*>

/V specifies that the search will be for records that do not contain the string.

/N specifies that the line number or record number will be included with each line of output.

/C specifies that only the count of the number of records that meet the search string criteria will be displayed, not the records containing the string.

/I specifies that the search should ignore the case of the string specified (uppercase or lowercase). Instead, search only on the character string itself. This parameter is new with DOS Version 5.00, and is not included with versions prior to 5.00.

<*"string"*> is the character string to be used in the search of each record. The character string must be enclosed in quotation marks.

<*filename*> is the name of the file or files to be searched for the specified string. If more than one file is to be searched, the filenames should be separated by spaces.

□ EXAMPLES

1. C:\> **FIND "Cons" < DATAB.TXT**
2. C:\> **FIND/V "Taxes" < ACCTS**
3. C:\> **FIND/C "William" < RECORDS**
4. C:\> **FIND/V/C "Smith" < DATAB.TXT**
5. C:\> **FIND/V/N/I "Mary" < RECORDS**
6. C:\> **DIR ¦ FIND " COM" ¦ MORE**
7. C:\> **DIR ¦ FIND/V "WK1" > PRN**

1. C:\> **FIND "Cons" < DATAB.TXT** A file named DATAB.TXT is searched for the string *Cons* in each of its records. Because no parameters associated with the command are specified, each record containing the string *Cons* will be displayed on the system console screen.
2. C:\> **FIND/V "Taxes" < ACCTS** A file named ACCTS is searched for the string *Taxes* in each of its records. Because the /V parameter is specified the records displayed will be those records that do not contain the string. The records not containing the string *Taxes* will be displayed on the console.
3. C:\> **FIND/C "William" < RECORDS** A file named RECORDS is searched for the string *William* in each of its records. Because the /C parameter is specified, only the count of the records containing the string *William* will be displayed. The number representing the count will be displayed on standard output.
4. C:\> **FIND/V/C "Smith" < DATAB.TXT** A file named DATAB.TXT is searched for the string *Smith* in each of its records. Because both the /V and the /C parameters are included, the search will be for records that do not contain the string. Only the count of the records will be displayed, because the /C parameter was specified as part of the command line.
5. C:\> **FIND/V/N/I "Mary" < RECORDS** A file named RECORDS is searched for the string *Mary* in each of its records. Because the /V and /N parameters are specified, the search will be for records not containing the string. The display of records will be preceded by the record number. Because the parameter /I was specified, the search will ignore upper- and lowercase distinctions; therefore, the search will be on the string *mary* and *MARY,* or any combination of upper- and lowercase letters such as *MaRy.*
6. C:\> **DIR ¦ FIND " COM" ¦ MORE** Three commands are chained together in this example: the DIR command will generate an output file that is sent to the FIND command. The FIND command will search for the string *COM*, but it is the *COM* string preceded by a space. This is essentially a search on the extension field COM. All records will be files with a COM extension. This listing will then be sent to the MORE command for display, one page at a time.
7. C:\> **DIR ¦ FIND/V "WK1" > PRN** The DIR command will generate an output file that is sent to the FIND command. This output file is searched for the string *WK1.* The listing produced will contain all of the files which do not have WK1 in them, the result of using the /V parameter. Redirection is used to send this list to the printer.

COMMON MISTAKES

Shown below are some common mistakes encountered when using these commands. Some mistakes generate error messages. Many mistakes, however, cause execution errors, but generate no messages.

1. C:\> **MORE**
2. C:\> **MORE > AUTOEXEC.BAT**
3. C:\> **SORT/ +10 < CUSTLST.TXT**
4. C:\> **DIR | SORT/ R**
5. C:\> **DIR | SORT < DIRLIST**
6. C:\> **FIND < A:\DATA\CUSTLST.TXT**
7. C:\> **FIND/N/C "CUST" < DATAB.TXT**
8. C:\> **FIND/V "Cust" < DATAB.TXT**

1. C:\> **MORE** The MORE command is used here, but no file has been specified as an input file. The command executes and the system hangs up because there is no file to read. Use Ctrl-C to cancel the command. Then retype the command and specify the file that is to be displayed in a paged format.

2. C:\> **MORE > AUTOEXEC.BAT** The MORE command is executed, but no file is specified as an input file. The greater-than (>) sign indicates redirection. Use the less-than symbol (<) to indicate that a file is to be read as an input file to the MORE command.

3. C:\> **SORT/ +10 < CUSTLST.TXT** The SORT command is executed and an input file is specified. When using a parameter with SORT, there can be no space between the slash symbol and +10. Retype the beginning of the command as SORT/+10 followed by the less-than symbol and the name of the file.

4. C:\> **DIR | SORT/ R** The DIR command will be chained to the SORT command. If the directory listing is to be sorted in descending order, there cannot be a space between the slash and the R. Retype the command as DIR | SORT/R.

5. C:\> **DIR | SORT < DIRLIST** This command indicates that the directory listing is to be sorted as well as the file DIRLIST. SORT cannot be used to sort two different files in a single operation. To save the sorted directory listing as a file, use the redirection symbol (>). This command should be typed as DIR | SORT > DIRLIST so that the directory listing is saved as a file on the disk.

6. C:\> **FIND < A:\DATA\CUSTLST.TXT** The FIND command is executed on the specified file CUSTLST.TXT. When using the FIND command, a string must be specified and enclosed in quotes. In this example, no search string is specified.

7. C:\> **FIND/N/C "CUST" < DATAB.TXT** The FIND command is used here, along with two parameters. The problem is that the parameters are not

consistent. The /C parameter indicates that only a count of the number of records meeting the criteria is to be displayed. The /N parameter indicates that each record satisfying the search string is to be displayed, along with the record number. The two parameters /N and /C are not consistent and should not be used together.

8. **C:\> FIND/V "Cust" < DATAB.TXT** A search is to be done on a string *Cust* as specified within the quotes. The search string is case-sensitive. The records contain a string *CUST* (all capitals), so what is specified in the search string is not consistent with what is stored in each of the records in the file DATAB.TXT. The search string used in the FIND command must always be consistent with the string appearing in the data records. This command should be retyped as FIND/V "CUST" < DATAB.TXT.

QUESTIONS AND PROBLEMS

1. What are the key characteristics of filter commands that make them different from other DOS commands?
2. What does the double-bar symbol (¦) do when used between two commands?
3. Can the MORE command be used with a file prepared by an application program?
4. Why is additional space needed on the default drive when commands are chained together using the double-bar symbol?
5. What happens to the temporary files that are written to the disk when commands are chained together?
6. What does the /V parameter do when used with the FIND command?
7. Will using the FIND command on the string "CUST" produce the same results as a FIND used on the string "cust"?
8. Can the FIND command be used to search multiple files for a given string such as "consumer"?
9. Can multiple parameters /V, /N, /C, and /I be used with the FIND command, such as FIND/V/N?
10. Is there an advantage to using the FIND command before the SORT command when searching a file on a string that is also to be sorted?
11. What parameter must be specified with FIND to make the string search insensitive to upper- and lowercase?
12. Write a Directory command and a filter command that will produce a listing sorted in ascending order by filename.

13. Write a filter command that will produce a directory listing of all the EXE extension files in the DOS directory on the printer.
14. Can the question in Problem 13 be solved without the use of a filter command?
15. Can SORT be used with text files created with EDLIN or EDIT in order to reorder information?

CHAPTER 15

INPUT AND OUTPUT CONTROL (EXTERNAL COMMANDS)

INTRODUCTION

One of the primary functions performed by any operating system is interfacing to various input and output devices connected to the computer. **Input and output** control allows the control of standard devices on the computer, such as the console (CON), the standard system printer (PRN), and the serial communications ports (COM1 through COM4). The control of nonstandard devices requires additional software.

DOS provides device drivers as part of the basic operating system for handling the DOS standard system devices. These standard devices include the keyboard and the display monitor addressed as CON, the standard system printer addressed as LPT1 or PRN, other parallel printers addressed as LPT2 and LPT3, the communications ports addressed as COM1 through COM4, disk drives addressed as A: through Z:, the auxiliary device addressed as AUX, and the null device addressed as NUL.

Nonstandard devices such as a mouse, a flat-bed scanner, extended and expanded memory, and other hardware require that device driver software be loaded and that a DEVICE= line be included in the CONFIG.SYS file. (A list of the additional device drivers included with DOS 5 is provided in Appendix G.) Some of these device drivers enhance operations on standard system devices. The ANSI.SYS file, for example, extends the capabilities of the console (CON) device.

This chapter discusses some of the DOS routines for setting up both standard and nonstandard devices, as well as commands used to take advantage of versatility built into many dot-matrix printers on the market today.

The external commands discussed in this chapter are:

DOSKEY
MODE
ASSIGN
PRINT
KEYB and KEYB*xx*
GRAFTABL
GRAPHICS

THE DOSKEY COMMAND

One of the new features added with the release of DOS 5 is the DOSKEY command, which was introduced briefly in Chapter 2. DOSKEY records and maintains in memory a sequence of commands that had been previously executed. In this chapter, we discuss the full range of features available through DOSKEY.

DOSKEY provides three basic capabilities to simplify and enhance keyboard operations. The first of these is maintaining a record of commands that have previously been executed. Using the default buffer size of 512 bytes, DOSKEY will maintain a record of approximately 25 commands. These can then be recalled, listed, edited, and executed using control-key sequences available at the keyboard.

The second feature available through DOSKEY is a capability to execute a series of commands. Chapter 14 discussed filter commands that could be chained together to execute a sequence of commands. The control symbol linking these commands was the chaining or double-bar (¦) symbol. With DOSKEY, any command can be linked with any other in a sequence. The control symbol linking the commands together through DOSKEY is the Ctrl-T key sequence, displayed as a paragraph symbol (¶).

Finally, DOSKEY can be used to create and save a command sequence for later use as a file. The file can be saved as a macro, a memory-based file much like a Terminate and Stay Resident routine (TSR). The file can also be saved as a batch file with a BAT extension. In the case of a macro file, you must enter it every time you start DOS, because everything in memory is lost when the computer is powered down. In the case of the batch file, it is available every time DOS is started because it is saved to disk as a permanent file. The format of the DOSKEY command is:

DOSKEY /H /Insert /M /Overstrike /Reinstall /bufsize=<*size*> <*macro*>=<*commands*>

/H or **/history** displays all commands that are currently in memory that DOSKEY has recorded. Macros that are created can use the /history parameter to send all the commands in the macro to a file using redirection (>).

/Insert specifies that DOSKEY should use the keyboard in insert mode rather than typeover mode. DOS inserts all characters typed into the text or commands, rather than replacing the characters.

/M or **/macros** displays all macros currently stored in memory. Remember that these will all be lost when the computer's power is turned off, because they are memory-resident rather than disk-based routines.

/Overstrike specifies that DOSKEY should use the keyboard in typeover mode. DOSKEY assumes /overstrike or typeover mode as its default value unless /insert is specified.

/Reinstall results in a new copy of DOSKEY being loaded into memory as a TSR. Previously recorded commands and macros are lost when a new copy is loaded. The old copy remains in memory, but the new copy takes over the command-recording function. Consider putting DOSKEY in your AUTOEXEC.BAT file and rebooting if DOSKEY needs reinstallation for some reason.

/bufsize=<*size*> specifies the size of the memory area in which command recording will be held. /Bufsize must be specified at the time DOSKEY is installed or reinstalled. The default value for /bufsize, if none is specified, is 512 bytes. This will generally record 20 to 25 commands of average size.

<macro>*=*<commands> specifies that DOSKEY should create a program whose name will be what is entered as macro and save it in memory. The name *macro* is then assigned to the command or set of commands that follow the equals sign (=). This set of commands is executed whenever the name *macro* is typed at the DOS prompt. To delete the macro, type its name followed by the equals sign, and press the Enter key.

When the DOSKEY command is executed, either through the AUTOEXEC.BAT file or by executing it at the DOS prompt, it begins keeping a record of all commands that are executed. DOSKEY maintains this file of commands for recall, modification, and execution. In general, you will want to include DOSKEY as part of your AUTOEXEC.BAT file so that its features are available every time you turn on the computer. To execute DOSKEY, if it is not already part of your AUTOEXEC.BAT file, type the sequence shown below:

```
C:\> DOSKEY
```

This command will install DOSKEY with the default 512-byte buffer for saving commands. To see how DOSKEY works, type the following sequence of commands:

```
C:\>cls
C:\>date
C:\>time
C:\>ver
C:\>vol
```

When DOS prompts for the entry of date, time, and so on, just press the Enter key. You have now entered five commands. Without the help of DOSKEY, the only command available through the keyboard buffer would be the last command typed (VOL). Press the function key F3 to recall the last command from the keyboard buffer. Press Enter to execute it. With DOSKEY, however, all the commands are available for recall.

To retrieve the five commands, press the F7 function key. DOSKEY now displays the entire sequence on the screen:

```
C:\>
1: cls
2: date
3: time
```

```
4: ver
5: vol
C:\>
```

In addition to displaying the entire sequence, the commands are numbered so they can be recalled by line number and executed. Press the Up Arrow key and DOS displays the last command (VOL). If Up Arrow is pressed again, VOL is replaced by the VER command. As you might guess, Down Arrow has just the opposite effect of Up Arrow.

To request a specific command by line number, use the F9 function key. To request the TIME command, press the function key F9. DOSKEY will display this message:

```
C:\>Line number: _
```

Type the number 3 to request the TIME command and DOS displays:

```
C:\>time
```

The Page Up key moves to the top of the list and recalls the first command in the stored list (CLS). Page Down moves to the bottom of the list and recalls the last command entered (VOL). To clear the buffer and delete the entire list, use the Alt-F7 key sequence where F7 refers to function key F7.

Table 15.1 describes the functions performed by various keys in using DOSKEY. These keys, combined with the four function key sequences F7, F9, Alt-F7, and Alt-F10, implement the capabilities of DOSKEY. The function key sequences are shown in Table 15.2

TABLE 15.1 DOSKEY Control and Editing Sequences

Key Sequence	Function
Up Arrow [↑]	Displays the previous command in the list based on the command pointer.
Down Arrow [↓]	Displays the next command in the list based on the command pointer.
Left Arrow [←]	Moves the cursor one character to the left from its current position.
Right Arrow [→]	Moves the cursor one character to the right from its current position.
Page Up	Moves the command pointer to the top of the list and displays the first command.
Page Down	Moves the command pointer to the bottom and displays the last command.
Ctrl-[←]	Moves the cursor one word to the right.

"continued"

TABLE 15.1 DOSKEY Control and Editing Sequences (continued)

Key Sequence	Function
Ctrl-[→]	Moves the cursor one word to the left.
Home	Moves the cursor to the beginning of the command
End	Moves the cursor to the end of the command
Ctrl-Home	Deletes from the current cursor position to the beginning of the command.
Ctrl-End	Deletes from the cursor location to the end of the command.
Ins	Puts the keyboard into insert mode so that characters are added at the position of the cursor.
Del	Deletes characters at the location of the cursor; the cursor remains in its current position.
Esc	Erases the command currently displayed.

TABLE 15.2 DOSKEY Function Key Sequences

Function Key	Function
F7	Recalls to the screen the entire list of commands in DOSKEY's command buffer.
Alt-F7	Delets all the commands from DOSKEY's command buffer and leaves it empty.
F9	Displays the message "Line number" and allows a specific command to be recalled from the DOSKEY command buffer, based on its line number.
Alt-F10	Deletes all macro definitions.

The second DOSKEY capability allows a sequence of commands to be executed in a manner similar to the filter commands discussed in Chapter 14. DOSKEY allows any set of commands to be executed as a sequence; it is not limited to just filter commands. Unlike filter commands, however, no input and output is passed from command to command. Each command executes as a separate command, but the entire sequence is executed much like a batch file, except that the sequence is initiated from the DOS prompt. Commands are separated using the Ctrl-T key sequence. Ctrl-T will display on the screen as a paragraph mark (¶). The example below illustrates a sample sequence using three commands:

```
C:\> CLS <Ctrl-T> MD \TEMP1 <Ctrl-T> DIR \TEMP1
```

The commands CLS, followed by MD \TEMP1, followed by DIR \TEMP1, will be executed in sequence. The MD \TEMP1 and DIR \TEMP1 commands will display on the screen as they execute, along with any messages generated. The screen should display the following:

```
C:\> MD \TEMP1

C:\> DIR \TEMP1
   Volume in Drive C has no label
   Volume Serial Number is 34E4-0DAF
   Directory of C:\TEMP1>
.            <DIR> 09-01-92 10:54 a
..           <DIR> 09-01-92 10:54 a
       2 file(s) 0 bytes
       4325376 bytes free
```

Command sequences of this type may be entered up to the limit of the keyboard buffer's capability to hold the characters. The typical keyboard buffer size is 132 characters. The Ctrl-T character sequence is useful in executing small sequences of related commands. For larger sequences and for sequences that you may wish to retain, use the macro feature or a batch file.

The third and final feature included in DOSKEY is the macro feature. If a command sequence is to be used several times in a computer session, create and save the command sequence as a macro. The command sequence becomes a memory-based file, much like a TSR. In the case of the macro file, it must be entered every time DOS is started because everything in memory is lost when the computer is powered down. In the case of a batch file, it is available every time DOS is started because it is saved to disk as a permanent file.

Table 15.3 shows character sequences that can be included to control command operations when defining a macro.

To create a DOSKEY macro, enter the command, type the macro name, then an equals sign, followed by the command or commands that are part of the macro. If multiple commands are entered, they must be separated by the Ctrl-T character. Some examples will illustrate the creation of several DOSKEY macros. Type the following at the DOS prompt, first making sure that DOSKEY has been installed:

1. `C:\>` **`DOSKEY QFORMT=format $1 /q /u`**
2. `C:\>` **`DOSKEY DIRN=dir $1$2 /o:n /p`**
3. `C:\>` **`DOSKEY DIRL=cd \temp $t dir /w`**

The first macro performs a quick and unconditional format of a diskette in the drive specified by $1. To perform a quick format on a diskette in Drive A, enter the command QFORMT a:. The a: will be substituted for $1 when the command is executed.

TABLE 15.3 Macro Character Control Sequences

Character	Function
$B or $b	Sends macro output to a command. This character sequence has the same effect as the piping character (¦) at the command line.
$G or $g	Use these special characters to redirect output to another device or to a file on disk instead of the screen. This is equivalent to the redirection character (>).
GG or gg	Appends output to the end of a file rather than overwriting the existing file. This is equivalent to the append symbol for output (>>).
$L or $l	Use this special character to redirect input. Input will then be read from another device or a file rather than the keyboard device. This is equivalent to the input redirection symbol (<).
$T or $t	Used to separate commands typed at the DOS prompt. Can also be used with commands contained in a DOSKEY macro.
$$	Specifies the dollar sign ($) character.
$1 thru $9	These characters represent a sequence of variables which can be entered at the command line. $1 is the first variable, $2 is the second variable, and so on. The $1 through $9 variables are used in the same way with macros that %1 through %9 are used as batch file variables.
$*	These characters are equivalent to all the information entered at the command line associated with a macro name.

In the second example, a macro called DIRN provides a directory listing on a drive and a directory specified at the time the macro is executed. The directory listing will be sorted alphabetically in filename order and will be displayed a page at a time. To execute this macro for the \DOS500 directory on Drive C, just enter the command DIRN C: \DOS500. C: substitutes in the command for $1 and \DOS500 substitutes for $2.

In the last example, two commands are chained together by the $t chaining parameter from Table 15.3. The macro DIRL first changes to a directory named \TEMP and then provides a directory listing in wide mode.

□ **EXAMPLES**

1. C:\> **DOSKEY /reinstall /bufsize=750**
2. C:\> **DOSKEY /m**
3. C:\> **DOSKEY /h > dkcommnd.TXT**
4. C:\> **DOSKEY /m > dkmacro.TXT**
5. C:\DOS500> **cls <Ctrl-T> cd \ <Ctrl-T> dir /o:g /p**
6. C:\> **DOSKEY DIRSUB=dir C:\ /o:g > PRN**

1. `C:\>` **`DOSKEY /reinstall /bufsize=750`** DOSKEY is reinstalled because that parameter has been specified. The new installation will include a DOSKEY buffer of 750 bytes instead of the default value of 512. This will provide an expanded space for storing commands and macros.
2. `C:\>` **`DOSKEY /m`** Here, DOSKEY will provide a list of all macros that have been stored in memory during this session. Macros are memory-resident programs and are only available during the current session. To save to a file the macros must be redirected using the redirection symbol (>).
3. `C:\>` **`DOSKEY /h > dkcommnd.TXT`** In this example, a list of all the DOS commands currently stored in memory by DOSKEY is saved as a file named dkcommnd.txt. The file is saved to the root directory of Drive C.
4. `C:\>` **`DOSKEY /m > dkmacro.TXT`** In this example, a list of all DOSKEY macros is redirected and saved as a file named dkmacro.txt.
5. `C:\DOS500>` **`cls <Ctrl-T> cd \ <Ctrl-T> dir /o:g /p`** Three DOS commands are chained together to be executed as part of one command line. The Ctrl-T key sequence is used to separate the commands. The second and third commands will display to the screen before executing. First, the display screen is cleared; then the root directory is set as the default directory; finally, the directory listing is displayed one page at a time. The directory listing is sorted, with directory entries displayed first, followed by files. The entries are not sorted in any order, only grouped by directories, then files.
6. `C:\>` **`DOSKEY DIRSUB=dir C:\ /o:g > PRN`** In the last example, a DOSKEY macro is created named DIRSUB. The macro consists of a directory command that displays the root directory listing on Drive C on the printer. The directory listing will be sorted, with directory entries grouped together and displaying before the group of files in the root directory.

THE MODE (MODE) COMMAND

The MODE command is used to control various devices that are part of DOS's standard devices. Standard devices include the console device, which includes the keyboard and the display screen (CON), the standard system printer (LPT1 or PRN), the communications ports (COM1, COM2, etc.), and others. In DOS Version 3.30 and later, MODE can also be used to set code-page information. MODE can be used to accomplish the following functions with the associated devices listed:

Console Device (CON)

- Set display screen characteristics—black and white or color.
- Set the number of columns to be displayed (either 40 or 80 characters per line).
- Set the number of lines to be displayed per screen.

- Set the keyboard repeat rate.
- Set up code pages associated with National Language Support.

System Printer (LPT1, LPT2, LPT3, or PRN)

- Set the number of lines per inch and the printer width for a parallel printer.
- Associate the printer to be used with a parallel printer port other than LPT1.
- Connect a serial printer by directing output from a parallel port to one of the serial ports.

Communications Port (COM1, COM2, COM3, or COM4)

- Set the communications parameters associated with one of the serial communications ports.

System Devices

- Check the status of various system devices.

MODE AND THE CONSOLE DEVICE

The following MODE commands are associated with control of the console device (CON). The keyboard is the console input device; the display screen is the console output device.

MODE: Set Display Screen Characteristics. The MODE command can be used to set the display screen characteristics, either color or monochrome, and to set the number of columns to be displayed, either 40 or 80 columns. A shift may occur in certain monitors so that the image is not centered on the screen. In that case, the MODE command can be used to shift the image either left or right for centering purposes, and to display a test pattern.

The form of the MODE command for display screen control is:

```
MODE <method>, <shift>,T
```

`<method>` selects the graphics adapter, either monochrome or color, and also allows you to specify the width of the display. Table 15.4 explains the values that can be specified by *<method>* and the meaning of each of the values.

`<shift>` can be specified as either *l* or *r* (left or right) to shift an off-center image either left or right on the display. For a 40-column display, the image can be shifted either one column left or one column right. For an 80-column display, the image can be shifted two columns either left or right.

`T` specifies that a test pattern should be displayed so that you can determine if the image is centered on the screen. A prompt is also displayed that asks if the leftmost and rightmost characters can be seen. If you reply "N" to the question, the image is shifted one character left or right and the prompt is again displayed. This continues until the image is centered and you reply "Y." DOS then returns to the standard DOS system prompt.

TABLE 15.4 **Display Screen Method Table**

Value	Characteristics
bw40	Color graphics adapter, color disabled, 40 column
bw80	Color graphics adapter, color disabled, 80 column
co40	Color graphics adapter, color enabled, 40 column
co80	Color graphics adapter, color enabled, 80 column
mono	Monochrome display adapter
40	Color graphics adapter, 40 column display
80	Color graphics adapter, 80 column display

MODE: Set Number of Lines to be Displayed. This form of the MODE command specifies the number of lines that can be displayed on the screen at a single time. For this command to be operational, the CONFIG.SYS file must specify DEVICE=ANSI.SYS when the system is initially booted. The MODE command can also be used to set the number of columns at the same time.

The format of the MODE command for display control is:

MODE CON cols=<*columns*> lines=<*lines*>

CON is the name of the output console device.

cols=<*columns*> specifies the number of columns in a line on the screen. <*Columns*> can be set to either 40 or 80.

lines=<*lines*> specifies the maximum number of lines to be displayed on the screen. <*Lines*> can be set to any one of three values: 25, 43, or 50.

Many applications reset the standard values associated with the standard system devices such as the keyboard and the display screen. These settings may override those settings made by the MODE command. To set the lines on the display screen permanently so that applications will not override the value, specify the lines setting as part of the DEVICE= line in the CONFIG.SYS file as DEVICE=ANSI.SYS/L, where L specifies the number of display lines (25, 43, 50). If problems arise with an application such as a spreadsheet, remove the L specification from the CONFIG.SYS and reboot.

MODE: Set Keyboard Repeat Rate. The MODE command provides control of how quickly a key repeats when held down, and how long the keyboard waits or pauses before beginning to repeat when held. The system has built-in settings, so under normal typing conditions, it is not necessary to change the settings. However, a very fast typist, or someone using a keyboard extensively throughout the day, may want to adjust these keyboard rates to maximize input speed. The format of the MODE command for keyboard repeat rate control is:

MODE CON rate=<*speed*> delay=<*pause*>

CON refers to the console input device—the keyboard.

rate=<*speed*> specifies the speed of repeat action when a key is held down. The rate is set by specifying a number between 1 and 32. A value of 1 results in the slowest repeat action (about two repetitions per second), whereas a value of 32 results in the fastest rate (about 30 repetitions per second).

delay=<*pause*> specifies the amount of time the system should wait, after a key is pressed, before beginning the repeating action. The values can range from 1 to 4, where each unit is approximately 0.25 seconds. A setting of 1 results in a delay of 0.25 seconds; a setting of 4 will cause a delay of approximately 1 second before beginning the repeating action.

MODE: Setting and Displaying Code Pages. The MODE command can be used to set and display code pages. To use this feature, code-page switching must have already been installed. Valid code pages include:

Value	Country/Language
437	United States
850	Multilingual
860	Portuguese
863	Canada (French)
865	Nordic

The format of the MODE command is:

MODE <*device*> cp select=<*code page*> <*refresh*> /Status

<*device*> is the name of the device, using standard system device names (CON, PRN, LPT1, LPT2, LPT3).

<*code page*> is the three-digit number of the code page to be used selected from the table above.

<*refresh*> specifies that a code page should be restored that was previously selected for a device.

/Status is optional. If used, it displays the code-page status of the device selected.

MODE AND THE SYSTEM PRINTER

The following MODE commands are associated with control of the system print devices (LPT1, LPT2, LPT3, or PRN). The MODE command can be used to set the format for the various print devices, to select an individual printer for use, and to redirect parallel printer output to a serial port. The various forms of the MODE command and their uses with the system print devices are discussed below.

MODE: Set Printer Format. The MODE command can be used to set the number of characters to be printed across the page, as well as the line spacing vertically on the page. Standard default settings are 80 characters per line across the page, with a standard spacing of six lines per inch. There are two formats for the MODE command to control the print devices, depending upon the version of DOS being used. If you are working with a version prior to Version 4.00, use the first form of the command:

```
MODE <printer:> <width>,<spacing>,P
```

If you are using Version 4.00 or later, use the second form of the command:

```
MODE <printer:> cols=<width> lines=<spacing>
retry=<action>
```

<*printer:*> is the name of the system device that is to be set or formatted. Values can be PRN, LPT1, LPT2, or LPT3. The printer device name must be followed by a colon, such as LPT1:.

<*width*> is the maximum number of characters that can be printed on the line. Values can be either 80 or 132 characters per line.

<*spacing*> is the number of lines per inch that will be printed in each inch of vertical spacing. Spacing is normally six or eight lines per inch.

/P specifies that DOS should try again when sending output to the printer if it finds the printer busy.

retry=<*action*> specifies what DOS should display when responding to a status request if the printer is busy.

MODE: Connect Serial Printer. The MODE command can be used to connect a parallel printer port to one of the serial ports. The serial port specified must be one that is available on your system. The number of serial ports on a typical system varies from one to four. DOS Versions 3.30 and later provide operating system support for COM1 through COM4. For versions earlier than Version 3.30, DOS supports COM1 and COM2. The format of the MODE command for redirecting output to a serial port is:

```
MODE <printer:>=<port>
```

<printer:> is the name of the parallel printer whose output will be redirected. Values for *<printer>* can be LPT1, LPT2, or LPT3. The printer device name must be followed by a colon.

<port> is the serial communications port to which the parallel printer will be connected.

To cancel redirection, enter the MODE command followed by the parallel printer whose redirection should be canceled.

MODE AND THE COMMUNICATIONS PORT

The following MODE commands are associated with control of the communications ports (COM1, COM2, etc.).

MODE: Set Communications Port Parameters. The first form of the MODE command for controlling the communications port is:

```
MODE <port> <baud>,<parity>,<databits>,<stopbits>,P
```

<port> is the code referring to the serial port whose communications settings are to be changed or set. The values of *<port>* can be COM1, COM2, COM3, or COM4, depending on your computer and the version of DOS installed on your system.

<baud> is the transmission rate or baud rate to be used in communications. The baud rate must match the hardware capabilities of the modem attached to the port. Baud rates have specific settings based on the hardware. Values for *<baud>* can be 110, 150, 300, 1200, 2400, 4800, 9600, 19200.

<parity> refers to the parity method used for checking loss of data bits. Values for parity can be *o* for odd, *e* for even, or *n* for none. The default value whenever parity is not specified is even.

<databits> is the number of bits used to represent a single character, such as a letter or number. Databits can be either 7 or 8 bits. The ASCII system uses 7-bit coding for characters; the EBCDIC system uses 8 bits. The default value is 7-bit coding based on the ASCII coding system.

<stopbits> is the number of bits used to mark the end of a character as part of the protocol used for transmission. Values for *<stopbits>* can be either 1 or 2.

P specifies that DOS should keep trying to send output to the specified serial *<port>* in the event that *<port>* is busy or not available for some other reason. If you are using a serial port for printing, you may want to specify P in setting up the serial port.

The second form of the MODE command for controlling the communications ports is:

```
MODE <port> baud=<rate> parity=<type> data=<databits>
stop=<stopbits> retry=<action>
```

<*port*> is the code referring to the serial port whose communications settings are to be changed or set. The values of <*port*> can be COM1, COM2, COM3, or COM4, depending on your computer and the version of DOS installed on your system.

Baud=<*rate*> is the transmission rate or baud rate to be used in communications. The baud rate must match the hardware capabilities of the modem attached to the port. Baud rates have specific settings based on the hardware. Values for <*rate*> can be 110, 150, 300, 1200, 2400, 4800, 9600, or 19200.

Parity=<*type*> refers to the parity method used for checking loss of data bits. Values for parity can be *odd, even, mark, space,* or *none*. The default value whenever parity is not specified is even.

Data=<*databits*> is the number of bits used to represent a single character, such as a letter or number. Databits can be either 7 or 8 bits. The ASCII system uses 7-bit coding for characters; the EBCDIC system uses 8 bits. The default value is 7-bit coding based on the ASCII coding system.

Stop=<*stopbits*> is the number of bits used to mark the end of a character as part of the protocol used for transmission. Values for <*stopbits*> can be either 1 or 2.

Retry=<*action*> specifies how the MODE command will respond when DOS tests the status of the serial port referenced. Values may be *b* for busy, *r* for ready, or *e* for error, depending on the hardware status when the serial port is tested. If you are using a serial port for printing, you may want to specify a retry action in setting up the serial port.

MODE AND SYSTEM DEVICE STATUS

Version 4.00 substantially expanded the capabilities of the MODE command and added parameters for existing capabilities available in prior versions. Among the capabilities added was the ability to check the status of a specified device on the system.

MODE: Check Device Status. To check the status of any device, use the format of the MODE command shown below. The device is the standard system device supported by DOS, including CON, PRN, LPT1, COM1, and so on. If no device is specified in <*device*>, DOS checks and reports on the status of all devices that it recognizes as connected to the system at the current time. The format of the command for device status checking is:

```
MODE <device> /STATUS
```

<*device*> specifies the system device to be tested for its status. Devices include CON, LPT1, PRN, COM1, and AUX1.

/STATUS specifies that DOS should check the specified device's status. /STATUS may be abbreviated /STA.

□ EXAMPLES

1. `C:\> MODE co80`
2. `C:\> MODE bw80,r,t`
3. `C:\> MODE mono`
4. `C:\> MODE 80`
5. `C:\> MODE CON lines=50`
6. `C:\> MODE CON rate=15 delay=2`
7. `C:\> MODE LPT1:132,8`
8. `C:\> MODE LPT1:,6`
9. `C:\> MODE LPT2: lines=8 cols=132`
10. `C:\> MODE LPT1:=com1`
11. `C:\> MODE LPT1:`
12. `C:\> MODE LPT1: /status`
13. `C:\> MODE con cp`
14. `C:\> MODE LPT1: cp refresh`
15. `C:\> MODE COM2 2400,n,8,,p`
16. `C:\> MODE COM1 baud=2400 data=8 stop=1 parity=odd`

1. `C:\> MODE co80` The MODE command sets the color graphics adapter controller to enable color and set the screen to display in 80-column mode.
2. `C:\> MODE bw80,r,t` In this example the display adapter is set for black and white mode, 80 columns wide. The *r* parameter shifts the display two columns to the right to center it on the screen. The *t* parameter causes a test pattern to display so that the centering can be checked.
3. `C:\> MODE mono` Here, the display adapter associated with a monochrome or black and white display will be enabled.
4. `C:\> MODE 80` In this example, only the number of columns for the display screen is specified. The color graphics adapter is selected and set to display the screen in 80-column mode.
5. `C:\> MODE CON lines=50` In this example, the second form of the MODE command is shown, using the keyword parameters. The output device for the console (CON) is selected. The display screen is set to display 50 lines per screen rather than the standard 25 lines per screen.
6. `C:\> MODE CON rate=15 delay=2` In this example, the keyboard repeat rate and delay settings are established with the MODE command. In this case, CON refers to the console input device—the keyboard. The keyboard is set for a 0.5-second delay, corresponding to delay=2. The repeat rate for displaying characters when a key is held down is approximately 15 characters per second, corresponding to a value for rate=15.

7. **C:\> MODE LPT1:132,8** The MODE command is used to control the standard system printer, commonly referred to as LPT1 or PRN. The printer will be set to display 132 characters across the page, with a vertical display of eight lines per inch.

8. **C:\> MODE LPT1:,6** In this example, the printer referenced as LPT1 is set to display at six lines per inch. Because nothing was specified in the first field (before the comma), the previous printer width value or setting is left unchanged. If the printer was printing 132 characters across the page, it remains at that setting. If it was printing in standard mode, 80 characters across the page, it remains at that setting. When using this form of the command, the parameters have place value, so the parameter for six lines per inch must be preceded by the comma, because there was no setting for the printer width.

9. **C:\> MODE LPT2: lines=8 cols=132** In this example, the settings for the printer are specified using the keyword form of the MODE command. The printer referred to as LPT2 is reset to a width of 132 columns across the page and a vertical spacing of eight lines per inch.

10. **C:\> MODE LPT1:=com1** The MODE command can be used to redirect the printer output to a serial port on the computer. This command redirects output sent to the printer LPT2 to the serial communications port COM1.

11. **C:\> MODE LPT1:** When a MODE command specifies only a reference printer, with no parameters, it serves the same purpose as to reset the printer. In this case, redirection of printer output for the printer LPT1 has been canceled. Output will be sent to printer LPT1.

12. **C:\> MODE LPT1: /status** The MODE command can be used to check the status of a specified device or all devices. This example requests that the status of the printer LPT1 be displayed. Rerouting, retry action specification, and code-page switching status are all reported.

13. **C:\> MODE con cp** In this example, the MODE command is used to request information regarding code-page status. The code-page status for the console keyboard device (CON) will be displayed.

14. **C:\> MODE LPT1: cp refresh** This is another example of using the MODE command with reference to code-page switching. The code-page that was selected for the printer LPT2 will be refreshed or restored.

15. **C:\> MODE COM2 2400,n,8,,p** The MODE command in this example is used to set up the serial or communications port associated with COM2. The port will be set for 2400-baud transmission speed; *n* specifies no parity, *8* specifies 8 data bits, and *p* specifies that DOS should continue to try to send information if it receives a busy signal. The number of stop bits was not specified, so DOS will use the default value of 1.

16. `C:\> MODE COM1 baud=2400 data=8 stop=1 parity=odd`
This example uses the keyword form of the MODE command to set the serial port associated with COM1. The transmission rate is set to 2400 baud, with 8 data bits and 1 stop bit used in data transmission. The communications device will use odd parity for error checking each byte of information transmitted.

THE ASSIGN (ASSIGN) COMMAND

The ASSIGN command physically reroutes an operation directed to one disk drive to the newly assigned disk drive. The ASSIGN command makes the actual type of drive (hard disk, floppy diskette, and so on) invisible to the operating system. Use this command with extreme care. Its primary use is with application programs that have drive addressing built into the application. An example is an application that has built-in addressing to the hard drive as Drive C. Suppose the application is actually installed on Drive D. Using the ASSIGN command, all references to Drive C can be rerouted to Drive D. Enter the command **ASSIGN C=D.** Now, every time the application addresses Drive C, DOS reroutes the request to Drive D.

Several DOS commands ignore drive assignments made with the ASSIGN command. These are the FORMAT, DISKCOPY, DISKCOMP, and SYS commands. These commands act as though the ASSIGN had never been in effect.

Because ASSIGN affects the operation of disk drives, there are some commands that should not be used when assigns are in effect. These commands are BACKUP, JOIN, LABEL, PRINT, RESTORE, and SUBSTITUTE.

One of the best ways to use the ASSIGN command, as well as other commands that physically modify the operation of devices, is in a batch file. By using ASSIGN in this way, any assignments that are put into effect at the beginning of the batch file can be canceled at the end of the batch file. When using commands such as ASSIGN, SUBSTITUTE, and JOIN, it is recommended that they only be used in specific situations and through a batch file that documents their use. A batch file can also be used in conjunction with application software that requires the special modifications that these commands can effect.

The format of the ASSIGN command is:

ASSIGN *<drive1>* = *<drive2>* /sta

<drive1> is the letter of the disk drive that is to be assigned. *Do not include the colon* as is normally done when addressing a disk drive.

<drive2> is the letter of the drive that will be accessed every time *<drive1>* is addressed. *Do not include the colon* as is normally done when addressing a disk drive.

/sta tells DOS to display a message reporting on the status of all assignments. The /sta parameter is available in Version 5 only.

Both <*drive1*> and <*drive2*> refer to physical drives that are installed on the system. The drive may be a hard disk drive, a diskette drive, or a virtual drive. The ASSIGN command can be used to assign a single drive or multiple drives with the same command. Separate the multiple drive assignments with a space.

As illustrated in the examples below, assignments can be issued and canceled. In DOS versions prior to 5.00, there is no form of the ASSIGN command that tells the user what assignments are currently in effect (see the /sta parameter above). As a result, unexpected operations of a disk drive cannot be determined by querying the system as to whether assignments have been made in some previous operation. For this reason among others, it is recommended that the ASSIGN command be used with care, that it be inside a batch file, and that all assignments be canceled as part of that same batch file's operation. Version 5 of DOS provides the /sta parameter for reporting drive assignments.

□ **EXAMPLES**

1. `C:\>` **`ASSIGN A=B`**
2. `C:\>` **`ASSIGN A=D B=D`**
3. `C:\>` **`ASSIGN C=E`**
4. `C:\>` **`ASSIGN`**
5. `C:\>` **`ASSIGN /sta`**

1. `C:\>` **`ASSIGN A=B`** In this example, Drive A has been reassigned to Drive B. When DOS searches for files, any file access that is addressed to Drive A will instead be sent to Drive B. A DIR command addressed to Drive A will provide the directory listing for Drive B. Note that colons are not used in the ASSIGN command.
2. `C:\>` **`ASSIGN A=D B=D`** This example shows that multiple drives can be assigned with one ASSIGN command. Here, both Drives A and B have been reassigned to Drive D. The assignment of drives is separated by a space.
3. `C:\>` **`ASSIGN C=E`** Hard drives can be assigned as well as floppy drives. Some personal computers support four floppy drives rather than two. Those systems have the first hard drive addressed as Drive E. In this example, Drive C has been reassigned to Drive E. A software application designed to run on an IBM PC using Drive C might require this assignment in order to run on a compatible with a hard drive having an address of Drive E.
4. `C:\>` **`ASSIGN`** Issuing an ASSIGN with no other fields resets all drive letters to their original physical assignments. This example would return all drive assignments to their normal status.
5. `C:\>` **`ASSIGN /sta`** The /sta parameter is available in DOS Version 5 only. In this example, DOS will report the status of all drive assignments currently in effect. A sample report is:

```
Original A:  set to E:
Original C:  set to D:
```

THE PRINT (PRINT) COMMAND

The PRINT command can be used to set up the operating characteristics for using the system printer, to manage the print queue, or to print a file. The PRINT command can be used with a minimum number of parameters, because all parameters have default values. Depending upon the amount of printing done with the computer and the type of operating environment (production, calculation, occasional use), it may be desirable to experiment with values different than the default settings. If experimenting with these settings, it is recommended that you only change one or two values at a time. The format of the PRINT command is:

PRINT /D:<*printer*> /Q:<*size*> /B:<*size*> /S:<*slice*> /M:<*max*> /U:<*wait*>

/D:<*printer*> specifies the printer device to be used. If no print device is specified, DOS assumes that the standard listing device PRN will be used. The <*printer*> device can be any of the following: PRN, LPT1, LPT2, LPT3, COM1, COM2, COM3, COM4, or AUX, depending upon the version of DOS being used.

/Q:<*size*> specifies the maximum number of files that can be in the print queue. The print queue size can be an integer number from 4 to 32. The default value for the print queue <*size*> is 10.

/B:<*size*> specifies the number of bytes that are set aside for the print queue buffer. The maximum value for the print buffer <*size*> is 16000 bytes. The default value is 512 bytes.

/S:<*slice*> specifies the number of time slices that are to be allotted to the printer in each second of time. The value for the number of time slices can range from 1 to 255 as an integer number. The default value for <*slice*> is 8.

/M:<*max*> specifies the length of time to be allotted to each time slice. The time is based on ticks of the internal clock of the computer. The value of <*max*> is an integer number between 1 and 255. The default value for <*max*> is 2.

/U:<*wait*> specifies the number of ticks of the internal clock that the PRINT command will wait before giving up its time slice. This occurs when the PRINT command finds the print device busy or unavailable when it is ready to print. The default value for <*wait*> is 1.

THE KEYBOARD LAYOUT (KEYB AND KEYB*xx*) COMMANDS

The Keyboard Layout command specifies a keyboard layout that matches the layout used with the country specified. In versions of DOS up to Version 3.20, the keyboard command was specified as KEYB*xx*, where *xx* specified the specific country, such as GR for Germany, FR for France, and so on. Beginning with Version 3.30, the country specification was changed to be a specified parameter (see Table 15.5), and the command became just KEYB.

Keyboards manufactured for use in the United States allow you to return to the U.S. layout after entering a KEYB command. In order to do this, issue the keyboard control command sequence Ctrl-Alt-F1, where F1 refers to function key number F1. To flip back to the keyboard you defined using the KEYB command, enter the keyboard control sequence Ctrl-Alt-F2, where F2 is the function key F2.

TABLE 15.5 Keyboard Layout Specifications for KEYB

Country	Keyboard Code	Code Pages	Keyboard ID
Belgium	BE	850, 437	120
Canada (French)	CF	863, 850	058
Denmark	DK	850, 865	159
Finland	SU	850, 437	153
France	FR	437, 850	120, 189
Germany	GR	437, 850	129
Italy	IT	437, 850	141, 142
Latin America	LA	437, 850	171
Netherlands	NL	437, 850	143
Norway	NO	850, 865	155
Portugal	PO	850, 860	163
Spain	SP	437, 850	172
Switzerland (French)	SF	850, 437	150
Switzerland (German)	SG	850, 437	000
Sweden	SV	437, 850	153
United Kingdom	UK	437, 850	168, 166
United States	US	437, 850	103

The format of the KEYB command is:

KEYB *<country> <code page> <keybfile>* /ID:*<keybid>*

<Country> is one of the country specifications listed in Table 15.5. *<Country>* is specified as a two-letter code, such as BE for Belgium, GR for Germany, and so on.

<Code page> is a three-digit number that specifies the code page associated with that country. For more information on code pages and the

National Language Support Function, refer to the NLSFUNC command and the index of this text.

<Keybfile> is the name of the file that contains keyboard layout information. If no keyboard file is specified, DOS uses its default filename of KEYBOARD.SYS and expects to find this file in the directory with other DOS-related files.

/ID:<keybid> is a keyboard ID code that specifies the keyboard layout when a country has more than one keyboard layout specification. If no keyboard ID is given, DOS assumes the ID code for the first keyboard layout for that country as shown in Table 15.5.

THE KEYBOARD (KEYB*xx*) COMMAND: VERSIONS PRIOR TO 3.20

The Keyboard (KEYB*xx)* command was used in versions of DOS prior to Version 3.30. To check to see if you have these keyboard commands rather than the KEYB command, check your DOS directory for a series of commands (KEYBdv, KEYBfr, . . . KEYBuk). In these versions of DOS, execute the specific command referencing the keyboard layout of the country of interest. As with the KEYB command, you may switch between the foreign keyboard of interest and the United States layout by using the keyboard control sequences. Ctrl-Alt-F1 returns to the default layout, which is US (for United States manufactured systems); use Ctrl-Alt-F2 to return to a keyboard selected with the KEYB*xx* command. To use any of these forms of the KEYB*xx* command, refer to Table 15.6 for the commands and the keyboard layout descriptions.

TABLE 15.6 Keyboard Country Commands for KEYB*xx*

Country	Keyboard Code	Command
France	FR	KEYBfr
Germany	GR	KEYBgr
Italy	IT	KEYBit
Spain	SP	KEYBsp
United Kingdom	UK	KEYBuk
Dvorak layout	DV	KEYBdv

THE ENABLE GRAPHICS CHARACTER SET (GRAFTABL) COMMAND

The GRAFTABLE command provides the ability to display special characters such as line-drawing characters, accented characters, and box-drawing characters. Use the GRAFTABL command to display these characters with the color graphics adapter in graphics mode. During normal DOS operations, the GRAFTABL command is not required. In cases where access is needed to any of the extended character set, execute GRAFTABL to gain access to the characters represented by these codes (ASCII characters 128 through 255). This command requires a color graphics adapter. The command has no effect when a monochrome display adapter is installed. The GRAFTABL command will normally be used only once in any single DOS session.

The format of the GRAFTABL command is:

GRAFTABL <*code page*> /status ?

<*code page*> is the three-digit number that specifies the code page that should be used in the DOS session. Code pages are part of DOS, beginning with DOS Version 3.30. Valid code pages include:

437	United States
850	Multilingual
860	Portuguese
863	Canada (French)
865	Nordic

/Status displays the current code page that is in effect.

? displays the current code page that is in effect, as well as a description of the parameters that are available and a list of other available code pages, along with the associated code-page numbers.

□ EXAMPLES

1. C:\> **GRAFTABL**
2. C:\> **GRAFTABL 865**
3. C:\> **GRAFTABL /status**
4. C:\> **GRAFTABL ?**

1. C:\> **GRAFTABL** This command must be typed in order to allow DOS to display the graphics characters in graphics mode. This command should be typed only once in a DOS session to set up the graphics mode.
2. C:\> **GRAFTABL 865** When a code page is used in conjunction with the GRAFTABL command, it enables DOS to display characters associated with that code page. In this case, the code page associated with the Nordic character set has been enabled by specifying code page 865.
3. C:\> **GRAFTABL /status** In this example, the /status parameter requests DOS to display information on the current code page that is in effect.
4. C:\> **GRAFTABL ?** In this command, the question mark requests that DOS display the current code page that is in effect, as well as a description of the parameters that are available and a list of other available code pages, and their associated code page numbers.

THE ENABLE GRAPHICS PRINTING (GRAPHICS) COMMAND

The GRAPHICS command is used to print displays produced when the system is in graphics mode. After entering the GRAPHICS command, the system will print graphics displays of the screen when a Shift-Prtsc keyboard sequence is entered.

For printers without color capability, the GRAPHICS command will print the image in several shades of grey. For color printers, the screen colors are produced with or without the background color. For screen resolutions exceeding 640 by 200 pixels, the GRAPHICS command results in the image being rotated to print in landscape mode.

The format of the GRAPHICS command is:

```
GRAPHICS <printer> <profile> /B /C /F /LCD /R
/P=<port> /PB:<id>
```

<printer> specifies the type of printer supported, including any of the following shown in Table 15.7. If *<printer>* is not specified, DOS assumes graphics as its default value.

<profile> specifies the filename that contains information about the printer or printers attached to the computer system. Details on all IBM-supported printers are contained in the DOS file GRAPHICS.PRO.

/B specifies that the background should be printed in color. This parameter is valid with a *<printer>* specification of color4 or color8 only.

/C specifies that the image to be printed should be centered on the page. This parameter is valid with screen resolutions of 640 by 200, or can be used with a 320 by 200 resolution printed with the /F parameter.

/F specifies that, with a screen resolution of 320 by 200, the image should be rotated to landscape mode (90-degree rotation).

/LCD specifies that the image from a liquid crystal display (LCD) screen should be printed. The IBM PC Convertible is one computer with an LCD screen.

/R specifies that the image be printed as seen on the screen. The image prints as light images on a dark background.

/P=<port> specifies which printer port should be used. Valid printer ports are 1 for LPT1, 2 for LPT2, and 3 for LPT3.

/PB:<id> specifies the aspect ratio that should be used when printing a graphics image. Valid values for *<id>* are STD for standard and LCD for a liquid crystal display.

TABLE 15.7 Printer Specifications for the GRAPHICS Command

Value	Description
color1	IBM PC Color Printer or compatible; black ribbon.
color4	IBM PC Color Printer or compatible; red-green-blue-black (RGB) ribbon.
color8	IBM PC Color Printer or compatible; cyan-magenta-yellow-black (CMY) ribbon
compact	IBM PC Compact Printer or compatible.
graphics	IBM PC Graphics Printer, IBM Quietwriter, IBM Proprinter, IBM Pageprinter, or compatible.
graphicswide	IBM Proprinter, IBM Quietwriter, or compatible with wide-carriage capability.
thermal	IBM PC Convertible Printer or compatible.

QUESTIONS AND PROBLEMS

1. What command is used to display the disk drive assignments currently in effect on your system?
2. Which command would be used to display a TREE diagram for the hard disk on a printer that cannot support graphics printing?
3. What standard system devices are affected by the GRAPHICS command?
4. What country keyboards are supported by the KEYB*xx* commands in DOS prior to Version 3.30?
5. What functions can be changed for the standard system console device using the MODE command?
6. What are the standard system printer widths and vertical print densities that can be set by the MODE command?
7. What baud rates are supported by the MODE command in controlling any of the serial communications ports?
8. What devices can be controlled using the PRINT command for sending output?
9. What command and associated parameters are used to determine the operating condition or status of the standard system devices?
10. What command is used to request code-page status for the console input device?

11. Write a command that can be included in the AUTOEXEC.BAT file that will allow previously typed commands to be recalled using the arrow keys.
12. Write a command that will set the repeat rate and delay for your keyboard.
13. Write a command to set the number of lines on the screen to 50 lines per screen instead of 25 lines.
14. Write a command that will allow DOS to print a graphics-based screen of information to the printer.
15. Approximately how many commands can be tracked by DOSKEY using a buffer size of 256 bytes?

CHAPTER 16

MEMORY MANAGEMENT (EXTERNAL COMMANDS)

INTRODUCTION

One of the most important functions performed by any operating system is memory management. Most of the memory management performed by the operating system while running programs and applications is invisible to the user. In Version 4.00, DOS provided a command (MEM) that gives some insight into the layout and use of memory. Version 5.00 expands on this memory management support to include additional device drivers, as well as support for extended memory and expanded memory. Currently, DOS provides no program for expanded memory management. Expanded memory management programs are supplied with the expanded memory board when it is purchased.

Early microcomputer systems had only conventional RAM memory, but most systems today have additional memory installed which goes beyond the standard 640 KB. Both extended and expanded memory are installed on many of today's systems, frequently bringing the total memory to 4 MB or more on many systems.

TYPES OF MEMORY

Systems today can have as many as four different kinds of memory. These are:

- Conventional or internal memory (RAM)
- Upper or high memory (HMA)
- Extended memory (XMS)
- Expanded memory (EMS)

The MEM command, discussed later in this chapter, is used to find out what kind and how much memory is installed on a computer. DOS provides support through the operating system to access conventional or RAM memory. No special programs are needed for DOS or application software to access this memory. Every byte of conventional memory is directly addressable. Only computers with an 80286 or higher processor can use memory other than conventional memory.

CONVENTIONAL MEMORY (RAM)

The conventional memory installed on a computer is usually 640 KB. On early PCs this memory may have been as small as 128 KB. Application programs, as well as DOS and other software, can use conventional RAM directly. No special programs are needed. Neither are any special commands required in CONFIG.SYS or AUTOEXEC.BAT. The COMMAND.COM file in DOS, along with device drivers and other storage areas, will typically require 70 KB to 125 KB of conventional memory. The balance is available for use by application programs, Terminate and Stay Resident programs (TSRs), and for data storage. Use the CHKDSK command to find out how much of the conventional memory area is free for programs after DOS is loaded.

UPPER MEMORY (HMA)

Upper memory is memory contiguous to conventional memory. It is sometimes referred to as the **high-memory area (HMA)**. Programs do not store information is this area of memory. Instead, it is used for holding parts of DOS, for holding device drivers, and for mapping memory blocks when expanded memory is installed. Systems with an 80386 or 80486 processor and extended memory can use the HMA to free up conventional memory, thereby expanding the memory available to application software. DOS Version 5.00 uses the upper memory area, if it is available, to substantially reduce the area required by COMMAND.COM and the associated device drivers and storage areas.

EXTENDED MEMORY (XMS)

Extended memory (XMS) may be installed on a system as purchased or can be added by purchasing an extended memory board. Extended memory, found on most systems with an 80286, 80386, or 80486 microprocessor, requires an additional program to recognize this storage space. That program is called an Extended Memory Manager. DOS Versions 4.00 and 5.00 provide a program that can recognize and provide access to extended memory. The DOS Extended Memory Manager is the device driver named HIMEM.SYS. HIMEM.SYS conforms to specifications laid down for use of extended memory by the Lotus/Intel/Microsoft/AST Extended Memory Specification (XMS). To install HIMEM.SYS on your system, include a command in CONFIG.SYS such as:

```
DEVICE=C:\DOS500\HIMEM.SYS
```

If this command is added to the CONFIG.SYS file after booting the computer, the system must be rebooted in order for DOS to execute this configuration command and load the associated device driver into memory.

EXPANDED MEMORY (EMS)

Expanded memory, like extended memory, is installed on many systems at the time of purchase. It too can be installed or increased through an expanded memory board. The purchase of an expanded memory product will also include software called an Expanded Memory Manager.

Expanded memory is not directly accessible by a program. Instead, expanded memory is divided into 16 KB segments, called *pages*. When information is requested from expanded memory, the expanded memory manager maps the information into page frames stored in the upper-memory area. The program then accesses the information from the HMA.

A program must be designed to use expanded memory. When considering the purchase of expanded memory, first check to see whether your application software programs can access this memory. This will be noted in the software documentation. Expanded memory management software conforms to the Lotus/Intel/Microsoft Expanded Memory Specification (LIM EMS) Version 3.2 or 4.0.

Because access to expanded memory is indirect through the page mapping process, software will run slightly slower when using this memory as compared to access of conventional memory or extended memory. Nevertheless, expanded memory greatly increases memory capabilities on a computer. With the introduction of Windows, and the development of large video and graphics-based programs, software can easily need memory in the 4 MB to 24 MB range. Extended and expanded memory has made this possible.

MEMORY MANAGEMENT

Versions 4.00 and 5.00 of DOS substantially expanded the capability of DOS to make use of memory beyond 640 KB. The MEM and EMM386 commands, coupled with the introduction of new device drivers, provide support for 80386 and 80486 processors. The external commands discussed in this chapter are:

MEM
EMM386

THE MEMORY MANAGEMENT (MEM) COMMAND

The MEM command can display information about all three types of memory: internal RAM, extended, and expanded memory. The format of the MEM command is:

MEM /PROGRAM /DEBUG

/PROGRAM or **/P** specifies that the name, location, size, and type of each program in memory is to be displayed.

/DEBUG or **/D** specifies that additional detailed data beyond that provided by the /P parameter should be included in the report.

DOS allocates memory for some basic functions at boot time. The DOS kernel requires part of RAM to store COMMAND.COM and its related programs. Additional amounts of memory are used for the DOS environment and by functions associated with commands in the CONFIG.SYS file, such as buffers, files, and so on. In addition, DOS device drivers such as the ANSI.SYS file which may be loaded at boot time require additional memory. More complicated CONFIG.SYS and AUTOEXEC.BAT files will require more memory for storing information related to the setup of your computer.

In some cases, as with extremely large application programs or compilers, the user may get an "Out of memory" message when attempting to load or run these applications. This usually occurs because the computer does not have sufficient data space for running the program. In these cases it is desirable to be able to examine the amount of memory required by the operating system.

Other situations arise that consume memory and may result in memory too small for running certain application programs. Virus programs are sometimes installed as Terminate and Stay Resident programs (TSRs). These programs reduce the amount of space available for application software such as word processors and spreadsheets. Other examples of TSRs are calculators, calendars, and notepad programs. These programs are loaded into memory and remain dormant until called up via a "hotkey" sequence. The function is then available for use, many times in a window on the display screen. If you use TSR programs, you may find that an application may run when no TSRs are loaded, but may produce error messages when some or all of your TSRs are loaded. The MEM command provides a method for examining memory and determining how best to increase the RAM that your application needs.

In most cases you will find little use for the MEM command. Program developers may find more use for the command, particularly if the programs are large and consume large amounts of RAM. Examples of uses of MEM are illustrated below, along with the typical reports generated by the command.

□ EXAMPLES

1. `C:\>` **`MEM`**
2. `C:\>` **`MEM /PROGRAM`**
3. `C:\>` **`MEM /DEBUG`**
4. `C:\>` **`MEM /DEBUG > PRN`**

1. `C:\>` **`MEM`** When used with no parameters, the MEM command provides a summary report similar to the CHKDSK report. The first section provides information about RAM, including the total bytes of RAM memory and the amount of memory available for a program, including the data area for the program. The second part of the report provides information about extended memory, if such memory is installed on your system. The report below provides an example:

```
655360 bytes total memory
654336 bytes available
560108 largest executable program size
393216 bytes total extended memory
327680 bytes available extended memory
```

2. `C:\> MEM /PROGRAM` In this example, the summary report will again be provided, but it will appear after a detailed listing of information about programs loaded in memory, including the address, name, size, and type. The locations of system data such as files and buffer information will also be provided. A complete sample report is shown below:

```
Address   Name      Size     Type
-------   ----      ----     ----
000000              000400   Interrupt Vector
000400              000100   ROM Communication Area
000500              000200   DOS Communication Area
000700    IO        000AC0   System Data
0011C0    MSDOS     0013F0   System Data
0025B0    IO        001C40   System Data
          SETVER    0001A0   DEVICE=
            ANSI    000630   DEVICE=
            HIMEM   000470   DEVICE=
                    000380   FILES=
                    000100   FCBS=
                    000200   BUFFERS=
                    0001C0   LASTDRIVE=
                    000740   STACKS=
004200    MSDOS     000040   System Program
004250    COMMAND   000940   Program
004BA0    MSDOS     000040    -- Free --
004BF0    COMMAND   000100   Environment
004D00    WP        000060   Environment
004D70    DOSKEY    001020   Program
005DA0    COMMAND   000040   Data
005DF0    WP        0660A0   Program
06BEA0    COMMAND   000090   Data
06BF40    COMMAND   000940   Program
06C890    COMMAND   000100   Environment
06C9A0    MEM       000090   Environment
06CA40    MEM       0176F0   Program
084140    MSDOS     01BAB0   -- Free --

655360 bytes total memory
654336 bytes available
209328 largest executable program size
393216 bytes total extended memory
327680 bytes available extended memory
```

3. `C:\> MEM /DEBUG` In this example, the summary report will again be provided at the end, but it will be a more detailed listing than that for the /PROGRAM parameter. The various device drivers associated with the

IBMBIO.COM file are shown. The address, name, size, and type will be provided. Again, you can see the location of system data such as files and buffer information. The complete sample report is shown below:

```
Address    Name       Size      Type
-------    ----       ----      ----
000000                000400    Interrupt Vector
000400                000100    ROM Communication Area
000500                000200    DOS Communication Area
000700     IO         000AC0    System Data
           CON                  System Device Driver
           AUX                  System Device Driver
           PRN                  System Device Driver
           CLOCK$               System Device Driver
           A: – D:              System Device Driver
           COM1                 System Device Driver
           LPT1                 System Device Driver
           LPT2                 System Device Driver
           LPT3                 System Device Driver
           COM2                 System Device Driver
           COM3                 System Device Driver
           COM4                 System Device Driver
0011C0     MSDOS      0013F0    System Data
0025B0     IO         001C40    System Data
           SETVER     0001A0    DEVICE=
           SETVERXXX            Installed Device Driver
           ANSI       000630    DEVICE=
           CON                  Installed Device Driver
           HIMEM      000470    DEVICE=
           XMSXXXX0             Installed Device Driver
                      000380    FILES=
                      000100    FCBS=
                      000200    BUFFERS=
                      0001C0    LASTDRIVE=
                      000740    STACKS=
004200     MSDOS      000040    System Program
004250     COMMAND    000940    Program
004BA0     MSDOS      000040    -- Free --
004BF0     COMMAND    000100    Environment
004D00     WP         000060    Environment
004D70     DOSKEY     001020    Program
005DA0     COMMAND    000040    Data
005DF0     WP         0660A0    Program
06BEA0     COMMAND    000090    Data
06BF40     COMMAND    000940    Program
06C890     COMMAND    000100    Environment
```

```
06C9A0      MEM        000090    Environment
06CA40      MEM        0176F0    Program
084140      MSDOS      01BAB0    -- Free --

655360 bytes total memory
654336 bytes available
209328 largest executable program size
393216 bytes total extended memory
327680 bytes available extended memory
```

4. `C:\>` **`MEM /DEBUG > PRN`** This example is similar to previous one, but instead of the report going to the display screen, it is sent as hard copy to the printer. The report is for the /DEBUG parameter.

THE EMM386 COMMAND

The EMM386 command is used in conjunction with the expanded memory device driver (EMM386.EXE). EMM386 controls access to expanded memory on computers that use an 80386 or 80486 microprocessor. The format of the EMM386 command is:

EMM386 <*on*> <*off*> <*auto*>

<*on*> enables access to expanded memory for software designed to use it. The default value is on.

<*off*> disables access to expanded memory.

<*auto*> provides access to expanded memory when a software program requests it.

The EMM386 command is used in conjunction with the expanded memory device driver (EMM386.EXE). This device driver, supplied with Version 5.00 of DOS, provides access to the upper memory area located above 640 KB. To activate this configuration command, it must be included in the CONFIG.SYS file with a DEVICE= line. The format of the command in CONFIG.SYS is:

DEVICE=<*path*>EMM386.EXE <*size*> ram noems

<*path*> specifies the pathname so that DOS can find the EMM386.EXE device driver file during the boot process. An example path is C:\DOS500\.

<*size*> specifies the amount of extended memory that should be used as expanded memory. The <*size*> parameter is entered in kilobytes, and stated in multiples of 16, because one page frame is 16 KB. The default value for <*size*> is 256. Sizes not in multiples of 16 KB are rounded down to the nearest multiple of 16.

ram provides access to expanded memory and the upper memory area (HMA).

noems provides access to the upper memory area, but prevents access to expanded memory.

Either the ram or noems switch must be used to access the high-memory area. EMM386 is normally used in conjunction with the HIMEM device driver. The HIMEM.SYS device driver will manage the use of extended memory and the high-memory area. The examples shown below are for commands included in a CONFIG.SYS file. As a result, the DOS prompt is not shown. These commands are only executed during the power-on or warm-boot process. For a list of the device drivers included with DOS, refer to Appendix G.

□ **EXAMPLES**

1.
```
DEVICE=C:\DOS500\himem.sys
DEVICE=C:\DOS500\emm386.exe
```
2.
```
DEVICE=C:\DOS500\himem.sys
DEVICE=C:\DOS500\emm386.exe 4096 ram
```
3.
```
DEVICE=C:\DOS500\himem.sys
DEVICE=C:\DOS500\emm386.exe noems
DEVICE=C:\DOS500\ansi.sys
DOS=high,umb
```

1.
```
DEVICE=C:\DOS500\himem.sys
DEVICE=C:\DOS500\emm386.exe
```

The HIMEM device driver is loaded to manage extended memory as well as the high-memory area above 640 K. The EMM386.EXE expanded memory manager will be executed; it allocates 256 KB of extended memory for use as expanded memory.

2.
```
DEVICE=C:\DOS500\himem.sys
DEVICE=C:\DOS500\emm386.exe 4096 ram
```

The HIMEM device driver is loaded to manage extended memory as well as the high-memory area above 640 K. The EMM386.EXE expanded memory manager is executed; it allocates 4096 KB of extended memory for use as expanded memory. The ram parameter provides access to the upper memory area as well as to expanded memory.

3.
```
DEVICE=C:\DOS500\himem.sys
DEVICE=C:\DOS500\emm386.exe noems
DEVICE=C:\DOS500\ansi.sys
DOS=high,umb
```

The HIMEM device driver is loaded into high memory for managing both the upper memory area and extended memory. The expanded memory device driver provides access to high memory, but not to any expanded memory. The ANSI.SYS device driver for expanded keyboard capability is loaded. Finally, the DOS=high, umb command loads much of the resident part of DOS into the upper memory area. The location of the device drivers can be checked and their location identified using the MEM command.

QUESTIONS AND PROBLEMS

1. Information displayed when using the /P or /D parameters with MEM is displayed using what number system for the format?
2. How could the information displayed using the /P parameter with MEM be used to make additional memory available for a large application program?
3. If several device drivers are not needed to run a large program, how can they be removed from memory?
4. Can the buffers and files areas allocated in RAM memory be reduced or totally eliminated?
5. What causes ANSI.SYS to be loaded into memory and can this file be removed from memory?
6. The two hidden files IBMBIO.COM and IBMDOS.COM consume large segments of RAM. Can these segments be reduced or eliminated?
7. What device driver is used to manage extended memory? How is it added to your system?
8. What program or device driver is used to provide access to the high-memory area on a computer?
9. What commands are required in CONFIG.SYS to load portions of DOS and device drivers into the high-memory area?
10. What are some differences between extended memory and expanded memory? What programs are used to manage each type of memory?

CHAPTER 17

THE DOS SHELL (EXTERNAL COMMANDS)

INTRODUCTION

Beginning with Version 4.00 of DOS, a program called the DOS Shell is provided. The purpose of this Shell program is to simplify the tasks of disk and file management. The Shell does away with the DOS prompt and provides menus and lists to select from, rather than typing DOS commands, as we have done in previous chapters.

If you have Version 4.00 or later of DOS, you can try out the Shell. You do not have to operate DOS from the Shell; use of the DOS Shell is optional. You decide whether to install it; if it installed automatically as part of the installation of DOS, it can be disabled, replaced with a batch file menu system (as shown in Appendix H), or replaced with some other operating environment. You can also continue to operate from the DOS prompt. Review this chapter and the major operating characteristics of the Shell, then decide whether operating from within the Shell, from a menu system, or from the DOS prompt is best for you. The choice is yours. The DOS Shell provides many functions and capabilities, so some installation time and experience will be required to master all of its capabilities and complexity.

The major operating characteristics of the Shell program are briefly outlined in this chapter. Determine how best to use the Shell and how you want to operate your system. Considerable flexibility is provided in both its setup and operating characteristics. This chapter discusses using the DOS Shell with a keyboard or a mouse, text and graphics modes, function keys and the Shell, and the major operating characteristics of the Shell environment.

COMMON FEATURES OF DOS SHELL VERSIONS 4.0 AND 5.0

The purpose of the DOS Shell is the same in both versions 4.0 and 5.0: to allow the user easy access to file and program management through a series of menus and selections. Although the basic functions are the same, particular screens and menus vary between DOS Shell for Version 4 and DOS Shell for Version 5. This section outlines the aspects that are the *same* between the two versions, while a later section covers aspects that are unique to version 5 of the DOS Shell.

GRAPHICS MODE AND TEXT MODE

The DOS Shell can operate in either graphics mode or text mode. If using a mouse, you will probably want to operate in graphics mode, although that is not a requirement. If operating from a keyboard input system, either mode is satisfactory. Examine the screen display associated with the Shell to determine what mode your system is in. Table 17.1 shows the key indicators for graphics mode and text mode.

TABLE 17.1 **DOS Shell Graphics Mode and Text Mode**

Function	Graphics Mode	Text Mode
Disk drive	Drive drawing	Drive letter displayed
Mouse	Pointer is an arrow	Pointer is a rectangle
Filenames	Symbol displayed to left of filename	No symbol
Menu names	Key letters underlined	Key letters highlighted
Menu choices	Key letters underlined	Key letters highlighted

THE KEYBOARD AND THE MOUSE

The DOS Shell can be used from either a keyboard having cursor control keys, or a mouse. For most IBM systems, a mouse has not been a standard hardware device, though that situation is changing. (By contrast, a Macintosh system has a mouse as a standard input device on all systems.) For this reason, it is useful to know how to operate the Shell from the keyboard. If your system has a mouse you will probably find it more convenient and efficient to operate the Shell using the mouse. Table 17.2 describes the basic Shell functions and how they are performed with both devices.

STARTING THE SHELL

The Shell can be started in one of two ways. You can initiate the Shell as part of the power-up or boot process. If done in this manner, the Shell is initiated via the AUTOEXEC.BAT and the CONFIG.SYS files, and is launched via the power-up or boot process or via a warm boot whenever you press the keyboard control sequence Ctrl-Alt-Del.

The Shell program can also be launched by typing the program name, just as you would execute any other DOS command. To initiate the Shell from the DOS prompt, type the command shown below:

```
C:\> DOSSHELL
```

TABLE 17.2 **Mouse and Keyboard Functions for the DOS Shell**

Key Sequence	Function
Keyboard Functions	
Alt Key or F10 (v. 5)	Select a menu. The key sequence activates the area of the screen that contains the menu. Use the key letter of the menu item or the arrow keys to highlight the menu name. The Enter key selects the item.
Key letter	Select a menu item. Press the key letter of the item desired or use the arrow keys to highlight the item desired. The Enter key selects the item.
Arrow keys	Select a file. Highlight the filename with the arrow keys, then press the Spacebar.
Arrow keys	Select a command. Highlight the command with the arrow keys, then press the Enter key.
Mouse Functions	
Click	Move the mouse pointer until it rests on the item, and press the left mouse button one time.
Double-click	Move the mouse pointer until it rests on the item, then press the left mouse button twice in rapid succession.
Drag	Move the mouse pointer until it rests on the item. Press and hold the left mouse button pressed. Move the mouse pointer to the new location. Release the mouse button once the item has been correctly positioned in its new location.

THE DOS SHELL VERSION 5

The DOS Shell for Version 5 offers several improvements over the Version 4 Shell. It's screens are more like the popular Windows graphical user interface, enabling you to simultaneously view the file-list and program-list areas. It also allows you to rename directories, search for files, and switch among active programs (up to the limit of your system's memory).

When the DOS Shell is started (either by the AUTOEXEC.BAT file or by entering DOSSHELL at the command prompt for the DOS directory), a screen like Figure 17.1 (shown in graphics mode) will appear.

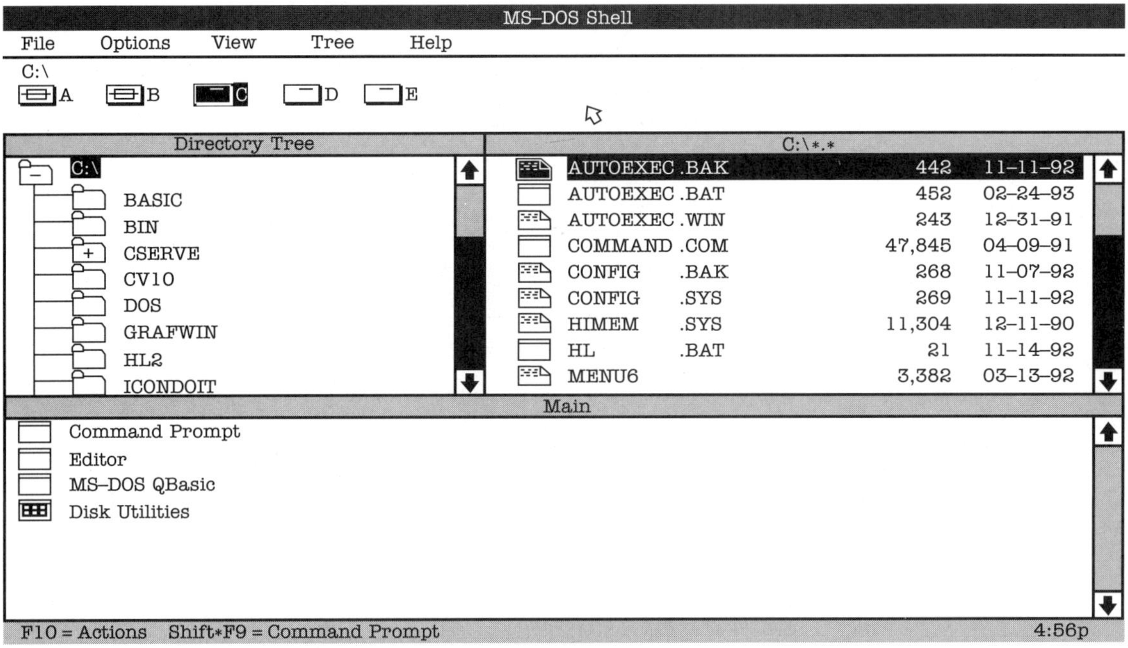

FIGURE 17.1 Initial screen of DOS Shell Version 5

The DOSSHELL screen has several parts, as shown in Figure 17.1. From the top of the screen to the bottom, they are:

- The *title bar*, which displays the name "MS-DOS Shell."
- The *menu bar*, with menus and lists of commands.
- The *drive selector*, which is used to select the disk drive whose files are to be displayed. In Figure 17.1, Drive C is selected (highlighted).
- Two windows for displaying the *directory tree* and a *file list*. In Figure 17.1, the directory tree shows the root directory on Drive C, and the *file list* shows the files in that directory.
- A *program list* window below the directory tree and file list. Figure 17.1 shows the Main *program group*. (Program groups are discussed later in this section.)
- A *status line* at the bottom of the screen, showing useful keys and the current time.

In Figure 17.1, note the arrow-shaped mouse pointer which appears if you have installed a mouse. Each window also has a set of *scroll bars* on its right edge that are used with the mouse to scroll the text displayed in the window.

Keyboard Commands for Version 5 DOS Shell

Table 17.3 lists keyboard commands common to all screens in the DOS 5 Shell.

TABLE 17.3 **Keyboard Commands for All Version 5 Shell Screens**

Key	Function
Enter	Executes the selected item
Esc	Cancels the current command or operation
F1	Accesses Help information on the current command, area, or dialog box option
Alt-F4 or F3	Exits the Shell permanently and returns you to the DOS command prompt
Shift-F5	Redraws the screen but does not update the file lists
Shift-F9	Temporarily exits to the DOS prompt. (Enter EXIT at the DOS prompt to return to the Shell.)

Moving Around the Shell Window

Either the keyboard or the mouse can be used to move to and select the various Shell functions. Using the mouse is probably easier, because all you have to do is move the mouse pointer to the item and click the left mouse button. If you don't have a mouse, or prefer to use keyboard commands, Table 17.4 lists keyboard commands to move around the Shell window.

Getting Help

The Shell's Help system is context-sensitive; that is, it provides Help information on the currently highlighted menu item or situation. You can also use the Help system to get help with any DOS Shell topic through the Help Index. For help with any particular menu item, highlight that item and press F1. For example, Figure 17.2 shows the screen that would appear if you highlighted the Rename item from the File menu and pressed F1. The Help text box briefly describes the Rename command and gives the name of a related topic to go to for more information. To explore a related topic, press Tab to highlight it and then press Enter, or just click on the topic with the mouse.

TABLE 17.4 Keyboard Commands for Cursor Movement in DOS Shell 5

Key	Function
F10 or Alt	Goes to the menu bar at the top of the screen
Alt-*letter*	Goes to the item on the menu bar beginning with *letter*
Tab	Moves to the next area of the Shell window; in a dialog box, moves to the next choice
Shift-Tab	Moves to the preceding area of the Shell window; in a dialog box, moves to the preceding choice
Home	Moves to the beginning of a line or list
End	Moves to the end of a list
Ctrl-Home	Moves to the beginning of a list
Ctrl-End	Moves to the end of a list
Up Arrow[↑]	Moves up one item in a list
Down Arrow[↓]	Moves down one item in a list
Any letter	Moves to the next item in the list beginning with that letter

FIGURE 17.2 Context-sensitive help for DOS Shell Version 5

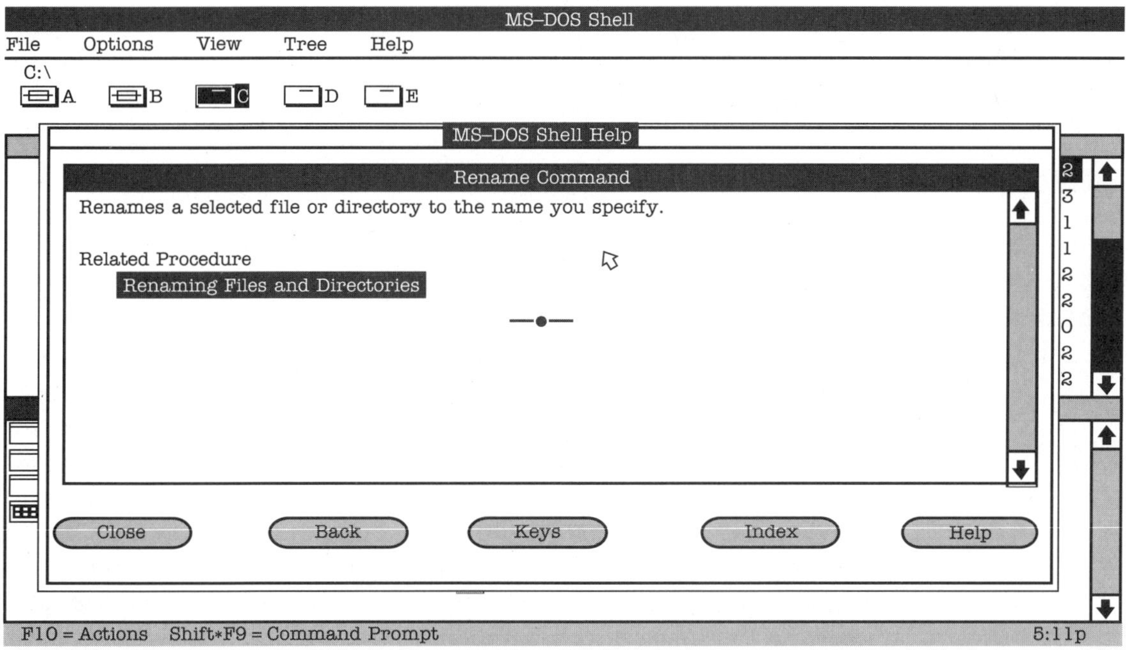

To get help from the Help Index, you can either select the "Index" button at the bottom of a context-sensitive help screen (as in Figure 17.2), or open the Help menu from the menu bar, as shown in Figure 17.3. The Shell Basics item on this menu is particularly helpful for reviewing the basic techniques for using Shell's windows, menus, and lists. The Commands and Procedures items give detailed information about specific commands and tasks.

FIGURE 17.3 DOS Shell Version 5 Help menu

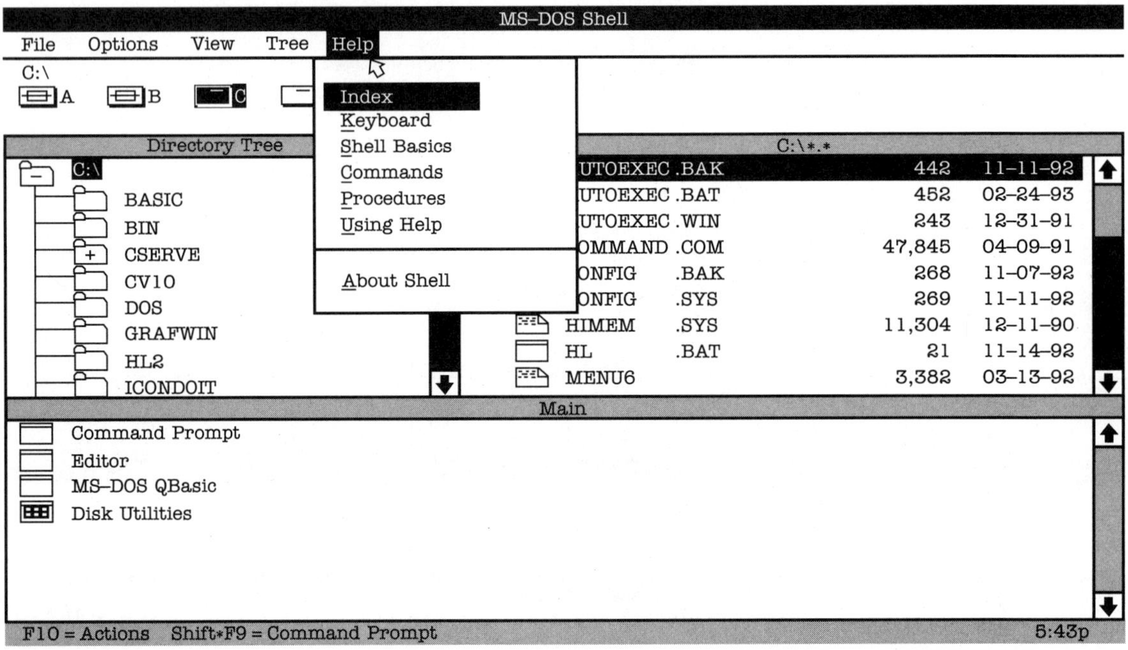

FILE MANAGEMENT

When the directory-tree or file-list areas of the Shell window are selected, you can perform operations on listed directories or files. You can search for files; copy, rename, delete, or move files; and create directories. You can also start programs by selecting the program filename from the file list (see "Executing Programs from the Shell," below). Table 17.5 shows keyboard shortcuts for handling files and directories.

In order to perform any file management functions, you must first have the appropriate drive selected. To select Drive A, for example, you would click on its symbol or letter in the drive specification area or highlight it and press Enter. Or

TABLE 17.5 Keyboard Shortcuts for File and Directory Handling

Key	Function
Drive-Selection Keys	
Left Arrow [←]	Moves selection cursor to previous drive
Right Arrow [→]	Moves selection cursor to next drive
Spacebar	Selects the drive at the selection cursor
Ctrl-*drive letter*	Selects the drive specified by the drive letter
Enter	Rereads the selected drive and displays its contents
File-Directory Keys	
F7	Moves selected file(s) from one directory to another; equivalent to Move command on File menu
F8	Copies selected file(s) from one directory to another; equivalent to Copy command on File menu
Del	Deletes selected file(s) or directory(s)
File-Selection Keys	
Shift-F8	Toggles Add mode on/off. (When Add mode is on, ADD displays in lower right corner of Shell window, and you can select multiple files from the file-list area.)
Shift [↑]	Adds the preceding file in file list to selection
Shift [↓]	Adds the next file in file list to selection
Shift-PgUp	Adds all files listed above current file to selection
Shift-PgDn	Adds all files listed below current file to selection
Ctrl-/	Selects all files in the selected directory
Ctrl-\	Deselects (clears) all files in selected directory
Shift-Spacebar	In Add mode, selects the group of files between the previously selected file and the cursor
Spacebar	In Add mode, adds the file at cursor location to the selection
Directory-Tree Keys	
[↑] or Ctrl-[↑]	Moves to preceding directory level
[↓] or Ctrl-[↓]	Moves to next directory level
–	Hides (collapses) directories below the selected directory

"continued"

TABLE 17.5 **Keyboard Shortcuts for File and Directory Handling (continued)**

Key	Function
+	Displays (expands) one level of directories below the selected directories
*	Displays (expands) all directories below the selected directory
File Display Keys	
F5	Rereads the selected drive and updates (refreshes) the file list for that drive
Ctrl-F5	Updates the file list for the current directory
F9	Views the contents of a selected file; while viewing a file switches between ASCII and hexadecimal display

you could use the shortcut of pressing Ctrl and the drive letter, in this case Ctrl-A. The Shell will then scan the selected drive and display a list of directories and files on the drive. If a directory has subdirectories, the directory icon will show a plus (+) symbol. To display subdirectories, you can click on a directory icon with a + symbol or select Expand One Level from the Tree menu.

Once you have selected the drive and directory, you can then select the file(s) you wish using the file-selection keys shown in Table 17.5 or the mouse, then select the operation you wish to perform on the file(s) from the File menu (Move, Copy, Delete, Rename, and so on) as shown in Figure 17.4.

When searching for a file, select Search from the File menu and enter to name of the file you are looking for. The Shell will search the entire drive for the file, unless you remove the check from the "Search Entire Drive" item in the Search dialog box (shown in Figure 17.5). Remove the check to search only the current directory. You can also use the * and ? wildcards in file searches. Figure 17.5 shows a Search dialog box for all files with a BAT extension on Drive C. The results of the search, a listing of all BAT files, will be displayed in a Search Results screen.

CREATING DIRECTORIES

You can create directories from the DOS Shell as an alternative to using the CD command from the DOS prompt. First you must select the parent directory under which you want to create a directory. To create a directory under the root directory (C:\), for example, that directory must be selected (highlighted) in the directory-tree area. Then choose Create Directory from the File Menu and enter the name of the new directory. Do not include a backslash as the first character of the new directory name.

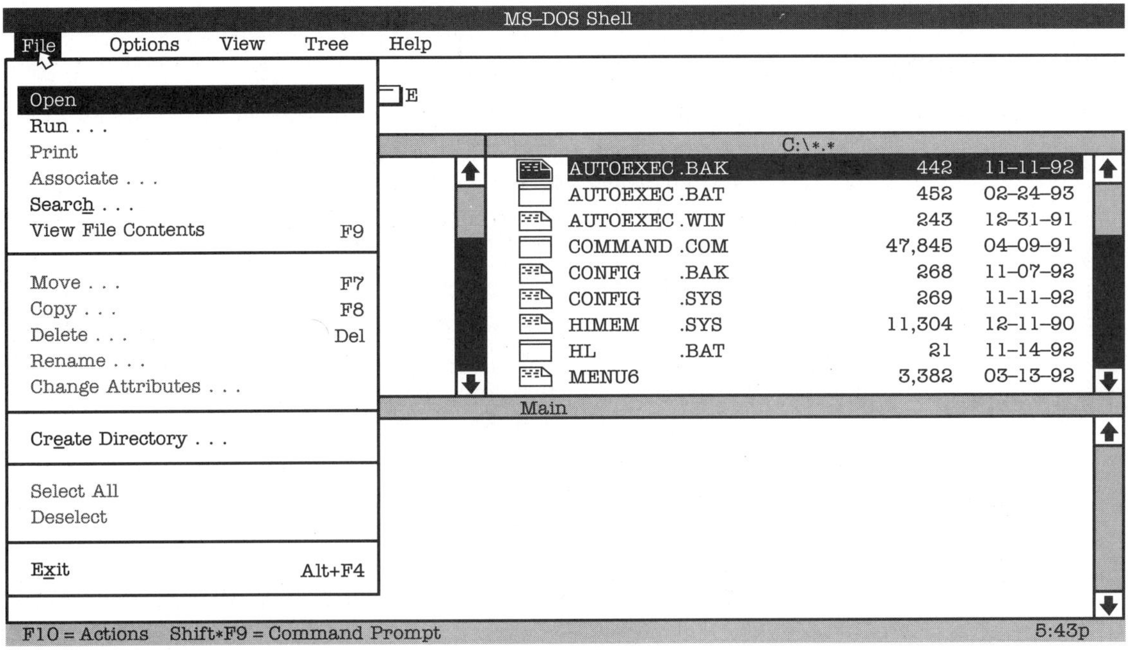

FIGURE 17.4 DOS Shell File menu

FIGURE 17.5 Search File dialog box

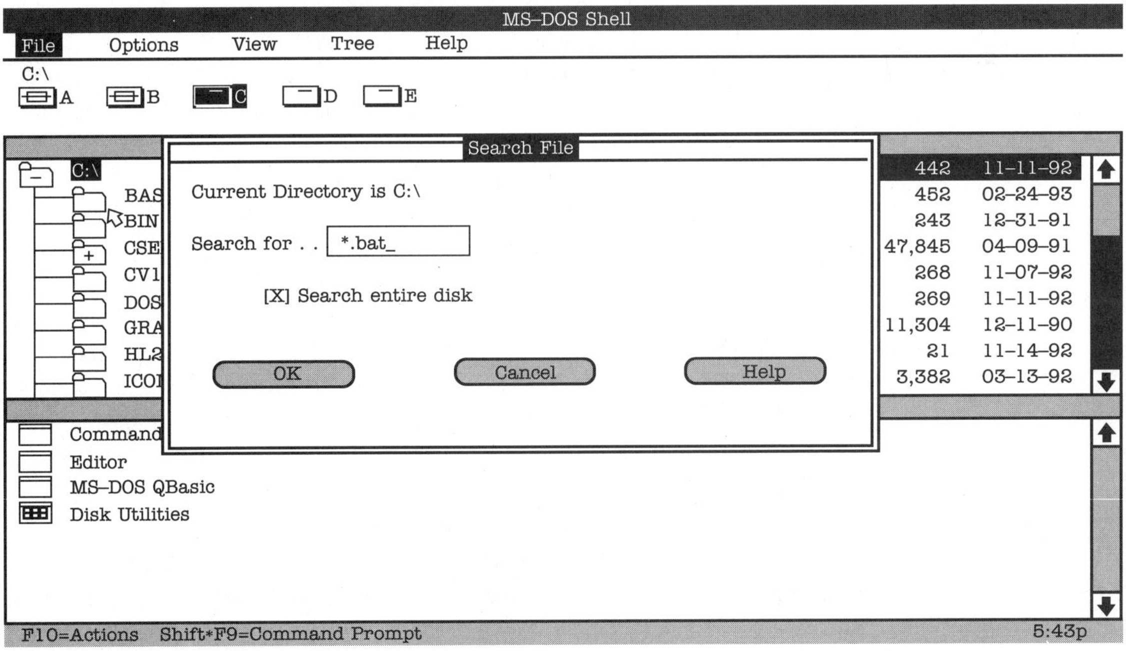

Running Programs

There are several options for executing programs (executable files with COM, EXE, or BAT extensions) from the DOS Shell. You can run programs from the DOS prompt, from the file list, from the File menu, or from the program list at the bottom of the screen. You can also create your own program group(s) to display in the program list area.

Using the DOS Prompt. To access the DOS prompt from the Shell, simply press Shift-F9 and the screen will clear and display the prompt. You can type whatever DOS commands you wish, run utilities or other programs, and then return to the Shell after exiting these programs by typing EXIT at the DOS prompt.

Running a Program from the File List. Another way to run a program is to select it in the file-list window and press Enter. With a mouse, you can double-click the program filename to run it. One disadvantage of running programs this way is that you can't specify command switches or other program parameters.

Using the File Run Command. There are two ways to run a program from the File menu. You can select the program filename from the file list, then select Run from the File menu. Or you can type in the program filename when you select File Run. When the program is finished, you will be returned to the Shell window.

Using the Program List. The program-list area of the Shell window enables you to set up your own menu of programs, or to choose programs from the default list, the Main group, as shown in Figure 17.6. The Main program group contains three programs: the MS-DOS command prompt (the COMMAND.COM program), the MS-DOS Editor (the EDIT program), and the MS-DOS BASIC program, QBASIC. It also includes a subgroup, Disk Utilities. You can tell that Disk Utilities is a group of programs because its icon has several small squares representing items within the group (In text mode, program groups are enclosed in square brackets).

To run a program from the program list, simply highlight the program name and press Enter, double-click the name with a mouse, or choose Open from the File menu. (In Figure 17.6, the MS-DOS Editor is selected.)

To select a program from a program group, first open the group (by pressing the arrow keys and Enter or by double-clicking the mouse). Figure 17.7 shows the program list for Disk Utilities group. To format a disk, for example, you would select Format and press Enter and a dialog box would appear where you could enter any parameters (switches) you wish to use, such as /f:720 to format a 720 KB disk.

Adding Program Items

When you are in the program-list area of the DOS Shell window, you can use the File New command to add your own program items or groups. A *program item* is

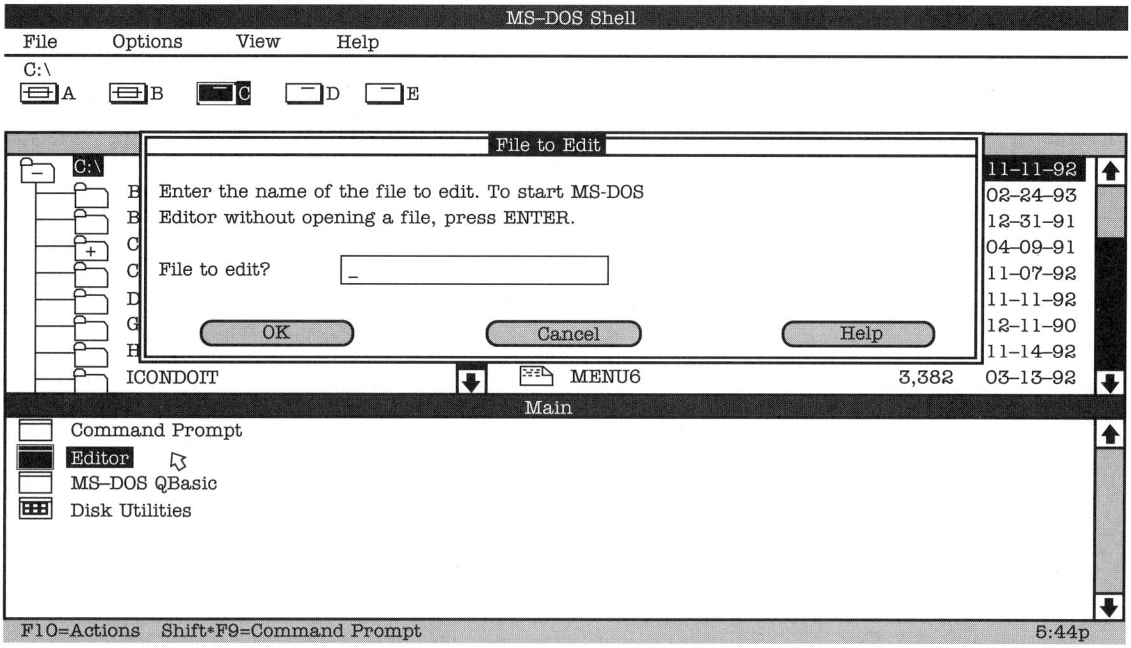

FIGURE 17.6 Main program group with Editor selected

FIGURE 17.7 Disk Utilities program group

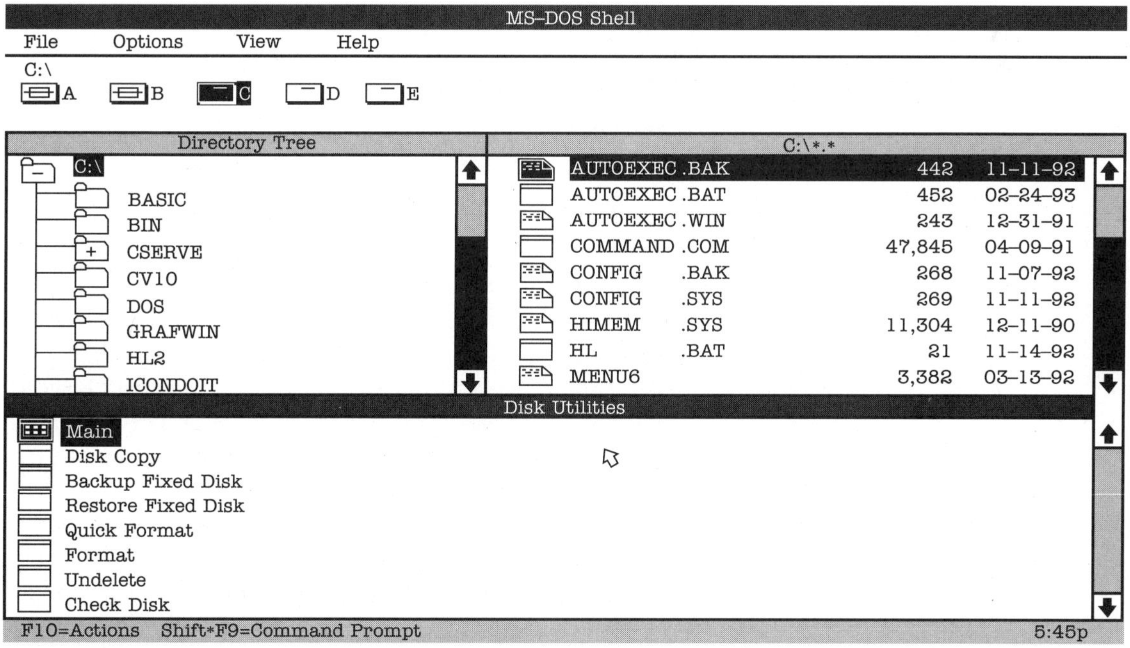

an individual program, and a *program group* is a menu item leading to a selection of programs. When you create program items, you can specify command switches or particular filenames for the program to open. When you select File and then New, the Shell asks if you want to create a program group or a program item. If you select Program Item, an Add Program dialog box similar to Figure 17.8 will appear.

FIGURE 17.8 Add Program dialog box

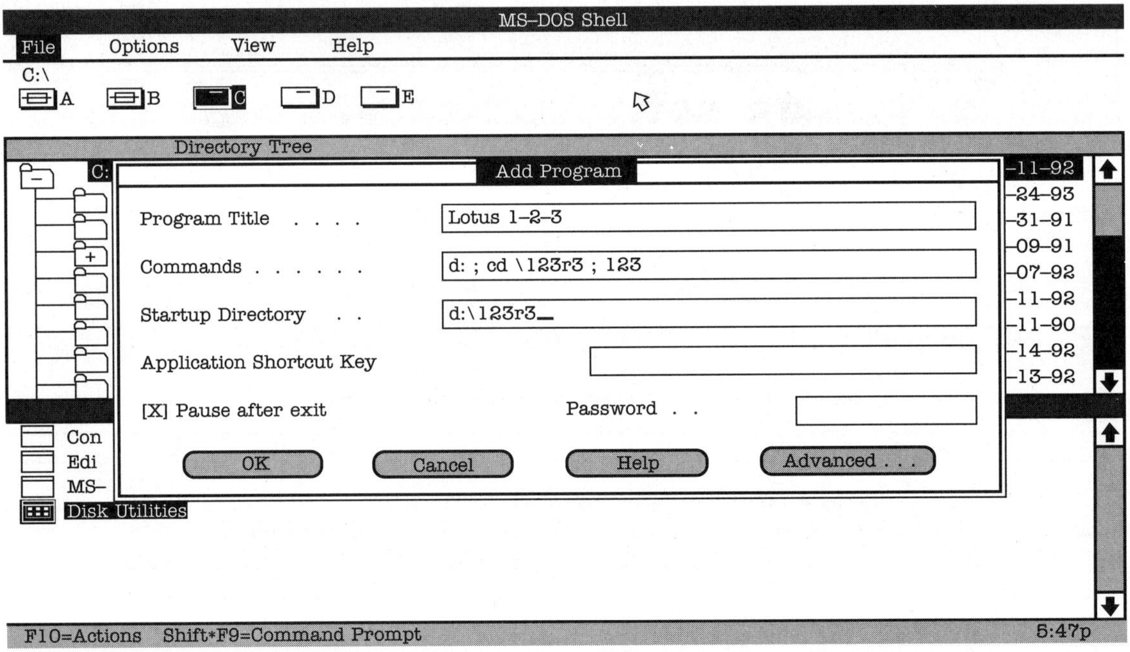

The Add Program dialog box shows the following items. Use the Tab key or the Shift-Tab key to move forward or backward among the boxes.

- *Program Title.* Here you type the title you want to appear in the Shell window. The title can be up to 23 characters.
- *Commands.* The commands entered here are the same you would enter at the DOS prompt to start the program. You can specify multiple commands (just as you would in a batch file) by separating each command sequence with a semicolon (;) preceded and followed by one or more spaces. Figure 17.8 shows the commands to start the spreadsheet program Lotus 1-2-3 on Drive D in the \123r3 directory. (To use batch files as the program commands, use the CALL command to run each batch file.)
- *Startup Directory.* This is normally the directory that contains the program you want to start. If you were creating a program to start WordPerfect, for example, you would enter the WordPerfect directory in this field.

- *Application Shortcut Key.* This enables you to specify a shortcut key to use to switch to the program automatically without having to select it. Use the Alt, Shift, or Ctrl key with a letter key to specify the shortcut key.
- *Pause after exit* is a check box that specifies if you want the "Press any key to continue" message to display after you exit a program and before you return to the Shell.
- *Password* is an optional field in which you can enter a password to be required to start the program. The password can contain up to 20 characters.

You will also note an *Advanced* button at the bottom of the Add Program dialog box. This button leads you to further options that control how a program runs. For more information consult your DOS manual or the online Help system.

Using Replaceable Parameters in the Command Line

It is possible to use replaceable parameters when you are specifying the commands to start a program in the Add Program dialog box. For example if you specify **CHKDSK %1** in the Command box, Shell will display a Program Item Properties dialog box like Figure 17.9 that asks for the value to use for %1. You can specify up to nine replaceable parameters in the Command box. For each you will need to fill out a Program Item Properties dialog box.

FIGURE 17.9 Program Item Properties dialog box

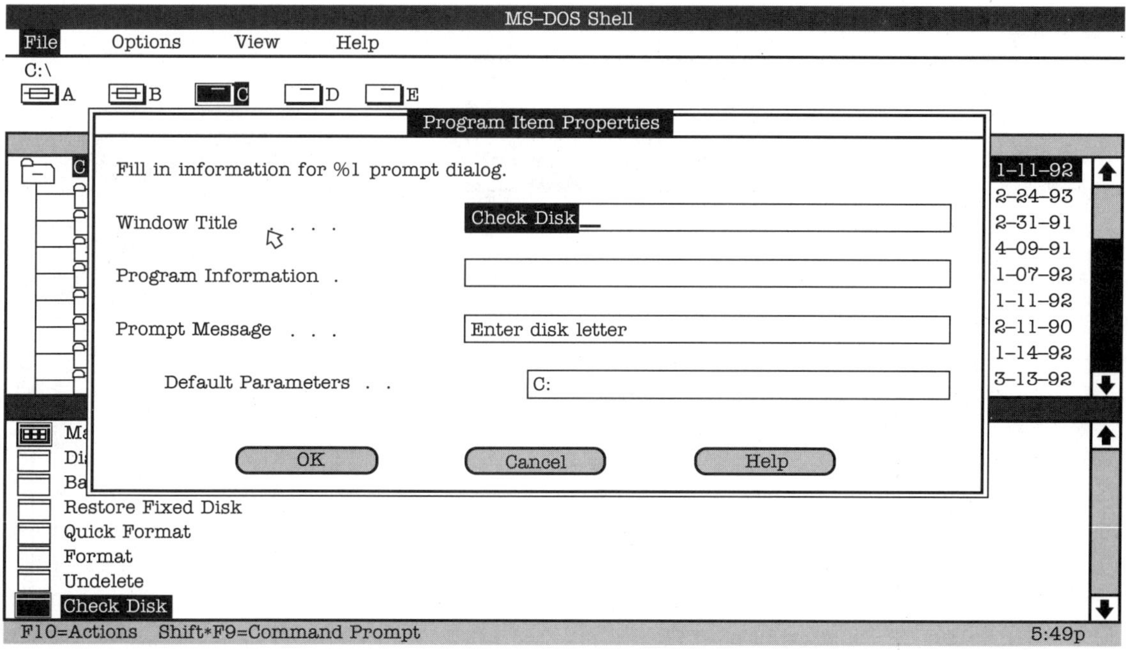

The Program Item Properties dialog box displays the following text boxes:

- *Window Title.* This is the title you want to appear at the top of the dialog box that appears when the program is selected.
- *Program Information.* This is for a descriptive message about the replaceable parameter, such as "Disk Drive Statistics" for a CHKDSK command.
- *Prompt Message.* Type the message you want to appear in front of the parameter entry area of the dialog box that appears when the program is selected.
- *Default Parameters.* This box enables you to specify a default value for the replaceable parameter, which can be overridden by the user's entry.

The Program Item Properties dialog box can also be accessed from the File menu by selecting the Properties command, if you want to change properties of already existing program items.

Adding a Program Group

It is sometimes helpful to group similar programs or most often used programs together. To create a program group, with the cursor in the program-list area, select File, then New, and choose the Program Group option button and then OK. The Shell will display the Add Group dialog box as shown in Figure 17.10.

FIGURE 17.10 Add Group dialog box

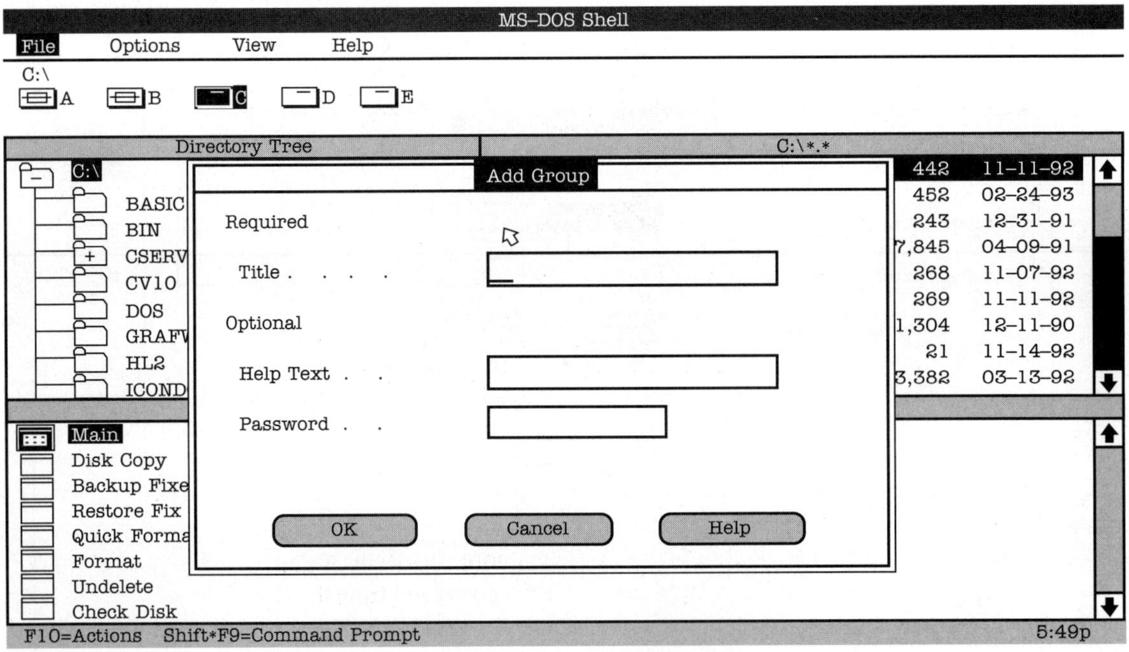

This dialog box has one required text box (Title) and two optional text boxes (Help Text and Password). The Title box contains up to 23 characters of text that you want to display as the title of your program group. Help Text can contain up to 255 characters of helpful information. Use the ^m character combination to indicate a line break. You can also enter a Password of up to 20 characters that must be entered in order to access the program group.

To add programs to a group, select that group, then use the File New command as detailed above under "Adding Programs" to add programs to that group. You can also copy a program item to another group by selecting the program item and using the File Copy command. To move a program item, copy it to its new location and then delete it from the old location with the Delete command from the File menu.

Switching Among Programs

DOS Shell Version 5 gives a new capability: you can have several programs active and switch among them with a keystroke. The DOS Task Swapper is not a true multitasking environment like Windows or DesqView; when you have one program running and switch to a second program, the first program is frozen and saved to disk. Likewise, when you switch back to the first program, the second program is frozen and saved to disk, freeing up the memory space it was using. Thus the Task Swapper is less memory-intensive than a true multitasking environment. If there is not enough room on the current drive to swap out the program(s) you have selected, the Shell will show an error message indicating you must either free up disk space or end the program before returning to the Shell.

To use more than one program, select the Options menu and then select Enable Task Swapper to open up the Active Task List area, which is shown in Figure 17.11.

To run a program, double-click the program name (or highlight the program and press Enter or select File Open). To switch to another program, use one of the following keys:

Ctrl-Esc	Switches back to the Shell from the current program
Alt-Esc	Switches back to the Shell from the current program
Alt-Tab	Cycles among active tasks (programs)
Shift-Enter	Adds a task to the Active Task List without switching to the program

Associating Data Files with Program Files

DOS Shell Version 5 offers one more way to make running programs easier and more efficient. With the Associate command from the File menu in the file-listing area, you can automatically correlate files with like extensions with a specified

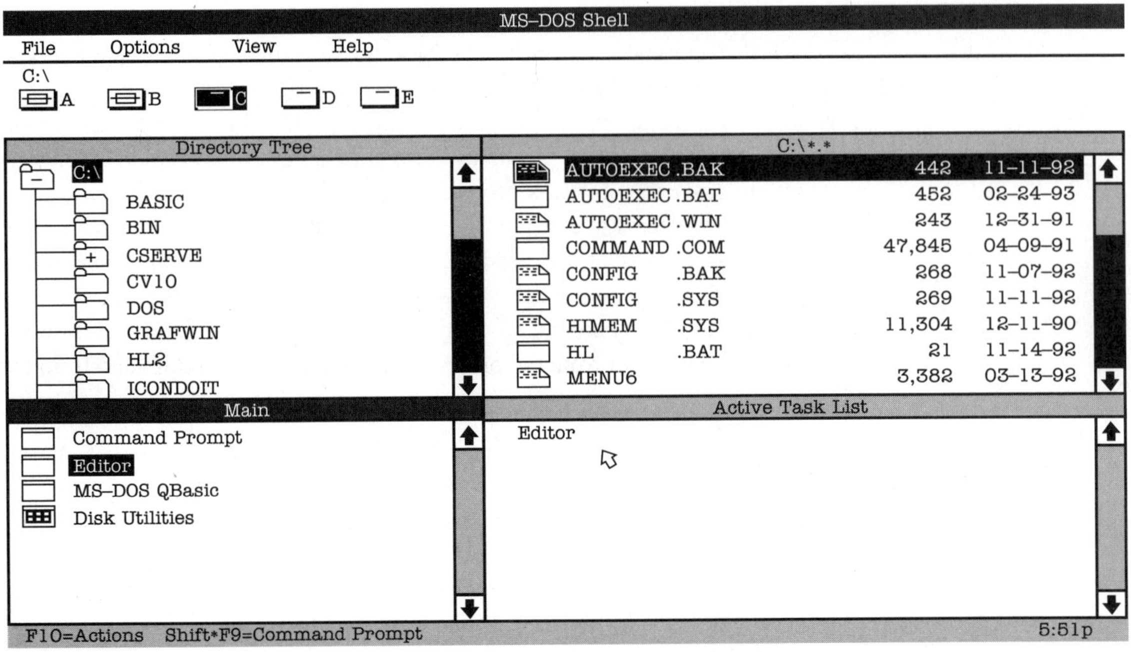

FIGURE 17.11 DOS Shell window with Active Task List

program. For example, suppose you wanted the Shell to load the EDIT editor every time you selected a file with the TXT extension, and to open that file in the editor. You could use the Associate command to associate all TXT files with the DOS EDIT command, as shown in Figure 17.12.

Now, if you select *any* file with the TXT extension and press Enter, or double-click the filename with the mouse, EDIT will be run and the file will be loaded.

One limitation of the Associate command is that a particular file extension can be associated with only one program. You cannot associate a group of files with the TXT extension with one program in one directory and with another program in another directory.

To remove a file association, select the program filename, then select File Associate and remove the file extension from the dialog box. Select OK to save the changes, and the program will no longer be associated with that extension.

EXITING THE SHELL TEMPORARILY

There are two ways to temporarily exit to the DOS prompt to execute commands. You can select the MS-DOS Command Prompt choice from the Main program group in the program-list area, or press Shift-F9 from any part of the Shell window. You can then run any command you want, and when you are finished type EXIT and Enter to return to the Shell.

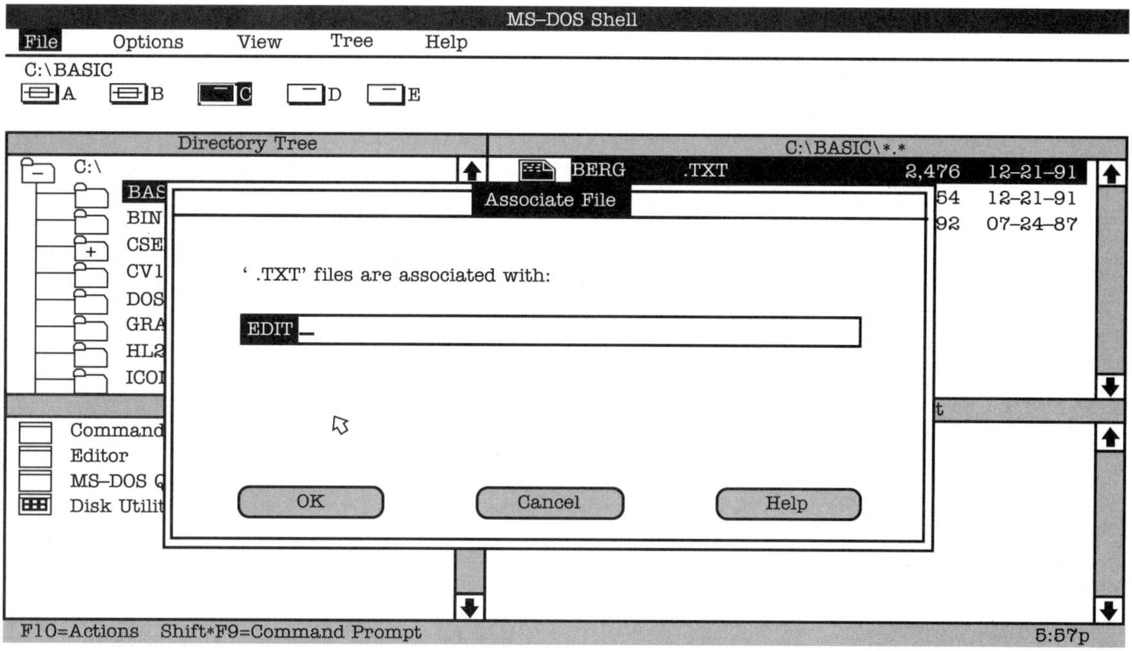

FIGURE 17.12 Associating a file extension with a program

QUITTING THE SHELL

To permanently quit the Shell and return to the DOS prompt, first make sure that you have exited all programs. (The Shell will not permit you to exit without first closing all active programs.) You shouldn't see any programs listed in the Active Task List area. If you do, press Alt-Tab to switch to any running programs and exit them properly. Then choose the File menu and Exit (or press F3) to quit the Shell.

QUESTIONS AND PROBLEMS

1. How is the DOSSHELL set to operate automatically at boot time or during a power-up of the computer?
2. What are the two modes in which the DOS Shell can operate and what are some differences between the two?
3. What are some advantages of operating the shell with a mouse?
4. What type of an executable file is the program DOSSHELL? In which directory will it normally be found?
5. What Function key is used to request help with a selected item or command?

6. What Function key is used to select the Menu Bar at the top of the Shell screen?
7. How are function keys used as part of the Shell?
8. What other files must be included as part of your system if a mouse is to be used to operate the Shell? Are there any boot control files that must be modified so that a mouse will operate with the DOS Shell?
9. Files are normally displayed in alphabetical order using the file system of the SHELL. What are some other File Display options available through the File Display menu?
10. What menu and options will allow you to find a file named BUDGET.FNL that is stored somewhere on Drive C?

CHAPTER 18

OTHER COMMANDS (EXTERNAL COMMANDS)

INTRODUCTION

DOS provides several other commands, in addition to the extensive list we have already discussed, that have limited or special purposes. These commands are briefly discussed in this chapter. Our purpose here is not to provide an extensive discussion of these commands, but to introduce their basic purpose and applications. Two of these commands, DEBUG and EXE2BIN, have primary applications for programmers and those desiring to create application software. Using these two programs requires a basic knowledge of programming and the hexadecimal number system. Some knowledge of assembly language and the link-edit process is also desirable.

The National Language Support Function was introduced with DOS Version 3.30, and is primarily useful when DOS is used as an international system. Code-page switching and foreign keyboard characters are supported as part of this system. For the vast majority of users in the United States, the NLSFUNC command will be of little or no interest.

The SELECT command was introduced, in Version 4.00 of DOS, as the command used to start the process for installing DOS on a new system. SELECT is not included in Version 5. For those with versions installed prior to Version 4.00, the SYS command can still be used to upgrade to a DOS 4.00 system. The external commands discussed in this chapter are:

SELECT
JOIN
DEBUG
EXE2BIN
NLSFUNC

THE START THE INSTALLATION (SELECT) PROGRAM

Beginning with Version 4.00, the process for installing DOS was changed significantly. The SELECT command is used to start the installation of a Version 4.00 system; this program then prompts for information regarding specifics of your system and does an initial installation of DOS on the hard drive. The use of SELECT and its installation process will not provide the tailoring and protection features discussed in Chapter 21 or the Appendices. It will provide a starting point from which further tailoring of your system can be done. For information on installing DOS 5, see Chapter 23.

Using SELECT with Version 4.00 provides a country-specific system because of the questions asked during the Install process. The CONFIG.SYS file created using Install contains a DEVICE= line that includes either the default value for the United States or information supplied about the country of choice. For most users, this includes a country code of 001 and a keyboard code of 437 for the United States.

The INSTALL diskette associated with Version 4.00 includes an AUTOEXEC.BAT file that automatically starts the installation process. To do this, just boot the system from this diskette, which should be mounted in Drive A on your computer. When the installation process is complete, both an AUTOEXEC and a CONFIG file will have been created with the extension 400. You can choose to use these two files directly with your system by renaming them to AUTOEXEC.BAT and CONFIG.SYS. You may want to begin with these two files, then modify them to your needs using one of the DOS text editors. See Chapters 21, 22, 23, and the Appendices for further information on installing DOS.

THE JOIN A DISK DRIVE TO A DIRECTORY (JOIN) COMMAND

The JOIN command is used to connect a disk drive to an empty directory on another disk drive. The operating system will then treat the joined disk as though it were a directory on the second drive. The joined drive acts as part of the second drive. If the JOIN command is entered without any other fields or parameters, DOS displays a list of the current joins that are in effect.

The format of the JOIN command is:

JOIN *<drive>* *<pathname>* /D

<drive> is the drive that will be joined to a directory on the second drive. The entire drive, including its directory structure, is joined beginning at the root directory. The drive letter that is joined may no longer be used in any command.

<pathname> is the drive letter, and the entire pathname, to which the *<drive>* is joined. The directory to which *<drive>* is joined must be empty. The directory to which *<drive>* is joined may not be the root directory of any drive.

/D is the parameter used to disconnect a previously created join. The specified directory remains on the drive.

THE DEBUG (DEBUG) COMMAND

The DEBUG command is primarily intended to provide programmers with various tools for debugging their programs. For the advanced DOS user, however, DEBUG has several useful features that allow you to look inside executable program files. (Other DOS utilities provide a similar capability and may be of interest to the advanced user.) DEBUG is not limited to use with a COM or EXE file;

it can also be used with any file, including executable files, formatted data files, and text files. DEBUG is an editor, just like EDLIN or EDIT are text editors. However, EDLIN or EDIT can only be used for editing text files; DEBUG can be used with any file. To use DEBUG you should be familiar with and understand, at a minimum, the hexadecimal number system. You should also refer to the reference manual that discusses all of the commands associated with DEBUG. Our discussion in this chapter will be limited to displaying some of the basic capabilities of DEBUG.

When using DEBUG, refer to a detailed reference on this program. It is also strongly recommended that precautions be taken such as backing up the programs that will be edited, or creating separate working copies that can be used in a test mode. DEBUG used indiscriminantly can cause major damage to your system and your files. **Use this program with extreme caution.**

DEBUG provides a group of commands that operate from its prompt in a manner similar to EDLIN. Many of the things you have learned earlier about the EDLIN editor can be applied to the DEBUG editor. The prompt for the DEBUG editor is the dash (-), just as the prompt for the EDLIN editor was the asterisk (*). To execute DEBUG, type its name followed by a filename, as shown below. This is similar to the manner in which you used EDLIN. This example uses the AUTOEXEC.BAT file as an illustration.

```
C:\> DEBUG autoexec.bat
```

DEBUG will respond by displaying its prompt character (-). A DEBUG command can then be entered to display the contents of the file. The dump command (d) is a DEBUG command that dumps a 128-byte section of the file. The d command, entered at the dash prompt, will display eight lines of information, 16 bytes per line. A sample display is shown below for a typical AUTOEXEC.BAT file. The right side of the screen displays the meaning of the hexadecimal codes for the beginning characters in each of the eight lines displayed in the example below:

```
-d

262E:0100 40 65 63 68 6F 20 6F 66 66 0D 0A 50 52 4F 4D 50 @echo off..
262E:0110 54 20 24 70 24 67 0D 0A 53 45 54 20 43 4F 4D 53 T $p$g..SET
262E:0120 50 45 43 3D 43 3A 5C 43 4F 4D 4D 41 4E 44 2E 43 PED=C:\COMM
262E:0130 4F 4D 0A 0A 70 61 74 68 20 43 3A 5C 3B 43 3A 5C OM..path C:
262E:0140 44 4F 53 33 33 30 0D 0A 66 61 73 74 6F 70 65 6E DOS330..fas
262E:0150 20 63 3A 3D 31 30 30 0D 0A 72 65 6D 20 56 65 72 c:=100..re
262E:0160 73 69 6F 6E 20 33 2E 31 38 4D 20 72 65 71 75 69 sion 3.18M
262E:0170 72 65 73 20 74 68 65 20 2F 44 2D 20 70 61 72 61 res the /D—
```

To display subsequent sections of the file, enter another dump (d) command. To exit DEBUG without saving the file, enter the quit (q) command. Most commands in DEBUG, just as in EDLIN, are single-character commands. Other DEBUG commands can be entered at the DEBUG prompt to modify, display, and save the contents of the file. DEBUG provides the ability to patch a command file, as long as the modification or patch leaves the file operational. DEBUG can also be used to compile a program script file. The advanced DOS user may well find reason to use DEBUG in conjunction with programs found in various PC magazines, through bulletin boards, or other information sources such as CompuServe. If using these sources, make sure that detailed information is also available on the commands associated with DEBUG and their applications.

THE CONVERT AN EXECUTABLE FILE (EXE2BIN) COMMAND

The EXE2BIN program supplied with DOS is primarily intended for use by programmers as opposed to the typical DOS application user. EXE2BIN converts a program file with an EXE extension to a program file with a COM extension. Both forms of the program file are executable. Because DOS uses a hierarchy of extensions in deciding what program to execute, both forms of the file should not exist on a system. In other words, you should never find a program file ABCD.EXE and a program file ABCD.COM on the same system, and certainly not in the same directory.

DOS only considers a file executable if it has an extension of COM, EXE, or BAT. The hierarchy of execution is COM, then EXE, and then BAT. If two files exist, ABCD.COM and ABCD.EXE, the ABCD file with the COM extension would execute every time you entered the command ABCD. You couldn't force the EXE file to execute by entering ABCD.EXE. DOS only uses the extensions to search for an executable file; it ignores the extension in loading the file and executing it. Therefore, typing ABCD.EXE would still result in the ABCD.COM file actually executing.

THE NATIONAL LANGUAGE SUPPORT FUNCTION (NLSFUNC)

The National Language Support Function tells DOS the pathname and the filename of the file that contains country-specific information, such as the date and time format and the currency symbol. The NLSFUNC command must be executed before any code-page command information can be entered.

The format of the NLSFUNC command is:

NLSFUNC *<country-specific file>*

<country-specific file> is the name of the file that contains country-specific information. DOS assumes that the file is the one specified in the country configuration command in COUNTRY.SYS. If there is no country configuration command in COUNTRY.SYS, DOS assumes that the file is named COUNTRY.SYS and searches for it in the root directory of the boot drive. Most versions of DOS supply a file named COUNTRY.SYS as part of the operating system.

□ EXAMPLES

1. C:\> **JOIN A: C:\DIRECT1**
2. C:\> **JOIN A: /d**
3. C:\> **JOIN**
4. C:\> **NLSFUNC C:\DOS401\country.sys**
5. **INSTALL C:\DOS401\nlsfunc.exe C:\DOS401\country.sys**
6. C:\> **EXE2BIN ABCD.EXE**
7. C:\> **DEBUG autoexec.bat**
8. C:\> **DEBUG ABCD.COM**
9. C:\> **DEBUG < text.scr**
10. C:\> **SELECT 049 gr**

1. C:\> **JOIN A: C:\DIRECT1** This command will join Drive A to the DIRECT1 directory on Drive C. References may no longer be made to Drive A as long as the join is in effect.
2. C:\> **JOIN A: /d** In this example, the join in effect for Drive A is deleted. Any other joins for other drives would remain in effect. Only the Drive A join is deleted.
3. C:\> **JOIN** The JOIN command used with no other fields or parameters displays all joins currently in effect. JOIN is like ASSIGN, SUBST, and similar commands. Exercise caution when using this command, because it alters the hardware operation of your system.
4. C:\> **NLSFUNC C:\DOS401\country.sys** If National Language Support is used occasionally, and you do not want to make it part of system operations, the NLSFUNC command can be entered at the DOS prompt. In this example, National Language Support is activated using the COUNTRY.SYS file, which is part of the \DOS401 directory.
5. **INSTALL C:\DOS401\nlsfunc.exe C:\DOS401\country.sys** To make National Language Support part of system operations, include a line in the CONFIG.SYS file such as the one shown in this example. The INSTALL command is included in CONFIG.SYS and will be executed as part of the power-up process or as part of a reboot process. The NLSFUNC command is executed and the COUNTRY.SYS file is loaded from the \DOS401 directory.
6. C:\> **EXE2BIN ABCD.EXE** The EXE2BIN program can be used to convert an EXE extension file to a COM extension file with the same filename. In

this example, a file, ABCD.EXE, is converted to a file named ABCD. COM. Both of these files are executable files.

7. `C:\> DEBUG autoexec.bat` The DEBUG program is executed and loads the AUTOEXEC.BAT file so that it has access to it. The DEBUG editor can then be used to display or modify the AUTOEXEC.BAT file.
8. `C:\> DEBUG ABCD.COM` The DEBUG program is used in this example to access the ABCD.COM program file. That file can then be modified using various DEBUG commands. Refer to reference material on DEBUG for the commands available for modifying or displaying a program file using the DEBUG editor.
9. `C:\> DEBUG < text.scr` In this example, DEBUG is used to assemble a script file text.scr, written in Assembly language in order to generate a COM file. That COM file can then be executed just as any other executable file from the DOS prompt.
10. `C:\> SELECT 049 gr` The SELECT command is used to generate a Version 4.00 system diskette with the German character set, using the appropriate country code: 049. The codes for various countries are part of the National Language Support Function tables.

QUESTIONS AND PROBLEMS

1. What types of files can be edited using DEBUG? What number system is used by DEBUG to display the characters in a file? What coding system is used on a personal computer to encode the characters that are displayed using DEBUG?
2. What type of user would need the facilities provided by the programs DEBUG and EXE2BIN?
3. What are some disadvantages of using the JOIN command?
4. What command must first be executed in order to use code-page switching?
5. What are two functions performed by the SELECT command?
6. What command is used to install code-page switching for a particular hardware device?
7. Write the command to compile an executable program from the script file named DISP.SCR.
8. What command is used to install code-page switching as part of the computer's operating environment? In what file must the command be included?
9. What requirement is imposed on a directory when a disk drive is joined to it?
10. Write the command to display the connections that are currently in effect as the result of using the JOIN command.

CHAPTER 19

BATCH FILE COMMANDS

INTRODUCTION

DOS provides a limited programming capability for use with the operating system through a technique known as **batch files.** A batch file is an executable program file, much in the same way that a COM or an EXE file is an executable program file. For a batch file to be executable, it must follow some fundamental rules. First, a batch file must have a BAT extension in order for DOS to treat it as an executable file. Second, an executable batch file can only contain internal commands, external commands, and batch file commands. As long as these two broad guidelines are followed, virtually any kind of batch file can be written and executed from within the DOS framework.

The most common example of a DOS batch file is the AUTOEXEC.BAT file that is written and automatically executed every time the computer is booted. A simple example of an AUTOEXEC.BAT file is given below:

```
@ECHO off
REM
REM             AUTOEXEC.BAT
REM
REM This file is used to control the boot process
REM The DOS prompt control is set by the PROMPT command.
REM The DOS path search is set by the PATH command.
DATE
TIME
PROMPT $P $G
PATH C:\;C:\DOS500;C:\UTIL
CLS
VER
```

This AUTOEXEC.BAT file obeys the two fundamental guidelines. Its filename contains an extension, BAT, and all of the commands within the batch file are internal commands, external commands, or batch file commands. In this example there are no external commands. The commands DATE, TIME, PATH, PROMPT, CLS, and VER are all internal commands. The remainder of the commands are batch file commands. In the case of AUTOEXEC.BAT, the file has a very specific name (AUTOEXEC), because that is what DOS requires if it is to execute this file automatically as part of the boot process. The file can also be executed by simply typing its name followed by pressing the Enter key.

What is the purpose of a batch file and how can it be used? Batch files have become quite common and have a wide variety of applications. Automating the boot process is one example; there are many others. Software suppliers use batch files to control and automate the software installation process. This cuts down on mistakes, saves support and documentation costs, and seeks to guarantee that software will be installed properly.

The BACKUP and RESTORE processes are frequently automated through batch files because of the large number of parameters or switches associated with them. Application programs such as WordPerfect or Lotus 1-2-3 are frequently executed through a batch file. The batch file can be used to guarantee that the user is operating from the correct directory. It can be used to make sure that data files are directed to diskette rather than to the hard drive; it can also be used to guarantee that the user-created files are automatically backed up as part of the exit process. Finally, menu systems are frequently implemented using a system of batch files. Personal computer laboratories in colleges or universities frequently use a menu system to control the student operating environment. Students can more easily use a system and its applications correctly when they begin learning to use personal computers and associated software through a menu system. (A sample batch file menu system is shown in Appendix H.)

These are but a few examples of the use of batch files. Fundamentally, any time you must use or duplicate a process many times through a series of DOS commands, you have a potential batch file application.

Batch files can also process **replaceable parameters.** Replaceable parameters are variables that are entered at the time the batch file is executed. When a batch file is programmed with replaceable parameters, the file will include references to %1 and %2 if the batch file contains two replaceable parameters. At the time of execution the user would enter the values to be given to each of these replaceable parameters as part of the command line. A command line as shown below, includes the value for two replaceable parameters, which must be separated by one or more spaces.

```
C:\> TEST A: FILE1.TXT
```

In this example, a batch file named TEST.BAT is executed. Two replaceable parameters are included in the command line. The disk drive reference A: will replace %1 every place it occurs in the batch file. The file reference FILE1.TXT will replace the variable reference %2 every place it occurs in the file TEST.BAT.

A second execution of TEST.BAT might use parameter references of B: and SAMPLE.DOC as the two replaceable parameter references. For more information on programming batch files and the use of replaceable parameters, see the examples later in this chapter or refer to a good book on batch file techniques.

This chapter is designed to introduce the user to the concept of batch files and to illustrate a few applications. It does not attempt to cover the topic of batch files in a comprehensive manner. The batch file commands discussed in this chapter are:

ECHO
REM
PAUSE
GOTO
IF
SHIFT
CALL

The ECHO Command

The ECHO command is used to turn on or turn off the echoing of commands to the display screen. When DOS is first booted, it sets the default mode for echoing of commands to ON. This means that any time a batch file is executed, each command in the batch file will be displayed on the screen (or *echoed* to the screen) before it is executed. When testing a batch file, it is helpful to leave ECHO on so that each command is displayed before it is executed. This provides information on which command was executing if error messages occur. Once the batch file is working, turn ECHO off to reduce screen clutter. The use of the @ symbol in front of the ECHO command works with DOS Version 3.30 and later. When used, it results in the ECHO command not being echoed to the display screen. The AUTOEXEC.BAT file example earlier illustrates the use of @ECHO off in its typical format.

The ECHO command can also display messages and comments to the screen. If text comments are included in the same line with the ECHO command, they will be displayed on the screen, regardless of the ECHO status set by ECHO on or ECHO off. The example below illustrates some sample ECHO statements as part of a batch file.

```
@ECHO off
REM This procedure copies a file from the hard drive
REM to a diskette mounted in Drive A.
REM %1 is the name of the file to be copied
ECHO Duplicate file to diskette
ECHO Place archive diskette in Drive A
PAUSE
C:
COPY %1 A:%1
```

The REM Command

The REM command is a nonexecutable command. It is used to place a comment in a batch file. Remarks will be displayed if ECHO is on; if ECHO is off, remarks do not display while the batch file is executing. A REM command that has no text after it is simply used to add blank lines to the comment. The REM command is normally used to place documentation comments in a batch file. The sample file below will display remarks since ECHO is set to on.

```
ECHO on
REM    Sample remarks statements
REM
REM    Sample Batch File Remarks
REM
REM Replaceable parameters should always be documented
REM %1 is an example of a replaceable parameter.
REM
```

THE PAUSE COMMAND

The PAUSE command, when included in a batch file, causes the batch file to stop executing or pause, and displays the message "Press any key to continue." Striking any key on the keyboard results in the batch file resuming execution and processing commands beginning at the next command following the PAUSE command. Use PAUSE to stop execution when some manual operation (such as loading a diskette) must be done. PAUSE can also be used to allow messages or instructions to be read from the display screen (the message or instructions should precede the PAUSE command.) The batch file can be canceled using Ctrl-C at the PAUSE message. The user is then queried on whether the batch file operation should be terminated. Respond y to terminate the batch file. The batch file below illustrates the use of PAUSE so that a diskette can be loaded into Drive A.

```
@ECHO off
REM This procedure copies a file from the hard drive
REM to a diskette mounted in Drive A.
REM %1 is the name of the file to be copied
ECHO Duplicate file to diskette
ECHO Place archive diskette in Drive A
PAUSE
C:
COPY %1 A:%1
```

THE GOTO COMMAND AND LABELS

The GOTO command is used in a batch file to branch to another line in the batch file identified by a label. A **label** is a line in the batch file identified by a colon (:), followed by a word called the *label identifier*. A GOTO followed by a label identifier causes DOS to branch to the label line and begin executing the commands immediately following the label line. In the example below, a test is done on the existence of a file on Drive A. If the test is true, the GOTO statement branches to the label CONTINUE.

```
@ECHO off
REM This procedure copies a file from the hard drive
REM to a diskette mounted in Drive A.
REM %1 is the name of the file to be copied
ECHO Duplicate file to diskette
ECHO Place archive diskette in Drive A
PAUSE
IF NOT EXIST A:%1 GOTO continue
ECHO A:%1 exists. Press CTRL-C to cancel execution
PAUSE
:CONTINUE
C:
COPY %1 A:%1
```

Labels are used as reference lines in the batch file so that the batch file programmer can use the line as a branching point in the file. The previous example illustrates the use of a label named :CONTINUE. Note that CONTINUE is not preceded by a colon in the GOTO statement. The colon is used only in the label statement itself.

THE IF COMMAND

The IF batch file command is used to test a condition. If the condition is true, the command in the line with the IF test is executed. If the condition is not met and is false, the batch file executes the next sequential statement in the batch file. There are six variations of the IF statement, depending on the type of condition to be tested. These are:

IF *<condition>* *<command>*

IF NOT *<condition>* *<command>*

IF EXIST *<condition>* *<command>*

IF NOT EXIST *<condition>* *<command>*

IF ERRORLEVEL *<condition>* *<command>*

IF NOT ERRORLEVEL *<condition>* *<command>*

The IF *<condition>* test is used to compare a string condition for equality. This could be testing against any set of string characters, including combinations of alphabetic characters, numeric characters, and punctuation characters. The IF NOT *<condition>* tests that the condition does not hold. This is also a string condition test. String condition tests use the double equals (==) sign. The example below illustrates the IF condition test. The IF NOT condition test could also be implemented in a similar manner.

```
@ECHO off
REM This is an example of string condition tests
IF %1 == A:     GOTO skip1
IF %1 == a:     GOTO skip1
GOTO end
:SKIP1
FORMAT %1%2 /u
:END
```

The IF EXIST *<condition>* test checks for the existence of a file on a disk drive. If the file is present on the drive, the condition is true. The IF NOT EXIST *<condition>* test determines if a file is not present on the particular disk drive (An example is shown below.)

Batch files frequently need to generate blank lines when displaying information. To generate a blank line type the word ECHO followed by a space. Then press the Alt key while typing the characters 255 on the numeric keypad portion of the keyboard. Then release the Alt key. The characters Alt and 255 will not display as part of the file, since this key sequence is used to display a blank line. As the example below illustrates, you can test for the presence of a single file or a series of files on a particular drive.

```
@ECHO off
REM This batch file tests for the presence of a file
REM on Drive A, before copying the file to Drive A.
REM
:START
IF "%1" == "" GOTO end
ECHO <ALT-255>
ECHO <ALT-255>
ECHO Copying %1 if not already present on A:
IF NOT EXIST A:%1 COPY %1 A:\
DIR A:\ /p
PAUSE
SHIFT
GOTO start
:END
```

The IF ERRORLEVEL test is a test for an error code set by DOS when it executes various commands. Error codes or levels are set as commands are executed. If a command executes successfully, an error level of 0 is normally set, as shown in the following example. If an error condition occurs as a result of the execution, various codes are set, depending on the error encountered. The IF NOT ERRORLEVEL *<condition>* tests that a particular level is not true as a result of executing a particular command.

```
@ECHO off
BACKUP C:\%1\*.* A: /s
IF ERRORLEVEL 0 GOTO done
ECHO Error occurred in backup procedure
ECHO Files backed up from directory %1
ECHO may be defective. Check messages from backup.
PAUSE
:DONE
```

When using the IF command, use the first set of tests (IF/IF NOT) if testing for a character string; use the second set of tests (IF EXIST/IF NOT EXIST) if testing for the presence or absence of a file; and use the third set of commands (IF ERRORLEVEL/IF NOT ERRORLEVEL) if testing for error conditions when executing particular commands. Refer to your DOS reference manual or books specializing on batch files for documentation on the ERRORLEVEL codes set by various commands when error conditions occur.

When typing an IF statement with a string test, the double equals sign (==) is used to test for equality. For example, a test on the string A: would read:

```
IF %1 == A: GOTO Label1
```

THE SHIFT COMMAND

The SHIFT batch file command moves the command line variables or replaceable parameters entered with a batch file one position to the left every time the SHIFT command is executed. The leftmost variable in the command line is then discarded. Up to 10 replaceable parameters can be processed using the SHIFT command. An illustration of the use of replaceable parameters as well as the use of SHIFT is shown below. Create the file using EDLIN or EDIT and name it FILETST.BAT.

```
@ECHO off
REM This batch file tests for the presence of a file
REM on Drive A, before copying the file to Drive A.
REM
:START
IF "%1" == "" GOTO end
ECHO <ALT-255>
ECHO <ALT-255>
ECHO Copying %1 if not already present on A:
IF NOT EXIST A:%1 COPY %1 A:\
DIR A:\ /p
PAUSE
SHIFT
GOTO start
:END
```

To execute this file and test two files named FILE1.DOC and FILE2.TXT, enter the following command:

```
C:\> FILETST FILE1.DOC FILE2.TXT
```

See the batch file examples later in this chapter for other illustrations of replaceable parameters.

THE CALL COMMAND

The CALL batch file command is used to process a batch file as though it was a subroutine of another batch file. When the CALL command is used from within a batch file, DOS branches to the batch file invoked by the CALL. Once the called batch file has completed execution, DOS returns to the original batch file and continues with the command immediately following the CALL command. In this example, a batch file named COPYALL is used as a subroutine to copy files. Files on the hard drive are copied to diskette. The batch file COPYALL.BAT contains a single COPY command to copy all files from the named directory on Drive C to a similar directory created on Drive A.

```
@ECHO off
REM
REM             Hard Drive File Protection
REM
REM This batch file uses a batch file subroutine named
REM COPYALL to copy files from named directories on
REM Drive C to similar directories on Drive A.
REM
REM %1 is the named directory
REM
:START
IF "%1" == "" GOTO end
ECHO <ALT-255>
MD A:\%1
CALL COPYALL
ECHO Files copied from %1 on Drive C to Drive A.
DIR A:\%1 /p
PAUSE
SHIFT
GOTO start
:END
```

☐ EXAMPLES

1. **An AUTOEXEC.BAT file that displays a menu.** An AUTOEXEC.BAT file stored in the root directory executes automatically whenever the computer is either cold-booted or warm-booted. The file is used to set up the computer for

normal operations and to tailor the setup to your individual needs. In the example below, the DATE and TIME are requested; the prompt is set to display the default drive and directory as well as the greater-than symbol; the search path for executing commands is set with the PATH command; and then a menu is displayed with a batch file named MENU.BAT. This batch file will execute automatically if AUTOEXEC.BAT is placed in the root directory on Drive C. (See also Appendix H for an example of a batch file menu system.)

```
@ECHO off
REM
REM             AUTOEXEC.BAT
REM
REM This file is used to control the boot process.
REM The DOS prompt control is set by the PROMPT command.
REM The DOS path search is set by the PATH command.
DATE
TIME
PROMPT $P $G
PATH C:\;C:\DOS330;C:\UTIL
CLS
MENU
```

2. **A batch file, REVIEW.BAT, to display a series of text files.** A batch file can be used with a replaceable parameter to display ASCII text files on the screen. The label START is used to identify the beginning of the loop. The IF statement tests to see when no more files exist to be displayed. When this condition is true, the file branches to the last statement in the batch file, represented by the label DONE. The name of the file to be displayed is echoed to the screen using the ECHO statement. After the display is cleared, a blank line is generated. To enter this statement, type the word ECHO followed by a space. Then press the Alt key while typing the characters 255 on the numeric keypad portion of the keyboard. Then release the Alt key. The characters Alt and 255 will not display as part of the file, since this is an Escape key sequence used to display a blank line. Following the blank line, the TYPE command is used to display the file, along with the MORE command, which provides a paging mechanism. Two more blank lines are displayed following the file, followed by a PAUSE command so that the end of the file can be reviewed. The SHIFT command then shifts the replaceable parameters, discarding the current one. The batch file then returns to the label START so that the next file can be displayed.

```
@ECHO off
REM
REM             REVIEW.BAT
REM
REM %1 represents the name of the file to be displayed.
```

```
REM
:START
IF "%1" == "" GOTO done
CLS
ECHO            ***** Filename %1 *****
ECHO <ALT-255>
TYPE %1 (¦) MORE
ECHO <ALT-255>
ECHO <ALT-255>
PAUSE
SHIFT
GOTO start
:DONE
```

An example of the use of this batch file is shown with the following command line. REVIEW.BAT is used to display two files—AUTOEXEC.BAT and CONFIG.SYS.

```
C:\> REVIEW AUTOEXEC.BAT CONFIG.SYS
```

3. **A FORMAT.BAT file to control disk formatting.** This batch file can be used to prevent accidental formatting of the hard drive. After the REMarks statements, IF statements are used to test to see that either Drive A or Drive B has been specified for disk formatting. Both upper- and lowercase letters are tested so that the command can be entered in upper or lowercase. If Drive A or B is specified, the batch file branches to the label SKIP1 to format the diskette. If neither Drive A or B is specified, an error message is echoed to the screen, followed by a PAUSE so that the user can read the message. The file then branches to the END label, then ECHO is turned back on. To format the diskette, use the INITIAL command. Since a directory cannot correctly contain two files by the same name, one with a COM extension and one with a BAT extension, the FORMAT.COM file has been renamed to INITIAL.COM. INITIAL.COM is now the DOS format routine used to format disk drives.

```
@ECHO off
REM
REM            FORMAT.BAT
REM
REM This batch file controls the formatting of floppy
REM disks mounted in Drives A or B.
REM It will not allow the hard disk to be accidentally
REM formatted.
REM
REM %1 is the disk drive to be formatted.
REM %2 is the parameters to be used to control the format.
REM
```

```
IF %1 == A:     GOTO skip1
IF %1 == a:     GOTO skip1
IF %1 == B:     GOTO skip1
IF %1 == b:     GOTO skip1
CLS
ECHO You have entered data to format the hard disk
ECHO This program cannot be used to format the hard
ECHO drive.
ECHO Now exiting back to DOS.
ECHO <ALT-255>
ECHO <ALT-255>
PAUSE
GOTO end
:SKIP1
REM
REM The FORMAT.COM file was renamed to INITIAL.COM
REM
INITIAL %1%2
:END
ECHO on
```

To execute the FORMAT.BAT file for Drive B with parameters /S/V, enter the command shown below.

C:\> **FORMAT B: /S/V**

4. **An application WP.BAT batch file with built-in backup.** This batch file executes WordPerfect from the \WP51 directory. It first establishes that the default drive is C and that the default directory is the \WP51\DATA directory, where all the application data files are stored. The WP.EXE file is then executed by fully addressing it as C:\WP51\WP. When the user exits the WordPerfect program, the screen is cleared and a message is displayed to load the backup diskette. Files are then copied to the diskette in Drive A. The message to store the diskette for safekeeping is displayed, and the batch file terminates. This batch file would be stored in a directory \BATCH, along with other application batch files. The directory \BATCH is on the PATH in the AUTO- EXEC.BAT file; the application directory \WP51 is not on the PATH.

```
@ECHO off
REM
REM                WP.BAT
REM
C:
CD \WP51\DATA
C:\WP51\WP
CLS
```

```
ECHO <ALT-255>
ECHO Files from the WP data directory will be copied
ECHO for safekeeping to a diskette in Drive A.
ECHO Now load the backup diskette into Drive A.
PAUSE
ECHO <ALT-255>
COPY C:\WP51\DATA\*.* A:
ECHO <ALT-255>
ECHO <ALT-255>
ECHO Store the backup diskette for safekeeping.
ECHO <ALT-255>
```

To execute this batch file, type:

```
C:\> WP
```

5. **A directory backup DIRBACK.BAT file for applications.** The DIRBACK batch file uses the BACKUP command to back up a specified directory on the hard drive, as well as all subdirectories of the specified directory to a specified diskette drive. The screen is cleared of all previous information. Then the default drive is set to C and the default directory is set to the root directory. The BACKUP command is issued using the %1 and %2 variables. The directory that will be backed up is that specified by %1. The data will be backed up to a diskette drive based on what is specified by %2. All subdirectories of the specified directory %1 will be backed up, since the /S parameter was included in the command.

```
@ECHO off
REM
REM               DIRBACK.BAT
REM
REM %1 is the name of the primary directory to back up.
REM %2 is the drive to use for the backup data.
REM
CLS
C:
CD \
BACKUP C:\%1\*.* %2:/S
```

An example of a command to back up the \LOTUS directory to Drive A is:

```
C:\> DIRBACK LOTUS A
```

QUESTIONS AND PROBLEMS

1. How can the comments in REMarks statements in a batch file be made to display when the file executes?

2. What is a replaceable parameter and how is it represented as a variable inside a batch file?
3. What batch file command is used to cause multiple variables typed at the command line to substitute for the %1 variable inside the batch file?
4. What effect does including an ECHO off as the first line in a batch file have on error messages and the report information produced by DOS commands?
5. What command is used to make a batch file execute as a subroutine from within another batch file?
6. What command or keyboard sequence is used to terminate the execution of a batch file?
7. What batch file command is used to display messages and information to the operator via the display screen?
8. What batch file command is used to test for the presence of a file CONFIG.SYS on the hard drive of your system?
9. What symbol must precede a label in a batch file in order to identify the word as a label?
10. What applications or problems best lend themselves to the use of a batch file as a practical solution technique?

CHAPTER 20

LANGUAGE TRANSLATORS (EXTERNAL COMMANDS)

INTRODUCTION

DOS provides access to a set of language translators in both the IBM PC-DOS version and in the Microsoft MS-DOS version. For an IBM PC with a copy of PC-DOS, your system will be supplied with the two translators, BASIC and BASICA. An IBM-compatible computer, will have a copy of MS-DOS and your system will, in all likelihood, have a copy of GWBASIC (or QBASIC for Version 5.) Each of these programs is a BASIC language interpreter. As such, it is the program that can be used to translate a BASIC program into a set of machine language statements that can be executed by your computer. Version 5.00 of DOS supplied in either original or upgrade format will include Microsoft's new QBASIC language translator.

The programs are normally supplied on the DOS diskettes and are loaded into the DOS directory on the hard drive during installation. Use the DIR command to display a list of the files in the DOS directory. You should see one or more of the following programs: BASIC and BASICA, or GWBASIC, or QBASIC, depending on your system. To execute any of the programs, just type their names at the DOS prompt as you would with any other DOS command. The language interpreter will execute and put you at the prompt character or introductory screen for that program.

You may also see one or several programs in your DOS directory with the extension BAS. This extension indicates that these are BASIC program files. BASIC program files will execute once the BASIC interpreter has been executed. Some versions of DOS provide a dozen or more BASIC programs for your use. Some versions provide only a few. Check your DOS directory or set of installation disks. The examples and discussion below use BASICA as the language interpreter. You can perform similar examples using BASIC, GWBASIC, and QBASIC. For more details on programming in BASIC, refer to the reference material supplied with your computer or purchase a good text on the BASIC language. You may never find a need to write a BASIC program. If not, the usefulness of your computer system will not be diminished. However, from time to time you may find that you need to write your own program. If so, BASIC is an easy-to-learn programming language for fundamental uses. For more complex problems you will want to refer to information on other language translators such as Pascal, C, COBOL, or FORTRAN, among others.

The external commands discussed in this chapter are:

BASICA
GWBASIC
QBASIC

A Sample BASIC Language Translator (BASICA)

To execute the BASICA program, just type its name at the DOS prompt, as shown below:

```
C:\> BASICA
```

The BASICA program executes, provides a message at the top of the screen, and supplies the OK prompt. This is the prompt used by some BASIC language interpreters to indicate that the BASIC interpreter is now loaded and in control of the computer. BASICA supports two modes of operation. The user can type a variety of commands at the OK prompt and they will execute. If you issue commands at the OK prompt, you are in command mode and remain there. You can also go into programming mode, in which case, you begin writing a BASIC program. To go into programming mode, (where the line numbers for the program are generated automatically) enter the command AUTO. BASICA will supply line numbers as you begin typing your program. You may also enter programming mode by typing a number at the beginning of a line, followed by a BASIC programming statement.

Some examples of commands are listed below and briefly described. The explanation here is introductory, and not comprehensive. Refer to the BASIC program documentation for more detail.

NEW
LIST
RUN
LOAD
SAVE
AUTO
SYSTEM

NEW tells BASIC that you want to begin writing a new program and to delete all references to any line numbers for any program previously in memory. Only use NEW if you no longer need the BASIC program already in memory and you have saved it to disk.

LIST causes the BASIC program already in memory to list to the display monitor line by line. The program will scroll across the screen until the entire program has been displayed. LIST has many forms so that you can view sections of the program without scrolling. Refer to the BASIC manual for more detail on the LIST command.

RUN causes the program already loaded into memory to execute using the BASIC language interpreter for translating your BASIC statements into machine language. To execute the MORTGAGE.BAS program for instance, you would first load MORTGAGE.BAS into memory (see "LOAD," below). Then type RUN. You will be allowed to enter data regarding a mortgage and see the results on the display screen.

LOAD followed by the name of a file results in that program being loaded into memory. To load the MORTGAGE.BAS program into memory from the \DOS401 directory, type the following:

```
LOAD "C:\DOS401\MORTGAGE"
```

After the program loads, you will be returned to the OK prompt. Type RUN to execute MORTGAGE.

SAVE results in the existing program in memory being saved to disk. When a BASIC program is saved, BASIC automatically adds a BAS extension to the filename. To save a program named SQUARES in the current directory on your hard drive, type the following:

```
SAVE "SQUARES"
```

A copy of the program is saved to disk. The program remains in memory for further use.

AUTO results in line numbers automatically being assigned when you write a program. As you type statements, end each the line with a carriage return by pressing the Enter key; BASIC will generate another line number. Line numbers will be in increments of 10 so that statements can later be inserted between two lines. To exit the AUTO mode when the program is finished, type Ctrl-C. BASIC will cease generating line numbers automatically.

SYSTEM is the command used to exit BASIC and return to the DOS prompt. When you are finished with BASIC, either in programming mode or running programs, type SYSTEM to exit to DOS.

These command examples were all executed from command mode and the OK prompt. The second mode of operation for BASIC is programming mode. If you execute the AUTO command, BASIC puts you in programming mode by automatically generating line numbers. You type the BASIC programming statements after the line number, then press the Enter key to terminate the line. Programming statement lines can be more than one line so that they wrap on the screen. Press the Enter key when the programming statement is complete, regardless of how many lines it requires on the screen. AUTO will automatically generate the next line number. Line numbers will be in increments of 10 unless specified otherwise. The format of a typical programming statement is:

NNN **STATEMENT FIELD**

NNN is the line number typed by you or generated automatically by AUTO.

STATEMENT is the BASIC statement or key word such as PRINT, LET, GOSUB, INPUT, etc.

FIELD is the modifier or specification associated with the STATEMENT command issued.

When using the AUTO mode, *NNN* (the line number) will be generated automatically, followed by a space. Type the necessary statement and fields associated with the program being written. For more information on programming in BASIC, refer to the documentation supplied with your system or purchase a good book on the version of BASIC that was supplied with your system. If you have an IBM-compatible and are using GWBASIC, make sure that the book is for GWBASIC, not just BASIC.

□ EXAMPLES

All of these examples after the first one are illustrated as though they were executed from the OK prompt, not the DOS prompt. For that reason, no prompt is shown with these examples.

1. C:\> **BASICA**
2. **NEW**
3. **LOAD "C:\DOS401\MORTGAGE"**
4. **LIST 100 – 200**
5. **RUN**
6. **SYSTEM**

1. C:\> **BASICA** In our first example, the BASICA program is executed from the DOS prompt. This program is now in control of your computer, just as would be any other application program that you executed such as WordPerfect or Lotus 1-2-3. Your screen should now display the OK prompt; you're ready to begin using BASIC.
2. **NEW** This command tells BASIC that you wish to begin using a new program. All references to a previous program are deleted. This command is normally issued when you wish to begin writing a new program.
3. **LOAD "C:\DOS401\MORTGAGE"** This command will load a new program from disk into memory. In this example the file MORTGAGE.BAS is loaded into memory from the hard drive and the \DOS401 directory. Almost every version of DOS includes a copy of this file as part of the DOS system. Other files with a BAS extension may be supplied as well. Refer to your version of DOS to see what was supplied with your system. The BAS extension files are generally not DOS version-dependent. That means that BASIC programs from DOS 2.10 can be copied to a DOS Version 4.00 system without problem. These files will not generate the "Incorrect DOS Version" message.

4. **LIST 100 – 200** In this example the LIST command has been used, but a specific sequence of line numbers has been specified. Lines from line number 100 through 200 will be displayed on the screen for the program currently in memory.
5. **RUN** The RUN command will cause the BASIC program already in memory to execute. If MORTGAGE.BAS was loaded as shown above, the MORTGAGE program will execute and begin asking for data related to mortgage calculations.
6. **SYSTEM** To exit BASIC and return to the DOS prompt, issue the SYSTEM command as shown in this example. This is a BASIC command and different from the SYS (System Transfer) command that is part of DOS. Only use SYSTEM when you are in BASIC at the OK prompt.

THE MICROSOFT BASIC LANGUAGE TRANSLATOR (GWBASIC OR QBASIC)

If you have an IBM-compatible computer, your system should contain a file named either GWBASIC or QBASIC. Which one is present depends on whether Version 5.00 of DOS is installed (QBASIC comes with Version 5). GWBASIC and QBASIC are executable programs. They are Microsoft's version of the BASIC language interpreter. BASIC and BASICA will generally not execute on an IBM compatible. One of several strange messages will appear on the screen which generally make no sense if you try to execute BASICA on an IBM compatible. One of the more typical messages is "Divide Overflow." Do not use BASIC and BASICA with a compatible. Instead, use GWBASIC or QBASIC.

GWBASIC and QBASIC contain many of the same commands and programming statements contained in BASIC and BASICA. Probably 80 to 90 percent of the commands and programming statements are identical. If you learned BASIC, you can very quickly become proficient in GWBASIC or QBASIC. There are, however, slight differences. Refer to a book on the version of BASIC that is installed with your system.

PART IV

SYSTEM MANAGEMENT

CHAPTER 21

INSTALLING DOS ON YOUR SYSTEM

INTRODUCTION

To install any version of DOS on your hard drive, first determine whether this is an initial installation or an upgrade of an earlier version. If this is an upgrade, proceed to Step 1, then skip to Step 4 in the procedure below. Whether you are installing DOS for the first time or upgrading DOS, it is important to recognize that several pieces of DOS must be put in place in order for your computer to operate correctly.

The DOS hidden files, along with COMMAND.COM, must be placed in the root directory of the hard disk drive. Two boot control files must be created—CONFIG.SYS and AUTOEXEC.BAT—and placed in the root directory. These are not strictly part of DOS; they are files that you create to control the setup and efficient operation of your system. The rest of the DOS files from your DOS master diskettes are then copied to a directory specifically created to hold these files. It is recommended that the name of the directory contain the DOS version number. For instance, if you are installing DOS Version 3.30, create a directory \DOS330 to hold all the DOS files other than the files placed in the root directory. If installing DOS Version 5, create a directory named \DOS500. It is generally recommended that you use either PC-DOS or MS-DOS Version 3.30 or later. Furthermore, there are several unique features that have been added to DOS in Version 5.00. If you are installing DOS Version 4.0, refer to Appendix E. For Version 3.XX, refer to Appendix D. The version number you are using will also affect the software applications that you buy and use.

INSTALLING DOS

The DOS diskettes supplied with the operating system manuals are known as master diskettes. These are the original diskettes and should be used in the initial installation only. After that, operate from working copies of these diskettes. The procedure described here will install DOS on your hard drive and create several working copy DOS diskettes that you can use in normal operations. Once this procedure is completed, use these master diskettes only if something happens to the working copies, or if this procedure must be repeated because your hard drive is damaged in some way. While you're thinking about it, establish a box or other safe place where all copies of master diskettes are kept, along with registration information for software. Whenever needed, you'll know exactly where to go to lay your hands on the master copies.

Most hard drives today are shipped with the hard drive already formatted. If the hard drive is not formatted, you must do so. Steps that may be skipped, such as the formatting of the hard drive, are noted below. This procedure assumes that you must complete the entire process. If installing DOS for the first time, begin with Step 1 of the process. If upgrading to Version 3.00 of DOS or a later version, perform Step 1 then skip immediately to Step 4. Refer to Chapter 23 if upgrading to Version 5. The upgrade for Version 5 can be used with either PC-DOS or MS-DOS. Make sure the correct one is used; they are not interchangeable. Purchase diskettes compatible in size with Drive A on your system.

1. Insert the master DOS diskette labeled *Startup* into the floppy Drive A. Turn on the power switch. Turn on the display unit if it is not already on. After a short time the computer should boot up and request date and time information. Enter the appropriate date and time and press the Enter key after each. The system should then display the DOS prompt as shown below, with a blinking cursor following the greater-than sign (>):

   ```
   A>
   ```

2. Enter the command shown below to determine if the hard drive has been formatted.

   ```
   A> DIR C:
   ```

   This command attempts to read the hard drive, which will normally be Drive C. It should display a list of files in the root directory of Drive C. If it does, the hard drive has been formatted; skip to Step 4. If an error message displays "Abort, Retry, or Fail," the hard drive has not been formatted and you must format it. Proceed to Step 3 in that case.

3. To format the hard drive, enter the command below. Press the Enter key after typing the command. This command not only formats the hard drive, but also makes it a bootable disk.

   ```
   A> FORMAT C:/S
   ```

   Once all the steps of this procedure are completed, boot from the hard drive for normal operations. For IBM PCs, DOS always tries to boot from Drive A first. If there is no diskette in Drive A, DOS then searches for the hard drive and boots from it. If booting from the hard drive, make sure there is no diskette in Drive A. The boot process for compatibles varies from machine to machine. Some boot in exactly the same way as an IBM PC; others boot from the hard drive regardless of whether there is a diskette in Drive A. These machines provide a special keyboard sequence to force booting from Drive A. Check your system documentation for more information on the boot process for your computer.

   The FORMAT command will display the tracks that are being formatted as it proceeds. If the program encounters any bad tracks, you may hear a whirring noise as it attempts several times to format that space on the disk. If particular tracks are bad, the program will flag them as bad so that they cannot be used. Once the formatting process is complete, the system files will be transferred and a message "System Transferred" will appear on the screen. You will then be asked to enter a volume label. Press the Enter key unless you wish to place a label on the hard drive. A label may be up to 11 characters in length. Press the Enter key after the label if you choose to enter one. A label is not typically necessary and will not affect the operation of your computer in any way. The hard drive has now been formatted as a bootable disk.

4. Execute the command shown below to copy the two hidden files to the hard drive. Press the Enter key after typing the command.

   ```
   A> SYS C:
   ```

   The computer should respond "System Transferred." If DOS responds "Insufficient Memory for System Transfer," back up your hard drive and repeat Step 3 to produce a bootable system disk on the hard drive.

5. Now copy the COMMAND.COM processor to your hard drive with the command shown below. As always, press the Enter key after typing the command:

   ```
   A> COPY command.com C:\
   ```

   COMMAND.COM will be copied from the Startup disk in Drive A to the hard drive and placed in the root directory. The message "1 File copied" will appear.

6. Now create a directory to store all the DOS files. It is recommended that the name of the directory include the version number of DOS. For instance, if installing DOS Version 3.30, the directory name will be \DOS330. In the command below, substitute the version number for *xxx* in the command. If you do not know the version number of DOS you are installing, type VER at the prompt and press the Enter key. A message will be displayed telling you the version number of DOS you are installing. Then copy all the files from the Startup diskette to this directory. Use the commands below to complete these operations:

   ```
   A> VER
   A> MD C:\DOSxxx
   A> copy *.* C:\DOSxxx
   ```

   All the files from the Startup disk are now in the new DOS directory. COMMAND.COM is also in the new directory, but this is a duplicate of the copy you placed in the root directory in Step 5. The duplicate copy of COMMAND.COM can be erased with the command below. Substitute the proper version number for *xxx*, just as you did above:

   ```
   A> DEL C:\DOSxxx\COMMAND.COM
   ```

7. In addition to the Startup diskette, most versions of DOS also come with an *Operating System* diskette or diskettes. Remove the Startup diskette from Drive A and insert the Operating System diskette into Drive A. Then execute the command below:

   ```
   A> copy *.* C:\DOSxxx
   ```

   All the files on the Operating System diskette will now be copied to the new \DOS*xxx* directory. If there are any other diskettes supplied with your copy of DOS, repeat Step 7 until all the diskettes have been copied into the \DOS*xxx* directory. When this operation is complete, DOS has been installed on the hard drive. Remove the Operating System diskette from Drive A. You're now ready to test that the hard drive is a bootable disk.

8. With no diskette in Drive A, press the three keys Ctrl, Alt, and Del at the same time, then release them. The computer will perform its normal boot operation. It will first attempt to boot from Drive A, and the Drive A light will come on. When the system finds no diskette in Drive A, it looks for the hard drive and boots from that disk. The system should boot from Drive C after approximately one to two minutes, depending on your computer, and then display the system prompt as shown below:

   ```
   C>
   ```

9. You're now ready to create two simple boot control files that will be stored in the root directory. You may later want to change these files once you have more experience. If you know the commands you wish to place in these files, substitute your file for the ones shown here. These are basic examples that will get you started in tailoring the computer to your specific needs. Refer also to Chapter 22 and Appendix C for hints on installing and protecting the system installation. Steps 10 through 13 below will create the two boot control files AUTOEXEC.BAT and CONFIG.SYS, then install them on the computer through the boot process.

10. Create the CONFIG.SYS file with the procedure below. Be careful to type the commands exactly as shown, with no typing mistakes. If you make a mistake, repeat the procedure. At the end of each line, press the Enter key as indicated in the first line. Once you have typed all lines of the file, use the F6 function key to generate the Ctrl-Z character, then press the Enter key. The file will be copied to the hard drive. The message "1 File(s) copied" will display on the screen.

    ```
    C> copy con C:\CONFIG.SYS <Enter>
    BREAK=on
    BUFFERS=30
    FILES=30
    LASTDRIVE=F
    ```

11. Create the AUTOEXEC.BAT file with the procedure below. Be careful to type the commands exactly as shown, with no typing mistakes. If you make a mistake, you will have to repeat the procedure. This is the same procedure you used in Step 10 for the CONFIG.SYS file. After typing the last line of the file, again press the F6 function key to generate the Ctrl-Z character and press the Enter key. The message "1 File(s) copied" will again display.

```
C> copy con C:\AUTOEXEC.BAT <Enter>
@ECHO off
DATE
TIME
PROMPT $p $g
PATH C:\;C:\DOSxxx
```

12. Now check to ensure that the two files are in the root directory and contain the correct commands. If you made mistakes in either Step 10 or Step 11, repeat that step to correct the file. The new file will replace the old file in the root directory. To check the root directory, type

    ```
    C> DIR C:\
    ```

    The Directory command will display the files in the root directory. Make sure that the CONFIG.SYS and AUTOEXEC.BAT files are listed in the directory report. If they are not, you have made a mistake in either Step 10 or Step 11, or both. Now check to see that each file contains the proper commands by displaying its contents. Execute the commands shown below:

    ```
    C> TYPE C:\CONFIG.SYS
    ```

    The CONFIG.SYS file will be listed to your display screen. Check to make sure that the contents of the file are the same as shown in Step 10 or agree with the copy of the file you entered. If not, repeat Step 10. Now list the contents of the AUTOEXEC.BAT file to the display screen by executing the command shown below:

    ```
    C> TYPE C:\AUTOEXEC.BAT
    ```

    The AUTOEXEC.BAT file will be listed to your display screen. Check to make sure that the contents of the file are the same as shown in Step 11 or agree with the copy of the file you entered. If not, repeat Step 11. Once you have ensured that these two files are correct and contain the commands appropriate for your system, proceed to Step 13.

13. Reboot the computer. Make sure there is no diskette in Drive A. Then press the three keys Ctrl, Alt, and Del at the same time. Then release all three. The boot process will execute, with both the CONFIG.SYS and the AUTOEXEC.BAT files as part of that process. Each of the commands in

these files will be executed to tailor the system to your particular needs. No error messages should appear indicating that any of the commands failed to execute correctly. Enter the date and the time when requested by the messages on the screen. When the process is completed, the DOS prompt should display as shown below, followed by a blinking cursor:

```
C:\ >
```

For additional information on tailoring the system to your needs, refer to Appendix C. As you gain more experience, you may want to modify this initial installation. Refer to Chapter 11 on EDLIN or EDIT to learn how to modify the CONFIG.SYS and AUTOEXEC.BAT files.

As a final step, create working copies of your DOS diskettes and one system boot diskette for use in the event that a problem arises with the hard drive and you cannot boot from it for some reason.

14. Make working copies of each of the original DOS diskettes by executing the command below. Prior to making the copies, however, determine how many diskettes are needed and then format them as data diskettes. To format the diskettes execute the format command FORMAT A:. Then execute the DISKCOPY command for each diskette to be duplicated:

```
C:\> DISKCOPY A: A:
```

When the program stops at the message, insert the first DOS diskette into Drive A as the source disk. The information will be copied from the disk into memory and stored there. At the appropriate message, insert a blank formatted diskette into Drive A as the target diskette. The information will be copied from memory to the target disk. Repeat this procedure as many times as necessary until all information has been copied from the master DOS disk as the source to the target disk. When the program asks if you want to copy another disk, reply **n** for No. Once this process is complete, enter the command shown below to ensure that the DOS diskette has been duplicated correctly:

```
C:\> DISKCOMP A: A:
```

The DISKCOMP command will now check to ensure that the two diskettes are duplicates. Once complete, the program should issue a message indicating that the two diskettes are exact duplicates. Use the master DOS diskette as the source disk or disk 1 and the new disk as the second. Once complete, remove the duplicated diskette and place a label on it similar to the label on the master diskette. Indicate also that this is a working copy of the DOS diskette. A label such as “DOS Startup diskette, Working Copy” might be appropriate.

Repeat Step 14 for any other master copies of the DOS diskettes. Depending on the size of your diskettes, either 31/2 inch or 51/4 inch, you may have to duplicate from one to five or more diskettes.

15. As a final step, create a floppy system boot diskette. This diskette is for emergency use when the hard drive does not boot for some reason. Use a blank diskette in this step. Insert the blank diskette into Drive A and type the command below:

```
C:\> FORMAT A:/S
```

The diskette will be formatted, then the nucleus of the operating system will be transferred to it. At the completion of the formatting process, the message "System Transferred" will be issued. At the completion, DOS will ask if you wish to format another diskette. Reply **n** to this message for No. Label this diskette "System Boot Disk."

Now store the System Boot diskette along with the Startup DOS diskette and any other master DOS diskettes in a safe place with other master diskettes.

You have completed the installation process for DOS, as well as protected yourself in case of emergencies. When using DOS diskettes in the future, use the working copies of the DOS diskettes rather than the master copies supplied as originals.

CHAPTER 22

ORGANIZING AND PROTECTING YOUR SYSTEM

INTRODUCTION

Today, most computers operate from a hard disk. This disk may have been formatted prior to your purchase. If not, then you must prepare the disk so that it can store information. You may also want to modify the setup of the disk based on your specific needs. For example, you may want to partition the disk into two or more logical drives. This chapter provides basic guidelines and suggestions for setting up a computer for normal operations. It is suggested that you read through the whole chapter first. Then select the parts that apply to the way you use your computer. These guidelines are intended to provide an efficient system as well as protection against both the typing errors and hardware failures that inevitably result from the use of a computer.

HARD DISK CAPACITY

For today's computers and applications it is wise to buy as much hard disk capacity as you can possibly afford. Many sophisticated application programs require 4 to 10 MB of hard disk space. If you are using your computer in a small business with accounting applications, you could easily require 20 to 40 MB for the accounting applications and your company's data. For the single-system user not running a business, a hard disk with a minimum of 80 to 100 MB is recommended. For a small to medium-sized business, a hard drive of 200 MB or more should be considered. You may also wish to consider a cartridge drive with 10 to 40 MB cartridges for your data. For systems without a cartridge drive and more than 40 MB of hard disk capacity, consider a tape backup system or an optical floppy drive rather than diskettes for performing system backup. Adapt these guidelines to your individual requirements. Use them as a starting point for designing your own system.

PARTITIONING THE HARD DRIVE

You can partition the hard disk into two or more partitions, depending on your specific requirements. For small hard disks (less than 32 MB), one partition is probably sufficient for most needs. For hard disks larger than 32 MB, or for computers running more than one operating system, a multipartitioned system may be necessary. If you regularly upgrade software or test systems or software applications, you may also want to partition the hard drive. The DOS FDISK program provides software necessary for partitioning the hard drive on the computer. Be careful when using FDISK, because all information on the hard disk is lost. It is strongly suggested that you make sure the entire system is backed up before using the FDISK command. For computer systems with at least 40 MB of space, a two-partition system is recommended, with approximately 65 to 75 percent devoted to the primary partition.

Format each partition for the operating system that will be used in that partition. If only a single operating system such as DOS is to be used, then format the first partition to be a bootable partition. The second partition will then operate as a separate disk or disks, such as Drive D, but will not be bootable. Remember when deciding on partition size that you will normally get about 80 percent utilization of space on the hard drive. Some space is always lost when storing files, because the last sector of a file will only partly use that allocation unit. When estimating total file space with accounting applications, and applications that keep their files on the hard drive, use the formula below to calculate the minimum disk space needed:

Disk space needed = file space estimate / (.80)

For instance, if your estimate of file space for your accounting system, including your company data, is 12.3 MB, then you should allocate a minimum of (12.3 MB/0.80) or 15.4 MB of hard disk space.

Select the active partition using the FDISK program. If there is only a single operating system, the bootable partition is the active partition by default.

ORGANIZING DIRECTORIES AND SUBDIRECTORIES

THE ROOT DIRECTORY

The root directory is established when any disk or diskette is formatted. All directories that are established at the first level become subdirectories of the root directory. Certain programs are generally stored or must be stored in the root directory. Learn these requirements. Generally, the system nucleus, including its hidden files, is stored in the root directory. Along with these, the CONFIG.SYS and AUTOEXEC.BAT files are also stored here. These files are automatically read and executed by the system at boot time if they are in the root directory. The DOS text editor EDLIN or EDIT can be used to build both the CONFIG.SYS and AUTOEXEC.BAT files. You can also use the procedure shown in Chapter 21 to establish an initial version of AUTOEXEC.BAT and CONFIG.SYS. If another program such as a word processor is used to build these files, remember to save these files as ASCII text files.

You may also wish to place the ANSI.SYS file in the root directory and make it part of your CONFIG.SYS file in order to extend the capability of your keyboard. Include a line in CONFIG.SYS such as DEVICE=C:\ANSI.SYS. ANSI.SYS provides keyboard redefinition as well as extended keyboard capabilities when using Escape sequences. It is a topic worth investigating by the advanced user.

Creating a Directory Structure

The directory structure for the hard disk should be built using the MD command. The directory structure will normally be related to the application software programs or packages you plan to use. For instance, if you were planning to use WordPerfect 5.1, Lotus 1-2-3 Version 3.1, and some games on your computer, you might make a set of directories just below the root directory named \WP51, \LOTUS31, \GAMES, as well as a DOS directory. If the version of DOS to be used is Version 5.00 then it is recommended that you name the DOS directory \DOS500. Then, there would be four subdirectories of the root directory: \WP51, \LOTUS31, \GAMES, and \DOS500. Any subdirectories of these four would be dictated by the installation instructions associated with the software applications. Avoid using directory names that are the same as the executable program name. For example, name your WordPerfect directory \WP51, not \WP, because the name of the executable program is WP.

Do not include application directories as part of the PATH command included in your AUTOEXEC.BAT file. Many application programs use the same executable filename, such as word processors that use the name WP.EXE. It is not unusual to find more than one word processor on a single computer, or two versions of the same software. If all application directories are on the PATH, then the file executed when you typed WP from the root directory is the first directory along the PATH; it may not be the WP you intended.

Always operate out of the proper directory when executing an application program. The advantage of using batch control files (see "Using Batch Files," below) is that you can guarantee that you operate out of the correct directory, not just the directory that happens to be the current directory.

When installing a new version of software or upgrading from an old version, do so in a new directory. Do not take a chance that you might damage the current production version of the software. This is particularly important with accounting applications, because your company cannot afford to be without its payroll system for a week while you debug some software installation problem. Likewise, you may not be able to do without your word processor for a week if you encounter installation problems during an upgrade.

Using Batch Files

Add a directory \BATCH and store all batch control files in this directory. Add the \BATCH directory to the PATH. Batch control files can be used to tailor the setup of an individual application such as WordPerfect, LOTUS 1-2-3, and others. This allows the tailoring of a program to an individual's needs, or perhaps the needs of a particular department within a company. Chapter 19 on batch files illustrates one example of this type of batch file. Put all your batch files in one directory so they are stored together.

Install a menu system built with batch files. (See Appendix H for an example of such a menu system.) Batch files take a relatively small amount of space per file and allow you to control the operation of your system, as well as ensure that program operations are set up properly for new or inexperienced users. For more details, see any one of several texts that provide information on menu systems and the use of batch files. Chapter 19 provides some example batch files.

PROTECTING YOUR SYSTEM

BACKING UP FILES

The software stored in the root directory of your hard disk is critical to the boot process for your computer. Should anything happen to these files, your computer may not boot successfully. Some software installation processes may attempt to modify the CONFIG.SYS or AUTOEXEC.BAT files. You may make these files inoperable in attempting to modify them. It is recommended that a directory named \BACKR be created on your system. Keep copies of all your critical root directory files in this subdirectory. You may want to keep a copy of every root directory file in this subdirectory. Then, if any of the key root directory files are damaged or changed, you can quickly restore them by copying the file or files back to the root directory from the \BACKR directory.

Once the hard disk is set up and the system is operating as you want it, the software should be backed up to a tape backup system or to diskettes. To back up the disk, use the BACKUP command that is part of DOS. Good backup procedures are an integral part of operating a computer. You may want to back up the entire system, or selected directory structures representing your installed software applications. There are many reasons to back up the system. Loss of the hard disk due to hardware failure, damage to key files, and software viruses are just some of the reasons to have a system backup. See Chapter 12 for more on the BACKUP and RESTORE commands and their applications.

PROTECTING KEY FILES

Damaging key files may result in hours of work to make the system operable again. Key files can be protected from accidental deletion or modification by hiding them or making them read-only, or both. Use the ATTRIB command to make a file read-only. There are several utility programs that can be used to hide and unhide files (see "Enhancing DOS with Utilities," below). The DOS program DEBUG can also be used to turn on the hide bit in the attribute byte. Recall that the attribute byte is stored in the system directory area, along with the filename and file extension fields. To make the AUTOEXEC.BAT and CONFIG.SYS files read-only, execute these two ATTRIB commands, as shown below:

```
C:\> ATTRIB +R C:\AUTOEXEC.BAT
C:\> ATTRIB +R C:\CONFIG.SYS
```

Then check to see that the read-only bit is on by displaying the attribute bits as shown below. The AUTOEXEC.BAT and CONFIG.SYS files should have an R displayed to the right of their filenames, showing that they are read-only files.

```
C:\> ATTRIB C:\*.*
```

The ATTRIB command in Version 5 of DOS can be used to make the files both read-only and hidden. Refer to Chapter 12.

VIRUS PROTECTION

Investigate the purchase of a virus detection program. Central Point Software, among others, sells a very good package. The package you choose should provide detection capability for a variety of viruses, as well as software for cleaning disks that become infected. Unfortunately, viruses have become one of the major operating problems when using PCs today. Take every precaution possible to avoid their infecting your computer. Even with care, however, this problem may arise, and you will have to deal with it. Even shrink-wrapped software received directly from a manufacturer has been known to contain a virus. You may infect your system when you boot from the installation disk as you install this new software. One estimate in the trade press placed the number of systems likely to be infected in excess of 20% of all personal computers. Make sure your system, your software, and important data are always backed up.

ENHANCING DOS WITH UTILITIES

Consider purchasing a good DOS utility program such as Norton Utilities, the Mace Utilities, or PC Tools. These programs provide many useful features that supplement DOS. They are available for sale through computer stores and mail-order catalogs. Other utilities are also available through bulletin boards, from diskettes sold with books on DOS, and as offers associated with magazine subscriptions. Some of the best sources are computer magazines such as *PC Magazine*, *PC World*, and others. This software is not part of the operating system, but rather an enhancement or supplement to it.

Rather than mix this software with the operating system, it is recommended that it be kept in a separate directory for this purpose. Set up a directory named \UTIL. Store the DOS supplemental or utility routines in the \UTIL directory. Include the \UTIL directory as part of the PATH so that this directory is always accessible for executing commands, just as is the \DOS*xxx* directory. PC Tools, Norton Utilities, etc. will be installed in their own directory.

APPENDIXES

APPENDIX A

THE ASCII CODING SYSTEM

The ASCII (American Standard Code for Information Interchange) coding system is based on a 7-bit code. It can generate 128 different codes (2^7). Those codes range from 0 to 127 in decimal or 0 to 7F in hexadecimal. Table A.1 shows the ASCII characters along with their decimal and hexadecimal values.

TABLE A.1 ASCII Character Table

ASCII	*Dec*	*Hex*	*ASCII*	*Dec*	*Hex*	*ASCII*	*Dec*	*Hex*	*ASCII*	*Dec*	*Hex*
	0	00	<space>	32	20	@	64	40	`	96	60
☺	1	01	!	33	21	A	65	41	a	97	61
☻	2	02	“	34	22	B	66	42	b	98	62
♥	3	03	#	35	23	C	67	43	c	99	63
♦	4	04	$	36	24	D	68	44	d	100	64
♣	5	05	%	37	25	E	69	45	e	101	65
♠	6	06	&	38	26	F	70	46	f	102	66
•	7	07	‘	39	27	G	71	47	g	103	67
◘	8	08	(	40	28	H	72	48	h	104	68
○	9	09	)	41	29	I	73	49	i	105	69
◙	10	0A	*	42	2A	J	74	4A	j	106	6A
♂	11	0B	+	43	2B	K	75	4B	k	107	6B
♀	12	0C	’	44	2C	L	76	4C	l	108	6C
♪	13	0D	–	45	2D	M	77	4D	m	109	6D
♫	14	0E	.	46	2E	N	78	4E	n	110	6E
☼	15	0F	/	47	2F	O	79	4F	o	111	6F
►	16	10	0	48	30	P	80	50	p	112	70
◄	17	11	1	49	31	Q	81	51	q	113	71
↕	18	12	2	50	32	R	82	52	r	114	72
‼	19	13	3	51	33	S	83	53	s	115	73
¶	20	14	4	52	34	T	84	54	t	116	74

"continued"

TABLE A.1 ASCII Character Table (continued)

ASCII	*Dec*	*Hex*	*ASCII*	*Dec*	*Hex*	*ASCII*	*Dec*	*Hex*	*ASCII*	*Dec*	*Hex*
§	21	15	5	53	35	U	85	55	u	117	75
▬	22	16	6	54	36	V	86	56	v	118	76
↨	23	17	7	55	37	W	87	57	w	119	77
↑	24	18	8	56	38	X	88	58	x	120	78
↓	25	19	9	57	39	Y	89	59	y	121	79
→	26	1A	:	58	3A	Z	90	5A	z	122	7A
←	27	1B	;	59	3B	|	91	5B	{	123	7B
∟	28	1C	<	60	3C	\	92	5C	|	124	7C
↔	29	1D	=	61	3D	|	93	5D	}	125	7D
▲	30	1E	>	62	3E	^	94	5E	~	126	7E
▼	31	1F	?	63	3F	–	95	5F	⌂	127	7F

The extended character set uses codes ranging from 128 to 255 decimal, or 80 to FF hexadecimal. Table A.2 shows the extended ASCII character set associated with these codes. These are implemented using the ANSI.SYS device driver in CONFIG.SYS.

TABLE A.2 Extended ASCII Character Set

ASCII	*Dec*	*Hex*	*ASCII*	*Dec*	*Hex*	*ASCII*	*Dec*	*Hex*	*ASCII*	*Dec*	*Hex*
Ç	128	80	á	160	A0	└	192	C0	α	224	E0
ü	129	81	í	161	A1	┴	193	C1	β	225	E1
é	130	82	ó	162	A2	┬	194	C2	Γ	226	E2
â	131	83	u	163	A3	├	195	C3	π	227	E3
ä	132	84	ñ	164	A4	─	196	C4	Σ	228	E4
à	133	85	Ñ	165	A5	┼	197	C5	σ	229	E5
å	134	86	ª	166	A6	╞	198	C6	µ	230	E6
ç	135	87	º	167	A7	╟	199	C7	τ	231	E7
ê	136	88	¿	168	A8	╚	200	C8	Φ	232	E8
ë	137	89	⌐	169	A9	╔	201	C9		233	E9
è	138	8A	¬	170	AA	╩	202	CA	Ω	234	EA
ï	139	8B	½	171	AB	╦	203	CB	δ	235	EB
î	140	8C	¼	172	AC	╠	204	CC	∞	236	EC
ì	141	8D	¡	173	AD	═	205	CD	Ø	237	ED
Ä	142	8E	«	174	AE	╬	206	CE	ε	238	EE

"continued"

TABLE A.2 Extended ASCII Character Set (continued)

ASCII	*Dec*	*Hex*	*ASCII*	*Dec*	*Hex*	*ASCII*	*Dec*	*Hex*	*ASCII*	*Dec*	*Hex*
Å	143	8F	»	175	AF	╧	207	CF	∩	239	EF
É	144	90	░	176	B0	╨	208	D0	≡	240	F0
æ	145	91	▒	177	B1	╤	209	D1	±	241	F1
Æ	146	92	▓	178	B2	╥	210	D2	≥	242	F2
ô	147	93	│	179	B3	╙	211	D3	≤	243	F3
ö	148	94	┤	180	B4	╘	212	D4	⌠	244	F4
ò	149	95	╡	181	B5	╒	213	D5	⌡	245	F5
û	150	96	╢	182	B6	╓	214	D6	÷	246	F6
ù	151	97	╖	183	B7	╫	215	D7	≈	247	F7
ÿ	152	98	╕	184	B8	╪	216	D8	°	248	F8
Ö	153	99	╣	185	B9	┘	217	D9	∙	249	F9
Ü	154	9A	║	186	BA	┌	218	DA	·	250	FA
¢	155	9B	╗	187	BB	█	219	DB	√	251	FB
£	156	9C	╝	188	BC	▄	220	DC	^{n}	252	FC
¥	157	9D	╜	189	BD	▌	221	DD	^{2}	253	FD
₧	158	9E	╛	190	BE	▐	222	DE	■	254	FE
ƒ	159	9F	┐	191	BF	▀	223	DF		255	FF

APPENDIX B
DOS INFORMATION

THE HISTORY OF DOS

As the power and capability of microcomputer hardware has increased over the years, the capabilities of DOS for microcomputers has increased to keep pace. Table B.1 below outlines the major improvements that have been part of new releases of DOS. This chart highlights but a few of the changes that were incorporated with each new release. For more details consult the technical reference manual included with the version of DOS that you are currently using.

TABLE B.1 The History of DOS

Version	Year	Characteristics
1.0	1981	Original Disk Operating System for the IBM PC.
1.1	1982	Double-sided floppy drive support.
1.25	1982	MS-DOS for non-IBM computers.
2.00	1983	Hard drive support introduced.
2.10	1983	IBM PC Jr. computer support included.
2.11	1983	Standard Version 2 for non-IBM customers.
3.00	1984	Support for IBM AT, 1.2 MB disk drives.
3.10	1984	Software support for computer networks.
3.20	1986	Floppy disk support for 3.5-inch disks.
3.30	1987	IBM PS/2 computer family supported.
4.00	1988	IBM DOS Shell introduced.
4.01	1989	Updates and corrections to Version 4.00.
5.00	1991	New DOS Shell, smaller nucleus, memory management, DOSKEY, delete file tracking.
6.00	1993	Includes disk compression feature nearly doubling storage capacity, anti-viralutility, multiple boot options, and improved backup and restore programs.

CONTROL-KEY SEQUENCES

The major control-key sequences associated with various combinations of keyboard keystrokes are listed in Table B.2. For a more detailed explanation, consult Chapter 2 of the text.

TABLE B.2 **Keyboard Control Sequences**

Key Sequence	Function
Ctrl-C	Cancels the command or program that is currently in execution.
Ctrl-Break	Same as Ctrl-C.
Ctrl-P	Puts the printer in echo mode.
Ctrl-Prtsc	Same as Ctrl-P.
Ctrl-S	Temporarily suspends processing and freezes the display screen.
Ctrl-Num Lock	Same as Ctrl-S.
Shift-Prtsc	Dumps the information on the display screen to the printer.
Ctrl-Alt-Del	Warm boot of the operating system.
Esc	Cancels the current line or command stored in the keyboard buffer.
Ins	Puts the keyboard in insert mode for inserting characters into a line.
Del	Deletes a single character from the keyboard buffer.
Backspace	Backspaces one character and deletes that character from the buffer.
Pause	Same as Ctrl-S.
Caps Lock	Toggles the keyboard between uppercase and lowercase.
Num Lock	Toggles the numeric keypad between numeric mode and cursor control mode.

Function-KEY SEQUENCES

In addition to providing control functions through ketboard sequences, DOS also provides function-key sequences that can increase your speed and skills at the keyboard. The function-key sequences associated with DOS are shown in Table B.3. For a more detailed explanation, refer to Chapter 2 in the text.

TABLE B.3 DOS Function-Key Sequences

Function Key	Description
F1	Recalls one character from the keyboard buffer each time it's pressed.
F2	Displays all characters up to the first occurence of the character typed from the keyboard buffer.
F3	Recalls all characters from the buffer, or the remaining characters in the buffer.
F4	Deletes all characters in the keyboard s buffer up to but not including the character pressed.
F6	Generates an EOF (end-of-file) character or Ctrl-Z when pressed.
F7	Recalls to the screen the entire list of commands in DOSKEY's command buffer.
Alt-F7	Deletes all the commands from the DOSKEY's commasnd buffer and leaves it empty.
F9	Displays the message "Line Number" and allows a specific command to be recalled from the DOSKEY command buffer, based on its number.

SYSTEM FILE SIZES

Table B.4 shows the size of the COMMAND.COM file, as well as the size of the I/O Manager and the File Manager hidden files for the various major versions of PC-DOS. If you are running MS-DOS, the sizes will be close to the numbers shown in the table below.

TABLE B.4 PC-DOS Control Program Sizes

DOS Version	Size of File	
1.0	COMMAND.COM	3231
	IBMBIO.COM	1920
	IBMDOS.COM	6400
1.1	COMMAND.COM	4959
	IBMBIO.COM	1920
	IBMDOS.COM	6400
2.0	COMMAND.COM	17664
	IBMBIO.COM	4608
	IBMDOS.COM	17152

"continued"

TABLE B.4 PC-DOS Control Program Sizes (continued)

DOS Version	Size of File	
2.1	COMMAND.COM	17792
	IBMBIO.COM	4736
	IBMDOS.COM	17024
3.0	COMMAND.COM	22042
	IBMBIO.COM	8964
	IBMDOS.COM	27920
3.1	COMMAND.COM	23210
	IBMBIO.COM	9564
	IBMDOS.COM	27760
3.2	COMMAND.COM	23791
	IBMBIO.COM	16389
	IBMDOS.COM	28477
3.3	COMMAND.COM	25307
	IBMBIO.COM	22100
	IBMDOS.COM	30159
4.0	COMMAND.COM	37888
	IBMBIO.COM	32810
	IBMDOS.COM	35984
5.0	COMMAND.COM	47845
	IBMBIO.COM	33430
	IBMDOS.COM	37394

DOS Additions

As DOS has expanded, services and utilities have been added to expand the functions available. In some cases additional features have been added to existing functions. Tables B.5 and B.6 show the additions to DOS for each of the major new releases. They also show major changes to existing routines. In most cases, additions to programs result in the addition of parameters supported by the program. Examples of these type of changes are the many additions to FORMAT.COM to accommodate new diskette formatting capabilities, as well as the support for 31/2 inch diskettes when they were introduced to the market.

TABLE B.5 New Internal, Configuration, and Batch File Commands

Version 2.0/2.1	Version 3.0/3.30	Version 4.0	Version 5.0
BREAK	COUNTRY	SWITCHES	
BUFFERS	DEVICE		DEVICE HIGH
CD	FCBS		DOS
CLS	LASTDRIVE		HIMEM.SYS
CTTY	CALL		
ECHO	CHCP		
IF ERRORLEVEL	@ (AT)		
IF EXIST	STACKS		
FILES	DRIVPARM		
FOR			

TABLE B.6 New External Commands

Version 2.0/2.1	Version 3.0/3.30	Version 4.0	Version 5.0
ANSI.SYS	ATTRIB.EXE	4208.CPI	APPEND.EXE
ASSIGN.COM	GRAFTABL.COM	FILESYS.EXE	DOSKEY.COM
BACKUP.COM	KEYBFR.COM	IFSFUNC.EXE	EDIT.COM
FDISK.COM	KEYBGR.COM	MEM.EXE	EMM386.EXE
FIND.EXE	KEYBIT.COM	SELECT.DAT	EXPAND.EXE
GRAPHICS.COM	KEYBSP.COM	SELECT.EXE	FC.EXE
MORE.COM	KEYBUK.COM	SHELLB.COM	HELP.EXE
PRINT.COM	LABEL.COM	SHELLC.EXE	MIRROR.COM
RECOVER.COM	SELECT.COM	XMA2EMS.SYS	QBASIC.EXE
RESTORE.COM	SHARE.EXE	XMAEM.SYS	SETVER.EXE
SORT.EXE	VDISK.LST		UNDELETE.EXE
TREE.COM	VDISK.SYS		UNFORMAT.COM
	BASIC.PIF		
	BASICA.PIF		
	JOIN.EXE		
	SUBST.EXE		
	DRIVER.SYS		
	REPLACE.EXE		
	XCOPY.EXE		
	APPEND.EXE		

"continued"

TABLE B.6 New External Commands (continued)

Version 2.0/2.1	Version 3.0/3.30	Version 4.0	Version 5.0
	COUNTRY.SYS		
	DISPLAY.SYS		
	EGA.CPI		
	FASTOPEN.EXE		
	KEYB.COM		
	KEYBOARD.SYS		
	LCD.CPI		
	NLSFUNC.EXE		
	PRINTER.SYS		

DISKETTE SPACE UTILIZATION

The space on a diskette is divided into two areas: a system area and a data area. Table B.7 shows the total diskette capacity for various diskettes based on their formatting parameters. The number shown under Data Capacity is the number of kilobytes displayed by DOS as the capacity of the diskette. This is the area available for storing files on the disk. For more detailed information, see Chapters 2 and Chapter 9.

TABLE B.7 Diskette Capacity Chart

Size	No. of Sides	Tracks per Side	Sectors per Track	Total Capacity*	Data Capacity*	System Area Capacity*
51/4	1	40	8	163,840 (320)	160,256 (313)	3,584 (7)
51/4	1	40	9	184,320 (360)	179,712 (351)	4,608 (9)
51/4	2	40	8	327,680 (640)	322,560 (630)	5,120 (10)
51/4	2	40	9	368,640 (720)	362,496 (708)	6,144 (12)
31/2	2	80	9	737,280 (1440)	730,112 (1426)	7,168 (14)
51/4	2	80	15	1,228,800 (2400)	1,213,952 (2371)	14,848 (29)
31/2	2	80	18	1,474,560 (2880)	1,457,664 (2847)	16,896 (33)

*Capacity figures are in bytes. Numbers in parentheses indicate number of sectors.

SYSTEM SPACE ALLOCATION ON DISKETTES

The system of a diskette is divided into three component parts. Table B.8 shows the sectors devoted to each of three parts, based on the size and format of the diskette. For a more detailed explanation, see Chapter 2 of the text.

TABLE B.8 Diskette System Area

Size	Data Capacity	Boot Sectors	FAT Sectors	Root Sectors	File Entries
51/4	160,256	1	2	4	64
51/4	179,712	1	4	4	64
51/4	322,560	1	2	7	112
51/4	362,496	1	4	7	112
31/2	730,112	1	14	14	224
51/4	1,213,952	1	6	7	112
31/2	1,457,664	1	18	14	224

FILE ATTRIBUTES

DOS keeps track of the characteristics of files by assigning a 1 to various bits in the attribute byte associated with each file. The attribute byte is stored in the system directory area of the disk, along with the file's name, extension, file size, and so on. The meaning of each of the bits in the attribute byte is shown in the Figure B.1. Some examples follow the figure. For a more detailed explanation and some example attribute byte patterns for various types of files, see Chapter 12.

FIGURE B.1 The File Attribute Byte

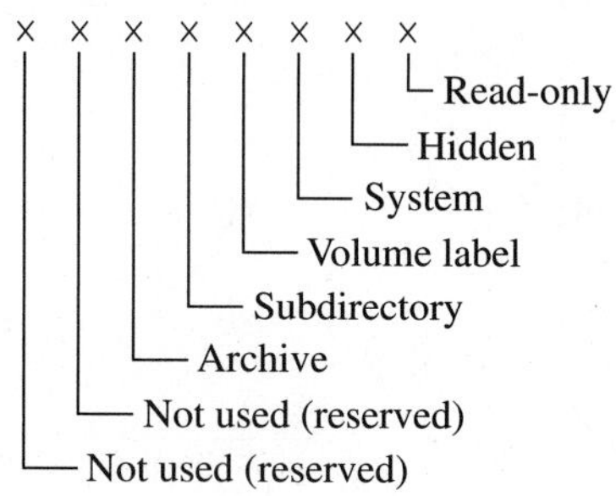

□ EXAMPLES

IBMBIO.COM	HEX = 27	BINARY = 0010 0111
IBMDOS.COM	HEX = 27	BINARY = 0010 0111
COMMAND.COM	HEX = 20	BINARY = 0010 0000
DISKLABL	HEX = 28	BINARY = 0010 1000
HIDDEN.FIL	HEX = 22	BINARY = 0010 0010
SUBDIR	HEX = 10	BINARY = 0001 0000
HIDDEN.SUB	HEX = 12	BINARY = 0001 0010
NORMAL.FIL	HEX = 20	BINARY = 0010 0000
READONLY.FIL	HEX = 21	BINARY = 0010 0001

APPENDIX C

SETTING UP YOUR HARD DISK

INTRODUCTION

Most computers today have a fixed disk or hard disk. This disk may have been formatted prior to purchase. If not, then you must prepare the disk so that it can store information. You may also want to modify the setup of the disk based on your specific needs. For example, you may want to partition the disk into two or more logical drives. This section will discuss setting up your hard disk from scratch. If your disk is already formatted, then you will want to skip over some of the information presented here and use only that part that fits your particular needs.

THE SETUP PROCEDURE

Outlined below is the general procedure to be used in setting up a hard disk. Each of these steps is discussed in detail. Chapter 22 provides additional information on designing a system to meet your specific needs. General guidelines on system setup are provided in Chapter 21. The general steps in setting up your hard disk are:

1. Divide the hard disk into one or more partitions depending on your specific requirements. For small hard disk computers or for hard disks less than 32 MB, one partition is probably sufficient. For hard disks larger than 32 MB or for computers running more than one operating system, a multipartitioned system will be necessary. If you regularly upgrade software or test systems or software applications, you may also want to partition your hard drive. The DOS FDISK program provides software necessary for partitioning the hard drive on your computer. **Be careful when using FDISK, since all information on the hard disk is lost. It is strongly suggested that you make sure the entire system is backed up before using the FDISK command.**
2. Format each partition for the operating system that will be used in that partition. If only a single operating system such as DOS is to be used, format the

first partition to be bootable. The second partition will then operate as a separate disk (such as Drive D) but will not be bootable.

3. Select the active partition using the FDISK program. If there is only a single operating system, then the bootable partition is the active partition by default.
4. The root directory is established when any disk or diskette is formatted. All directories that are established at the first level become subdirectories of the root directory. Certain programs are generally stored or must be stored in the root directory. Learn what these requirements are. Generally the system nucleus including its hidden files is stored in the root directory. Along with these, the CONFIG.SYS and AUTOEXEC.BAT files are stored in the root directory. These files are automatically read and executed by the system at boot time if they are in the root directory. The DOS text editors, EDLIN or EDIT, can be used to build both the CONFIG.SYS and AUTOEXEC.BAT files. If another program such as a word processor is used to build these files, remember to save them as ASCII text files.
5. The directory structure for the hard disk should be built using the MD command. The directory structure will normally be related to the application programs or packages you plan to use. If you were planning to use Wordperfect 5.1, Lotus 1-2-3, and some games on your computer then you might make a set of directories just below the root directory named \WP51, \LOTUS, \GAMES, as well as a DOS directory, for example. If the version of DOS to be used is Version 5 then it is recommended that the DOS directory be \DOS500. These would be four subdirectories of the root directory—\WP51, \LOTUS, \GAMES, and \DOS500. Any subdirectories of these four would be dictated by the installation instructions associated with the software applications WordPerfect 5.1, Lotus 1-2-3, and the specific games to be installed.
6. There are numerous utility routines available to enhance your microcomputer. They are available for sale as DOS utilities through computer stores and mail-order catalogs. They are also available through bulletin boards, from diskettes sold with books on DOS, as offers associated with magazine subscriptions, and so on. Some of the best sources are computer magazines such as *PC Magazine*, *PC World*, and others. This software is not part of the DOS operating system, but rather an enhancement or supplement to it. Rather than mix this software with the operating system, it is recommended that it be kept in a separate directory for this purpose. Create a directory named \UTIL for this purpose. Store the DOS supplemental or utility routines in the \UTIL directory. Consider also installing a virus protection program on your computer.
7. The software stored in the root directory of your hard disk is critical to the boot process for your computer. Should anything happen to these files, your computer may not boot successfully. Some software installation processes may attempt to modify the CONFIG.SYS or AUTOEXEC.BAT files. You

may make these files inoperable in attempting to modify them. It is recommended that a directory named \BACKR be created on your system. Keep copies of all your critical root directory files in this subdirectory. You may want to keep a copy of every root directory file in this subdirectory. If any of the key root directory files are damaged or changed, you can quickly restore it by copying the file back to the root directory from the \BACKR directory.

8. Damaging key files may result in hours of work to make the system operable again. Key files can be protected from accidental deletion or modification by hiding them or making them read-only or both. Use the ATTRIB command to make a file read-only. ATTRIB can also be used to hide the file using the DOS 5 version of ATTRIB. There are several third-party utility programs that can be used to hide and unhide files if you are using versions of DOS earlier than Version 5. The DOS program DEBUG can also be used to turn on the hide bit in the attribute byte. The attribute byte is stored in the system directory area along with the filename and file extension fields as well as other information associated with managing that file.
9. Once the hard disk is set up and the system is operating as you want it, the software should be backed up to a tape backup system or to diskettes. To back up to diskettes, use the BACKUP command that is part of DOS. Good backup procedures are an integral part of operating a computer. You may want to back up the entire system or back up selected directory structures representing your installed software applications. There are many reasons to back up the system. Loss of the hard disk due to hardware failure, damage to key files, and software viruses are just some of the reasons to have a system backup. See Chapter 12 for more on the DOS BACKUP and RESTORE commands and their application.

SYSTEM UPGRADE PROCEDURE

If DOS is already installed on your hard drive, but you wish to upgrade to a later version, use the procedure below for versions before DOS 5. To upgrade to DOS 5, refer to Chapter 23. To use this procedure, the DOS hidden files must already be installed in the root directory of your hard drive. You can use the CHKDSK command to verify that you have the two hidden files on your disk. If you wish to check that the specific files are there, use CHKDSK /V to get a list of all the files. If you are using an IBM (PC-DOS) computer the two hidden files will be IBMBIO.COM and IBMDOS.COM. If you are using an IBM-compatible (MS-DOS) computer the hidden files will be IO.SYS and MSDOS.SYS. To upgrade to a later version of DOS (prior to Version 5) use the step-by-step procedure below.

1. Boot your computer from Drive A using the diskettes supplied with the new version of DOS you plan to install. Use the SYS command to transfer the hidden files for the new system to the hard drive (See Chapter 13 on the SYS command.) Then copy COMMAND.COM to the hard drive using the COPY command. The commands to do this are shown below.

```
A\> SYS C:
A\> COPY A:COMMAND.COM C:\COMMAND.COM
```

   Once the hidden files are transferred, the message "System Transferred" will display on the screen. Copying COMMAND.COM will result in a message, "1 File Copied." The DOS nucleus or kernel has now been transferred to your hard drive.

2. Since you are already operating from the hard drive, a directory structure already exists on the hard drive. Add a directory for the new version of DOS. If you were upgrading to Version 3.18 of MS-DOS for a compatible, build a directory \DOS318 using the MD command. Then copy all the DOS files from the new DOS diskettes to this directory. The commands are shown below.

```
A\> MD C:\DOS318
A\> COPY A:*.* C:\DOS318
```

   Normally DOS is supplied as a set of diskettes rather than a single diskette. Once all the files from the first diskette are copied to the hard drive, eject that diskette and insert the second diskette. Use the same COPY command as shown above in Step 2 to copy the second and subsequent diskettes to the hard drive. Repeat this procedure until all the DOS diskettes have been copied to the hard drive. You have now transferred the new DOS system to the hard drive. In copying all the DOS files to the new \DOS318 directory used in this example, you have placed a copy of COMMAND.COM in both the root directory and the \DOS318 directory. This is a duplication and wastes valuable disk space. The file is not needed both places. Remove COMMAND.COM from the \DOS318 directory by executing the Delete command shown below.

```
A\> DEL C:\DOS318\COMMAND.COM
```

3. You now must delete the old version of DOS from your hard drive. If the old version of DOS is in a directory named \DOS then all the files in this directory must be deleted and the directory should be removed. If the old version of DOS is in some other directory, then substitute that directory name for \DOS in the example below. If the old version of DOS is in the root directory on your hard drive then you must delete the files selectively so that you do not destroy non-DOS files that may be in the root directory. To delete all the operating system files in the \DOS directory and to remove the \DOS directory, execute the commands shown below.

```
A\> DEL C:\DOS\*.*
A\> RD C:\DOS
```

Once this step is completed, the new version of DOS will be installed on your hard drive. Likewise the old version has been removed.

4. Now reboot your computer to make sure that the system will boot successfully from the hard drive. To do this eject any diskette that might be in Drive A. Then hold down the Ctrl and Alt keys and depress the Del key, then release them all to warm boot the computer. The computer should boot successfully. Use the VER command to make sure that you are now running the new version of DOS. The DOS version number will display when the VER command is given. If any problems arise check to see that the steps above have been completed successfully. If there are any problems, insert the DOS boot disk into Drive A and do a warm boot from that diskette. Check for mistakes in performing all the parts shown in steps 1 through 3 above.
5. Now that the computer boots from the hard drive, the CONFIG.SYS and AUTOEXEC.BAT files must be modified for the new version of DOS. For versions of DOS up through Version 3.30 the changes to these two files should be minimal unless other hardware devices have been added. The one change that must be made is to modify the PATH command that is normally part of the AUTOEXEC.BAT file. Use EDLIN to call up AUTOEXEC.BAT. Use EDLIN commands to modify the PATH command that is part of this file. You will want to delete the old DOS directory from the path and add the new DOS directory. Based on the example above, the directory \DOS would be changed to \DOS318. Use whatever directory is appropriate for your particular system. Then save the new version of AUTOEXEC.BAT. Now warm boot again so that DOS recognizes any changes you made to AUTOEXEC.BAT or to CONFIG.SYS. Any time changes are made to these two files or to the DOS nucleus you must warm boot so that the new system setup is recognized. Proceed with the remaining steps below if necessary. If you have not previously used the suggestions in steps 6 through 9, you may want to make these changes to your system now. If not, the new version of DOS is now installed on your hard drive and you have completed the upgrade process.
6. There are numerous third-party utility routines available to enhance your microcomputer's operating system. They are available for sale as DOS utilities and are also available through bulletin boards, out of magazines, and so on. Some of the best sources are computer magazines such as *PC Magazine*, *PC World*, and others. This software is not part of the operating system, but rather an enhancement or supplement to it. Rather than mix this software with the DOS operating system, it is recommended that it be kept in a separate directory for this purpose. It is recommended that a directory named \UTIL be

set up for this purpose. Store all of these DOS supplemental programs in the \UTIL directory.

7. The software stored in the root directory of your hard disk is critical to the boot process for your computer. Should anything happen to these files your computer may not boot successfully. Some software installation processes may attempt to modify the CONFIG.SYS or AUTOEXEC.BAT files. You may make these files inoperable in attempting to modify them. It is recommended that a directory named \BACKR be created on your system. Keep copies of all your critical root directory files in this subdirectory. You may want to keep a copy of every root directory file in this subdirectory. If any of the key root directory files are damaged or changed, you can quickly restore them by copying the file or files back to the root from the \BACKR directory.
8. Damaging key files may result in hours of work to make the system operable again. Key files can be protected from accidental deletion or modification by hiding them or making them read-only or both. Use the ATTRIB command to make a file read-only. There are several utility programs that can be used to hide and unhide files. The DOS program DEBUG can also be used to turn on the hide bit in the attribute byte. The attribute byte is stored in the system directory area along with the filename and file extension fields. To make the AUTOEXEC.BAT and CONFIG.SYS files read-only, execute the first two ATTRIB commands as shown below. Then check to see that the read-only bit is on by displaying the attribute bits as shown in the third command following. The AUTOEXEC.BAT and CONFIG.SYS files should have an R displayed to the left of their filenames showing that they are read-only files.

```
C:\> ATTRIB +R C:\AUTOEXEC.BAT
C:\> ATTRIB +R C:\CONFIG.SYS
C:\> ATTRIB C:\*.*
```

9. Once the hard disk is set up and the system is operating as you want it, the software should be backed up to a tape backup system or to diskettes. To back up to diskettes, use the BACKUP command that is part of DOS. Good backup procedures are an integral part of operating a computer. You may want to back up the entire system or back up selected directory structures representing your installed software applications. There are many reasons to back up the system. Loss of the hard disk due to hardware failure, damage to key files, and software viruses which may damage your software are just some of the reasons to have a system backup. See Chapter 12 for additional information on the DOS BACKUP and RESTORE commands and their applications.

APPENDIX D

INSTALLING DOS VERSION 3.*xx* ON A HARD DRIVE

INTRODUCTION

To install Version 3.*xx* on your hard drive, you must first determine whether this is an initial installation on the hard drive or an upgrade to an earlier version. If this is an upgrade of an earlier version, proceed to Step 1, then skip to Step 4 in the procedure below.

Whether you are installing DOS for the first time or upgrading DOS, it is important to recognize all the steps that must be accomplished in order for your computer to operate properly.

To install DOS, several pieces must be positioned. The DOS hidden files, along with COMMAND.COM, must be placed in the root directory of the disk. Two boot control files are created—CONFIG.SYS and AUTOEXEC.BAT—and are placed in the root directory. These are not strictly part of DOS; they are files that you create to control the setup of your system. They are important to the efficient operation of your computer. The rest of the DOS files from the DOS master diskettes are then copied to a directory specifically created to hold these files. It is recommended that the name of the directory contain the DOS version number. For instance, if you are installing DOS Version 3.30, create a directory \DOS330 to hold all the DOS files other than the files placed in the root directory.

INSTALLING DOS 3.*xx*

The DOS diskettes supplied with the operating system manuals are known as *master diskettes*. These are the original diskettes and should be used in the initial installation only. After that, you should operate from working copies of these diskettes. The procedure described here will install DOS on your hard drive and create working diskettes that you can use in normal operations. Once this procedure is completed, use the master diskettes only if something happens to the working copies. While you're thinking about it, establish a box or other safe place where all copies of master diskettes are kept along with registration information for software. In that way, you'll know where to go to retrieve master copies of software and registration information.

Most hard drives purchased today are shipped to the customer with the hard drive already formatted. If the hard drive is not formatted, you must first format the hard drive. Steps that may be skipped in the installation, such as the formatting of the hard drive, are noted below. This procedure assumes that you must complete the entire process. If you are installing DOS for the first time, begin with Step 1. To upgrade to Version 3 of DOS, perform Step 1, then skip immediately to Step 4.

1. Insert the master DOS diskette labelled *Startup* into the floppy Drive A. Turn on the power switch. Turn on the display unit if it is not already on. After a short time the computer should boot up and request date and time information. Enter the appropriate date and time and press the Enter key after each has been typed. Your system should then display the DOS prompt as shown below, with a blinking cursor following the greater-than sign (>):

   ```
   A>
   ```

2. Enter the command shown below to determine if your hard drive has been formatted:

   ```
   A> DIR C:
   ```

   This command attempts to read the hard drive, which will normally be Drive C. It should display a list of files in the root directory of Drive C. If it does, your hard drive has been formatted and you can skip to Step 4. If an error message displays "Abort, Retry, or Fail," the hard drive has not been formatted and you must format it. Proceed to Step 3 in that case.

3. To format the hard drive, enter the command below. Press the Enter key after typing the command. This command not only formats the hard drive, but also makes it a bootable disk. Once all the steps of this procedure are completed you will boot from the hard drive for normal operations.

   ```
   A> FORMAT C:/S
   ```

   The command will display the tracks that are being formatted as it proceeds. If the program encounters any bad tracks, you may hear a whirring noise as it attempts several times to format that space on the disk. If particular tracks are bad, the program will flag them as bad so that they cannot be used. Once the formatting process is complete, the system files will be transferred and a message "System Transferred" will appear on the screen. You will then be asked to enter a volume label. Press the Enter key unless you want to place a label on (give a name to) the hard drive. A label may be up to 11 characters in length. Press the Enter key after the label if you choose to enter one. A label is not typically necessary and will not affect the operation of your computer in any way. You have now formatted the hard drive and made the hard drive a bootable disk.

4. Execute the command shown below to copy the two hidden files to the hard drive. Press the Enter key after typing the command:

```
A> SYS C:
```

   The computer should respond "System Transferred." If DOS responds "Insufficient Memory for System Transfer," back up your hard drive and perform Step 3 above to produce a bootable system disk on the hard drive.

5. Now copy the COMMAND.COM processor to your hard drive with the command shown below. As always, press the Enter key after typing the command:

```
A> COPY COMMAND.COM C:\
```

   COMMAND.COM will be copied from the *Startup* disk in Drive A to the hard drive and placed in the root directory. The message "1 File copied" will appear.

6. Now create a directory to store all the DOS files. It is recommended that the name of the directory include the version number of DOS. For instance, if you are installing DOS Version 3.20, the directory name will be \DOS320. In the command below, substitute the version number for the *xxx* in the command. If you do not know the version number of DOS you are installing, type VER at the prompt and press the Enter key. A message will be displayed telling you the version number of DOS you are installing. Then copy all the files from the *Startup* diskette to this directory. Use the commands below to complete these operations:

```
A> VER
A> MD C:\DOSxxx
A> copy *.* C:\DOSxxx
```

   All the files from the *Startup* disk have now been copied to the new DOS directory. COMMAND.COM is also in the new directory, but this is a duplicate of the copy you placed in the root directory in Step 5. The duplicate copy of COMMAND.COM can be erased with the command below. Substitute the proper version number for the *xxx* just as you did above:

```
A> DEL C:\DOSxxx\COMMAND.COM
```

7. In addition to the *Startup* diskette, most versions of DOS also come with an *Operating System* diskette. Now remove the *Startup* diskette from Drive A and insert the *Operating System* diskette into Drive A. Then execute the command below:

```
A> copy *.* C:\DOSxxx
```

All the files on the *Operating System* diskette will now be copied to the new \DOS*xxx* directory. If there are any other diskettes supplied with your copy of DOS, repeat Step 7 until all the diskettes have been copied into the \DOS*xxx* directory. When this operation is complete, DOS has been installed on your hard drive. Remove the *Operating System* diskette from Drive A. You're now ready to test that your hard drive is a bootable disk.

8. With no diskette in Drive A, press the three keys Ctrl, Alt, and Del at the same time, then release them. The computer will perform its normal boot operation. It will first attempt to boot from Drive A, and you will see the Drive A light come on. When the system finds no diskette in Drive A, it looks for the hard drive and boots from that disk. The system should boot from Drive C after approximately one to two minutes, depending on your computer, and then display the system prompt as shown below:

```
C>
```

9. You're now ready to create two simple boot control files that will be stored in the root directory. You may later want to change these files once you have more experience. If you know the commands you want to place in these files, substitute your file for the ones shown here. These are basic examples that will get you started in tailoring your computer system to your specific needs. Refer also to Chapter 22 and Appendix C for hints on installing and protecting your system installation. Steps 10 through 13 below will create the two boot control files—AUTOEXEC.BAT and CONFIG.SYS—and then install them on your system through the boot process.

10. Create the CONFIG.SYS file with the procedure below. Be careful to type the commands exactly as shown, with no typing mistakes. If you make a mistake, you will have to repeat the procedure. At the end of each line, press the Enter key as indicated in the first line. Once you have typed all the lines of the file, use the F6 function key to generate the Ctrl-Z character, then press the Enter key. The file will be copied to the hard drive. The message "1 File(s) copied" will display on the screen.

```
C> COPY CON C:\CONFIG.SYS
   BREAK=on
   BUFFERS=30
   FILES=30
   LASTDRIVE=F
```

11. Create the AUTOEXEC.BAT file with the procedure below. Be careful to type the commands exactly as shown, with no typing mistakes. If you make a mistake, you will have to repeat the procedure. This is the same procedure as used in Step 10 for the CONFIG.SYS file. After typing the last line of the file, again press the F6 function key to generate the Ctrl-Z character, and press the Enter key. The message "1 File(s) copied" will again display.

```
C> COPY CON C:\AUTOEXEC.BAT
        @ECHO off
        DATE
        TIME
        PROMPT $p $g
        PATH C:\;C:\DOSxxx
```

12. Now check to ensure that the two files (AUTOEXEC.BAT and CONFIG.SYS) are in the root directory and contain the correct commands, using the DIR command as shown below. If you made mistakes in either Step 10 or Step 11, repeat that step to correct the file. The new file will replace the old file in the root directory.

    ```
    C> DIR C:\
    ```

    The Directory command will display the files in the root directory. Make sure that the CONFIG.SYS and AUTOEXEC.BAT files are listed in the directory report. If they are not, you have made a mistake in either Step 10 or Step 11, or both. Now check to see that each file contains the proper commands by displaying its contents. Execute the command shown below:

    ```
    C> TYPE C:\CONFIG.SYS
    ```

    The CONFIG.SYS file will be listed on your display screen. Check to make sure that the contents of the file are the same as shown in Step 10 or agree with the copy of the file you entered. If not, repeat Step 10.

    Now list the contents of the AUTOEXEC.BAT file to the display screen by executing the command shown below:

    ```
    C> TYPE C:\AUTOEXEC.BAT
    ```

    The AUTOEXEC.BAT file will be listed on your display screen. Check to make sure that the contents of the file are the same as shown in Step 11 or agree with the copy of the file you entered. If not, repeat Step 11. Once you have ensured that these two files are correct and contain the commands appropriate for your system, proceed to Step 13.

13. Now reboot the computer. Make sure there is no diskette in Drive A. Then press the three keys Ctrl, Alt, and Del at the same time. Then release all three. The boot process will execute, with both the CONFIG.SYS and the AUTOEXEC.BAT files as part of that process. Each of the commands in these files will be executed to tailor your system to your particular needs. You should see no error messages that indicate that any of the commands failed to execute correctly. Enter the date and the time when requested by the messages on the screen. When the process is completed, the DOS prompt should display as shown below, followed by a blinking cursor:

```
C:\ >
```

DOS has now been installed on your hard drive and the system has been tailored to your computer. For additional information on tailoring the system to your needs, refer to Appendix C and Chapters 21 and 22. As you gain more experience, you may want to modify this initial system installation. Refer to Chapter 11 on EDLIN to learn how to modify the CONFIG.SYS and AUTOEXEC.BAT files.

Create working copies of your DOS diskettes and one system boot diskette for use in the event that a problem arises with your hard drive and you cannot boot from it for some reason.

14. Make working copies of each of the original DOS diskettes by executing the command below. Execute the DISKCOPY command for each diskette to be duplicated.

    ```
    C:\ > DISKCOPY A: A:
    ```

    When the program stops at the message, insert the first DOS diskette into Drive A as the source disk. The information will be copied from the disk into memory and stored there. At the appropriate message, insert a blank formatted diskette into Drive A as the target diskette. The information will be copied from memory to the target disk. Repeat this procedure as many times as necessary until all information has been copied from the master DOS disk as the source to the target disk. When the program asks if you want to copy another disk, reply **n** for No. Once this process is complete, enter the command shown below to ensure that the DOS diskette has been duplicated correctly:

    ```
    C:\ > DISKCOMP A: A:
    ```

    The DISKCOMP command will now check to ensure that the two diskettes are duplicates. Once complete, the program should issue a message indicating that the two diskettes are exact duplicates and that the results of the comparison are OK. Use the master DOS diskette as the source disk (or disk 1) and the new disk as the second disk. Once complete, remove the blank diskette and place a label on it similar to the label on the master diskette. Indicate also that this is a working copy of the DOS diskette. A label such as DOS Startup diskette, Working Copy might be appropriate. Repeat step 14 for any other master copies of the DOS diskettes. Depending on the size of your diskettes, you may have to duplicate from one to five diskettes.

15. As a final step, create a floppy system boot diskette. This diskette is for emergency use when your hard drive does not boot for some reason. Use a blank diskette in this step that will be saved for emergency use. Insert the blank diskette into Drive A and type the command below:

```
C:\ > FORMAT A:/S
```

The diskette will be formatted and the nucleus of the operating system will be transferred to the floppy diskette. At the completion of the formatting process, the message "System Transferred" will be issued. At the completion DOS will ask if you wish to format another diskette. Reply **n** for No. Label this diskette as a *System Boot disk.*

Now store the System Boot diskette along with the Startup DOS diskette and any other master DOS diskettes in a safe place with your other master diskettes. You have completed the installation process for DOS, as well as protected yourself in case of emergencies. When using DOS diskettes in the future, use the working copies of the DOS diskettes rather than the master copies supplied with DOS.

APPENDIX E

INSTALLING DOS VERSION 4.*xx* ON A HARD DISK

INTRODUCTION

Beginning with DOS Version 4.00, the process for installing or upgrading DOS was modified substantially. Version 4.00 of DOS introduced a new command named SELECT. The SELECT command initiates the installation process and takes the user through a step-by-step process for installing DOS. It also allows customization for specific countries and keyboards, in effect making DOS an international system. Table E.1 defines the country and keyboard codes that can be used with the SELECT command.

TABLE E.1 **SELECT Command Codes**

Country	Country Code	Keyboard Code
Australia	061	US
Belgium	032	BE
Canada (English)	001	US
Canada (French)	002	CF
Denmark	045	DK
Finland	358	SU
France	033	FR
Germany	049	GR
International (English)	061	
Israel	972	
Italy	039	IT
Latin America	003	LA
Middle East (Arabic)	785	
Netherlands	031	NL
Norway	047	NO
Portugal	351	PO
Spain	034	SP

"continued"

TABLE E.1 SELECT Command Codes (continued)

Country	Country Code	Keyboard Code
Sweden	046	SV
Switzerland (French)	041	SF
Switzerland (German)	041	SG
United Kingdom	044	UK
United States	001	US

The format of the SELECT command is:

```
SELECT <source> <target> <country> <keyboard>
```

The SELECT installation specifications include language and keyboard layout selections, and, as a result, are country-specific. The installation thus becomes country-specific on your hard disk. The DOS installation diskette to be loaded in Drive A contains an AUTOEXEC.BAT file that automatically starts the Version 4.00 Select program.

INSTALLING DOS VERSION 4.*xx*

To start the installation process, load a diskette in Drive A and either power up the computer if it is turned off, or do a warm boot using the Ctrl, Alt, and Del keys if it is already turned on.

Prior to the installation of Version 4.*xx*, you need to obtain certain information about your hardware configuration so that the installation can be tailored to your system and optimized based on the size of your computer's memory. You should obtain answers to the following questions prior to booting from the Version 4.*xx* installation diskette:

1. How much RAM memory is installed on your computer?
2. What version of DOS is currently installed? Is it an IBM version (PC-DOS) or a compatible version (MS-DOS)?
3. What make and model printer is connected to your computer?
4. Is your printer a serial printer or a parallel printer?
5. What port is your printer connected to? (Normally this is LPT1 for a parallel printer and COM1 for a serial printer.)

To complete the installation of Version 4.*xx*, you will need one or more diskettes to complete the operation, even if you are installing DOS on a hard drive. Use Table E.2 to find out the number of diskettes needed for Drive A on your system.

The installation program is quite detailed and will prompt you for answers to questions as it proceeds. Online help is also available. The SELECT program will prompt for answers and tell you which of the original DOS diskettes should be loaded as it proceeds.

If your computer has less than 512 KB of internal RAM, choose the first option (*Minimum DOS function*) when requested. If your system has 512 KB of internal RAM, choose the second option (*Balanced DOS function*) when requested. If your system has 640 KB of memory or more, choose option 3 (*Maximum DOS function*) when prompted. It is recommended that you format the number of diskettes required based on Table E.2, but that is not absolutely required. If the diskettes you need are unformatted, DOS will format them as part of the process.

When SELECT finishes, it will have created two files that contain specific boot control information for your system. These two files are AUTOEXEC.400 and CONFIG.400. In order to use these files with your system, they must first be renamed as AUTOEXEC.BAT and CONFIG.SYS. You may not be able to rename the *.400 files to these names since your system may already have an AUTOEXEC.BAT and a CONFIG.SYS file installed. Furthermore, your current files may contain commands or information that you want to incorporate into the new Version 4 files. In order to do this, execute the sequence of commands below.

This set of commands first saves your current files so that you will have access to their information. Then it renames the *.400 files to their appropriate names so that the Version 4 boot control information is incorporated. If you want to include any of the commands in your old boot control files into the new

TABLE E.2 **Diskette Requirements for Installation**

Type of Disk Installation	Diskette Capacity	No. of Diskettes (PC-DOS)	No. of Diskettes (MS-DOS)
360 KB	360 KB	4	5
1.2 MB	360 KB	4	5
720 KB	720 KB	2	3
1.44 MB	1.44 MB	1	2
Hard disk with 5 1/4-inch	360 KB	1	1
Hard disk with 3 1/2-inch	Any	1	1

versions, refer to Chapter 11 on EDLIN for information on how to modify a text file. If you want to display the contents of any of the files, use the TYPE command, along with the name of the appropriate file.

The sequence of commands below assume that Version 4.*xx* has been installed from the DOS Version 4.*xx* installation diskettes. Execute the sequence below after pressing the F3 function key to exit the DOS Shell installed by Version 4.

```
C:\> REN autoexec.bat autoexec.sav
C:\> REN config.sys   config.sav
C:\> REN autoexec.400 autoexec.bat
C:\> REN config.400   config.sys
```

Now warm-boot the computer using the Ctrl-Alt-Del key sequence so that you are now running under the Version 4 just installed and using the new AUTOEXEC and CONFIG files. You should now see a display related to the DOS Shell, which provides several function-key options. It is now up to you to decide how you want the system to operate and whether you want to run under the DOS Shell or under some other system better suited to your needs.

You may want to review from Step 6 on in Appendix D as well as Appendix C for more information on system installation options. You may also want to incorporate some of the protection hints given there and in Chapter 22 into your Version 4 system.

APPENDIX F
DOS COMMAND SUMMARY

INTRODUCTION

This command summary is organized in four groups: internal commands, external commands, batch file commands, and configuration commands. Within each category, commands are organized alphabetically. The commands and their parameters are summarized briefly. For more details and examples of command usage, refer to the chapter that discusses the individual command.

INTERNAL COMMANDS

BREAK

In normal operations, DOS checks for a BREAK (generated by Ctrl-C) only when it reads or writes to a device such as the monitor or the printer. With BREAK turned on, DOS checks for a break signal each time a system call is generated as well as when writing to a device. There are no parameters.

BREAK=<*On* or *Off*>

CHANGE DIRECTORY (CD)

This command changes or displays the current directory for the specified disk drive.

CD <*drive:*><*path*>

<*drive:*> is the letter, followed by a colon, of the drive whose current directory is to be changed.
<*path*> is the name of the directory that is to become the current directory.

CD, entered by itself, will display the current drive and directory. For a detailed discussion of this command, including examples and common mistakes, see Chapter 6.

CHANGE CODE PAGE (CHCP)

Change Code Page tells DOS which code page to use for any devices that support code page switching. Changing the code page changes the language or character set that DOS is using at the current time. Commands associated with CHCP are the NLSFUNC command, which must be loaded prior to use, and the MODE command. The COUNTRY.SYS file must be available to the CONFIG.SYS file. Note: Oriental language codes are available; however, hardware modifications must be made prior to use. Not all codes are available in all DOS versions. Check the documentation that came with your version of DOS to determine codes that can be used.

CHCP <*codepage*>

<*codepage*> is the three-digit number that specifies which code page DOS is to use. The default value is 437 for the United States. Table F.1 is a list of common international code page numbers.

TABLE F.1 Code Page Numbers (CHCP Command)

Code Page Number	Code Page
437	United States
850	Multilingual (Latin I)
852	Slavic (Latin II)
860	Portuguese
862	Hebrew
863	French Canadian
864	Arabic
865	Nordic

CLEAR SCREEN (CLS)

This command clears the screen of any displayed information and moves the cursor to the top lefthand corner of the screen. The prompt is then displayed at the top-left corner of the screen. This may be the system prompt or a user-designed prompt. This command is used frequently in batch files to remove clutter from the screen.

CLS

CLS is always entered alone, there are no parameters. For more information and some examples, see Chapter 8.

COPY

The COPY command copies a file or group of files from one device to another. Files can also be combined using this command. The results of the copy can be checked or verified using the /V parameter or by setting the Verify status (see VERIFY).

```
COPY <source> /A /B + <source> <target> /A /B /V
```

<source> is the file or group of files to be copied or the device to be used as the input device.

<target> is the file or device to which the source information is to be copied.

Parameters

/A causes files to be treated as ASCII text files. Source files are copied up to the first EOF mark.

/B causes the file or files to be treated as binary or nontext files. With /B specified, the file or files are copied in their entirety.

/V causes the copy process to be verified. DOS verifies the copy by first turning on the VERIFY status during the copy, and then turning off VERIFY once the copy process is complete.

For a detailed discussion of this command including examples and common mistakes, see Chapter 7.

Change Console (CTTY)

This command allows a choice of default devices for input and output. Normally the keyboard and display screen are used for this purpose. If a device other than CON, AUX, or COM is used, the CONFIG.SYS file must contain a device driver for the assigned device. The device named must be capable of input and output.

```
CTTY <device name>
```

<devicename> is the name of the device to be used as the source of input and as the destination of output.
Examples of the use of this command are provided in Chapter 8 along with a discussion of usage rules.

DATE

The DATE command sets the computer's system date. If there is no clock card present in the system to keep track of the date, a default date will be used. The date, which is stamped on files as they are created or modified, can be used with other commands as a means of identifying groups of files.

DATE ***<mm-dd-yy>***

<mm-dd-yy> or ***<mm/dd/yy>*** is the form in which the date should be entered; month, day, and year, separated as shown by hyphens or slashes; no spaces are permitted.

DATE, entered with no other information, displays the current system date and provides the user an opportunity to change the date. DATE is frequently used in association with the TIME command. Both are discussed in Chapter 5.

Delete (DEL)

A useful, but sometimes dangerous command, DELETE removes the specified file or files from the directory. DELETE can be used with wildcards to delete groups of files with a single command. Special software may be needed to recover files that have been deleted.

DEL ***<filename>*** **/P**

<filename> is the name of the file or files, including the drive and pathname if needed, that are to be deleted.

Parameters

/P signals DOS to ask for confirmation of the deletion before it takes place. This is very helpful if wildcards are used.

A discussion of file-recovery utilities is included in a general discussion of this command in Chapter 7.

Directory (DIR)

This is one of the most useful DOS commands. It provides a list of the files in a directory. The names of directories are included in the report. Hidden files do not appear as a result of this command unless the appropriate parameters are specified. The output may be controlled in several ways, or redirected to the printer. In addition, see the DIRCMD command in the Configuration Commands section for information about customizing your DIR displays. See Chapter 2 for information on the redirection of files and Chapter 6 on DIR.

DIR ***<pathname>*** **/P /W /A:FileType /O:Sequence /S /B /L**

<pathname> provides a listing of files from a specific drive and/or directory. This may also be used with wildcards to search for groups of files.

DIR, entered without a specified drive or directory, returns a report from the default drive and directory.

Parameters

/P stops the scrolling of the file list after the screen is full and waits for the user to press a key before displaying the next screen of entries.

/W arranges the file report so that the listing appears in columns. This permits the maximum number of filenames to be displayed on the screen at one time.

/A:FileType displays the file type(s) specified by the use of a character from the list below. Used without a specified value, all files of all types are displayed. These values may be used in combination; do not separate the values with spaces or punctuation marks. (Available in MS-DOS Version 5 only.)

h	Hidden files
-h	Files not hidden
s	System files
-s	Nonsystem files
d	Directories
-d	Files only
a	Files not backed up
-a	Backed-up files
r	Read-only files
-r	Not read-only

/O:Sequence changes the order of the display of filenames by specifying one of the values from the list below. Used without a specified value, the files are listed in alphabetical order. These values may be used in combination; do not separate the values with spaces or punctuation marks. (Available in MS-DOS Version 5 only.)

n	Alphabetical order
-n	Reverse alphabetical order
e	Alphabetical order by extension
-e	Reverse alphabetical order by extension
d	Listing by date and time of creation
-d	Reverse listing of date and time of creation
s	File size, smaller files first
-s	File size, largest files first
g	Group directory entries before files

-g	Group directory entries after files
/S	searches all subdirectories of the current or specified directory for the specified filename.
/B	gives a simple list of filenames, with no other information.
/L	displays all filenames in a lowercase format.

A complete discussion of the DIR command is found in Chapter 4 and Chapter 6.

ERASE

This command is sometimes used in place of DELETE. See the section on the DELETE command in Chapter 7 and DELETE in this Appendix.

EXIT

This command is used from within the COMMAND.COM program to return to the calling processor. This command will have no effect if the /P parameter is used when issuing a COMMAND command. (See COMMAND under External Commands, this Appendix.)

```
EXIT
```

LOADHIGH (LH)

Programs may be loaded into the upper memory area in order to save conventional memory. If an upper-area memory manager has been installed concomitant with an extended memory manager, programs may take advantage of unused upper memory. A sequence might be: (1) HIMEM.SYS is installed, (2) EMM386.EXE is installed, and (3) LOADHIGH is executed. If sufficient space is not available in the upper memory area, conventional memory will be used without warning from DOS. (Available in MS-DOS Version 5 only.)

LH *<program>* *<parameters>*

<program> is the program to be loaded into upper memory.

<parameters> are any parameters normally required to execute the program.

MAKE DIRECTORY (MD)

This command is used to create a directory on a disk or diskette in order to organize large numbers of files. Directories must be created in a top-to-bottom order; the parent directory must first exist before a subdirectory can be created.

```
MD <directory name>
```

<*directory name*> is the name of the directory to be created, including the drive, if necessary. The use of this command is discussed in conjunction with the Remove Directory and Change Directory commands in Chapter 6.

PATH

PATH is used to define a search path along which DOS can look for executable files. When the name of an executable file is entered at the prompt, DOS attempts to find it in the default directory on the default drive. With a PATH command in effect, DOS will also search other specified directories to find the file.

```
PATH <pathname1>;<pathname2>;<etc.>
```

PATH ; (entered with a semicolon) returns the path to a default mode in which no other directories are searched.

<*pathname*> is the name, including the drive, of a directory to be searched for executable files. Each must be chained with a semicolon and no spaces are permitted.

PATH, entered without pathnames, returns the current search path. Search paths are discussed in Chapter 8 with other System Control commands.

Set System (PROMPT)

The PROMPT command allows you to modify the system prompt to show a customized prompt. You may show the time, date, current drive and/or directory, or a message to the user. The normal system prompt is the drive letter followed by the greater-than sign (>).

```
PROMPT <message> <code>
```

<*message*> is a string entered by the user.

<*code*> refers to a two-character code DOS uses to display specific information as part of the prompt. See the list in Table F.2.

PROMPT, entered by itself, restores the prompt to the system default. Examples of the use of this command may be found in Chapter 8.

Remove Directory (RD)

This command removes a directory from a disk or diskette. In order to be removed, a directory must be empty of all files, including hidden files, and all subdirectories. Directories must be removed from the bottom of the structure to the top. A directory cannot be removed if it is the default directory.

```
RD <directory name>
```

TABLE F.2 DOS Prompt Codes

Code	Display
$$	$ character
$q	= character
$g	Greater-than (>)
$l	Less-than (<)
$b	¦ character
$d	Date
$p	Default drive and directory
$n	Default drive only
$v	DOS version number
$t	Time
$h	Backspace
$e	Escape character
$_	Move to new line in the display

<directory name> is the name of the directory to be removed, including the drive letter, if needed.

The use of this command is discussed in conjunction with the Make Directory (MD) and Change Directory (CD) commands in Chapter 6.

RENAME (REN)

RENAME changes the name of a file or group of files that have already been created. This command does not move the file to another directory. A new filename must be unique to that directory.

```
REN <oldname> <newname>
```

<oldname> is the name with which the file is currently identified, including the drive and directory, if needed.

<newname> is the name the file will have after the command is executed. It does not include a drive or directory name; the file will remain in the drive and directory in which it is currently located.

A complete presentation of the uses of this command, including the use of wildcards in the renaming process can be found in Chapter 7.

SET ENVIRONMENTAL VARIABLE (SET)

SET allows the user to make certain values, associated with a variable, part of the system environment. These variables are associated with specific application software packages, or software used with hardware such as a sound card. See the last section of commands in this appendix, Configuration Commands, for more information.

SET *<variable>*=*<value>*

<variable> is the environmental variable required, by software or hardware, to be in the system environment area of memory. Used without a *<value>*, it erases the *<variable>* from the system environment.

<value> given to the *<variable>*, which may include a drive, pathname, or other data.

SET, entered without the *<variable>* or *<value>* displays the status of all environmental variables. Further discussion of this command is included in Chapter 8.

TIME

This command sets the system time for the computer. If there is no clock card present in the system to keep track of the time, a default time will be used. The time is stamped on files as they are created or modified, and can be used with other commands as a means of identifying groups of files.

TIME *<h:mm>*:<ss>.<xx> <*A* or *P*>

<h:mm> represents the hour (*h*) based on the 24-hour military system; followed by minutes (*mm*).

<ss> represents seconds which may be entered if a very accurate time is desired.

<xx> represents hundredths of seconds, also an optional entry that may be specified if seconds are entered.

<*A* or *P*> specifies AM (*A*) or PM (*P*). *A* is the default.

TIME, entered with no other information, displays the current system time and provides the user an opportunity to change it. TIME and other fundamental internal commands are discussed in Chapter 5.

Display Contents of File (TYPE)

This command displays the contents of an ASCII text file. Normally, the output is directed to the display screen. Output may be directed to the printer using the hardware controls discussed in Chapter 2, or by using output redirection, also discussed in Chapter 2. Screen display of a long file will result in text scrolling on the screen. The use of filter commands as described in Chapter 13 will be useful in this situation.

TYPE *<filename>*

<filename> is the name of the file, including the drive and directory, if needed.

Chapter 7 includes this command as well as other internal commands concerned with file management.

VERSION (VER)

VERSION displays the version number of DOS, either PC-DOS or MS-DOS, that was loaded as part of the boot process.

VER

VER is always entered alone; there are no parameters. Additional information about this command is located in Chapter 8.

VERIFY

This command is a toggle that turns on or off the Verify feature of DOS. VERIFY confirms that data transferred by a COPY command is copied accurately. This is similar to the /V parameter available with the COPY command.

VERIFY <*Off* or ***On*>**

<*Off* or ***On*>** is either Off or On, depending on whether VERIFY is to be deactivated or activated.

VERIFY, used without a status statement, returns the current state of the Verify feature. VERIFY and COPY are part of Chapter 7.

VOLUME (VOL)

This command displays the disk's volume label if there is one. This label uniquely identifies the disk. The label is normally created at the time the disk is formatted, as part of the FORMAT command. The label may be changed using the LABEL command discussed in Chapter 9.

VOL <*drive*:>

<*drive*:> is the drive containing the disk for which a volume label is requested. If no drive is specified, the default drive is used.

VOL is a disk management command. Details of the use of this command are found in Chapter 5.

EXTERNAL COMMANDS

APPEND

APPEND functions with data files the way PATH works with executable files. With an APPEND statement in effect DOS can look for data files in directories other than the default drive and directory. DOS may, however, fail to tell you where it found the file and therefore save it in the current directory instead of the source directory.

APPEND <*pathname;pathname;etc.*> /E /X /Path:<*On or Off*>

<*pathname*> is the name of a drive, or a drive and directory combination, that DOS will search to find a specified data file. Multiple pathnames must be chained with a semicolon (;).

APPEND, entered with no parameters, displays the current search path. APPEND entered with a semicolon (APPEND;) removes any data search paths.

Parameters

/E allows DOS to put the APPEND information into the environment. The /E parameter can be used only the first time an APPEND command is used, and no other parameters except the /X can be specified at the same time. A second APPEND command must be entered to establish the data search path. This switch is only available in Versions 3.3 and later.

/X makes the data search path available to a wider variety of DOS commands. Follows the same basic rules as the /E parameter. This switch is only available in Version 3.3 and later.

/Path:<*On or Off*> is only available in DOS Version 4.00 or later. The effect of the command, when turned on, is to include data files that have a pathname as part of the filename, that is, a drive letter and/or a directory name.

Examples of the use of this command, along with commonly made mistakes, are found in Chapter 12.

ASSIGN

This command redirects any I/O requests made for one drive to go to another drive instead. These requests include file saving and file retrieving. I/O requests may come from the user or from an application package. This command is available in Version 3.0 and later. There are, however, several warnings that should be noted with the use of this command:

1. Do not use BACKUP, RESTORE, LABEL, JOIN, SUBSTitute or PRINT commands with assigned drives.
2. FORMAT, DISKCOPY, and DISKCOMP ignore the ASSIGN command.
3. The ASSIGN command should be used with caution and not for normal run-time procedures.
4. There is no way to have DOS display the assignments of affected drives if you are using a version of PC-DOS or MS-DOS prior to Version 5.00. You must keep track of any ASSIGN commands issued.

ASSIGN <*drive1=drive2*> <*drive3=drive4*> /S

<*drive1=drive2*> allows multiple assignments to be made in an ASSIGN command. More than one drive can be assigned to another drive (Drive1 and Drive3 could both have been assigned to Drive2). Each pair of drive assignments are separated by a space; no colons are used.

ASSIGN alone cancels all assignments made previously.

Parameters

/S displays the results of the ASSIGN command in effect.

Available in MS-DOS Version 5.00 only.

A more complete explanation of this command is found in Chapter 15.

ATTRIBUTE (ATTRIB)

This command controls certain characteristics of a file. It is useful for file group selection in several DOS operations, and for a first level of file security to prevent accidental deletion. Wildcard characters are permitted. Use of this command is limited to Versions 3.2 and later.

ATTRIB <*+R* or ***–R*> <*+A*** or ***–A*> <*+S*** or ***–S*> <*+H*** or ***–H*>**
<*Pathname*> /S

<*+R* or ***–R*>** controls whether or not a file is read-only. Setting the read-only byte to +R mode allows users to look at a file, but not to make any changes to that file. The –R parameter lets modifications be made to a file.

<*+A* or ***–A*>** sets the archive bit of a file. Turning on the archive bit indicates that the file has been created or modified since the last file backup. This bit is read whether the DOS BACKUP or other commercial programs are used. Turning off the bit indicates that a file has not been modified since the last file backup.

<*+S* or ***–S*>** marks the file(s) as a system file. Available in MS-DOS Version 5 only.

<*+H* or ***–H*>** marks the file(s) as a hidden file. This may be useful as a method of preventing inadvertent deletions of files or changes in files such as AUTOEXEC.BAT or CONFIG.SYS. Available in MS-DOS Version 5 only.

<*Pathname*> is the name of the file or files to be modified.

Parameters

/S extends the command's influence to all subdirectories of the specified parent directory.

For further information about this command and its security uses, see Chapter 12.

BACKUP

BACKUP is a useful command that makes a copy of a file, groups of files, an entire directory, or a whole hard disk. This procedure provides a method by which lost or damaged data can be retrieved from secondary storage. The information, which includes the directory structure of the files involved, is stored compactly. Files restored to a disk will reflect the same directory structure they had on the original. Do not back up files on disks affected by an ASSIGN, SUBST or JOIN command.

BACKUP <*pathname*> <*drive2*:> /S /M /A /F:Size /D:Date /T:Time /L:Pathname

<*pathname*> is the drive and/or directory and/ or filenames to be backed up.

<*drive2*:> is the target drive that must be specified. DOS will write the backup files to this disk. Usually this is a floppy drive or a tape drive.

Parameters

/S backs up all of the files in all of the subdirectories of the specified parent directory.

/M checks the archive attribute to see if specified files have been modified since the last backup. If so, they are backed up.

/A adds the files to be backed up to a diskette already containing backup files. Without this switch, DOS will write the new files over the old ones, which are then lost.

/F:Size formats the target disk if it is not already formatted. Size may be any legitimate disk size, as indicated below.

Single-sided	5.25"	160KB
Single-sided	5.25"	180KB
Double-sided	5.25"	320KB
Double-sided	5.25"	360KB
Double-sided	3.50"	720KB
Double-sided	5.25"	1.2MB
Double-sided	3.50"	1.44MB
Double-sided	3.50"	2.88MB

/D:<Date> checks the date stamped on each file as it was created or last modified and will back up only those files with a date equal to or greater than the specified date.

/T:<Time> functions like the /D:Date parameter but uses the time stamp on the file or files.

/L:<Filename> generates a file that is a log of the names of the files backed up, including the source drive information, the time of backup, and the date. Filename is a pathname specifying drive, directory, and filename. If no filename is specified, DOS will use a default name—BACKUP.LOG—and place it in the root directory of the source drive.

Examples of the use of this command are included in Chapter 12, along with instructions for restoring files that have been backed up.

BASIC, BASICA, GWBASIC, QBASIC

BASIC stands for Beginners All-purpose Symbolic Instruction Code. It is a beginning programming language included in DOS. Files created in BASIC have a BAS extension. You may return to DOS by entering SYSTEM. The BASIC program on your system may be BASIC, BASICA, GWBASIC, or QBASIC (MS-DOS Version 5).

BASIC

BASIC is invoked at the command prompt like any other program. The name of the version present on your computer would be substituted: BASIC, BASICA, GWBASIC, or QBASIC.

Chapter 20 contains a general discussion on the BASIC language translators.

CHECK DISK (CHKDSK)

This command analyzes the data storage distribution for a disk and reports the volume name, the number of user-created files, the number of hidden files, total disk space available, the number of bytes in bad sectors, the number of bytes free, the total memory units available, and the memory units used. It also notifies the user if lost clusters of data have been detected. The command can also be used to correct these cluster errors. CHKDSK can list the name and directory structure of all the files on the specified drive. Do not use this command when an ASSIGN, JOIN, or SUBST command is in effect, or with a drive assigned to a network.

CHKDSK *<drive:>* *<filename>* /F /V

<drive:> is the drive to be checked.

<filename> is an individual file or group of files to be checked for storage in contiguous sectors.

CHKDSK entered alone checks the default drive for the information listed above.

Parameters

/F checks for errors in cluster allocation and corrects them when a positive response is given to the prompt.

/V responds with a tree-like report of all files on the specified drive. At the conclusion of this list, the normal CHKDSK report will be given.

Chapter 9 includes more information about this command.

COMMAND PROCESSOR (COMMAND)

This command can be used to invoke a copy of the command processor, COMMAND.COM, in order to modify some of its characteristics without rebooting. If this technique is used, the AUTOEXEC.BAT and CONFIG.SYS files already invoked must be compatible with the new command processor. Also, the use of a new processor, even temporarily, is not equivalent to rebooting the computer. It was also a method used by earlier versions of DOS to execute a batch file and then return to the original processor. In order to return to the original processor, type EXIT at the system prompt.

COMMAND *<pathname> <device name>* /E:Num /P /C *<file-name>* /MSG

<pathname> is the location of the processor to be invoked.

<devicename> is the device to be used instead of the default monitor and keyboard combination.

Parameters

/E:NUM permits the user to decide how many bytes will be used for the environment of the new processor. The default value for Num is 160 bytes, although up to 32768 bytes may be specified.

/P indicates that the processor to be invoked will remain permanently in control.

/C *<filename>* is the name of the executable program or batch file to be invoked. When execution of the program has been completed, control will be returned to the original processor.

/MSG is used only when working on a system that does not have a hard drive. It stores all error messages in memory instead of in a file. The /P parameter must be used concurrently. (Available in MS-DOS Version 5 only.)

COMPARE (COMP)

This command compares two files or sets of files on a byte-by-byte basis to see if their contents are identical. When very important data is being copied, COMPARE is sometimes used to ensure the integrity of the copy. While the information given about the differences is available only in hexadecimal format for versions prior to MS-DOS Version 5.00, COMPARE does alert you to the fact that the files are not exact duplicates. A message indicating that the files are identical is displayed if the files match. COMPARE is available in Versions 3.3 or later.

COMP *<pathname1> <pathname2>* /A /C /D /L /N=Number

<pathname1> is the first file or group of files to be used in the comparison.

<pathname2> is the second file or group of files to be used in the comparison.

Parameters (Available in MS-DOS Version 5 only.)

/A provides an alphabetical display of the differences in the specified files.

/C compares the specified files without case sensitivity.

/D provides a decimal display of the differences in the specified files.

/L is the number of the line with a discrepancy. The number is displayed instead of the discrepancy.

/N=Number compares the specified Number of lines in the file.

The differences between the Disk Compare (DISKCOMP) and COMPARE (COMP) commands are discussed in Chapter 12.

DEBUG

DEBUG is a method of examining and/or changing a file on a byte-by-byte basis. The information is displayed in a hexadecimal format. DEBUG functions in much the same manner as a line editor. The prompt is an underscore (_). This advanced command is used for specialized tasks.

DEBUG *<pathname>*

<pathname> is the name of the file to be examined, including drive and directory information if needed.

DEBUG is more fully explained in Chapter 18.

Disk Compare (DISKCOMP)

DISKCOMP compares two diskettes on a track-by-track basis. Diskettes must be of like configuration, size, and capacity. Hard drives may not be compared; neither can virtual or RAM drives. This command should not be used when an ASSIGN or JOIN command is in effect. It should also not be used in a network situation. One other factor to keep in mind is that two diskettes can contain the same files, merely be arranged differently, and be reported as having differences. Files must be in the same order on the disk in order for the comparison to be valid. This command is most often used when diskettes have been duplicated using DOS.

DISKCOMP *<drive1:>* *<drive2:>* /1 /8

<drive1:> is the first diskette to be compared.

<drive2:> is the second diskette to be compared.

Parameters

/1 compares only the first side of the diskette even if it is a two-sided diskette.

/8 compares only the first eight sectors of a track, even if it is a nine-sectored diskette.

DISKCOMP, entered with no drives specified, causes DOS to prompt you to insert disks.

Further details about this command can be found in Chapter 9.

DISK COPY (DISKCOPY)

Duplication of whole diskettes can be accomplished quickly and accurately with this command. DISKCOPY can be used only for two disks of like construction, of the same size and capacity. Like DISKCOMP, DISKCOPY should not be used with an ASSIGN, SUBST, or JOIN command in effect. Also, note that in versions prior to 3.3, the target disk must be formatted before the copy procedure is initiated.

DISKCOPY *<drive1:>* *<drive2:>* /1 /V

<drive1:> is the source diskette drive letter.

<drive2:> is the target diskette letter.

DISKCOPY may be entered without parameters in order to accommodate single-drive systems. This allows the changing of disks in and out of a single drive. Use of this command in a single-drive system may be somewhat slow.

Parameters

/1 copies only the first side of a diskette.

/V verifies the copy procedure to ensure accuracy.

(Available in MS-DOS Version 5 only.)

Examples of the use of this command are found in Chapter 9.

DOSKEY

This utility, available in MS-DOS Version 5 only, enhances keyboard control sequences. It allows previously typed commands to be recalled and modified, therefore eliminating retyping. It also provides the capability of defining macros. Table F.3 presents a list of DOSKEY keyboard control sequences. Table F.4 provides a list of macro commands.

DOSKEY /Reinstall /Bufsize=Bytes /M /H /Insert or **/Overstrike MacroName=*<string>***

Parameters

/Reinstall installs a new copy of DOSKEY, therefore permitting changes in the installation. It also clears the DOSKEY buffer.

/Bufsize=Bytes allows specification of the buffer size used to store DOSKEY commands. The default size is 512; the minimum size is 256 bytes.

TABLE F.3 **DOSKEY Keyboard Control Sequences**

Key Sequence	Action
Up Arrow [↑]	Recalls the previous command.
Dn Arrow [↓]	Recalls the next command stored.
PgUp	Recalls the first command stored in the buffer.
PgDn	Recalls the last command stored in the buffer.
Left Arrow [←]	Moves the cursor one space to the left.
Right Arrow [→]	Moves the cursor one space to the right.
Ctrl-[←]	Moves the cursor one word to the left.
Ctrl-[→]	Moves the cursor one word to the right.
Home	Moves the cursor to the beginning of the line.
End	Moves the cursor to the end of the line.
Esc	Clears the command from the display.
F1	Recalls one character at a time from the last command entered.
F2	Displays all characters up to the first occurrence of a character typed on the keyboard.
F3	Recalls all characters from the buffer, or the remaining characters in the buffer.
F4	Deletes all characters in the keyboard buffer up to, but not including, the character pressed.
F5	Accepts the line edited as the current buffer line.
F6	Generates an EOF character, Ctrl-Z, when pressed.
F7	Displays all commands stored in the buffer with their line numbers.
Alt-F7	Clears the buffer.
F8	Searches the buffer for a command that matches a string entered at the keyboard prior to pressing the F8 key.
F9	Used to enter a command number so that it may be recalled.
Alt-F10	Deletes all macro definitions stored in the buffer.

/M displays a list of all of the DOSKEY macros available.

/H displays a list of all of the commands that have been entered and are still stored in the buffer. The resulting list may be redirected to a file or the printer.

/Insert or **/Overstrike** determines whether the keyboard is in a typeover or insert mode. The default status is typeover mode.

MacroName=<*string*> is a two-part parameter. *Macro name* is the name you want to assign to your macro. String represents the sequence of DOS commands you want to execute. Note that macros cannot be invoked from within a batch file, although a batch file may create them. Macro Name= deletes the file from the buffer.

Macros are executed by entering their name, along with any parameters required, on the command line. See Chapter 15.

TABLE F.4 DOSKEY Macro Commands

Macro	Action
$g	Redirects the output of a command to a device other than the screen.
gg	The output of a command is appended to a previously existing file.
$1	Redirects the input of a command from the keyboard to a specified file.
$b	Redirects the output of a macro-invoked command to another command.
$t	Inserts a space between multiple commands entered in a single command. This is necessary to issue several commands within one macro.
$$	Used to specify the $ in a command.
$1 . . . $9	Used similarly to the %1 characters in batch files to allow for a replaceable parameter.
&*	Permits multiple parameters entered on a command line to be accepted into a macro as one parameter.

DOS Shell (DOSSHELL)

DOSSHELL, first available in MS-DOS Version 4.00 and upgraded and improved in Version 5.00, invokes a graphic interface that allows greater flexibility and ease of use for those wishing to access DOS from screens and menus rather than the DOS prompt.

```
DOSSHELL /T< :screen<resolution> > /G< :screen
<resolution> > /B
```

Parameters

/T< :*screen<resolution>* > invokes the Shell in text mode, where *<screen>* may one of three values below, and *<resolution>* depends on the hardware in use. The value of *<resolution>* may be changed after the Shell is in use.

/G< :*screen<resolution>* > invokes the Shell in graphics mode, where *<screen>* may one of three values below, and resolution depends on the hardware in use. The value of *<resolution>* may be changed after the Shell is in use. See the Options menu in DOSSHELL for a complete list of resolutions available for your hardware.

/B invokes the Shell in a black-and-white mode.

Screen values

l low
m medium
h high

DOSSHELL is presented in Chapter 17.

EDIT

A companion to QBASIC, EDIT is a full-screen editor that uses menus to allow the user to create, edit, and save ASCII documents. QBASIC must be present on the system and available through the PATH command or present in the same directory in order for EDIT to be used.

EDIT *<pathname>* /B /G /H /Nohi

<pathname> is an ASCII text file to be edited. If the file does not previously exist, it will be created.

Parameters

/B is black-and-white mode, used for monochrome monitors that are having difficulty displaying EDIT.

/G is used in conjunction with a CGA monitor; it allows faster screen updating.

/H causes the maximum number of lines of text that are allowable by the monitor in use to be displayed.

/Nohi causes only eight colors to be used in the display instead of the default of 16.

EDIT and EDLIN are both discussed in Chapter 11.

EDLIN

This is a line editor included with DOS. It can be used for short letters or notes. Its primary use, however, is to create or modify batch or configuration files (AUTOEXEC.BAT, CONFIG.SYS, and the like). If the specified filename already exists, EDLIN will notify the user so that a file is not unintentionally written over an existing file. A new file is reported as such. Table F.5 gives EDLIN commands.

EDLIN *<pathname>*

<pathname> is the name of the file to be created or modified, including drive and directory if needed.

See Chapter 11 for examples of using EDLIN to its best advantage.

TABLE F.5 EDLIN Commands

Command	Action
x, *y*, *d*C	Copy range, *x* to *y*, to point before line *d*.
x, *y*D	Delete a group of lines, *x* through *y*.
E	Exit EDLIN and save file.
*x*I	Insert lines starting at line *x*.
x, *y*L	List lines from *x* to *y*.
x, *y*, *d*M	Move range, *x* to *y*, to point starting at line *d*.
*x*P	Display page beginning at line *x*.
x, *y*R <s1> <F6><S2>	In range *x* to *y*, replace string 1 with string 2.
x, *y*S<string>	Search for string in range *x* to *y*.
Q	Quit EDLIN without saving.
*d*T*file2*	Transfer *file2* into current file at line *d*.
<num>W	Write a number of lines to the specified drive to free memory when editing a large file.

Expanded Memory Support for 80386 Processors (EMM386)

This command facilitates the use of expanded memory in computers with an 80386 processor. It also enables or disables support for a Weitek coprocessor. Once the device drivers for 386 support have been installed, the status may be modified by using the following command. (Available in MS-DOS Version 5 only.)

EMM386 ***<On*** or ***Off*** or ***Auto>*** ***<W=On*** or ***W=Off>*** **Ram Noems**

Parameters

<On or **Off** or **Auto>** specifies whether the support is active or not, or allows for support only when a program calls for such support.

<W=On or **W=Off>** turns support for the Weitek coprocessor on or off.

Ram facilitates access to upper-memory blocks and expanded memory.

Noems allows only upper-memory blocks to be accessed.

The memory management command EMM386 is discussed in Chapter 16.

Executable To Binary Conversion (EXE2BIN)

Converts files with EXE extensions to files with COM extensions. This is not the same as renaming the file; you may, however, rename the file in the process. Files that are successfully converted will run faster than they did as EXE files.

EXE2BIN ***<pathname1> <pathname2>***

<*pathname1*> is the file to be converted, including the drive and directory if required.

<*pathname2*> renames the file as part of the conversion process.

Information about this command can be found in Chapter 18.

EXPAND

Files supplied with Version 5 of MS-DOS come in a compressed format. This command will allow the transfer of a file or files from DOS diskettes to a specified destination. Most often this command is used to replace deleted files. Each diskette in the DOS package contains a file called PACKING.LST, an ASCII text file that contains a list of the files on that disk. Compressed files may be identified by their extension, which ends in an underscore character (_). One or more files may be expanded at a time; however, wildcard characters are not permitted.

EXPAND <*sourcefile*> <*target*>

<*source file*> is the name of the file to be expanded, including the pathname if required. More than one file may be specified on the command line. Each filename must be separated by a space.

<*target*> is the drive and/or directory to which the file is to be copied. A new filename may be specified as part of <*target*>.

Chapter 12 describes the use of this command.

EXPANDED COPY (XCOPY)

See XCOPY for a summary of this command.

FASTOPEN

FASTOPEN speeds up the file location process. A list of file addresses is kept in memory so that DOS will not have to look for the address on the disk. This command relieves hard drive wear and tear. Each file, up to the number specified, is added to the list after it is used the first time. FASTOPEN can be issued only one time during a session; the computer must be rebooted in order to change the parameters. This is important to note if the command is included in the AUTOEXEC.BAT file—it must be rewritten and the computer rebooted to effect the change. This command should not be used when an ASSIGN, JOIN, or SUBST command is in effect.

FASTOPEN <*drive1:*>=<*(num,file-x)*> /X

<*drive1:*> is the letter of the drive on which the files are located. A maximum of four drives can be listed in a single command. Separate them by a space.

num is the number of files DOS will keep track of.

file-x is the number of file-extent entries DOS will keep track of. If this feature is used, the *num* and the *file-x* must be separated by a comma and the whole expression enclosed in parentheses.

Parameters

/X is an extended memory switch which causes FASTOPEN to use extended memory instead of conventional memory.

FASTOPEN is discussed in Chapter 9, including the advantages and disadvantages of its use.

FILE COMPARE (FC)

FC and COMP perform similar functions. However, FC does not allow the use of wildcard characters. Only two files may be compared at one time. Files may be compared on either a byte-by-byte or line-by-line basis.

FC /A /B /C /L /LB*Number* /N /*Number* /T /W <*file1*> <*file2*>

<*file1*> is the first of the two files to be compared, including any path information needed to locate the file.

<*file2*> is the second of the two files to be compared, including any path information needed to locate the file.

Parameters

/A Results in an abbreviated report. Only the first and last lines of each group of mismatched lines are displayed.

/B indicates that the files will be compared on a byte-by-byte basis. When this switch is used, no other switches are allowed.

/C ignores case distinctions when comparing the files.

/L results in a line-by-line comparison except when the files have an EXE, COM, BIN, SYS, OBJ, or LIB extension.

/LB*Number* allows specification of the number of lines to be held in the line buffer in the search for matching lines. The default is 100 lines.

/N indicates that line numbers will be included in the display.

/*Number* indicates that a value of 1 through 9 may be specified as the number of lines that must match to consider that the files match up again. The default is 2 lines.

/T indicates that tab characters will be literally compared instead of being treated as a series of spaces.

/W indicates that all spaces and tabs will be ignored, whether in the beginning, middle, or end of the text.

Chapter 12 discusses this command, along with similar commands, in greater detail.

FIND

This command locates files containing a specified string. The results of the operation are usually sent to the screen; however, output redirection may be used to send the results to a file or the printer. This can be helpful if you can't remember what files contain what information.

FIND /V /C /N /I <*"string"*> <*pathname*>

<*"string"*> is the string of characters to be found. It must be enclosed in quotation marks.

<*pathname*> is the file or files to be searched for the string.

Parameters

/V finds lines in the file(s) that do not contain the string.

/C sends a count of the lines in the file(s) containing the string rather than the lines themselves.

/N adds a line number to the lines in the file that contain the string. Do not use /C and /N at the same time.

/I instructs DOS to ignore case in performing the search. (Available in MS-DOS Version 5 only.)

FIND and other filter commands are discussed in Chapter 14. Redirection is discussed in Chapter 2.

FIXED DISK(FDISK)

Invokes a menu-driven program to create, display, or delete partitions on a hard disk. This command should be used with care. It should not be used when an ASSIGN, JOIN, or SUBST command is in effect.

FDISK

See Chapter 9 for additional notes on usage with hard drives.

FORMAT

All new diskettes must be prepared to receive data. To do so, use the FORMAT command. Hard drives must also be prepared in this way. Formatting a disk will destroy any data already stored on the it. FORMAT should not be used when the SUBST, JOIN, or ASSIGN commands are in effect. Take caution when using this command to ensure that you do not inadvertently format your hard disk or a floppy diskette with important information on it.

FORMAT <*drive:*> /V /8 /1 /S /B /4 /N:*Numsectors* /T:*Numtracks* /F:*Sizedisk* /Q /U

<*drive:*> is the letter of the drive containing the diskette you want to format.

Parameters (See also Table F.6)

/V lets the user create a volume label at the time of formatting.

/8 formats floppy diskettes with eight sectors per track instead of nine.

/1 formats a single-sided diskette. This switch is available only in versions 3.1 and later.

/S places the system files on the diskette making it bootable.

/B formats a diskette with eight sectors. It allocates room for system files that can be added later using the SYS command.

/4 formats double-density, double-sided diskettes in a high-capacity drive. Diskettes formatted in this way are not always reliable. Available in Version 3.2 and later.

/N:*Numsect* allows you to specify the number of sectors per track to be allocated during formatting. Available in Version 3.3 and later.

/T:*Numtracks* allows you to specify the number of tracks you want to have on your diskette. Available in Version 3.3 and later.

/F:*Sizedisk* allows you to specify the floppy diskette size. Available in Version 4.00 and later only.

/Q specifies that the FAT and the directory area of a previously formatted diskette should be deleted as part of a new format operation. However, the diskette is not scanned for errors. (Available in MS-DOS Version 5.00 only.)

/U initiates a permanent, nonreversible format. Caution should be exercised with the use of this command. (Available in MS-DOS Version 5 only.)

TABLE F.6 FORMAT Parameters

Disk Size	Parameters Allowed
160/180KB	/1 /4 /8 /B /N:*Numsect* /T:*Numtracks* /V /S /F:*Sizedisk*
320/360KB	/1 /4 /8 /B /N:*Numsect* /T:*Numtracks* /V /S /F:*Sizedisk*
720KB	/N:*Numsect* /T:*Numtracks* /V /S /F:*Sizedisk*
1.2MB	/N:*Numsect* /T:*Numtracks* /V /S /F:*Sizedisk*
1.44MB	/N:*Numsect* /T:*Numtracks* /V /S /F:*Sizedisk*
Hard Disks	/V /S

A complete explanation of the many varieties of the FORMAT command can be found in Chapter 9.

GRAPHICS

DOS must have help in order to print graphic displays with certain graphics adapter cards. This command was primarily used before the advent of enhanced graphic display adapters, and will not function with them. If a monochrome monitor or display is used, the printer will print up to four shades of gray. A color printer may be selected to reproduce the graphic in color.

GRAPHICS *<printercode>* /R /B /LCD /C /F /P=*ComPort* /PB:Standard or **/PB:LCD**

<printer code> selects the type of printer to be used. See Table F.7.

TABLE F.7 **Printer Codes for the GRAPHICS Command**

Codes	Printer
Color1	IBM or compatible color printer with a black ribbon.
Color4	IBM or compatible color printer with a four-color ribbon.
Color8	IBM or compatible color printer with an eight-color ribbon.
Compact	IBM or compatible compact printer. (Not available in MS-DOS Version 5.)
Hpdefault	Hewlett-Packard PCL printers, any model.
Deskjet	Hewlett-Packard DeskJet printer.
Graphicswide	IBM printer with an 11-inch carriage.
Graphics	IBM Graphics, IBM Proprinter, or compatible. The default printer.
Laserjet	Hewlett-Packard LaserJet printer.
Laserjetii	Hewlett-Packard LaserJet II printer.
Paintjet	Hewlett-Packard PaintJet printer.
Quietjet	Hewlett-Packard QuietJet printer.
Quietjetplus	Hewlett-Packard QuietJet Plus printer.
Ruggedwriter	Hewlett-Packard RuggedWriter printer.
Ruggedwriterwide	Hewlett-Packard RuggedWriterwide printer.
Thermal	IBM convertible or compatible thermal printer.
Thinkjet	Hewlett-Packard ThinkJet printer.

Parameters

/R prints the graphics as displayed; light image on a dark background.

/B indicates that the background will be printed in color if a color printer has been selected.

/LCD displays the image on a Liquid Crystal Display monitor, usually found on portable computers.

/C centers the image to be printed on the page. It may be used with the /F option listed below. (Available prior to MS-DOS Version 5 only.)

/F rotates wide images to print in a landscape mode. (Available prior to MS-DOS Version 5 only.)

/P=*ComPort* indicates the communications port to be used. This can be LPT1, LPT2, or LPT3. (Available prior to MS-DOS Version 5 only.)

/PB:Standard or **/PB:LCD** selects the printbox size, depending on the printer type used. (Available in MS-DOS Version 5 only.)

GRAPHICS is described in Chapter 15.

Graphics Table (GRAFTABL)

This command loads a table for the color/graphics mode into memory. This will allow DOS to display special characters associated with individual languages. The adapter card must be in graphics mode. This command is available in Version 3.3 and later.

GRAFTABL <*code*> /Status ?

<*code*> is the code number for the language desired. See Table F.8.

TABLE F.8 **Language Codes (GRAFTABL)**

Code-Page Number	Code Page
437	United States
850	Multilingual
852	Slavic (Available in MS-DOS Version 5 only.)
860	Portuguese
863	French Canadian
865	Nordic

GRAFTABL entered alone loads the default code, English.

Parameters

/Status generates a display showing the current code page.

? sends a request to DOS to display the list of alternative code pages. (Available in MS-DOS Version 5 only.)

Chapter 15 includes information regarding the circumstances in which this command might be used.

HELP

This utility program, available in MS-DOS Version 5 only, supplies information about any specified command. HELP may be invoked in either way described below.

HELP *<command>* or
***<command>* /?**

<command> is the command for which HELP is requested.

Parameters

/? entered after a command results in HELP information being displayed rather than the execution of the command.

HELP is discussed in Chapter 4.

JOIN

Sometimes it is convenient to treat a diskette as if it were a subdirectory on another drive. Some application packages demand that data be stored in the same location as the program itself. The JOIN command will let you store information on another diskette. The directory must be an empty subdirectory of the root directory on the first diskette. If the directory does not exist, it will be created on the specified drive. Once a JOIN command has been issued, the connected drive is no longer available for use until the JOIN is canceled or the computer is rebooted. Commands that would read or write to this drive will not function. These include BACKUP, RESTORE, FORMAT, DISKCOPY, DISKCOMP, CHKDSK, LABEL, RECOVER, FDISK, and SYS.

JOIN *<drive:>* *<pathname>* /D or
JOIN *<drive:>* /D

<drive:> is the letter of the drive to be connected to the specified drive and directory combination in *<pathname>*.

<pathname> is the name of the directory to be joined, including the drive letter and directory name.

JOIN by itself displays any JOIN commands in effect.

Parameters

/D cancels any JOIN command in effect. *<drive:>* must be specified.

Illustrations of this command may be found in Chapter 18.

KEYBOARD (KEYB)

If you want to type in a foreign language, you must change the keyboard configuration. The commas shown must be typed, even if the variable is not entered. This may result in two commas in a row. This function is interwoven with several others, including MODE and NLSFUNC. Read the sections about these commands before trying to change the language of your keyboard. Also note that this command has changed from version to version of DOS. Check the documentation for your version for specific details.

KEYB *<country>*,*<codepage>*,*<pathname>* /Id:*IdNum* /E

<country> is the two-character code selected from Table F.9.

TABLE F.9 Keyboard and Country Codes (KEYB Commands)

Country	Country Code	Keyboard Code	Keyboard ID Code
Belgium	437	BE	120
Brazil	437	BR	
Canada (French)	863	CF	058
Czechoslovakia	852	CZ	
Czechoslovakia	852	SL	
Denmark	865	DK	159
Finland	437	SU	153
France	437	FR	189 or 120
Germany	437	GR	129
Hungary	852	HU	
International	850	—	—
Italy	437	IT	141 or 142
Latin America	437	LA	171
Netherlands	437	NL	143
Norway	865	NO	155
Poland	852	PL	
Portugal	860	PO	163
Spain	437	SP	172
Sweden	437	SV	153
Switzerland (French)	437	SF	150
Switzerland (German)	437	SG	000
United Kingdom	437	UK	166 or 168
United States	437	US	103
Yugoslavia	852	YU	

<*codepage*> must also be selected from Table F.9. It represents the code page appropriate to the desired keyboard style.

<pathname> is the location of the KEYBOARD.SYS file, usually in the root directory or a \DOS*xxx* directory.

Parameters

/Id:*IdNum* is specified when a country code uses more than one keyboard style. Selected from Table F.9.

/E indicates to DOS that an enhanced keyboard has been installed.

Chapter 15 discusses this and other input/output controls.

LABEL

You may change, create, or delete, a label on a disk using this command. The label is a unique identifier for your disk. Up to 11 characters may be specified for the label. LABEL is available in Version 3.0 and later.

```
LABEL <drive:><newname>
```

<*drive:*> is the drive containing the disk whose label is to be created or changed.

<*newname*> may be specified if replacing the old volume label or adding a new label.

LABEL displays the volume label of <*drive:*>. Disk-management commands, including LABEL, are found in Chapter 9.

MEMORY (MEM)

This is a recently introduced command that will display the amount of memory, both free and used, on the computer. A listing of memory allocation is displayed. This might be of interest if "Out Of Memory" messages are returned by the system. More specific information is also available if the parameters discussed below are used.

```
MEM /Program /Debug /Classify
```

MEM, used without parameters, displays the amount of free and used memory.

Parameters

/Program returns a list of any programs that are loaded in memory.

/Debug provides technical information about the programs loaded into memory and other information generally used by programmers.

/Classify provides a listing of the programs in memory, both for upper memory and conventional memory. This switch may only be used by itself. (Available in MS-DOS Version 5 only.)

MEMORY is examined in Chapter 16.

MIRROR

MIRROR provides information that may be used by the UNDELETE or UNFORMAT commands to restore inadvertently erased files or diskettes. This command should not be used when an ASSIGN, JOIN, or SUBST command is in effect. Available in MS-DOS Version 5 only.

MIRROR *<drive1:>* /L /T*<drive2:><entrynumber>* /*Partn*

<drive1:> is the drive containing the diskette or the hard drive for which information is desired.

Parameters

/L results in DOS recording only the most recent information about the disk.

/T*<drive2:><entrynumber>* invokes a Terminate and Stay Resident (TSR) program to track file deletions. It also indicates that the information is to be stored somewhere other than in the current drive and directory. *Drive2* is the drive and/or directory desired; *Entry Number* is the number of entries to be kept in the deletion-tracking file. The default values for *Entry Number* are shown in Table F.10.

TABLE F.10 **Number of Entries (MIRROR Command)**

Disk	Entries	File Size
360KB	25	5KB
720KB	50	9KB
1.2MB	75	14KB
1.44MB	75	14KB
20MB	101	18KB
32MB	202	36KB
>32MB	303	55KB

/U unloads the TSR loaded by using the /T parameter described above. This parameter may not be used with other parameters.

/*Partn* stores information about the partitions set up on a hard drive. UNFORMAT can use this information to restore a hard drive if it has been unintentionally formatted.

MIRROR is fully explained in Chapter 9.

MODE

MODE is a multipurpose command. There are several forms that must be considered independently. Each form is described below. These forms allow DOS to communicate with the display and communications ports, such as the printer. This allows the user to customize these communications.

Display control. This use of MODE allows the user to center the display, control how many columns are displayed on the monitor, and to turn the color display on or off.

MODE <*characteristic*>,<*shift*>,T

<*characteristic*> controls whether the display will be in monochrome or color and how many columns will be used. (See Table F.11.)

<*shift*> shifts the display to the left if an L is entered or to the right if an R is entered. This command may have no effect on EGA or VGA monitors.

Parameters

T indicates that in order to determine if the display has been centered, DOS will display a test pattern. The user will then be prompted to reply yes or no to whether the display is properly centered.

Line display control. In Version 4.00 or greater, it is possible to specify how many columns and lines are to be displayed on the screen. Note that some monitors may be unable to respond to this command. Also note that DEVICE= ANSI.SYS must be included in the CONFIG.SYS file. Be sure to include a pathname if necessary.

MODE Con <cols=*colnum*> <lines=*linenum*>

Con is the console device used for display.

<cols=*colnum*> is the number of columns displayed on the monitor, which can be either 40 or 80.

TABLE F.11 **MODE Display Codes**

Characteristic	Code
Monochrome display	Mono
Color/graphics, 40 columns	40
Color/graphics, 80 columns	80
Color/graphics, 40 columns, color enabled	Co40
Color/graphics, 80 columns, color enabled	Co80
Color/graphics, 40 columns, color disabled	Bw40
Color/graphics, 80 columns, color disabled	Bw80

<lines=*linenum*> is the number of lines displayed on the monitor, which can be 25, 43, or 50.

Keyboard repeat speed. In Version 4.00 or greater of DOS, the user is able to specify how long to wait before beginning to repeat a key that is continuously pressed. The user may also control how fast the repeated character is generated.

```
MODE Con <rate=speed> <delay=wait>
```

Con is the console device used for data input.

<rate=*speed*> may be a value from 1 to 32, where 1 is the slowest rate and 32 is the fastest.

<delay=*wait*> determines the wait until a pressed key begins to repeat. This may be a value from 1 to 4.

Serial communications control. This form of MODE is primarily concerned with the control of a modem associated with a serial communications port. Control of this function may also be needed to send data to a serial printer. This command has changed significantly with the various versions of DOS. Check your documentation for specific information before using this command.

```
MODE <port> <baud=rate> <data=databits> <parity=type>
<stop=bit> <retry=action>
```

<*port*> is the serial port to be used, which can be COM1, COM2, COM3, or COM4.

<baud=*rate*> sets the baud rate for transmission, which can be 110, 150, 300, 1200, 2400, 4800, or 9600.

<data=*databits*> is the number of bits used to represent a character. The default value is 7, but 5, 6, or 8 may be used.

<parity=*type*> defines the error checking to be performed. This can be:

N	None
S	Space
M	Mark
O	Odd
E	Even

<stop=*bit*> is the specific electric signal marking the end of character, this is usually l, but can be l.5 or 2.

<retry=*action*> is the response generated by DOS when receiving a busy signal from the serial port. The default value is Ready. The possible values are:

E	Error
R	Ready
B	Busy

Parallel printer control. A printer attached to a parallel port can be controlled to print in wide- or narrow-carriage formats. This is important if you have a wide-carriage printer and wish to print in a narrow format. The number of lines per inch can also be controlled.

MODE <*port*> <cols=*width*> <lines=*spacing*> <retry=*action*>

<*port*> is the parallel port to which the printer is connected, which can be either LPT1, LPT2, or LPT3.

<cols=*width*> is the width of the output sent to the printer, which can be 80 for standard format or 132 for wide carriage.

<lines=*spacing*> controls the number of lines per inch; spacing can be 6 or 8.

<retry=*action*> causes a specific action to be taken if DOS receives a busy signal from the parallel port. The possible actions are:

E	Error
B	Busy
R	Ready
N	None

Parallel to serial port redirection. At times the user may want to send data to a printer connected to a serial port rather than a parallel port. See the section above for serial communications control before proceeding.

MODE <*printer*>=<*port*>

<*printer*> is the parallel port currently connected to the printer, which can be LPT1, LPT2 or LPT3.

<*port*> is the communications port to which the data is to be sent: COM1, COM2, COM3, or COM4.

Code-page preparation. In order to prepare a device to conform to a code page other than the default, it is necessary to use the MODE command.

MODE <*device*> <CP prepare=*codes*> <*pathname*>

<*device*> is the device for which the code page is to be changed; CON, PRN, LPT1, LPT2, or LPT3.

<CP prepare=*codes*> are the code-page numbers associated with a language. See Table F.12.

<*pathname*> is the file, including the drive and directory if needed, containing the file with the code-page information. See Table F.13.

TABLE F.12 Code Page Numbers

Language	Code Page
American	437
Multilingual	850
Portuguese	860
French-Canadian	863
Nordic	865

Code page selection. To select a previously prepared code page for a specified device, you must use this command. See the section above.

```
MODE <device> <CP select=codepage>
```

`<device>` is the appropriate device, this can be CON, PRN, LPT1, LPT2, or LPT3.

`<CP select=codepage>` is a three-digit code selected from Table F.12.

Code-page status. To check the status of a previously installed code page, you may use this form of the MODE command.

```
MODE <device> CP /Status
```

`<device>` is the device whose status is to be checked: CON, PRN, LPT1, LPT2, or LPT3.

Parameters

`/Status` is an optional parameter.

Code-page restoration. If a previously installed code page has been erased for a particular device, it can be restored using this command.

```
MODE <device> CP Refresh
```

`<device>` is the device whose code page is to be restored.

Device status. Version 4.00 or greater allows the user to check the status on any device in the system.

```
MODE <device> /Status
```

`<device>` is the device for which the status is to be reported.

Parameters

`/Status,` used without a specified device, will report the status of all devices on the system.

Many of the uses of the MODE command are mentioned in Chapter 15.

TABLE F.13 **Information Files (MODE Command)**

CPI Files	Device Controlled
EGA.CPI	IBM PS/2 video adapter or EGA card
4201.CPI	IBM 4201 Proprinters
4108.CPI	IBM X24 and XL24 Proprinters
5202.CPI	IBM Quietwriter III
LCD.CPI	Liquid Crystal Display

(MORE)

MORE is one of a group of commands that let you work with data on a DOS level. MORE is specifically designed to let you view a text file one page at a time. This becomes increasingly important as the speeds of computers increase. After each page of text is displayed, a message will be shown that prompts the user to press a key to continue. MORE can be used when displaying data on the screen or in conjunction with output redirection to send text to the printer one page at a time. One page refers to one screen on the display monitor.

MORE < *<filename>*

<filename> is the name of the file to be displayed, including the drive and directory if needed, or the command whose output is to be controlled.

Filter commands, including MORE, are discussed in Chapter 14.

National Language Support Function (NLSFUNC)

This command provides extended country information. It must be used before the CHCP command to change the default country. Country support includes such areas as the format of the time, date, and currency. The name of the file containing the country-specific information must be specified at this time, unless the file, usually COUNTRY.SYS, is supplied as part of the CONFIG.SYS file. See Chapter 16 for information regarding the CONFIG.SYS file and its uses.

NLSFUNC C:\COUNTRY.SYS

NLSFUNC is entered without stating the filename if it has already been listed in the CONFIG.SYS file.

COUNTRY.SYS is the file containing the country-specific information. A directory may be specified if required. NLSFUNC is discussed in Chapter 18 with other seldom-used commands.

PRINT

Text can be printed on a DOS level in a controlled manner using the PRINT command. Many controlling parameters can be specified to modify the command according to job requirements. Another benefit is that the list of files to be printed (called the print queue) can be managed in the background while the system is doing something else. Some of the available parameters—D, B, Q, S, U, and M—may be used only the first time the command is entered . Not all of the parameters are available with all versions of DOS. Please check the reference book that accompanied your DOS diskettes for specific information. This command should not be used when an ASSIGN command has been issued.

PRINT /D:*device* /B:*buffersize* /U:*busy ticks* /M:*max ticks* /S:*time slice* /Q:*queue size* /T <*pathname* /C or **/P>**

Parameters

/D:*device* is the device used for printing, usually PRN.

/B:*buffersize* is the amount of memory used as a buffer. The default is 512; however, a range of 512 through 16384 may be specified.

/U:*busyticks* is the number of clock ticks that the PRINT command will wait if the printer is busy before giving up its time slice.

/M:*maxticks* represents how many clock ticks the PRINT command keeps under control during each time slice.

/S:*timeslice* is the number of time slices per second controlled by the PRINT command.

/Q:*queue size* indicates how many files to hold in the print queue during a given session.

/T stops all printing.

<*pathname* /C or **/P>** /C removes the file specified from the print queue. /P adds the specified file to the print queue. Both will continue to function until the other is encountered.

Input/output controls are discussed in Chapter 15.

QBASIC

This the version of BASIC released with MS-DOS Version 5.00. See the section on BASIC for further discussion.

QBASIC is described in more detail in Chapter 20, along with other language translators.

Recover Files (RECOVER)

Occasionally one or more sectors in a file will become corrupted. This results in the file being unreadable. The RECOVER command attempts to pull the rest of the sectors together so that the file will become usable again, even if a portion of the file is lost. The command may also be used to recover the files on an entire disk. Do not use this command when a JOIN or SUBST command has been used, or in a network environment. This command can trash your disk. Use it with extreme caution. The use of this command is *not* recommended.

RECOVER *<pathname>* *<disk>*

<pathname> is the name of the file to be acted on, including drive and directory name if needed.

<disk> directs RECOVER to act on the entire disk in the specified drive. Do not use this parameter with *<pathname>*.

RECOVER is a disk-management command discussed in Chapter 9. Use it with extreme caution.

REPLACE FILES (REPLACE)

REPLACE selectively copies files from a specified source to a specified destination. It can use one or more parameters to select which files to copy.

REPLACE *<pathname1>* *<pathname2>* /A /P /R /S /W /U

<pathname1> is the source of the file or files.

<pathname2> is the destination of the file or files.

Parameters

/A copies only files that do not exist in the specified destination. May not be used with /S or /U.

/P indicates that the user will be prompted to confirm each file transfer.

/R allows copying over files marked as read-only.

/S searches all subdirectories for a match with the specified source files, may not be used with /A.

/W waits for the user to press a key before continuing, providing an opportunity to change disks if necessary.

/U checks the date stamped on both files, only copying files with a more recent date over older files. (Available in Version 4.00 and later only.)

External file-management commands are discussed in Chapter 12.

RESTORE FILES (RESTORE)

This is the opposite half of the BACKUP/RESTORE combination. Files which have been stored with the BACKUP command must be reinstalled with the RESTORE command. Many of the associated parameters are similar to those used with BACKUP. RESTORE will notify the user to insert the Backup diskette, which will be Backup diskette #1.

RESTORE ***<drive name:> <pathname>*** **/A:*Date* /B:*Date* /S /P /M /N /E:*Time*/L:*Time* /D**

<drive name:> is the drive which contains the Backup diskette.

<pathname> is the directory and/or drive on which the restored files are to be placed.

Parameters

/A:*Date* restores all files modified on or after the date specified.

/B:*Date* restores all files modified on or before the date specified.

/S restores all files into the subdirectories of the specified directory.

/P causes each restoration to be prompted for confirmation before it is initiated.

/M restores files modified or deleted since the last BACKUP command.

/N restores files that no longer exist on the target drive.

/L:*Time* restores files modified on or after the Time specified.

/E:*Time* restores files modified on or before the Time specified.

/D provides a listing of files that meet the specified criterion, without actually restoring any files. The pathname must be specified. (Available in MS-DOS Version 5 only.)

Chapter 12 gives several examples of the use of this command.

SELECT COUNTRY/LANGUAGE (SELECT)

This is another of the commands associated with the control of country-specific configuration and/or language-specific configuration. In this instance, a disk that is both country- and language-specific is created. SELECT is not available in Version 5.

SELECT ***<pathname1> <pathname2> <code> <kybcode>***

<pathname1> is the source of the information needed to create the disk. Usually this will be the DOS directory.

<pathname2> is the drive containing the disk that is to be created. The disk will be formatted in the process. If the disk is a hard disk, DOS will prompt for the volume label to be entered.

<code> is the code to be used for the country information. (See Table F.14.)

<kybcode> is the keyboard code to be used.

This command is discussed in Chapter 18 along with several other infrequently used commands. See also Appendix E.

TABLE F.14 Country and Keyboard Codes (SELECT Command)

Country	Code	Keyboard Code
Australia	061	US
Belgium	032	BE
Canada (English)	001	US
Canada (French)	002	CF
Denmark	045	DK
Finland	358	SU
France	033	FR
Germany	049	GR
International	061	—
Israel	972	—
Italy	039	IT
Latin America	003	LA
Middle East	785	—
Netherlands	031	—
Norway	047	NO
Portugal	351	PO
Spain	034	SP
Sweden	046	SV
Switzerland (French)	041	SF
Switzerland (German)	041	SG
United Kingdom	044	UK
United States	001	US

Set up Installation of DOS Version 5 (SETUP)

This command is not found on most systems after the upgrade process is complete. It is used to initiate the installation (upgrade) of DOS to Version 5. Further discussion may be found in Chapter 23.

Share Files (SHARE)

SHARE is used in a networking environment. File sharing and locking are supported. SHARE is not available in Version 5.

```
SHARE /F:Space /L:Locks
```

Parameters

/F:*Space* allocates memory for file sharing. The default is 2048.

/L:*Locks* is the number of file-region locks. The default is 20.

SHARE is a system control command examined in Chapter 13.

Set Version (SETVER)

Occasionally you will encounter a program that will operate only with a specific version number of DOS. This command facilitates the operation of that program. The SETVER command can be used to update the version table to include the appropriate program. (Available in MS-DOS Version 5 only.)

SETVER *<pathname>* *<filename>* *<versionnumber>* or **/D /Q**

<pathname> is a drive and directory that contains the SETVER.EXE file. Specified without any other parameters, it will result in a listing of the current version table.

<filename> is the name of the program to be added to the table. These must be executable files.

<versionnumber> is the version of the operating system to be added to the version table.

Parameters

/D will cause the entry of the program file specified to be deleted. *<version number>* and the /D parameter should not be used at the same time.

/Q prevents the deletion message from being displayed. May be used only with /D.

SORT

SORT physically rearranges the contents of a field into alphabetical or reverse alphabetical order. The output can be redirected to a new file or another device such as the printer. See the Chapter 2 section on file redirection for help. The source of the data can also be controlled. Information on the use of file piping (¦) is found in Chapter 13, Filter Commands.

<pathname> **¦ SORT /R /+N**

<pathname> is the file to be sorted, including the drive and directory.

Parameters

/R sorts files in reverse alphabetic order.

/+N sorts the file on a letter in column N.

SORT is the last of the filter commands addressed in Chapter 14.

SUBSTITUTE (SUBST)

A directory pathname can be referred to by a drive letter. Commonly, the drive letter is a drive letter not in use, such as E: or F:. Be sure that the LASTDRIVE command has been specified in your CONFIG.SYS file. Once the command is in effect, any I/O requests directed to the drive letter will go to the directory specified. Many commands that affect the system environment will not function with this command in effect. Some of these are FORMAT, ASSIGN, BACKUP, and RESTORE.

> **SUBST *<drive:>* *<pathname>*** or **SUBST *<drive:>* /D**

> ***<drive:>*** is the drive letter that will be used to substitute for the directory path.

> ***<pathname>*** is the full directory name that is to be referred to by the drive letter.

SUBST entered alone displays a list of any substitutions in effect.

Parameters

> **/D** cancels the substitution assigned to the specified drive letter. *<drive*:> must be specified.

SUBST is discussed in Chapter 10.

SYSTEM (SYS)

Primarily, SYS is used when upgrading the version of DOS on your system. See Chapter 21, or Appendix C, D, or E for further information on the version of DOS that you want to install. SYS transfers the hidden DOS system files, IBMBIO.COM and IBMDOS.COM (or their MS-DOS equivalents IO.SYS and MSDOS.SYS) to a specified disk. It also transfers these files to a diskette that is to be made bootable. The SYS command must be on the disk with the files to be transferred, and this must be the default drive and directory.

> ***<pathname>* SYS *<drive:>***

> ***<pathname>*** is the drive and directory where the system files are located. Usually this will be a floppy drive diskette.

> ***<drive:>*** stands for the destination of the system files. This is usually a hard drive.

This external command is discussed with other system control commands in Chapter 13.

SHOW DIRECTORY STRUCTURE (TREE)

As the name suggests, the command gives a listing of the directory structure. All directory names are listed, along with the names of any subdirectories. If requested, the command will also list the names of the files in each directory, subdirectory, and the root directory. This command is available only in Version 3.2 and later.

> **TREE *<drive:>* /F /A**

> ***<drive:>*** is the drive to be acted upon. If none is specified, the default drive is used.

Parameters

> **/F** lists all of the files as well as the directory names.

> **/A** indicates that ASCII characters are used instead of graphics in the display. Available in Version 4.00 and later.

TREE is a useful organizational tool reviewed in Chapter 10.

Undelete Files (UNDELETE)

This newly introduced utility provides a much-needed method of retrieving files that have been accidentally deleted. Files may not be recovered if the directory in which they were contained has been removed. UNFORMAT can sometimes retrieve erased directory names. Available in MS-DOS Version 5 only.

> **UNDELETE *<pathname>* /List /All /Dos /Dt**

> ***<pathname>*** is the file or files to be undeleted. If no files are specified, all of the files that have been deleted will be retrieved.

Parameters

> **/List** provides a listing of files which may be deleted, but does not actually restore them. May be used with the /Dos or the /Dt parameter.

> **/All** recovers all possible files without prompting for confirmation on each file. If the MIRROR command has been used, the deletion-tracking file will be used.

> **/Dos** recovers all files deleted by MS-DOS. Any existing deletion-tracking file is ignored.

> **/Dt** recovers only files listed in the deletion-tracking file. The user will be prompted for confirmation before a file is undeleted.

UNDELETE is described in Chapter 9.

UNFORMAT

UNFORMAT can be used in several ways. It can assist in recovering files that have been rendered unusable due to reformatting of a diskette or hard drive. It can also rebuild, at least in part, a partition structure that has been corrupted. UNFORMAT cannot be used on hard drives associated with a network. Caution should be exercised before using this command. (Available in Version 5 only.)

```
UNFORMAT <drive1:> /J /U /Test /P /Partn /L
```

`<drive1:>` is the drive containing the disk to be unformatted.

Parameters

/J verifies that the MIRROR command has successfully saved the pertinent information, and that it matches the information currently on the disk or diskette. This parameter is used only by itself.

/U can be used if there is not a MIRROR file available.

/Test provides a sample showing the result of using the UNFORMAT command. No actual unformatting occurs. MIRROR files are not used if this parameter is specified.

/P echoes DOS messages to the printer so that the user can keep a hard copy of resulting displays for reference.

/Partn restores damaged partition tables to a hard drive. A file created by the MIRROR command is required for this operation.

/L displays a list of all files and directories; otherwise, only fragmented files and directories will be displayed. If used with the /Partn parameter, /L will list partition information.

A more complete explanation of this command is found in Chapter 9.

EXTENDED COPY (XCOPY)

This command provides a way to copy large groups of files selectively. It will also copy files from an entire directory structure, including subdirectories.

```
XCOPY <pathname1> <pathname2> /A /M /E /P /S /V /W
/D:Date
```

`<pathname1>` is the file to be copied. If only a drive is specified, the files on the entire drive will be copied. If a directory is specified, the files in that directory will be copied.

`<pathname2>` is the destination intended for the files.

Parameters

/A copies all files with the archive bit set, but the archive bit is not modified.

/M copies all files with the archive bit set, and the archive bit is turned off.

/E copies all subdirectories, even if they are empty. The /S parameter must be used if /E is used.

/P prompts the user to verify that each file needs to be copied.

/S copies subdirectories and their contents, unless they are empty.

/V verifies that each file copied is identical to the original file.

/W prompts the user for verification before each file is copied.

/D:*Date* copies files created or modified on or after the specified date.

XCOPY is an undervalued command. See Chapter 12 for examples of its use.

BATCH FILE COMMANDS

The following batch file commands are discussed in Chapter 19.

@ (AT)

Commonly called the "at" parameter. This prevents a command from being echoed on the screen. Most often it is on the first line of the batch file with the ECHO command to prevent even the first command from echoing to the screen.

@ *<command>*

<command> is the command prevented from echoing to the screen.

CALL

A second batch file can be executed from within the first batch file. Information can be passed to this second file. Once the new batch file has completed its assigned task, control is returned to the parent or "calling" batch file.

CALL *<batchname> <parameters>*

<batch name> is the name of the batch file to be called, including the drive and directory if needed.

<parameters> contains any information the second batch file needs to complete its assignment.

ECHO

This command controls whether or not commands are echoed onto the screen as they are executed. The user can also use ECHO to display messages on the screen to provide directions or warnings as the file executes. A third use of the ECHO command is to send internal messages to devices such as the printer. These messages can be sent in or out of a batch file.

ECHO <On or **Off> *<message>***

<On or **Off>** turns the ECHO feature on or off as specified. Note that this affects only commands, not messages.

<message> is any statement the author of the batch file wants to make. This should not be used with the off or on switches.

Note:

ECHO Alt-255 can be used to echo a blank line. The Alt key is pressed and held while the numeric keypad numbers 255 are pressed.

FOR

FOR is a conditional statement that provides the capability to have a batch command act on a list of files or parameters. If this command is used in a batch file, as is most often the case, two percent (%) signs are used. If the command is entered on the DOS command line, only one % sign is used.

FOR %%*<variable>* IN *<list>* DO *<command>*

%%*<variable>* is a one-letter variable name assigned by the author.

IN signals the file that a set of parameters or filenames follows.

<list> is a set of filenames on which specific action is to be taken. Wildcards can be used in specifying filenames. If a set of names is to be entered, they must be separated by spaces.

DO precedes the command that is to be executed.

<command> is the DOS command to be executed on each member of the list.

GOTO

GOTO allows the user to control the order of execution of the commands in a batch file. Frequently, GOTO is used in a conditional situation in which if a certain condition is true, execution is skipped down or up to another point in the file. GOTO is used with a label (see LABEL, below) that indicates the precise point to which control is to move. Note that the label itself is preceded with a colon; but when a label is referred to in a GOTO command, the colon is omitted.

GOTO *<label>*

<label> is an author-supplied variable name.

IF

Without the IF command, batch files would have very little flexibility. Conditions may be tested and found to be true or false. False statements can also be tested for with NOT.

IF <NOT> *<condition>* *<command>*

<NOT> can be used to see if a condition does not exist.

<condition> is one of several conditions for existence that can be evaluated. (See Conditions, below.)

<*command*> is the action to be taken if the condition is found to exist or not to exist. Frequently, it results in a change in the execution order. See the GOTO command discussion in Chapter 19.

Conditions

EXIST is used with IF to see if a file or files already exist in the directory specified.

ERRORLEVEL <*number*> signals DOS to store the number returned as a result of a command having been entered. The number returned depends on the results of the command. A successful completion will return one number; an unsuccessful one will return a different number. The numbers returned for DOS commands are explained in the DOS manual supplied with each version of PC-DOS or MS-DOS.

<*string1*>==<*string2*> tests to see if two character strings match. These strings can be filenames or user-specified characters.

LABEL

Indicates the point to which a GOTO command has sent control. Each label must be preceded by a colon (:).

:<*label*>

<*label*> is an author-supplied variable name.

PAUSE

This command halts the execution of a batch file and optionally displays a message. This command can be useful in providing options to users, such as changing disks, or an opportunity to halt the program. If no message is entered the default message, "Press any key to continue," will be displayed.

PAUSE <*message*>

<*message*> is author-supplied to provide directions or information.

REMARK (REM)

This command enables the author to place comments in the batch file. Comments about any program enable the author to remember what was done and why. If ECHO is on, comments will be displayed as the file executes. Note that you can also place comments in the CONFIG.SYS file when you are using Version 4.00 or greater.

REM <*comment*>

SHIFT

Batch files have a limited number of variable parameters (0 through 9) that they are able to manipulate. In order to extend that number, a SHIFT command is used. The %0 parameter content is discarded and replaced with the %1 parameter, and so on until the %9 parameter is empty. An eleventh parameter can then be placed into %9. This continues until all listed parameters have been moved into place.

```
SHIFT
```

Configuration Control Commands

These commands affect the system configuration, and are used in the CONFIG.SYS file. For information on configuration commands, system setup, and memory management, see Chapter 16 and Part IV on System Installation and System Management. A list of device drivers is provided in Appendix G.

BREAK

In normal operations, DOS checks for a BREAK (generated by Ctrl-C) only when it reads or writes to a device such as the monitor or printer. With BREAK turned on, DOS checks for a break signal each time a system call is generated as well as when writing to a device.

BREAK=<On or **Off>**

BUFFERS

DOS reserves an area of memory to store data read from or written to storage media. How many areas are reserved affects how often read/write operations are performed, and therefore affects program efficiency and the amount of wear and tear on the hard drive. Many programs make recommendations on the appropriate number of buffer areas to reserve. Note that buffers are portions of memory. If a large number (over 25 or 30 in many cases) is specified, programs may have insufficient memory to function properly.

BUFFERS=<*number*>,<*maxsects*> /X

<*number*> is the number of buffer areas to reserve.

<*maxsects*> specifies the number of sectors handled in an I/O operation. The default is 1; up to 8 can be specified. Available only in Version 4.00 or greater.

Parameters

/X instructs DOS to use extended memory for the buffer areas. Available only in Version 4.00.

Possible Buffers

Version 1–3.2	1–99
Version 3.3	2–255
Version 4	1–99

Default Buffers

128–255 KB	5
256–511 KB	10
512 KB or more	15

COUNTRY

Conventions for time, currency, and numeric expressions vary from country to country. This command modifies these and other conventions according to the country selected. See Change Code Page for related information.

COUNTRY=<*countrycode*>,<*codepage*>,<*pathname*>

<*countrycode*> is selected from Table F.15. The default code is the one in which the operating system was manufactured. Leading zeros must be entered where appropriate.

<*codepage*> is selected from Table F.16. It specifies the selected code page.

<*pathname*> is the location of the file containing country-specific conventions. COUNTRY.SYS is used as the default if none is specified.

Oriental language codes are available; however, hardware modifications must be made prior to use. Not all codes are available in all versions. Check the documentation to determine codes that can be used.

TABLE F.15 **Country Codes (COUNTRY Command)**

Country	Code
Australia	061
Belgium	032
Canada (English)	001
Canada (French)	002
Denmark	045
Finland	358
France	033
Germany	049
International	061
Israel	972
Italy	039
Japan	081
Korea	082
Latin America	003

"continued"

TABLE F.15 Country Codes (COUNTRY Command) continued

Country	Code
Middle East	785
Netherlands	031
Norway	047
People's Republic of China	086
Portugal	351
Spain	034
Sweden	046
Switzerland (French)	041
Switzerland (German)	041
Taiwan	088
United Kingdom	044
United States	001

TABLE F.16 Code Page Numbers (COUNTRY Command)

Code Page Number	Code Page
437	United States
850	Multilingual
860	Portuguese
862	Hebrew
863	French Canadian
864	Arabic
865	Nordic

Specify Device Driver (DEVICE)

Device driver programs enable DOS to control specific devices such as a mouse, the monitor, and the keyboard. DEVICE establishes the location of the specific driver needed for a device. Frequently, there will be several DEVICE statements in the CONFIG.SYS file. These drivers will also have a SYS extension.

```
DEVICE=<pathname>
```

<*pathname*> is the location and name of the device driver, including the drive letter if needed.

Load Device Drivers Into Upper Memory (DEVICEHIGH)

This configuration command functions exactly like DEVICE, except that the device drivers are loaded into upper memory. HIMEM.SYS must be installed prior to use, and a **DOS=Umb** statement must be loaded into memory as well. Available in MS-DOS Version 5 only.

DEVICEHIGH=<*pathname*>

<*pathname*> is the location and name of the driver program, including the drive letter if needed.

Directory Command (DIRCMD)

This command allows you to customize the results of a DIR command. The features added to DIR in Version 5 can be set in AUTOEXEC.BAT using the SET command with DIRCMD.

SET DIRCMD=<*parameters*>

<*parameters*> are any of the parameters available with the DIR command.

DOS

Greater amounts of available memory have produced more memory management commands. This command provides a link to upper memory and facilitates loading itself into the high-memory area. Multiple parameters can be chained with commas; no spaces are permitted. EMM support must be already installed. Available in MS-DOS Version 5 only.

DOS=<High or **Low> <Umb** or **Noumb>**

Parameters

High causes DOS to attempt to load itself into the high memory area.

Low causes all of DOS to be kept in conventional memory.

Umb causes link to be maintained between conventional memory and the upper-memory area.

Noumb disconnects the link between the memory areas.

Driver Parameter (DRIVPARM)

DOS relies on an internal default table for the characteristics of read/write devices. These characteristics can be controlled if desired. Multiple statements, controlling different devices, can be included in the same CONFIG.SYS file. This command is available only in non-IBM versions of DOS.

```
DRIVPARM=/D:DriveNumber /F:DeviceType /S:Sectors/track
/T:Tracks/side /C /I /N
```

Parameters

/D:*DriveNumber* is a number correlating to each drive, A=0, B=1, C=2, D=3, and so on.

/F:*DeviceType* is the type number of the device, see Table F. 17.

/S:*Sectors/track* is the number of sectors per track. Nine is the default; a number up to 99 can be specified.

/T:*Tracks/side* is the number of tracks per disk side, a number up to 99 can be specified.

/C indicates that door lock support is required.

/I indicates that the device is an electrically compatible 31/2-inch diskette. Available in Version 4.00 and greater only.

/N indicates a nonremovable device.

TABLE F.17 **Device Types (DRIVPARM Command)**

Device	Type Number
51/4″, 360 KB diskette	0
51/4″, 1.2 MB diskette	1
31/2″, 720 KB diskette	2
Fixed disk	5
Tape drive	6
31/2″, 1.44 MB diskette	7

File Control Blocks (FCBS)

This command controls the maximum number of files that can be open at any one time using file control blocks. It allows the user to specify how many files to protect against automatic closure, as the number of files that can be open at a time fail to meet the demand. Some software uses these blocks to store information needed to create, delete, and open files, as well as for writing to or reading from files.

```
FCBS=<maxopen>,<maxprotected>
```

<maxopen> indicates how many files can be open at a time. A maximum of 255 may be specified. The default is 4.

<maxprotected> is the number of files that will be protected from automatic closures as memory requirements change. This number must always be lower than *<maxopen>*. A maximum of 255 may be specified.

FILES

This command is often thought of in conjunction with BUFFERS. The two are frequently set at the same time. FILES dictates the number of files that can be open at a time.

FILES=<*number*>

<*number*> indicates how many files are desired.

INSTALL

Selected commands can be loaded in CONFIG.SYS. These commands then become part of the environment.

INSTALL=<*filename*> <*parameters*>

<*filename*> is the name of the desired command, including the drive and directory if needed. The file extension must be included as part of the name.

<*parameters*> are the parameters normally used with the specified command from the list below:

FASTOPEN.EXE
KEYB.COM
NLSFUNC.EXE
SHARE.EXE

LASTDRIVE

DOS permits the user to decide how many drives it is possible to address on a system. This permits logical drives for use with such commands as JOIN and SUBST, and RAM drives to be accessed.

LASTDRIVE=<*letter*>

<*letter*> is the letter, from A through Z, of the last accessible drive. The default is E.

REMARK (REM)

This addition to DOS, which was introduced in Version 4.00, permits an explanatory note or remark to be included in the CONFIG.SYS FILE. This is similar to the REM command for batch files.

REM <*statement*>

<*statement*> is a comment made by the user.

SET ENVIRONMENTAL VARIABLE (SET)

This command allows a modification of the environment from the keyboard during a session. The commands that are discussed can be used in either the

CONFIG.SYS file as discussed in Chapter 21, or at the keyboard from the DOS prompt.

SET *<variable><value>*

<variable> is the environmental variable. If no *<value>* is specified, the variable is deleted from memory.

<value> is an assigned value or status given to the variable.

SET, entered without parameters, displays all environmental variables in effect. SET is examined in Chapter 8.

SHELL

SHELL is most often used to indicate the location of COMMAND.COM, the default processor, if it is not in the root directory. A command processor other than COMMAND.COM can be used if so specified. Any parameters that would normally be used with the command processor can be specified at this time.

SHELL=*<filename>*

<filename> is the name and location of the command processor to be loaded.

STACKS

Stacks are contiguous areas of memory some software requires to operate properly.

STACKS=*<number>,<size>*

<number> is the number of stacks desired. Permissible values range from 0 to 64. The default for 8088 processors and some portables is 0, while the default for more recent computers is 9. Check the documentation that came with your computer for the exact default if necessary.

<size> is the size, in bytes, of each stack. The default size is 128 for most computers. Check the documentation for specific information. The default for 8088 processors and some portables is 0.

SWITCHES

Version 4.00 or greater of DOS permits the user to select standard keyboard functions even when an enhanced keyboard is installed.

SWITCHES=/K

/K disables extended keyboard functions and must be specified.

APPENDIX G
DEVICE DRIVERS

THE STANDARD SYSTEM DEVICES

DOS supports the standard system devices through the command processor (COMMAND.COM) and the two hidden files normally installed with it (IO.SYS and MSDOS.SYS). These standard devices include the display screen, the keyboard, and the standard system printer, among others. These devices are referred to through their device names such as CON, PRN, LPT1, COM1, AUX, and NUL. For more information on the standard devices, refer to the Index and Chapter 15 on Input/Output Control.

NONSTANDARD DEVICES AND DOS DEVICE DRIVERS

DOS can also support other devices that might be connected to your personal computer. DOS includes a set of device drivers (SYS extension files) in support of these devices. The device drivers included here are either part of DOS Version 5 or likely to be part of an upgraded system because they were included in earlier versions, such as DOS 3.30 and DOS 4.01. In addition to these device drivers, others may be included on your computer because they were part of a hardware purchase. The most common example of an additional device driver not included as part of DOS is the MOUSE.SYS device driver supplied when you purchase a mouse.

The device drivers described here are included with the operating system.

DEVICE DRIVERS

ANSI.SYS. Defines functions associated with the console keyboard and display screen. These allow changes to graphics display, cursor control movement, and individual key reassignment on the keyboard.

CONFIG.SYS. This is a user-supplied device driver associated with the startup process on the computer. This file can contain configuration commands associated with the setup and operation of the computer. Refer to Chapters 21 and 22 for system guidelines on setup and sample CONFIG.SYS files. Some versions of DOS create a starting version of CONFIG.SYS that you can modify for specific needs.

COUNTRY.SYS. Provides country support associated with code-page switching and the National Language Support function (NLSFUNC).

DISPLAY.SYS. Supports code-page switching for the console in cases where an international system capability is needed.

DRIVER.SYS. Creates a logical drive that can then be used to refer to a physical floppy disk drive. Specific parameters are provided that refer to the type of drive desired.

EGA.SYS. Will save and restore the display screen in cases where Task Swapper is used with an EGA-type monitor.

EMM386.EXE. Used to simulate expanded memory in an extended memory partition. It will also provide access to the upper-memory area on a 80386- or 80486-based processor.

HIMEM.SYS. Manages the use of extended memory on a computer with an 80286 or higher microprocessor.

KEYBOARD.SYS. Provides keyboard support for using an international system and using the KEYB and KEYB*xx* commands with other keyboard layouts.

PRINTER.SYS. Supports code-page switching for the printer in cases where an international system capability is needed.

RAMDRIVE.SYS. Creates a virtual or simulated disk drive in RAM. Information stored in a RAM drive must be saved prior to system shutdown or it will be lost.

SETVER.EXE. Loads the MS-DOS version table into memory. This is a feature incorporated with Version 5.00 to support the DOS 5.00 upgrade.

SMARTDRV.SYS Creates a disk cache in extended or expanded memory in order to speed up standard disk operations.

VDISK.SYS. Similar to RAMDRIVE.SYS and performs the same general functions associated with support for a virtual or RAM disk. Some systems may have either RAMDRIVE.SYS or VDISK.SYS. Version 5 includes the RAMDRIVE.SYS device driver.

XMAEM.SYS. Provides extended and expanded memory support on IBM PS/2 model computers with an 80286 microprocessor. Included with PC-DOS Versions 4.00 and 4.01.

XMA2EMS.SYS. Provides expanded memory support associated with the Lotus-Intel-Microsoft standard specification for memory support. Software using this standard will refer to a LIM or LIM EMS specification. Included with DOS Version 4 systems.

APPENDIX H

BATCH FILE MENU SYSTEMS

BATCH FILE MENUS

The use of batch files along with batch file commands provides the ability to create various programs for setting up and controlling a microcomputer. Menu systems are one example of such control. A batch file menu system allows a user to merely select options from a menu in order to execute various programs including application software such as WordPerfect, Lotus 1-2-3, and other programs.

The files to install a sample batch file menu system are labeled and listed below. A one-page menu system and a two-page menu are shown. To install either of these systems on your computer, first create a directory named \FRTEND on the hard drive. Then create each of the files below, using either of the DOS text editors—EDIT or EDLIN. Store all of these batch files in the directory \FRTEND. These menu systems can be executed as part of the boot process, by including the statement MENU as the last line of your AUTOEXEC.BAT file. To execute the menu system without using AUTOEXEC.BAT, create the files and then execute the MENU.BAT file by typing MENU at the C (or default system) prompt.

ONE-PAGE BATCH FILE MENU SYSTEM

1. **MENU.BAT** The MENU.BAT file is executed from the command line or can be executed through AUTOEXEC.BAT. To execute as part of the boot process, include the command MENU as the last line in the AUTOEXEC.BAT file.

```
@ECHO OFF
REM
REM    MENU.BAT File
REM
CLS
REM
REM BATCH FILE CALLED TO PUT UP MENU SCREEN
```

```
REM
C:
CD \FRTEND
TYPE MENU.TXT
PROMPT PLEASE MAKE A SELECTION?
```

2. **MENU.TXT** Below is listed the MENU.TXT file. Create this file with a text editor and save it with the name MENU.TXT. This file is used together with the TYPE command to display the menu on the display screen. The file begins with the line "MAIN MENU."

```
                      MAIN MENU
 SELECT AN APPLICATION BY TYPING THE NUMBER TO THE LEFT,
              THEN PRESS THE [ENTER] KEY.

1. WORDPERFECT 5.1
2. VENTURA
3. HARVARD GRAPHICS
4. EXCEL (STUDENT EDITION)
5. UNUSED
6. UNUSED
7. FORMAT Data Disk (Drive A:)
8. FORMAT Data Disk (Drive B:)
9. Exit to Root Directory
```

3. **1.BAT** The 1.BAT file is used to execute the WordPerfect 5.1 application software. The name of the program to execute is WP.EXE. Data files are automatically sent to a diskette mounted in Drive A. The default directory is set to be the root directory on Drive A. Upon exiting from WordPerfect, the user is sent back to the Menu screen.

```
@ECHO off
REM
REM  1.BAT
REM
CLS
REM
REM BATCH FILE USED TO EXECUTE WORDPERFECT 5.1
REM
PROMPT $p$g
C:
CD \WP51
REM
REM All data files are redirected to Drive A
REM
A:
CD \
```

```
C:\WP51\WP
C:
CD \FRTEND
MENU
```

4. **2.BAT** The 2.BAT file is used to execute the Ventura Publisher application software. The name of the program to execute is VP.EXE. There is no automatic redirection of data files with this batch file. Upon exiting from Ventura, the user is sent back to the Menu screen.

```
@ECHO off
REM
REM  2.BAT
REM
CLS
REM
REM BATCH FILE TO EXECUTE VENTURA PUBLISHER
REM
PROMPT $p$g
C:
CD \VENTURA
VP
C:
CD \FRTEND
MENU
```

5. **3.BAT** The 3.BAT file is used to execute the Harvard Graphics application software. The name of the program to execute is HG.EXE. The HG.EXE file is stored along with the application software files in the \HARVARDG subdirectory. There is no automatic redirection of data files with this batch file. Upon exiting from Harvard Graphics, the user is sent back to the Menu screen.

```
@ECHO off
REM
REM 3.BAT
REM
CLS
REM
REM BATCH FILE TO EXECUTE HARVARD GRAPHICS
REM
PROMPT $p$g
C:
CD \HARVARDG
HG
```

```
C:
CD \FRTEND
MENU
```

6. **4.BAT** The 4.BAT file is used to execute the student version of Excel. The name of the program to execute is EXCEL.EXE. The EXCEL.EXE file is stored along with the application software files in the \WINDOWS subdirectory. There is no automatic redirection of data files with this batch file. Upon exiting from Excel, the user is sent back to the Menu screen.

```
@ECHO off
REM
REM  4.BAT
REM
CLS
REM
REM BATCH FILE TO EXECUTE EXCEL
REM
PROMPT $p$g
C:
CD \WINDOWS
EXCEL
C:
CD \FRTEND
MENU
```

7. **5.BAT** The 5.BAT file is only a shell batch file since this particular menu selection has not been assigned to a particular function. This batch file sends a message to the display and then returns to the menu. Use other example batch files as models when modifying this for a particular application.

```
@ECHO off
REM
REM  5.BAT
REM
CLS
REM
REM THIS BATCH FILE IS UNUSED AT THIS TIME
REM
PROMPT $p$g
ECHO:
ECHO NO APPLICATION IS INSTALLED ASSOCIATED WITH THIS
ECHO MENU ITEM. RETURNING YOU TO THE MENU. IF YOU NEED
ECHO FURTHER HELP PLEASE SEE YOUR INSTRUCTOR.
ECHO:
PAUSE
```

```
C:
CD \FRTEND
MENU
```

8. **6.BAT** The 6.BAT file is only a shell batch file since this particular menu selection has not been assigned to a particular function. This batch file sends a message to the display and then returns back to the menu. Use other example batch files as models when modifying this for a particular application.

```
@ECHO off
REM
REM  6.BAT
REM
CLS
REM
REM THIS BATCH FILE IS UNUSED AT THIS TIME
REM
PROMPT $p$g
ECHO:
ECHO NO APPLICATION IS INSTALLED ASSOCIATED WITH THIS
ECHO MENU ITEM. RETURNING YOU TO THE MENU. IF YOU NEED
ECHO FURTHER HELP PLEASE SEE YOUR INSTRUCTOR.
ECHO:
PAUSE
C:
CD \FRTEND
MENU
```

9. **7.BAT** The 7.BAT file is used to format data diskettes for a 31/2-inch diskette drive. The 7.BAT file calls FORMATA.BAT to do the formatting. (See Step 12 to create FORMATA.BAT.) Diskettes are automatically formatted as data disks, so they are not bootable. The example shown assumes that DOS is stored in the \DOS330 directory. Modify as necessary for individual systems.

```
@ECHO off
REM
REM  7.BAT
REM
CLS
PROMPT $p$g
REM
REM THIS BATCH FILE FORMATS DATA DISKS FOR DISKETTES
REM MOUNTED IN DRIVE A.
REM
C:
```

```
CD \DOS330
ECHO:
ECHO This program will FORMAT a data disk in Drive A
ECHO using the default format parameters for this
ECHO disk drive and system.
ECHO:
ECHO To FORMAT a disk with parameters such as /S or /V
ECHO Use the FORMATA batch file shown later.
ECHO:
ECHO:
PAUSE
CALL FORMATA
C:
CD \FRTEND
MENU
```

10. **8.BAT** The 8.BAT file is used to format data diskettes for a 51/4-inch diskette drive. The 8.BAT file calls FORMATB.BAT to do the formatting (see Step 13). Diskettes are automatically formatted as data disks, so they are not bootable. The example shown assumes that DOS is stored in the \DOS330 directory. Modify as necessary for individual systems.

```
@ECHO off
REM
REM  8.BAT
REM
CLS
PROMPT $p$g
REM
REM THIS BATCH FILE FORMATS DATA DISKS FOR DISKETTES
REM MOUNTED IN DRIVE B.
REM
C:
CD \DOS330
ECHO:
ECHO This program will FORMAT a data disk in Drive B
ECHO using the default format parameters for this
ECHO disk drive and system.
ECHO:
ECHO To FORMAT a disk with parameters such as /S or /V
ECHO Use the FORMATB batch file shown later.
ECHO:
ECHO:
PAUSE
CALL FORMATB
```

```
C:
CD \FRTEND
MENU
```

11. **9.BAT** The 9.BAT file exits from the Menu back to the DOS prompt and sets the default directory to the root directory. The directory listing of the root directory for Drive C is displayed one screen at a time.

```
@ECHO off
REM
REM  9.BAT
REM
CLS
REM
REM Exit to the Root Directory
REM
PROMPT $p$g
C:
CD \
DIR /p
```

12. **FORMATA.BAT** The FORMATA.BAT batch file formats diskettes for Drive A only. If executing directly, it checks the first variable entered to make sure that Drive A is specified. If the diskette drive is not specified or is incorrectly specified, it exits from the batch file with a message. Store this batch file in the DOS directory such as \DOS500.

```
@ECHO off
REM
REM  FORMATA.BAT
REM
REM This batch file controls the formatting of floppy
REM disks. It will only allow the A: drive diskettes
REM to be formatted.
REM
REM %1 is the disk drive to be formatted
REM %2 is the format control parameter
REM
IF %1 == A: goto skip1
IF %1 == a: goto skip1
CLS
ECHO:
ECHO You have entered data to format a drive other than
ECHO Drive A. You may only format floppy disks using
ECHO Drive A. This batch file will exit to the DOS
ECHO Prompt.
```

```
ECHO:
ECHO:
PAUSE
GOTO end
:SKIP1
REM
REM The FORMAT.COM file from DOS must be renamed to
REM INITIAL.COM.
REM
INITIAL %1%2
:END
ECHO on
```

13. **FORMATB.BAT** The FORMATB.BAT batch file formats diskettes for Drive B only. If executing directly, it checks the first variable entered to make sure that Drive B is specified. If the diskette drive is not specified or is incorrectly specified, it exits from the batch file with a message. Store this batch file in the DOS directory such as \DOS500.

```
@ECHO off
REM
REM  FORMATB.BAT
REM
REM This batch file controls the formatting of floppy
REM disks. It will only allow the B: drive diskettes
REM to be formatted.
REM
REM %1 is the disk drive to be formatted
REM %2 is the format control parameter
REM
IF %1 == B: goto skip1
IF %1 == b: goto skip1
CLS
ECHO:
ECHO You have entered data to format a drive other than
ECHO Drive B. You may only format floppy disks using
ECHO Drive B. This batch file will exit to the DOS
ECHO Prompt.
ECHO:
ECHO:
PAUSE
GOTO end
:SKIP1
REM
REM The FORMAT.COM file from DOS must be renamed to
REM INITIAL.COM.
```

```
REM
INITIAL %1%2
:END
ECHO on
```

TWO-PAGE BATCH FILE MENU SYSTEM

1. **MENU.BAT** The MENU.BAT file is executed from the command line or can be executed through AUTOEXEC.BAT. To execute as part of the boot process, include the command MENU as the last line in the AUTOEXEC.BAT file.

```
@ECHO OFF
REM
REM  MENU.BAT File
REM
CLS
REM
REM BATCH FILE TO DISPLAY Page 1 of the MENU SCREEN
REM
C:
CD \FRTEND
TYPE MENUP1.TXT
PROMPT PLEASE MAKE A SELECTION?
```

2. **MENUP1.TXT** Below is listed the MENUP1.TXT file. Create this file with a text editor and save it with the name MENUP1.TXT. This file is used together with the TYPE command to display the first page of the menu on the display screen. The file begins with the line "MAIN MENU - Page 1."

```
                    MAIN MENU - Page 1
SELECT AN APPLICATION BY TYPING THE NUMBER TO THE LEFT,
               THEN PRESS THE [ENTER] KEY.
1. WORDPERFECT 5.1
2. VENTURA
3. HARVARD GRAPHICS
4. EXCEL (STUDENT EDITION)
5. UNUSED
6. UNUSED
7. FORMAT Data Disk (Drive A:)
8. FORMAT Data Disk (Drive B:)
9. Page 2 of Main Menu
```

3. **MENUP2.TXT** Below is listed the MENUP2.TXT file. Create this file with a text editor and save it with the name MENUP2.TXT. This file is used

together with the TYPE command to display the second page of the menu on the display screen. The file begins with the line "MAIN MENU - Page 2."

```
                    MAIN MENU - Page 2
 SELECT AN APPLICATION BY TYPING THE NUMBER TO THE LEFT,
               THEN PRESS THE [ENTER] KEY.
10. DOS500
11. UNUSED
12. UNUSED
13. UNUSED
14. UNUSED
15. UNUSED
16. UNUSED
17. Return to Previous Menu
18. EXIT to Root Directory
```

4. **1.BAT through 8.BAT** Use same files as used for a one-page menu system shown earlier in this appendix.

5. **9.BAT** The 9.BAT file is used to display the second page of the menu system. Two batch files (9.BAT and 17.BAT) are used to move between the two pages of the menu.

```
@ECHO off
REM
REM  9.BAT
REM
CLS
REM
REM BATCH FILE CALLED TO PUT UP Page 2 of MENU SCREEN
REM
C:
CD \FRTEND
TYPE MENUP2.TXT
PROMPT PLEASE MAKE A SELECTION?
```

6. **10.BAT** The 10.BAT file is used to exit to the DOS directory. DOS commands can then be executed directly from that subdirectory. In this example, DOS Version 5 is installed in a \DOS500 directory.

```
@ECHO off
REM
REM  10.BAT
REM
CLS
REM
REM DOS VERSION 5.00 INSTALLED
REM
```

```
PROMPT $P$G
C:
CD \DOS500
DIR \DOS500 /w
ECHO:
ECHO:
ECHO PLEASE MAKE A SELECTION OR TYPE MENU TO RETURN
```

7. **11.BAT through 16.BAT** These batch files are the same as the 5.BAT shown with the one-page menu system.

```
@ECHO off
REM
REM  11.BAT
REM
CLS
REM
REM THIS BATCH FILE IS UNUSED AT THIS TIME
REM
PROMPT $p$g
ECHO:
ECHO NO APPLICATION IS INSTALLED ASSOCIATED WITH THIS
ECHO MENU ITEM. RETURNING YOU TO THE MENU. IF YOU
ECHO NEED FURTHER HELP PLEASE SEE YOUR INSTRUCTOR.
ECHO:
PAUSE
C:
CD \FRTEND
MENU
```

8. **17.BAT** The 17.BAT file is used to return to the previous page (Page 1) of the menu.

```
@ECHO off
REM
REM  17.BAT
REM
CLS
REM  REM BATCH FILE CALLED TO PUT UP MENU PAGE 1
REM
C:
CD \FRTEND
TYPE MENUP1.TXT
PROMPT PLEASE MAKE A SELECTION?
```

9. **18.BAT** The 18.BAT file is used to exit to the root directory.

```
@ECHO off
```

```
@ ECHO off
REM
REM  18.BAT
REM
REM
REM BATCH FILE TO EXIT TO Root Directory
REM
CLS
PROMPT $p$g
C:
CD \
DIR /p
```

10. **FORMATA.BAT and FORMATB.BAT** Use the files shown earlier with the one-page menu system to control formatting on diskette drives A and B.

ANSWERS TO QUESTIONS AND PROBLEMS

Answers to Questions and Problems

Chapter 1 DOS as an Operating System

1. DOS is a disk operating system. The term has been used for a wide variety of computers and operating systems. Over the last 10 years the term DOS has been largely associated with personal computers. DOS provides the software that operates the hardware. It also provides a control program that interfaces with application software; DOS provides a communications link between the user, the software being used, and the computer hardware. Without an operating system the computer will not operate.
3. *Compatibility* refers to the degree to which to computers can communicate or operate the same software and read the same files. Computers can be boot compatible, file compatible, and/or software compatible. Personal computers using an INTEL microprocessor and running DOS are usually file compatible and software compatible.
5. No. Files written by one version of DOS such as Version 3.10 can be read and retrieved by another version of DOS such as Version 5 on a completely different machine. Both must be running DOS; and, both must be running an INTEL microprocessor 808*x*, or an 80286 or higher processor.
7. Version 3.20 of DOS introduced support for 31/2-inch disk drives. Double-density capacity is approximately 720 KB and high-density capacity is 1.44 MB. This substantially increased the storage capacity of diskettes as compared to the old standard of 360 KB. The diskettes are more durable and better protected from dust and dirt with the new design.
9. PC-DOS was developed for the IBM line of personal computers. MS-DOS was developed for IBM compatibles. Each manufacturer licenses their version of DOS from Microsoft and many contain features or programs unique to their machine. Even an upgrade to MS-DOS Version 5 may show slight differences from machine to machine since DOS 5 is an upgrade to an earlier version of DOS for that computer.

Chapter 2 Hardware and Software

1. A *keyboard control sequence* is a function that is implemented by pressing a combination of keys. The Ctrl-C combination cancels the command that is

currently being executed. The sequence Ctrl-Alt-Del warm boots the computer.

3. The three keys which perform no function when pressed singly are the Ctrl, the Alt, and the Shift keys. They are frequently used in combination with other keys to implement control key sequences.

5. The *keyboard buffer* is a special memory associated with the keyboard used to store commands typed at the keyboard. The keyboard buffer generally holds 132 characters of information.

7. The *read/write notch* of a 51/4-inch diskette and the read/write slide switch on a 31/2-inch diskette perform the same function. These place the diskette in a read-only mode in one position and make the diskette read/write when placed in the opposite position. A 51/4-inch diskette is read-only when the notch on the protective sleeve is covered. A 31/2-inch diskette is read-only when the slide switch is open so that light shines through the hole.

9. Structured filenames allow groups of files to be displayed together. They also allow files to be easily identified based on the name without examining the contents of the file.

11. The *default directory* is the directory that will be displayed by the command PROMPT pg. It is also referred to as the *current directory*. When executing an external command, DOS first looks in the current directory for the command it is to execute.

13. Use the redirection symbol (>) to redirect output to a device other than the console. To send output to the system printer, redirect the output by including **> PRN** in the command line.

Chapter 3 Commands and Command Groups

1. DOS performs functions such as disk management, file management, input/output control, and memory management to name a few. Some functions are implemented using both internal and external commands.

3. The CHKDSK program can be used to assess and keep track of storage space usage and bytes available on a diskette.

5. The DIR command can be used to list all the COM and EXE files that are stored in the DOS directory. These should be all the external command files associated with DOS.

7. The programs associated with the execution of an internal command are part of the command processor (COMMAND.COM).

9. Most versions of DOS are too large to fit on a single floppy disk. Therefore a floppy can only hold part of DOS rather than the entire operating system. Other advantages include the access speed of hard drives compared to

floppies.

Chapter 4 Introductory Commands

1. The HELP command supplied as part of DOS 5 supplies a brief description of a command along with short descriptions of all switches or parameters associated with each command.
3. No. The DISKCOPY command duplicates a diskette. The diskettes must be identical in format. A double-density diskette can be duplicated or disk copied onto another double-density diskette.
5. The FORMAT command along with the /S switch must be used to build a bootable system diskette. Personal computers in general can only be booted from Drive A or the hard drive, which is normally Drive C.
7. Use the CHKDSK command to display space utilization about disks and diskettes as well as about the amount of internal memory. To see all the files on a disk including hidden files, use **CHKDSK C:/V.**
9. Hidden files and system files will generally not be copied since the COPY command never recognizes these types of files.
11. Type the forward slash (/) followed by a question mark (?). To get help with the command FORMAT type **FORMAT/?**
13. The source and target diskettes must be formatted identically. Therefore the target diskette must be double-sided double-density.

Chapter 5 Disk Management (Internal Commands)

1. The total storage capacity of a diskette includes all sectors that are available for storing data. There are a total of 2880 sectors available, each holding 512 bytes. The total storage capacity of a 31/2-inch high-density diskette is 1,474,560 bytes (1.44 MB).
3. The system area is used to store information for the boot sector, the File Allocation Table (FAT), and the directory area. Every disk, including both hard disks and diskettes, has space allocated for system storage for that disk. As a result, each diskette or disk is self-contained, because it stores FAT and directory information as well as the actual files on the disk.
5. A clock card allows the computer to update the date and time information automatically once the clock has been initially set. A clock card contains a small battery for powering the clock even when power is turned off on the computer. A battery will normally last 4–5 years before needing replacement.
7. A volume label can be used to identify the disk. One use is to use the label to store your name in a lab situation. The label can also be used to identify the type of information on the disk such as correspondence, budget information, etc. The volume label can be up to 11 characters in length.

9. The *default directory* is the directory DOS expects to use whenever that disk is addressed for accessing files or finding commands for execution. Each disk or diskette has a default directory setting associated with that disk or diskette. The default is stored on the disk or diskette and stays with it even if removed from the computer.

Chapter 6 Directory Management (Internal Commands)

1. The \WORD and the \WORD\GR directories. The parent directory must always exist before a subdirectory can be created.
3. All of the files must have been deleted from the directory. All subdirectories of the specified directory must also be removed before the directory itself can be removed. To remove a directory, the default directory cannot be the directory that is being removed. If the prompt is C:\WP50, the \WP50 directory cannot be removed. If you cannot remove a directory when it appears to be empty, it may contain hidden files or hidden subdirectories. See the CHKDSK /V command to view hidden entries in a directory, or use the ATTRIB command if using DOS 5.
5. The Change Directory command. **CD A:\DIR1** would make the default directory on Drive A the \DIR1 directory.
7. The name and the extension field of each user file are displayed. The size, date, and time fields are not displayed with a filename when the /w parameter is used with DIR. No hidden files are displayed.
9. The single-dot (.) symbol refers to the current directory.
11. Use the **CHKDSK /V** command along with MORE to page through the entire directory structure. A batch file could also be written that also used the DIR command and the FIND command searching for and displaying the filename field.
13. Use the DIR command followed by the switch **/o:n** to sort the directory names in ascending alphabetic order.
15. Either the CHKDSK command or the ATTRIB command can be used in Version 5. In earlier versions of DOS before 5 only the CHKDSK command would display all files regardless of the status of their attributes.

Chapter 7 File Management (Internal Commands)

1. The DOS TYPE command can correctly display ASCII text files, such as those created by the DOS text editors EDIT or EDLIN.
3. The VERIFY command turns the verify feature of DOS on or off. The purpose of VERIFY ON is to assure that data is accurately written to disk.
5. Use /A with COPY to tell DOS to treat the files as ASCII text files. Use /B to

tell DOS to treat the files as binary files. Use /V to have COPY verify that the copy was made without errors.

7. Yes. The Rename command (REN) can change the filename, or the file extension, or both can be changed as part of the same command line.

9. Eight files will be copied based on the *.* reference. Hidden files are not referenced when using the *.* wildcard.

Chapter 8 System Control (Internal Commands)

1. CLS positions the cursor in the upper lefthand corner of the screen, just after the DOS prompt.

3. Some application software requires that a minimum version of DOS be installed in order for the application software to operate properly. The parameters available with certain DOS commands are based on the version of DOS installed. Some DOS commands are only available with particular versions. DOS Version 5 contains some new commands such as DOSKEY, MIRROR, and UNFORMAT.

5. The PATH command controls this function. To add directories to the search path as part of the startup process, include a PATH command as part of the AUTOEXEC.BAT file on your system. A PATH command can also be entered at the command prompt to add an entry to the path or to change the path.

7. SET, PATH, PROMPT, and CTTY among others.

9. The root directory and the DOS directory would always be included so that external DOS commands could be executed regardless of the current directory. See Chapters 21 and 22 or the Appendices for additional suggestions on these commands and the installation/protection of your system.

Chapter 9 Disk Management (External Commands)

1. The CHKDSK command, used with the /F parameter, will attempt to recover lost clusters and place them in the root directory. Each file recovered will be given a filename FILE*nnnn*, where *nnnn* is a sequence number. Each file has an extension of CHK. These files can then be renamed, deleted, viewed, etc., depending upon the content of the recovered information.

3. `FORMAT d:/S,` where d: is the drive letter of the disk drive.

5. The FASTOPEN command can be part of CONFIG.SYS or AUTOEXEC.BAT. If used in a CONFIG.SYS file, it is normally used along with the INSTALL configuration command.

7. The COPY command copies visible files from one place to another. The DISKCOPY command duplicates a diskette. It cannot be used with hard disks. DISKCOPY duplicates everything on the source diskette including

hidden files, directories and subdirectories, and volume labels. DISKCOPY can also format a diskette, if necessary, as part of the duplication process.

9. Use the CHKDSK command with the /V parameter to display all files on the disk by directory. Use the filter command MORE to display all the files in paged format or redirect the output to the printer if hard copy is desired. The ATTRIB command in Version 5 will also display all files in a single directory along with the status of some of the file's attributes.
11. The MIRROR command is used to install delete tracking for any disk. Place the MIRROR command in the AUTOEXEC.BAT file to install delete tracking as part of system initialization.
13. The hard drive can be temporarily unbootable if the system nucleus files are damaged or AUTOEXEC.BAT or CONFIG.SYS become inoperable. Accidentally deleting COMMAND.COM will give the error message, "Non-system disk." If COMMAND.COM is not the same version as IO.SYS and MSDOS.SYS, the error message "Incorrect DOS Version" will be the result. Having a system disk that will boot the computer from Drive A allows these problems to be corrected.
15. Use the UNDELETE command (Version 5) along with the /dos parameter if delete tracking is not installed. UNDELETE may be able to recover a deleted file using information from the FAT table.
17. Use the UNFORMAT command with either the /j parameter or the /test parameter. Both cannot be used in the same command line. These two parameters cause the UNFORMAT command to test the disk for recovery without attempting to rebuild the disk.

Chapter 10 Directory Management (External Commands)

1. The SUBST command allows a disk drive letter to substitute for a long pathname. It can substantially reduce typing and, therefore, reduce potential typing errors when long pathnames must be used in addressing files.
3. Some printers are not capable of printing graphics characters. The /A parameter allows an alternate character set to be used to draw the tree structure for the disk.
5. Commands such as JOIN, SUBST, and ASSIGN modify the way the hardware operates. It is suggested that certain commands not be used when these commands are in effect, such as BACKUP and RESTORE commands. Some commands, such as DISKCOPY, ignore the ASSIGN and SUBST commands. By using these commands as part of a batch file, they can be reset to normal operation at the end of the batch file. This also prevents problems with hardware operations in many cases. The ASSIGN command provides no method for displaying assigns currently in effect in versions prior to DOS 5, thereby

making their installation invisible to a new user on a system. Many commands will not work when a SUBST command is in effect, and others will not have the desired effect. Exercise caution when using any command that modifies the normal hardware operations and standard device references such as disk drives.

7. The directory structure for the named directory will be displayed to the console. In this case, the directory structure for \WP51 will be displayed.

Chapter 11 The DOS Text Editors (External Commands)

1. The # refers to the line after the last line of the file. In effect, you can think of it as referencing the end-of-file (EOF) mark in the file.
3. EDLIN can be used to edit text files which are sometimes referred to as ASCII files. A batch file is an example of an ASCII text file.
5. Typing the number 20 will display that line in the file and provide the opportunity to modify the contents of that line.
7. The Copy (c) command will copy part or all of the contents of a file. The command **1,25,#,20c** will produce 20 additional copies of a file 25 lines in length. The command **1,#,#,20c** will not function correctly on most systems because of the double # reference. Use the actual line number, as shown, to reference the last line in the file. In the example shown here, the contents of a 25-line file was duplicated 20 times.
9. Use the Ctrl-C key sequence to exit back to Command mode.
11. Both EDIT and EDLIN are line editors for text files. EDIT provides a help feature along with full-screen editing features and pull-down menus. Files created with EDLIN are version independent in DOS (they will work with any version of DOS). EDIT was added in Version 5 of DOS.
13. Use the F6 function key. The display at the bottom of the screen in EDIT lists the function keys available for use with EDIT.
15. Use the control key sequence Ctrl-Home to move to the top of the file when using EDIT. Use the key sequence Ctrl-End to move to the end of the file.

Chapter 12 File Management (External Commands)

1. All of the files located in the named directory \WP51, as well as any subdirectories of \WP51, will be backed up. Use the /S parameter to back up an application directory as well as all its subdirectories.
3. The BACKUP command issued should be **BACKUP C:*.* d: /S,** where d: is the diskette drive to be used for backup diskettes. The named directory is the root directory of Drive C and /S specifies all subdirectories of the root.
5. By specifying *.WK1 as the designated filename as part of a RESTORE

command, such as **RESTORE B: C:*.WK1 /S,** to restore all files with the extension WK1 to all subdirectories from the backup diskettes.

7. Yes. Just specify the file or files to be replaced as part of the file specification in the RESTORE command.
9. XCOPY copies visible files (not hidden files) from one place to another. XCOPY can also copy entire directory structures if the /S parameter is specified. XCOPY can be used with either hard drives or floppy drives. DISKCOPY is a diskette duplication program. It copies all files, including hidden files, and places them in the same location on the target disk as they had on the source diskette. DISKCOPY cannot be used with hard disk drives.
11. To make the CONFIG.SYS file read-only issue a command such as **ATTRIB +r C:\CONFIG.SYS.** With DOS Version 5 only, issue the command **ATTRIB +h C:\CONFIG.SYS.** With Version 5, both operations can be given in a single command by including both +r and +h in the same command line.
13. Use the COMP command along with the /n=*number* parameter to specify the number of lines. To compare FILE1.scr and FILE2.scr, use the command **COMP FILE1.scr FILE2.scr /n=100.**
15. Use the RESTORE command **RESTORE A: C:\LOTUS22*.* /S** to restore from diskettes mounted in Drive A that contain the entire hard drive backup. If the diskette containing the beginning of the backup for the \LOTUS22 directory is known, the backup can be started directly from that diskette, otherwise begin with diskette #1 of the backup.

Chapter 13 System Control (External Commands)

1. The hidden files, IO.SYS and MSDOS.SYS for a version of MS-DOS, or IBMBIO.COM and IBMDOS.COM for a version of PC-DOS, are transferred. The COMMAND.COM file is transferred to the target drive when the SYS command is executed only in Version 5.
3. The two hidden files, IO.SYS and MSDOS.SYS for MS-DOS, or IBMBIO.COM and IBMDOS.COM for PC-DOS, and the COMMAND.COM file.
5. The command processor (COMMAND.COM) is visible and can be seen using the DIR command. It can also be copied with any of the copy commands including COPY, XCOPY, and REPLACE.
7. Files are locked on a network so that two or more people are not accessing and modifying the same file at the same time. Without file locking updates might be lost.
9. The diskette in Drive A must be a bootable diskette.

11. The SHARE.EXE file would most likely be found in the \DOS*xxx* directory of the file serving computer. The *xxx* represents the version of DOS installed such as \DOS401.

Chapter 14 Filter Commands (External Commands)

1. Filter commands can be chained to other DOS commands. They can receive data through the chaining process from another command; they can also send output through the chaining process to another DOS command. The process of receiving and sending data to another command is sometimes referred to as *piping*.
3. No. The MORE command can only provide paging for ASCII text files.
5. These temporary files are automatically deleted by DOS.
7. No. The FIND search is sensitive to upper- and lowercase letters since it uses the binary code representation of the character. A search on the string "CUST" will produce different results than one done on the string "cust". The strings must be exact matches. With Version 5, specify the /I parameter if case sensitivity should be ignored.
9. Yes. However, the parameters should be compatible, and not produce conflicting results.
11. Ignoring case sensitivity cannot be specified in versions prior to Version 5. In Version 5 specify the /I parameter if case sensitivity is to be ignored in a search on a string.
13. Use the command **`DIR C:\DOS500 | FIND "EXE" > PRN.`** This command sends all the DOS directory files to the FIND command that then searches for a string EXE that is preceded by a single blank character. This will produce a list of all EXE extension files which are then sent to the printer to be listed.
15. Yes. Use the SORT command along with the less-than symbol (<) to read them as input files into SORT. Then use the parameter /+*n* where *n* is the character number in the record on which the sort should begin. If the sort is to be on a first name field which is character 20 in each record, specify /+20 as part of the sort.

Chapter 15 Input/Output Control (External Commands)

1. Disk drive assignments are made using the ASSIGN command. It does not have the capability to display current assignments in effect in any version of DOS prior to Version 5. In Version 5 the ASSIGN command can also be used to display the assignments that are currently in effect.
3. The GRAPHICS command is used with the printer. A port can be specified. The standard system devices affected are LPT1, LPT2, and LPT3.

5. The MODE command for the console (CON) can affect both the keyboard and the display screen. The display characteristics affected can include color, number of columns, and number of lines displayed on the screen. Code-page switching is also a feature associated with the console. In addition, the keyboard repeat rate, as well as the pause or delay when using the repeat key feature, can be set using the MODE command.
7. The baud rate represents the transmission rate for sending or receiving characters through a modem. Baud rate settings using the MODE command can be any of the following: 110, 150, 300, 1200, 2400, 4800, 9600, or 19200 (Version 5). The baud rate selected with software must be matched to the capability of the physical hardware (the modem).
9. The MODE command is used with the /STATUS parameter. MODE will report a status for standard system devices including CON, PRN, LPT1, LPT2, and LPT3.
11. Include the DOSKEY command in the AUTOEXEC.BAT file. If desired, the parameter /bufsize may be specified. The default buffer size is 512 bytes for storing previously typed commands. The command would be **`DOSKEY /512`.**
13. The MODE command can increase the number of lines displayed on the monitor to 50 instead of 25. Use **`MODE CON lines=50`** to change the number of lines on the screen from 25 to 50. The number of columns would remain unchanged in this example, but could have been changed also as part of the same command.
15. Approximately 15–20 commands can be stored using a buffer size of 256 bytes. The length of the commands will determine the actual number that will fit in a 256-byte buffer.

Chapter 16 Memory Management (External Commands)

1. The hexadecimal number system is used to display numbers and memory addresses.
3. By altering the CONFIG.SYS file to remove these device drivers. Before altering CONFIG.SYS, it is suggested that a copy of the original be made for safekeeping. After CONFIG.SYS has been modified, reboot to put the commands into effect.
5. Include a line in the CONFIG.SYS file such as DEVICE=ANSI.SYS in order to have this file loaded and available for use. To remove this file from memory, remove the DEVICE=ANSI.SYS line from CONFIG.SYS and reboot.
7. The HIMEM.SYS device driver provides a way to manage extended memory. It is included in the CONFIG.SYS file, usually in conjunction with another

line that allows DOS to use extended memory. The two lines are **DEVICE=C:\DOS*xxx*\HIMEM.SYS** and **DOS=High.**

9. The HIMEM.SYS statement must be the first of the lines in the CONFIG.SYS file to open access to available memory in areas other than conventional memory. The second line might load DOS into upper memory. Other lines could load specific device drivers into memory. An example might be:

```
DEVICE=C:\DOS\HIMEM.SYS
DEVICEHIGH=SMARTDRV.SYS
DOS=High
```

Chapter 17 The DOS Shell

1. To cause the computer to load the shell automatically during either a cold boot or a warm boot, include the command DOSSHELL as the last line in the AUTOEXEC.BAT file. This allows the computer to be set up with other commands such as PROMPT, PATH, etc. prior to loading the Shell. The command DOSSHELL must be on the path, so the PATH command in the AUTOEXEC.BAT file should include C:\DOS*xxx* as one of its entries.
3. A mouse allows the user to merely click on an entry to display a pull-down menu, for example. Commands can be executed by double clicking. Once mastered, mouse operations are generally much faster and less prone to mistakes than are similar commands from the keyboard.
5. The F1 function key is used to request help when using the DOS Shell.
7. Function keys are used to operate the Shell. The F10 key activates the Menu Bar so that menus can be selected and items can be executed from various menus. SHIFT-F9 exits the Shell to the DOS prompt without quitting the Shell. SHIFT-F8 can be used with the File Menu to select a group of files. Other function keys perform other functions. If operating from the keyboard rather than with a mouse, learn the various operations performed by the function keys.
9. Files may be displayed in a variety of orders, based on information contained in the file directory area. The File Display order can be by Name, Extension, Date, Size, and Disk order. The file display can include hidden and system files if desired. Ascending or descending order can be selected. A group of files can be selected by specifying a group in the Name field, such as *.COM to only display files with a COM extension..

Chapter 18 Other Commands (External Commands)

1. DEBUG can be used to edit any type of file since it deals with each individual byte. Program files, formatted data files, and text files can all be edited.

DEBUG displays characters as a hexadecimal number representing that byte. Bytes are encoded on most personal computers using the ASCII coding system.

3. The JOIN command attaches a disk drive to another drive and treats it as a directory. The disk drive attached can no longer be directly addressed as long as it is joined.
5. The SELECT command is used to install Version 4.00 of DOS from the INSTALL diskette. SELECT can also be used to build a country-specific diskette.
7. To compile the script file DISP.SCR, use the DEBUG program. The command executed from the DOS prompt is **DEBUG < DISP.SCR.**
9. A directory must be empty and cannot be the root directory in order to be used in a JOIN command.

Chapter 19 Batch File Commands

1. The actual statements in a REMarks line will display if the REM is replaced with an ECHO command. REMarks will also display if the first line of a batch file turns ECHO on. Then all statements in the batch file will be displayed on the screen before each command is executed. If scrolling is a problem, insert PAUSE statements at appropriate places in the batch file.
3. The SHIFT command performs this replacement. The current value is thrown away and replaced with the variable next in line.
5. Use the CALL batch file command to invoke a batch file from within another one. Once the called batch file completes execution, control returns to the statement immediately following the CALL in the original batch file.
7. The ECHO command can be used to send messages or any other information you wish displayed on the monitor screen.
9. The colon (:) should precede a label. The label should be the only thing on that line in the batch file. When referencing the label in another command such as **GOTO label1**, label1 is not preceded by the colon.

GLOSSARY

A

Alt An abbreviation used to refer to the Alt key on the keyboard. The Alt key does nothing when pressed by itself. It must be used with other keys to perform control key sequence operations.
application program A program that performs a general function or task, such as word processing or data management.
archive To copy or duplicate files onto a separate disk or tape for safekeeping. The BACKUP command is used to back up or archive files to protect software and important data.
ASCII A 7-bit coding system that is used to represent letters, numbers, punctuation characters, and other symbols. A total of 128 codes can be represented. ASCII stands for American Standard Code for Information Interchange.
attribute byte One byte of information stored in the system directory area of a disk to encode information about a directory entry. Individual bits of the byte indicate the characteristics of the entry, including archive, system, hidden, subdirectory, volume label, and read-only.
AUTOEXEC.BAT A batch file DOS uses during the boot process to set operating characteristics of the system. DOS automatically searches for this file during the startup process. The commands in the batch file must obey the rules for writing batch files.
AUX The abbreviation for the Auxiliary device. DOS uses this as a communications port. AUX can be either COM1 or COM2 in DOS Versions through 3.2. In Versions of DOS later than 3.2 AUX can be COM1, COM2, COM3, or COM4.

B

backslash Character on the keyboard used in addressing files. Backslash is also another term for the root directory, sometimes referred to as the backslash directory.
backslash directory See *backslash.*
back up To copy a file or group of files to tape or disk as a protection against accidental damage or loss.
BAK An extension used by many programs, including EDLIN, to represent the previous version of a file before it was updated and saved. When a file is saved with EDLIN, the previous copy on the disk is given a BAK extension. The current copy is then saved under the filename.
BASIC A programming language included with many versions of DOS. PC-DOS includes both BASIC and BASICA. MS-DOS versions through Version 4.01 have normally included GWBASIC. The DOS upgrade for Version 5.00 includes QBASIC from Microsoft.
batch file A file whose extension must be BAT in order for it to be executable. Batch files can contain internal, external, and batch file commands. Batch files are ASCII text files and can be displayed using the TYPE command.
baud A term used to represent the rate at which data is transmitted over a communications channel.
binary A number system that uses base 2 and whose digits are 0 and 1. The binary system is used extensively with computers to represent the state of various digital signals, where 0 represents *off* and 1 represents *on.*
BIOS An abbreviation for the Basic Input/Output System. The BIOS refers to the startup program and the low-level hardware control program used to control various devices such as the keyboard, display, and disk drives.
bit The smallest piece of information used with computers. Eight bits are used to make one byte, which is the memory needed to store a single character.
boot A term used to refer to the process of starting up the computer. It was derived from the idea that the control program of the operating system must be loaded into RAM. To do that, a small program, sometimes referred to as the *bootstrap loader,* must first be loaded so that it can read the DOS kernel into RAM.
boot compatibility A term used to refer to the compatibility between an IBM microcomputer and a microcomputer from another manufacturer. If the two computers are boot compatible, either the IBM or the compatible can be booted from the same boot or startup disk.
byte A unit of memory that is required to hold a single character. One byte contains eight bits. A byte can store a letter, a number, a punctuation mark, or any character that is part of the coding system used on that computer. Microcomputers use the ASCII coding system.

C

character string A group of characters that DOS treats as a single unit. The string can be alphanumeric. Both the DOS text editors, EDLIN and EDIT, and the filter command FIND can treat character strings.

COM1 . . . COM4 Device names for the communications ports supported by DOS. Versions of DOS up to Version 3.2 recognize COM1 and COM2. Versions 3.30 and later recognize COM1 through COM4.
command A filename that is used to execute a computer program, whether a DOS program or an application program.
command file A DOS file that is executable because it is a program. Command files under DOS have the extensions COM, EXE, or BAT. Files other than BAT contain machine instructions. BAT command files contain DOS commands.
command groups Groups of related software commands that perform a similar function under the operating system. File management, disk management, directory management, and system control are some of the operating system functions performed by DOS. See Chapter 3.
command processor The processor loaded at boot time under DOS. The DOS command processor is the COMMAND.COM file.
COMMAND.COM See *command processor.*
communications port The electrical terminal through which the computer communicates with an outside source. The communications port is normally connected through the telephone system so that it can communicate with other computers.
compatibility A term used to refer to the compatibility between an IBM microcomputer and a microcomputer from another manufacturer. The two computers may have varying degrees of compatibility. The two will always be *file-compatible* if they are running DOS. They may also have a high degree of *software compatibility*, meaning that they can run the same software.
CON An abbreviation used to address the console device. DOS refers to the keyboard as the standard input device (CON), and refers to the display console (CON) as the standard output device when addressing the display unit or monitor.
CONFIG.SYS A configuration file stored in the root directory of the boot disk that is processed during computer startup. This file contains configuration commands that determine the setup of the computer.
CPU An abbreviation that refers to the central processing unit of the computer. The CPU is that part of the computer that processes data, performs calculations, and executes instructions.
Ctrl An abbreviation that refers to the Control key on the keyboard. The Control key does nothing when pressed by itself. It must be used with other keys to perform control key sequence operations.
current directory The current directory is also referred to as the *default directory*. This is the directory that DOS searches when executing instructions or searching for files, unless it is instructed otherwise.
current drive Also referred to as the *default drive*, this is the disk drive that DOS searches for commands and files unless instructed to do otherwise.

D

data file A file that contains data for a program.
default The base value for a feature or software specification. Default values provide information or values to DOS when executing commands in the absence of more specific information from the user.
default directory See *current directory.*
default drive See *current drive.*
default format The base format values for a disk drive when formatting a floppy diskette. The base format is either high-density or double-density for either 51/4-inch or 31/2-inch drives. The base format can be overridden if the drive is a high-density drive, provided that high-density diskettes are used.
device An input/output piece of equipment that performs a specific function. A keyboard, a display, and a printer are the most common examples of devices.
device driver A software program used to control a specific input/output device that is connected to the computer system. Nonstandard devices require device drivers in order for them to function with the DOS operating system.
device name The name by which DOS addresses a specific device such as the keyboard, display, or the printer. CON and PRN are two examples of device names.
directory An area on the disk used to hold files. Directories have names that are addressed when the directory entries are to be displayed.
disk A magnetic media used to store information. The disk can be either a fixed disk or a removable floppy diskette.
disk drive An electromechanical device that spins the disk or diskette so that information may be stored on or retrieved from the media.
diskette A removable disk used to store computer files. The magnetic media are enclosed in a protective jacket that may be flexible or made of a hard plastic material.
display The screen used to display the command or data typed at the keyboard, as well as the output results. DOS assumes the display is the standard output device and addresses it as the console device (CON).
DOS An abbreviation used for Disk Operating System. DOS is also used as a shorthand notation for either PC-DOS or MS-DOS when that term refers to microcomputers.
DOS Shell See *Shell.*
double-density A media density specification for some diskettes. Double density is sometimes referred to as low density. For 51/4-inch diskettes, double-density formatting provides 362,496 bytes of usable data space on the diskette. For 31/2-inch diskettes, double-density provides 730,112 bytes of usable data space.
drive letter The letter used as a means of addressing a disk drive or referring to a specific drive.

E

EDIT A full-screen text editor included with DOS 5.
editor A program used to create or modify text files. EDLIN and EDIT are the text editors included as part of either MS-DOS or PC-DOS. EDIT is only included with Version 5 of DOS.
EDLIN A text editor included as part of MS-DOS or PC-DOS in all versions including DOS 5.

executable file A program containing instructions that can be executed by typing the file's name, followed by pressing the Enter key. Executable files under DOS have an extension of COM, EXE, or BAT.
expanded memory (EMS) Additional memory that can be installed on an IBM or compatible computer. A memory management program is required to set up and use this memory. Software must include the necessary features in order to use this memory. Use of expanded memory is governed by the LIM (Lotus-Intel-Microsoft) specification. Up to 8 MB of expanded memory may be installed.
extended memory (XMS) Additional memory that can be installed on some models of IBM and compatible computers. An 80286, 80386, or 80486 microprocessor is required. Up to 15 MB of extended memory can be installed.
extension A part of a filename that contains up to three characters. The extension is an optional part of a file specification. The characters used in the extension or file suffix must obey the same rules as for filenames.

F

FAT table DOS uses the File Allocation Table (FAT) to manage the space on a disk. This table, along with the system directory on the disk, keeps track of the status of all space on the disk and the pieces of all files stored on the disk.
file A collection of related data or information, or a program for performing a specific task. Files are normally stored on magnetic media such as tape or disk.
file compatibility A term that refers to the degree of compatibility between an IBM microcomputer and a microcomputer from another manufacturer with regard to reading and storing files. The two computers are file-compatible if files written to a diskette on one computer can be read by the compatible computer and vice versa.
file extension See *extension.*
file manager A program that is part of DOS and used to manage the files on disk drives. The file manager and the input/output manager are hidden files invoked by COMMAND.COM when needed to process files.
filename A name of one to eight characters that is assigned to identify a file. Specific rules must be followed in assigning a name to a file.
filespec The complete specification used to address or find a file. The filespec can include a drive letter, a pathname, a filename, and an extension.
filter command A DOS command that can be chained to other commands as part of a single command line sequence. Filter commands can pass files to other DOS commands by reading standard input and writing standard output. The vertical or *pipe* symbol (¦) is used to chain commands together.
fixed disk A large-capacity disk that cannot be removed from the computer system unit or its housing if it is a stand-alone, fixed disk. It is sometimes referred to as a hard drive or *hard disk.* Fixed disks are normally of 20 MB or larger in size.
floppy diskette See *diskette.*
format The process of preparing a disk, either a hard disk or a diskette, for use on a computer. Formatting the disk prepares the disk for use by the computer and makes the disk compatible with the operating system that formatted it. The root directory is created at the time the disk is formatted.
formatted file A file prepared by an application software program. Formatted data files contain control characters inserted by the software application in order to display information to the screen, as well as print the file in a formatted way on the printer. Examples of some of these control characters are soft carriage returns, margin and justification control, and indents in a word processing data file. Formatted data files usually also contain the print control codes for printing the file, including the default printer identification.
function key One of 10 or 12 keys on the computer that can invoke special commands or functions usually preceded by F, as in F1. DOS uses several of the function keys on the computer. See *Appendix B.*

H

hard disk See *fixed disk.*
hard sectored A formatting feature of some diskettes, where the number of sectors per track is built into the diskette itself. Most diskettes are soft-sectored rather than hard-sectored.
hardware The equipment that makes up a computer system, normally including the system unit, the display, the keyboard, and the disk drives. It may include other special equipment such as a mouse or a scanner, depending on the types of work done using the computer.
hexadecimal The base 16 number system used by computers. The digits in the number system range from 0 through F, where F represents the decimal number 15. The hexadecimal system is convenient in computing because of the ease of use in converting binary numbers to hexadecimal. One hexadecimal number requires four binary digits when making the conversion.
hidden file A DOS file that is normally hidden from display when the DIR command is invoked. Files are hidden by setting the hide bit to 1 in the attribute byte. Files are normally hidden so they cannot be accessed directly under DOS.
hide bit See *hidden file.*
high density A media density specification for some diskettes. For 51/4-inch diskettes, high density provides 15 sectors per track and 1,213,952 bytes (1.2 MB) of usable data space on the diskette. For 31/2-inch diskettes, high density provides 18 sectors per track and 1,457,664 bytes (1.44 MB) of usable data space.
hub Part of a diskette that is used to clamp the diskette so that it can be spun in the drive at the proper speed. On better diskettes, it may be reinforced for strength.

I

index hole A hole in the diskette that marks the beginning of each track for soft-sectored diskettes.
initialize See *format.*
input/output A term referring to the processes involved in reading and writing data to the devices connected to the computer system.
interface The point at which two units or systems are brought together or

interconnected. Control cards are used to interface devices, such as a disk drive or a printer, to the computer's system unit. Information on the display screen can be the interface between a human and a piece of software. DOS uses a command line interface between the operating system and the user.
I/O Abbreviation for *input/output.*
I/O manager A DOS program that provides input/output services on the system. The I/O manager and the file manager are hidden files. The I/O manager is invoked by COMMAND.COM to process any input or output, including the reading and writing of files.
I/O redirection See *redirection.*

K

kernel See *nucleus.*
keyboard The device used for preparing input and issuing commands to the computer. It is laid out similar to a typewriter keyboard with alphabetic, numeric, and special keys. DOS assumes that the keyboard is the standard input device unless it is otherwise assigned.
keyboard control A set of hardware control sequences that can be used to control the display of information. See *Chapter 2.*

L

label The label encoded on a disk using the LABEL command. The label can be up to 11 characters and can be displayed using the VOL command. It is sometimes referred to as the *volume label.* In a batch file, a label is a line that starts with a colon (:) followed by a label identifier.
LPT1 . . . LPT3 Device names used to refer to the printers that can be addressed by DOS. DOS uses these device names to refer to the ports that can be used to attach parallel printers.

M

memory An electronic or magnetic device used to store information on the computer. Memory that can be both read from and written to is referred to as random access memory (*RAM*). Memory that stores programs and only can be read is referred to as read-only memory (*ROM*).
microcomputer A small computer, usually a single-user system, used with various application software programs.
microprocessor An integrated circuit, usually on a single chip, that acts as the engine of the computer. The microprocessor is used for processing, and communicates with the other parts of the computer system.
modem A device used to transmit data over the telephone system between two computers. For two computers to communicate, each must have its own modem.
monitor A device attached to the computer that displays both input and output information. It is sometimes referred to as the computer display unit.
monochrome A term used to describe a one-color computer display. The display is usually in amber or green.
MS-DOS An operating system for IBM-compatible microcomputers developed by Microsoft Corporation.

N

network A group of computers linked via cables and related circuitry so that they can share resources and communicate with each other.
nucleus The resident part of DOS that resides in RAM when the computer is booted. It is also referred to as the *kernel.*

O

operating system A group of system programs that control and manage the resources of a computer system. DOS is an example of an operating system that is used to control a microcomputer.
output The results of executing a program. Output is usually in the form of a report sent to the computer display or to the printer.

P

parallel interface An interface to an I/O device in which all the bits of the entire byte are transmitted to or from the device at the same time. A parallel interface requires multiple data lines, as opposed to the single data line used in a serial interface. The LPT printer interfaces on the computer are parallel interfaces.
parallel port The port that is usually used to connect the printer.
parameter A letter, number, or other code used with a command file to define the specific way the program should operate. Some commands such as BACKUP, RESTORE, XCOPY, and REPLACE have many parameter options. Some commands such as TYPE, VER, and CLS have no parameter options.
parity An error detection or encoding scheme used to ensure accuracy when storing data and retrieving data from secondary storage. A parity system used this way is normally referred to as an even-parity system or an odd-parity system.
path The string of directory names that defines the location of a specific directory. The string of directory names originates at the root directory.
pathname The portion of a file specification that defines the directory location of the file. The pathname relates to the specific disk drive referred to by its drive letter where the file can be found.
PC-DOS An operating system for IBM microcomputers. It was originally developed for the IBM PC when it was first released in 1981.
pipe To direct the output of one command as input to a second command that has been chained to it. The broken vertical bar (¦) is used to pipe input and output between commands.
port See *communications port.*
print queue A list of files that are to be printed by DOS. The DOS PRINT command can handle a print queue list of files. Application software may also develop a print queue when printing multiple files of output.
printer A device that produces printed material. DOS refers to the standard printer as the PRN device. It may also reference the device as LPT1.

PRN The abbreviation refers to the standard system printer under DOS. The device name LPT1 can also be used.

program A set of instructions stored as a file that can be executed by typing the name of the file under DOS. Files with the extension COM and EXE are typical DOS program files.
prompt A character, symbol, or group of characters displayed to indicate what program is currently in control of the computer system. The greater-than (>) sign is sometimes referred to as the standard DOS prompt. The EDLIN program uses the * prompt; BASIC uses the symbol OK as its prompt. Application programs may also use prompt characters to indicate that they are currently in control.

R

RAM An abbreviation for the random access memory or internal memory of the computer. In most computers the contents of RAM are lost when the computer's power is turned off.
RAM disk See *virtual disk*.
read-only bit See *read-only file*.
read-only file A file that can be read from disk or loaded into memory. A file that is read-only cannot be changed. A read-only file has its read-only attribute bit set to 1.
redirection The process of having a DOS command or other program take its input from a device other than the keyboard (standard input) or send its output to a device other than the display (standard output). DOS uses the less-than (<) sign to redirect standard input and the greater-than (>) sign to redirect standard output.
replaceable parameter A reference consisting of a percent (%) sign followed by a number. Replaceable parameters are used in batch files to refer to variables entered with the batch file at the time of its execution.
ROM An abbreviation for read-only memory. ROM is a type of computer memory that is permanently encoded in the circuitry. ROM chips typically contain programs used in processes such as computer startup and BIOS operations. ROM memory is not lost when the electrical power is turned off.
root directory The main directory under DOS that is created when a disk is formatted. Every formatted disk has a root or backslash directory.

S

serial port A communications port to which serial devices are connected to the computer. COM1 through COM4 are the serial ports supported by DOS. Modems and serial printers are two examples of devices that might use the serial port on the computer.
shell A program that acts as an interface to the user of a computer. Commands processed by the shell program are then passed to the appropriate software program for processing. DOS 4.00 introduced the DOS Shell interface.
shift The Shift key on the keyboard. The Shift key does nothing when pressed by itself. It must be used with other keys to perform control key sequence operations. With the Caps Lock key off, the Shift key produces capital letters when any alphabetic key is pressed. With Caps Lock on, the Shift Key produces lowercase letters when an alphabetic key is pressed.
soft-sectored A method of formatting a diskette in which the software determines the number of sectors on each track on the disk. Diskette formatting under DOS uses soft-sectored formatting of either 8, 9, or 15 sectors per track on 51/4-inch diskettes, and 9 or 18 sectors per track on 31/2-inch diskettes.
software The programs that are used with a computer system. The software makes the hardware function.
software compatibility A term that refers to the compatibility between an IBM microcomputer and a microcomputer from another manufacturer. The two computers are software compatible if they can run the same software. System software is normally not interchangeable between the two, but application software may be.
special characters Characters that are part of a coding system such as ASCII that are other than alphabetic, numeric, or punctuation characters. ASCII includes graphics and other characters that are part of the coding system but cannot be typed from the keyboard.
standard input The device from which a program reads its input in the default mode. Normal DOS operation uses the keyboard as standard input. Standard input can be redirected using the less-than (<) symbol. Standard input normally comes from the CON device.
standard output The device to which a program sends its output in the default mode. Normal DOS operation uses the display as standard output. Standard output can be redirected using the greater-than (>) symbol. Standard output normally is sent to the CON device.
stop bit A signal used in data communications, such as modem operations, to signal the end of a character.
subdirectory An area on a disk or diskette that has been named and stores related files such as a software application program or a related set of data files.
system default The base value for a feature or hardware or software specification. Default values provide information or standard operating procedures for the computer. An example of a system default is the boot process for the computer. System defaults can be overridden by the user to modify the operating procedure or to set up the software or system.
system program A program used to control the operation of all or a part of the computer system and its hardware. The DOS nucleus or kernel is one example of hardware control programs that are part of DOS.
system prompt The character or group of characters that a program uses to display the fact that it is in control of the computer. The DOS prompt is usually denoted by displaying the > symbol, following the default disk drive.

T

telecommunications The transmission of data between two computers, usually via the telephone network.
temporary file A file DOS creates when piping output or redirecting output. DOS deletes the temporary file when the command completes execution.
text Characters that include alphabetic characters (both lower- and uppercase), numeric characters, and punctuation and related special characters that can be typed at the keyboard.
text editor A program that can be used to create or modify text files. The DOS

text editors are EDLIN and EDIT.
text file A file that contains text characters. See *text.*

V

version of DOS A number that represents a particular release of DOS. It includes a major release number, followed by a modification level number. The two numbers are separated by a period. For example, Version 3.20 represents modification level .20 of DOS Release 3.
virtual disk A section of RAM reserved for use as a simulated disk. It is also referred to as a *RAM disk.* Because they are part of RAM, the contents of a virtual disk are lost when power is turned off, unless they have been previously saved to a hard disk or a floppy diskette.
volume label A label encoded on the disk that can be up to 11 characters. The volume label is placed in the filename and extension fields in the directory area on the disk.

W

warm boot The process of reloading the control programs of the operating system by simultaneously pressing the Ctrl-Alt-Del keys.
wildcard character A special character that represents a single character or a group of characters in a filename. For instance, the question mark (?) can represent a single character. The asterisk (*) can represent several characters, an entire field, or part of a field.
write protect To prepare a diskette so that information can only be read from the disk. If the diskette is write-protected, information cannot be written to the diskette.

INDEX

NOTE: DOS Commands are boldfaced.